CONSPIRACY TO MURDER

Also by Linda Melvern

Techno-Bandits (Co-authored, 1983)

The End of the Street (1986)

The Ultimate Crime: Who Betrayed the UN and Why (1995)

A People Betrayed: The Role of the West in Rwanda's Genocide (2000)

United Nations (World Organisations series, 2001)

CONSPIRACY TO MURDER

The Rwandan Genocide

LINDA MELVERN

London • New York

First published by Verso 2004

3 5 7 9 10 8 6 4 2

Verso
UK: 6 Meard Street, London W1F 0EG
USA: 180 Varick Street, New York, NY 10014–4606
www.versobooks.com

Verso is the imprint of New Left Books

ISBN-13: 978-1-84467-542-5
ISBN-10: 1-84467-542-4

British Library Cataloguing in Publication Data
A catalogue record for this book is available from the British Library

Library of Congress Cataloging-in-Publication Data
Melvern, Linda.
Conspiracy to murder: the Rwanda genocide / Linda Melvern.
p. cm.
Includes bibliographical references and index.
ISBN 1-85984-588-6 (alk. paper)
1. Genocide–Rwanda–History–20th century. 2. Rwanda–Ethnic relations–History–20th century. 3. Tutsi (African people)–Crimes against–Rwanda–History–20th century. 4. Hutu (African people)–Rwanda–Politics and government–20th century. 5. Rwanda–History–Civil War, 1994–Atrocities. I. Title.

DT450.435.M423 2004
967.57104'31–dc22

2004000822

Typeset in Bembo
Printed in the USA

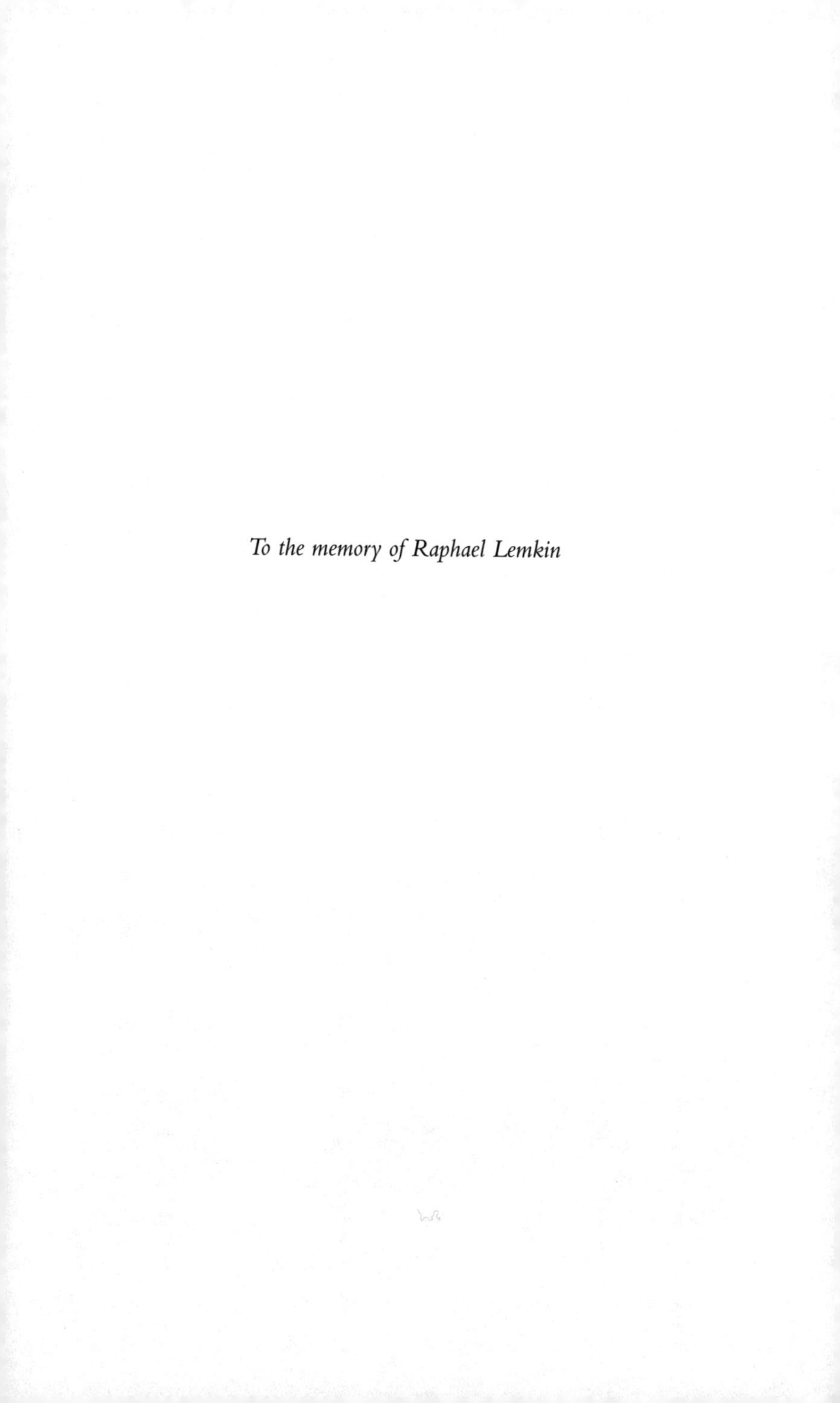

To the memory of Raphael Lemkin

CONTENTS

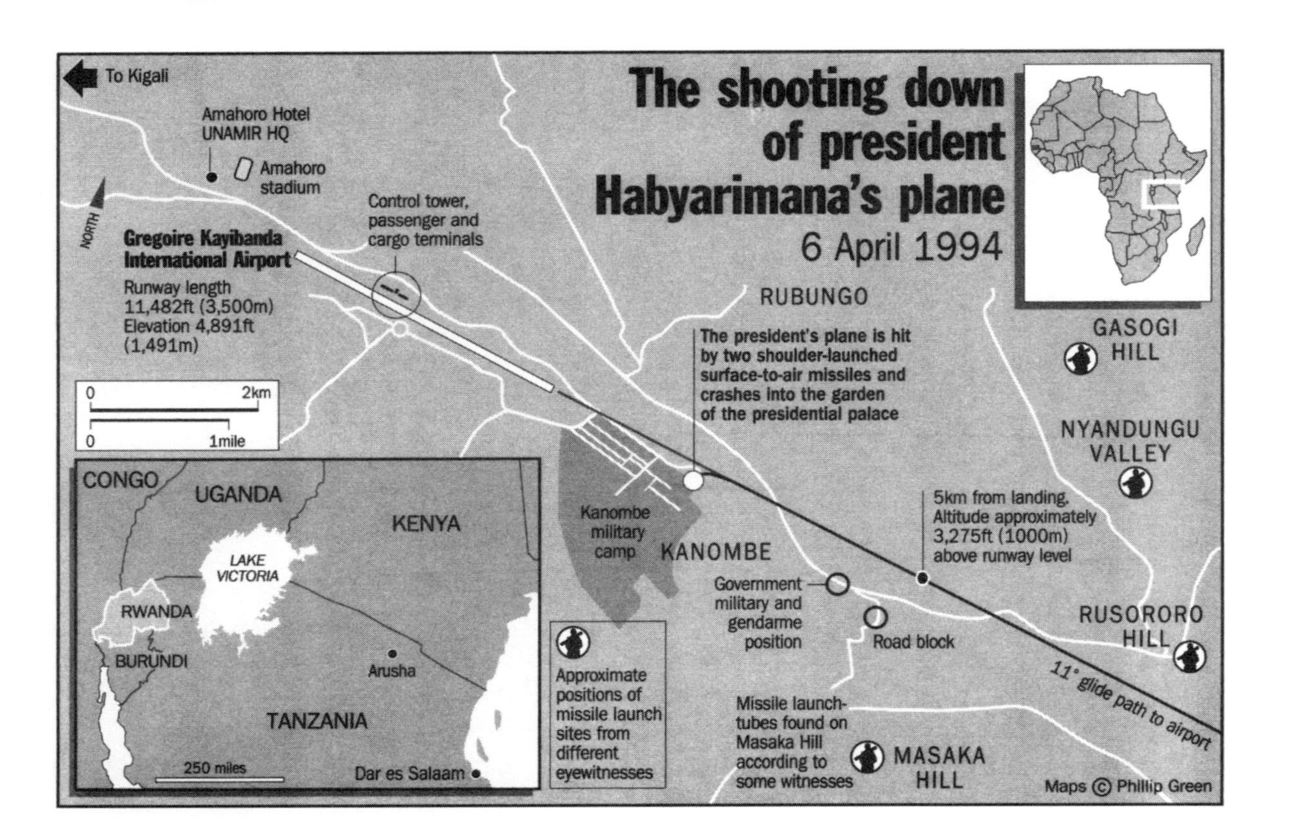
The shooting down of president Habyarimana's plane
6 April 1994
To Kigali
Amahoro Hotel
UNAMIR HQ
Amahoro stadium
NORTH
Gregoire Kayibanda International Airport
Runway length 11,482ft (3,500m)
Elevation 4,891ft (1,491m)
Control tower, passenger and cargo terminals
0 2km
0 1mile
RUBUNGO
The president's plane is hit by two shoulder-launched surface-to-air missiles and crashes into the garden of the presidential palace
GASOGI HILL
NYANDUNGU VALLEY
Kanombe military camp
KANOMBE
5km from landing. Altitude approximately 3,275ft (1000m) above runway level
Government military and gendarme position
Road block
RUSORORO HILL
11° glide path to airport
Missile launch-tubes found on Masaka Hill according to some witnesses
MASAKA HILL
Approximate positions of missile launch sites from different eyewitnesses
CONGO
UGANDA
KENYA
LAKE VICTORIA
RWANDA
BURUNDI
Arusha
TANZANIA
250 miles
Dar es Salaam
Maps © Phillip Green

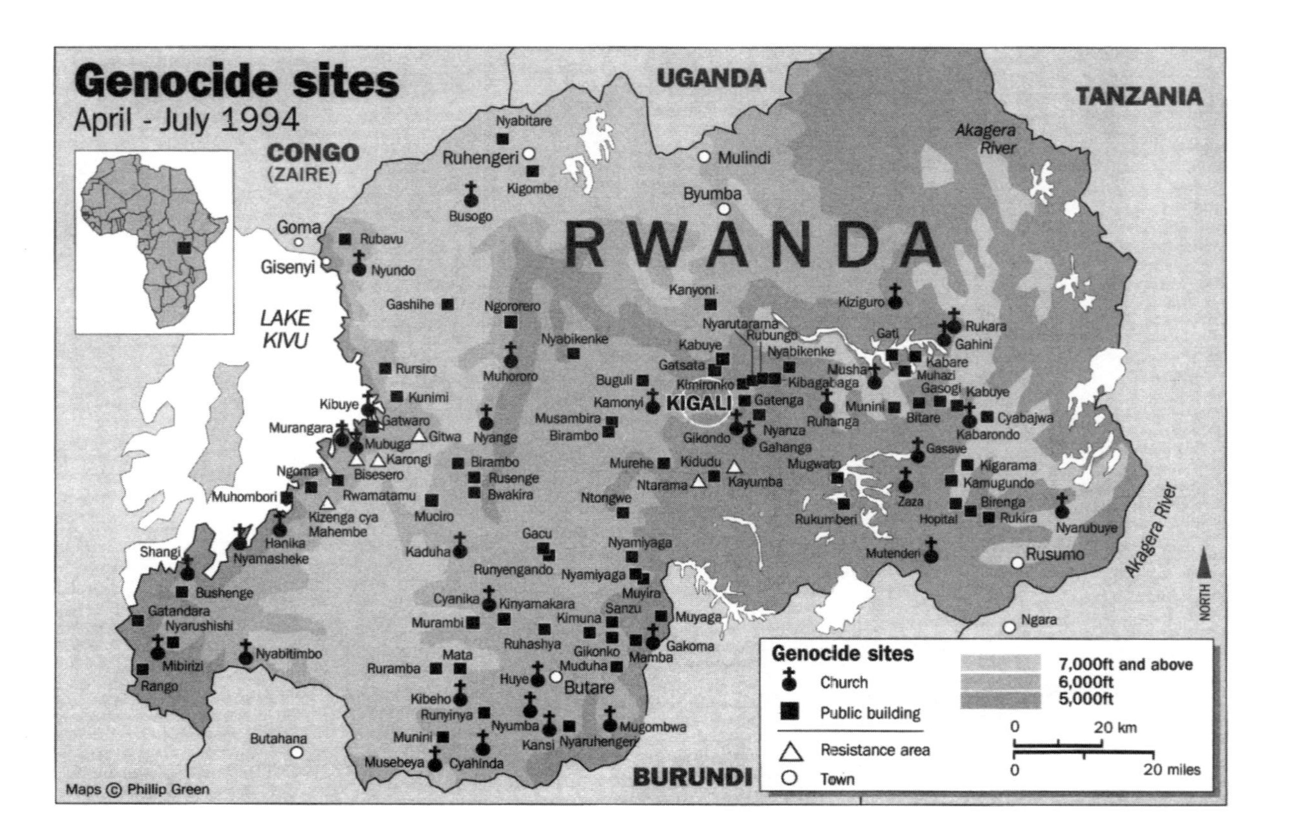
Genocide sites
April - July 1994
UGANDA
TANZANIA
CONGO
(ZAIRE)
BURUNDI
RWANDA
LAKE KIVU
Akagera River
Akagera River
KIGALI
Ruhengeri
Mulindi
Byumba
Goma
Gisenyi
Kibuye
Butare
Rusumo
Ngara
Butahana
Nyabitare
Kigombe
Busogo
Rubavu
Nyundo
Gashihe
Ngororero
Nyabikenke
Muhororo
Rursiro
Kunimi
Gatwaro
Murangara
Mubuga
Gitwa
Karongi
Bisesero
Nyange
Musambira
Birambo
Biramo
Rusenge
Bwakira
Ngoma
Rwamatamu
Muhombori
Kizenga cya Mahembe
Muciro
Hanika
Nyamasheke
Shangi
Bushenge
Gatandara
Nyarushishi
Mibirizi
Rango
Nyabitimbo
Kaduha
Gacu
Runyengando
Nyamiyaga
Nyamiyaga
Muyira
Sanzu
Muyaga
Cyanika
Kinyamakara
Murambi
Kimuna
Ruhashya
Gikonko
Gakoma
Mamba
Muduha
Mata
Ruramba
Huye
Kibeho
Runyinya
Nyumba
Kansi
Nyaruhengeri
Mugombwa
Munini
Musebeya
Cyahinda
Ntongwe
Murehe
Kidudu
Ntarama
Kayumba
Kanyoni
Nyarutarama
Rubungo
Kabuye
Gatsata
Nyabikenke
Buguli
Kimironko
Kibagabaga
Kamonyi
Gatenga
Gikondo
Nyanza
Gahanga
Kiziguro
Rukara
Gahini
Gati
Kabare
Muhazi
Musha
Gasogi
Kabuye
Munini
Bitare
Ruhanga
Cyabajwa
Kabarondo
Gasave
Mugwato
Kigarama
Kamugundo
Zaza
Rukumberi
Birenga
Hopital
Rukira
Nyarubuye
Mutenderi
NORTH
Genocide sites
Church
Public building
Resistance area
Town
7,000ft and above
6,000ft
5,000ft
0 20 km
0 20 miles
Maps © Phillip Green

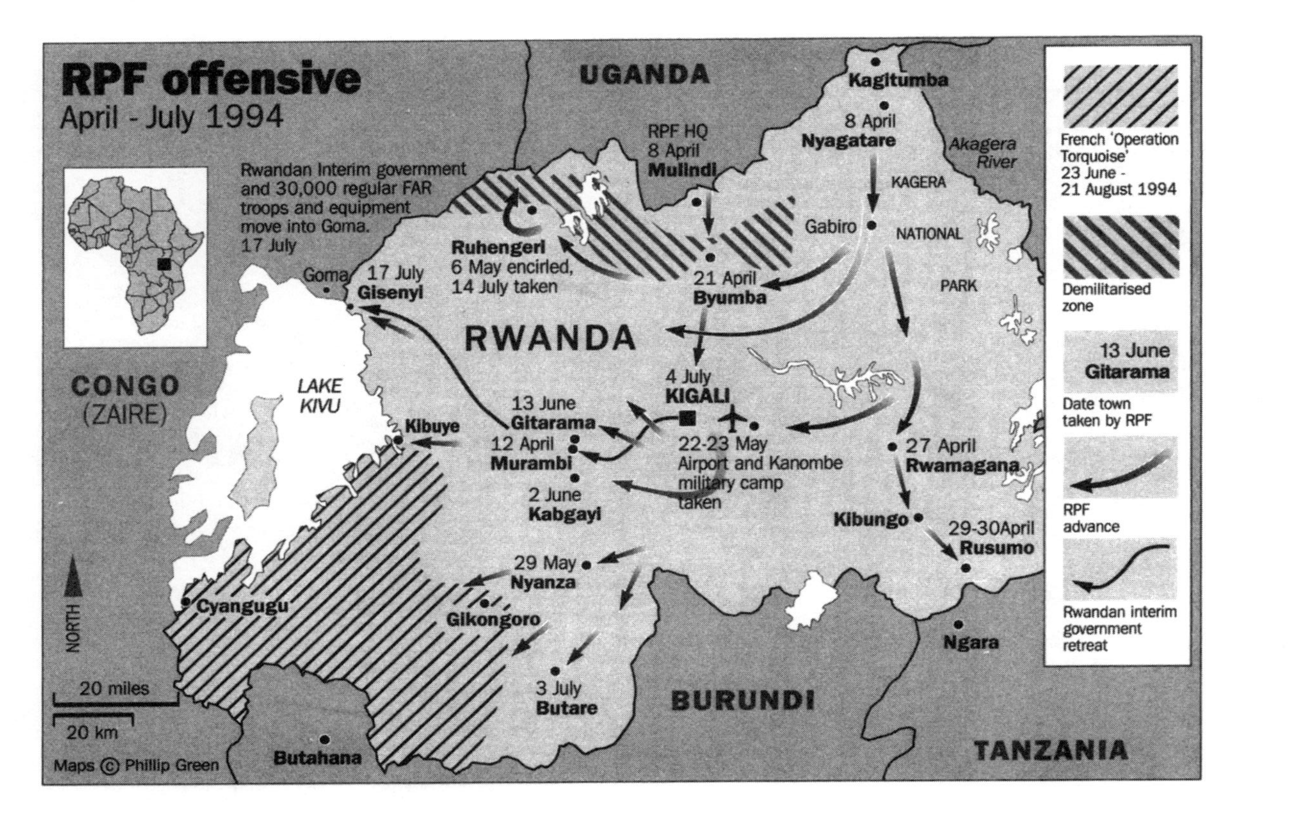
RPF offensive
April - July 1994
UGANDA
Kagitumba
8 April
Nyagatare
Akagera River
RPF HQ
8 April
Mulindi
KAGERA
NATIONAL
PARK
Gabiro
Rwandan Interim government and 30,000 regular FAR troops and equipment move into Goma.
17 July
Ruhengeri
6 May encirled,
14 July taken
21 April
Byumba
Goma
17 July
Gisenyi
RWANDA
CONGO
(ZAIRE)
LAKE KIVU
4 July
KIGALI
13 June
Gitarama
Kibuye
12 April
Murambi
22-23 May
Airport and Kanombe military camp taken
2 June
Kabgayi
27 April
Rwamagana
Kibungo
29-30April
Rusumo
29 May
Nyanza
Cyangugu
Gikongoro
NORTH
3 July
Butare
Ngara
20 miles
20 km
BURUNDI
TANZANIA
Butahana
Maps © Phillip Green
French 'Operation Torquoise'
23 June -
21 August 1994
Demilitarised zone
13 June
Gitarama
Date town taken by RPF
RPF advance
Rwandan interim government retreat

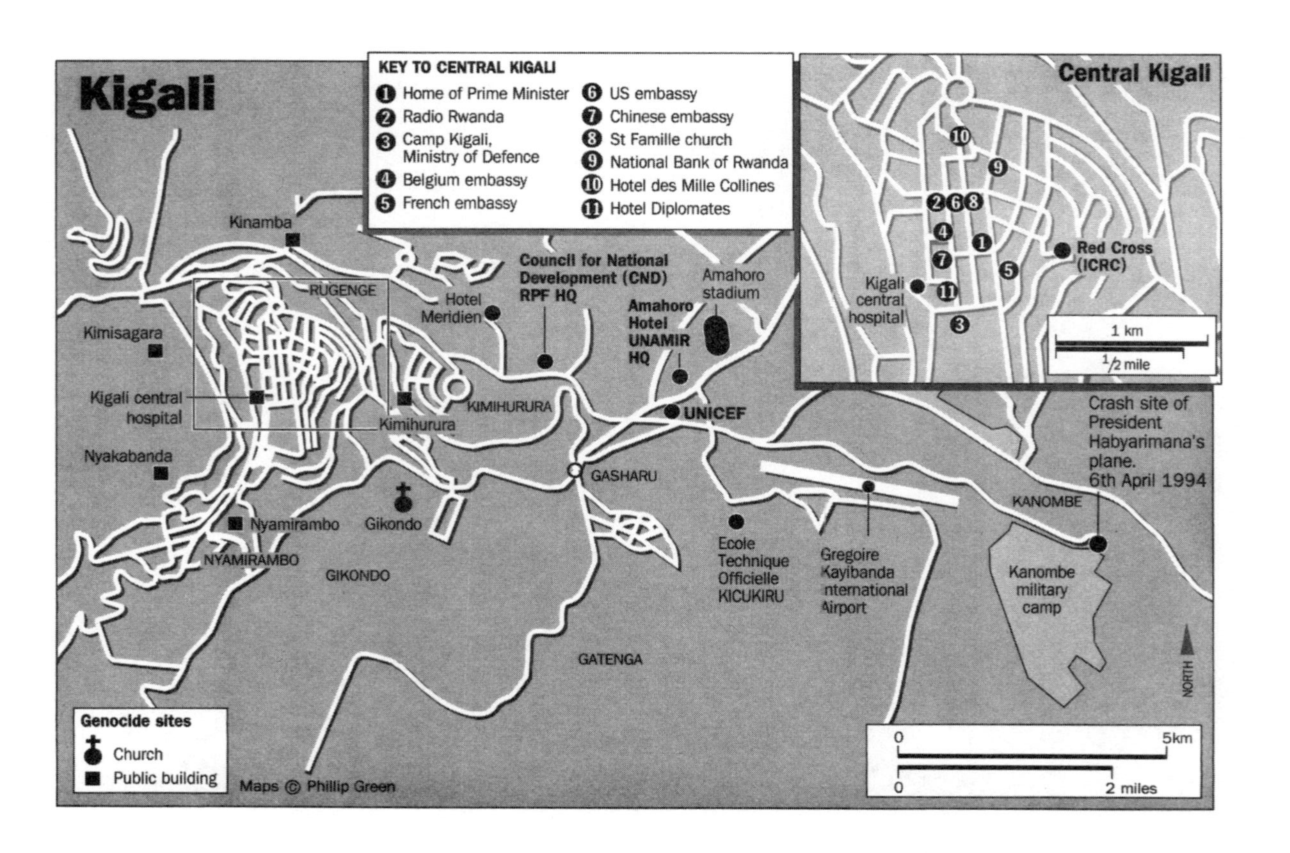
Kigali
KEY TO CENTRAL KIGALI
1 Home of Prime Minister
2 Radio Rwanda
3 Camp Kigali, Ministry of Defence
4 Belgium embassy
5 French embassy
6 US embassy
7 Chinese embassy
8 St Famille church
9 National Bank of Rwanda
10 Hotel des Mille Collines
11 Hotel Diplomates
Central Kigali
Red Cross (ICRC)
Kigali central hospital
1 km
1/2 mile
Kinamba
RUGENGE
Hotel Meridien
Council for National Development (CND) RPF HQ
Amahoro stadium
Amahoro Hotel UNAMIR HQ
UNICEF
Kimisagara
Kigali central hospital
KIMIHURURA
Kimihurura
Nyakabanda
GASHARU
Nyamirambo
Gikondo
NYAMIRAMBO
GIKONDO
Ecole Technique Officielle KICUKIRU
Gregoire Kayibanda nternational Airport
Crash site of President Habyarimana's plane. 6th April 1994
KANOMBE
Kanombe military camp
GATENGA
NORTH
Genocide sites
Church
Public building
Maps © Phillip Green
0
5km
0
2 miles

PREFACE

In April 1994 I was at the United Nations secretariat building in New York completing a book on the fifty-year history of the organisation which was being filmed for a Channel Four television series called *UN Blues*. My first interviews about the genocide in Rwanda took place then including with ambassadors who were sitting in the Security Council. This was when I first began to investigate the circumstances of the genocide. I published the earliest account of the failure over Rwanda in a lengthy article in *The Scotsman* in January 1995. This article described the abandonment by the Security Council of Lieutenant-General Roméo Dallaire and his tiny garrison of peacekeepers in the UN Assistance Mission for Rwanda (UNAMIR), who stayed in Rwanda for the three months of genocide. It also gave an account of the secret and informal meetings of the Security Council held to devise UN policy towards Rwanda. The first crucial hours of the genocide, the murder of the ten Belgian peacekeepers, and the systematic elimination of Rwanda's political opposition were described. Ever since that first article I have investigated and written about this event. In September 2000 I published *A People Betrayed: The Role of the West in Rwanda's Genocide*.

The idea behind a second book was to examine more extensive material and a wide range of a new information obtained subsequently. This shed new light on how the genocide was planned and perpetrated and who was responsible. The new material, upon which a great deal of this book relies, gave a unique insight into the minds of the conspirators and how they determined that genocide and the racist ideology that underpinned it should become a part of government policy.

In the Rwandan capital, Kigali, I gained access to files and records that were found when the Rwandan government army abandoned the city. These neatly typed letters, memoranda, reports and other documents, all written in French, filed neatly in ring-binders, include evidence of the planning of genocide. Many of them are from the G2 department, military intelligence, in the Rwandan government army. I also had access to documents taken into exile by the "génocidaires", the files later abandoned in refugee camps. These included documents from the records of the interim government whose cabinet members perpetrated the genocide. They also show how government ministers waged a campaign of international spin to persuade the world that the large number of deaths in Rwanda was due to civil war.

The information in the book also includes material obtained from the International Criminal Tribunal for Rwanda (ICTR). The prosecution case against the defendants, which is outlined in the on-going trials, has benefited from research undertaken by others, particularly an investigation carried out within weeks of the genocide by Belgium military authorities and intelligence agents and the Commission of Experts created by the Security Council and which reported to it in October 1994. The prosecution has drawn on information from independent agencies and relied on evidence from Human Rights Watch, the UN's own enquiry and from the commissions of the enquiry undertaken by two governments, France and Belgium. The evidence produced in court includes documents from my archive. A series of prosecution witnesses together with a documentary trail, indicates important links between a group of colonels in the army, and extremist politicians hostile to the peace agreement.

A picture of how the genocide was perpetrated comes from the confession of the prime minister of the interim government, Jean Kambanda. Kambanda enters the history books as the first person in an international court to plead guilty to the crime of genocide. His 1,800-page interrogation has not yet been made publicly available by the

ICTR. It is a remarkable document in which Kambanda describes how Rwanda's full state apparatus was used to carry out the killing. Kambanda told his interrogators how cabinet meetings were devoted to the progress of the genocide, and how visits to local areas were made by ministers to drum up support for the killing. Genocide is a deliberate policy to reconstruct the world. In order to commit genocide a group of people must make an agreement requiring a concerted plan of action.

In Kigali there are soldiers from the former Rwandan government army who provided me with information, and I obtained valuable accounts from interviews conducted with category one genocide convicts who have been sentenced to death by Rwanda's national courts. In years to come more details will emerge. In Rwanda the remains of the victims continue to be unearthed, while the confessions of perpetrators are heard in courts at community level in the Gacaca trials, the current Rwandan government's policy of local justice.

At the UN Secretariat in New York I was allowed to study the records of the Department of Peacekeeping Operations (DPKO), the decision to grant access provided by the Secretary General, Kofi Annan. These documents include the twice-daily reports sent to UN headquarters while the genocide progressed. This archive must be one of the world's most extraordinary collections.

The crime of genocide is the most serious crime against humanity, and its prevention the single most important commitment of the countries who join together as the UN. The Security Council of the UN is central to the application of the 1948 Convention on the Prevention and Punishment of the Crime of Genocide. This convention was the world's first truly universal, comprehensive and codified protection of human rights. It stood for a fundamental and important principle: that whatever evil may befall any group, nation or people, it was a matter of concern not just for those people but for the entire human family. This must surely call in to question why, when it came to Rwanda in 1994, the Council not only failed to prevent genocide but actually helped to create the conditions that made it possible.

The combination of revelations about the scale and intensity of the genocide, the complicity of western nations, the failure to intervene and the suppression of information about what was actually happening is a shocking indictment, not just of the UN Security Council, but more so of governments and individuals who could have prevented what was happening but chose not to do so. This must surely be one of the defining scandals of the twentieth century.

There is so much more to uncover, and the research into this great crime will continue for decades to come. It is to be hoped that this book and the archive of documents upon which it is based, will benefit those who wish to continue to investigate such a terrible event.

Linda Melvern
January 2006

1

GENOCIDES

On 1 May, 1998, an immaculately dressed man in a blue suit, with a neatly trimmed beard and spectacles, stood in a courtroom to plead guilty to genocide. And so it was that Jean Kambanda entered the history books, the first person ever to plead guilty to the crime of genocide at an international court hearing.

Kambanda was the prime minister of the government in Rwanda that planned and perpetrated genocide in 1994. He had controlled the administration of genocide, eliminated those unwilling to take part and made sure that local authorities had enough people available to engage in the killing. He had sanctioned a climate of hatred and paranoia, incited violence and ultimately sanctioned mass murder. Kambanda was convicted on all six counts and was sentenced to life imprisonment.[1]

Jean Kambanda was first educated by missionaries. Later he went to Brussels and studied economics. After graduating, he worked in insurance before joining a bank, which helped finance his political career. Politics became a passion. But his politics were extreme, founded on an ideology of exclusion. Kambanda was radically anti-Tutsi and he believed that the Tutsi were racially alien. The national policy of his government had been to create a Hutu state without them.

On the run for three years after the genocide was over, Kambanda was arrested in the early morning of 18 July, 1997 in Nairobi. He was taken to Arusha in Tanzania by plane the same day, accompanied by Pierre

Duclos and Marcel Desaulniers, two investigators for the International Criminal Tribunal for Rwanda, the ICTR. Once in Arusha he was taken to a safe house, an apartment in a modern building. Kambanda immediately offered his cooperation and told investigators that he wanted to tell the truth, confiding to the deputy prosecutor that he wished to do so for the sake of his children. In exchange for a full confession he wanted protection for them. A deal was struck. It was negotiated with Bernard Muna, the then deputy prosecutor of the ICTR.

On 3 August, 1997, he was moved to the United Nations detention facility just five miles outside Arusha, but he was kept apart, and out of reach of his fellow detainees, for his own safety. On 26 August Kambanda was moved again, this time some 500 kilometres away in Dodoma, to a mansion the investigators had nicknamed the Palais Royal. He was the only detainee and apart from his interrogators and members of the prosecution team he saw no other person. Nor was he allowed to communicate with anyone. It was here that his plea agreement was signed, on 29 April, 1998.[2]

The agreement incorporated Kambanda's plea of guilty to genocide and his acknowledgement of the fact that a genocide had taken place. The purpose of the mass killings of the Tutsi in Rwanda had been to exterminate them. Kambanda accepted that as prime minister he had exercised *de jure* authority over the government of nineteen ministers and *de facto* authority over senior civil servants and senior officers in the military. His confession was a breakthrough because he promised to testify against the other ringleaders, the only genocide suspect to do so.

The transcript of Kambanda's interrogation, based on sixty hours of interviews, is an extraordinary document.[3] It gives an unprecedented insight into how the genocide was perpetrated. But Kambanda is completely unrepentant. He defies his interrogators. When one of them mentions a "Hutu moderate" he is irritated. No such person exists for him. The phrase "Hutu moderate" was just political propaganda. He told them that the problem in Rwanda was between Hutu and Tutsi. "I am a Hutu," he said. He told them of a state commission that had toured the country to verify the ethnicity of those who wanted further education. It was 1972; he was sixteen and had to appear before it with his father by his side and the members of the communal council where he lived to vouch that he was a Hutu. "We were always Hutu," he said. "Everyone knew that this was the issue. No one wanted to bring it up."

The cells in the United Nations detention facility in Arusha house the world's worst criminals. The engineers of a new Holocaust, they planned the genocide with the utmost cunning. They live comfortably enough; their compound has gardens, a gym, and they eat fresh food and vegetables.[4] Their world is far removed from that of the foot soldiers of the genocide, the more than 100,000 Rwandans accused of taking part in the killing, who live in Rwandan prisons in the direst conditions.

The Arusha prisoners remain convinced of the rectitude of their actions. They have formed an association to plan and coordinate their defence and to maintain contact where possible with their co-conspirators who are still at large, those still planning and agitating for Hutu Power. They blame their fate on the skill of the Tutsi in attracting the sympathy of the "international community". They claim the Tutsi are the masters of deceit and accuse them of undertaking a campaign to compare themselves with the Jews in order to get sympathy.

The leader of the prison group is Colonel Théoneste Bagosora, the military officer who took control of elite units in the armed forces when the genocide began. "The Tutsi never had a country of their own to make themselves into a people," he writes. "They are people who came to Rwanda and were naturalised." Bagosora believes that the Tutsi should have lived peacefully in neighbouring countries where they were given a home, but "with arrogance and pride" they had imposed "their supremacy" on the Hutu of Rwanda. The Tutsi had eliminated all the Hutu kings and their descendants and ruled the Hutu with cruelty until the colonisers had arrived. Bagosora explains how the characters of "the two protagonists" were different: the Tutsi were proud, arrogant, tricky and untrustworthy and were convinced that the only good Tutsi was a Tutsi in power. The Hutu were modest, honest, loyal, independent and impulsive.[5] This ideology underpinned the genocide in Rwanda.

But neither historians nor anthropologists can agree on the origins of the divisions that were so crucial to Rwanda's terrible history. Some anthropologists contest the idea that Hutu and Tutsi are distinct groups.

Others maintain that the Tutsi came to Rwanda from elsewhere, originating in the Horn of Africa and migrating south where they gradually achieved dominance over the other two groups, the majority Hutu and the small number of Twa. The latter view appears to have originated with the English colonial agent and explorer John Hanning Speke, whose odious theories decreed that the Tutsi formed a superior race, different from the majority of common and savage "negroes". So superior was the culture in this part of Africa that it must surely have originated from somewhere else, somewhere nearer to the Europeans, and probably nearer Egypt than anywhere. This theory held that the Tutsi were intelligent and with a refinement of feelings "rare among primitive people".[6]

Others insist that the race idea was conceived in Europe, that the idea that Tutsi and Hutu were different races came with the European colonisers. In this view it was the coloniser who thought up the idea that the Tutsi had come to Rwanda from somewhere else and had "invaded" a country that "belonged" to the Hutu. The Hutu extremists used this version of history to good effect during the genocide by portraying the Tutsi as "aliens".

In the Kinyarwanda language, common to all Rwandan people, the word Hutu meant subject or servant and the word Tutsi rich in cattle. But the differences were not solely based on wealth or class; there were Hutu and Tutsi in the same class with Tutsi pastoralists as poor as their Hutu neighbours. In Rwanda all the people shared the same language, lived side by side and worked together.

More recent studies tell us that the word Tutsi was first used to describe the ruling elite and the word Hutu used to convey contempt for inferiors, both Tutsi and Hutu. It was the imposition of *uburetwa*, or communal labour, that exacerbated the differences and there were anti-Tutsi revolts even before the advent of colonial rule.[7]

One hundred years before the genocide of 1994 an unsuspecting king of Rwanda welcomed a German count, Gustav Adolf von Götzen, to his court. He had no idea that ten years previously, at the Berlin Conference of 1884, the European superpowers had agreed to divide the African continent among themselves. Rwanda was gifted to Germany. The Germans found a unique and extraordinary country, an organised and structured monarchy, semi-feudal with aristocrats and vassals, and an administrative structure that emanated from the court. It was organised on four levels: province, district, hill and neighbourhood. High chiefs managed the provinces, two chiefs for each district appointed by the king, a land chief in charge of agricultural levies and a cattle chief who collected cattle taxes. The hills were administered by hill chiefs. Each layer of this hierarchy was linked in a relationship of mutual dependence based on reciprocal arrangements regarding goods and services. In Rwanda there were three groups of people, the Hutu, Tutsi and Twa. The Twa were pygmies and comprised a small part of society. The Hutu, the most populous group of the society, generally ran the neighbourhoods in Rwanda's highly controlled hierarchy; they obeyed the orders of those from above, most of whom were Tutsi. The monarchy was Tutsi, and most of the hill, district and provincial chiefs were Tutsi. In the King's army the warriors were Tutsi, the Hutu were the camp followers and the Twa provided pots and iron implements.[8] There was also a marked physical difference between Hutu and Tutsi; the former were generally shorter and stockier; the Tutsi were tall and willowy with angular features.

German rule did not last. After the First World War the western provinces of German East Africa, Ruanda (Rwanda) and neighbouring Urundi (Burundi) were given to Belgium under a League of Nations mandate, a system intended to help those of the world's peoples who were considered incapable of ruling themselves. The wellbeing of the Rwandans and Burundians would be a "sacred trust of civilisation and development". Belgium was pledged to ensure freedom of speech and religion for its colonies. But Belgium did no such thing. Colonial rule eroded the power of the king of Rwanda and disrupted the old state apparatus. Money was introduced and western education was organised for the sons of the chiefs. A system of forced labour was instigated, mainly to build roads, and cruelty, particularly the practice of whipping, became so prevalent that some people fled to become migrant workers in Uganda. The conditions of the Hutu masses worsened and their suffering was more extreme than ever before.

The divisions in society were enforced. In 1933 the Belgian administration organised a census. Teams of Belgian bureaucrats arbitrarily classified the whole population as Hutu, Tutsi or Twa, giving everyone an identity card with the ethnic grouping clearly marked. Every Rwandan was counted and measured: the height, the length of their noses, the shape of their eyes. For many Rwandans, though, it was not always possible to determine ethnicity on the basis of physical appearance: Rwandans in the south were generally of mixed origin and were classified as Hutu although many of them looked like Tutsi. In the north mixed marriages were rare. Some people were given a Tutsi identity card because they had more money or more cows. The divisions in society became more pronounced with the Hutu discriminated against in all walks of life.[9]

Jean Kambanda, the future prime minister of Rwanda, was born, in 1955, in Gitarama in the last years of the monarchy. He was two years old when the Hutu first called for an end to their subservient status. Their bitter and ultimately violent struggle began in 1957 with the publication of a Hutu manifesto calling for majority rule.

The manifesto maintained that the problem in Rwanda was Tutsi supremacy. Many Belgian priests who lived in Rwanda agreed and helped the Hutu in their struggle, providing access to the outside world and a lobby in Europe. A rallying point for this so-called social revolution was a belief that the Tutsi were not really Rwandans at all; they had overrun the country years before. For the Hutu the future of Rwanda meant freedom from Tutsi rule and for the Tutsi it meant a restoration of their dynastic customs and an end to Belgian colonisation. In turn, there were Tutsi supremacists who believed that the Hutu were by their very nature subservient.[10]

The United Nations also considered Rwanda's problems in terms of a "racial" divide. When the Hutu manifesto was published a UN report had loftily claimed that there was little hope for a "rapprochement between the races" and called on the Belgians to help to emancipate the downtrodden Hutu.

And then, in 1959, a series of events led to terrible and devastating violence. The king died in mysterious circumstances after being treated by a Belgian doctor. To this day, his death remains a mystery. The Tutsi elite blamed the Belgians and Hutu extremists. The Tutsi decided to try to destroy the emerging Hutu leadership. In November a Hutu leader was attacked by young Tutsi and a series of killings of Tutsi began. The country was put under martial law and curfew. A campaign of terror against the Tutsi was instigated with the killing of Tutsi spreading from hill to hill. Tutsi families fled for their lives as waves of violence spread.

One Tutsi family in Gitarama fled in a matter of hours from their home. In the race to escape, the mother bundled the family and a few belongings into the car and drove off quickly, as their would-be assassins were already approaching the house. Shortly afterwards their home was razed to the ground by the attackers. Years later one of the children, Paul Kagame, revisited his birthplace to find a still empty hill and one or two older survivors of the massacres who bore witness to the horrors of that day. Today Kagame is the president of Rwanda.[11]

In 1959 thousands of people were killed and thousands more families fled when Belgian authorities proceeded to oust Tutsi chiefs and sub-chiefs and replace them with Hutu. Dozens of petitions were sent to the UN from Tutsi in fear of their lives and revealing a suspicion that the killing was organised: "… the officials report that fighting is between two groups of inhabitants which is not true … for a long time they have been living together and mixed up … burning and killing are being done during the daylight sometimes in the presence of so-called police … how can people with no proper communications have organised such a thing?"[12]

The UN General Assembly sent a special commission to Rwanda. It reported that racism bordered on "Nazism against the Tutsi minorities" and that the government together with the Belgian authorities were to blame. The commission reported that the hostility between the ethnic groups had been artificially engineered and had led to the murder of an estimated 2,000 people. The Tutsi had been brutally expelled from social and political life. Unless there was national reconciliation, the commission concluded, the outlook for Rwanda was bleak.[13] They were right. When the first political parties were formed, they were created along strict ethnic lines. Unlike in other colonies, there was no emerging national liberation movement in Rwanda; no celebration of Rwanda as a state or a people.

For the next three decades in Rwanda political life would fall under the influence of a monstrous racist ideology that preached intolerance and hatred. The killing of Tutsi in 1959 was the first of several alleged genocides. The number of victims would vary widely but the methods used to trap and kill victims would remain largely the same.[14] And in each case the role of propaganda and a distortion of history were paramount.[15] In the years between 1959 and 1994 the idea of genocide, although never officially recognised, became a part of life.

Rwanda was declared an independent republic in July 1962 by its first president, Gregoire Kayibanda, a Hutu from the south and a former school teacher. His victory was due to the support he received from Belgium, and his government was comprised entirely of Hutu. Kayibanda, an authoritarian and secretive man, was the founding father of Hutu nationalism and he ruled through a local network of Hutu on every hill, and a small group of politicians from his home town of Gitarama. The Tutsi were considered to be the eternal enemy.

Thousands of Tutsi families had by now fled the country. They were living as stateless refugees on subsistence levels in neighbouring countries and were denied entry to Rwanda. An estimated quarter of a million lived in camps in Uganda. The camps, for those who were able to reach them, were poorly equipped and infrequently supplied, and many of those seeking refuge did not survive the early months of exile. Some inferior land was allocated by the local Ugandan authorities to the Rwandans, but most ended up working as cheap labour for the local farmers in order to scratch a living. Later, the United Nations High Commission for Refugees (UNHCR) helped to establish more permanent refugee settlements providing food and non-food items, which went part of the way to sustaining the livelihood of the refugees.

Then, in an effort to enforce their return home, on 14 November, 1963 about 1,500 men recruited from refugee camps[16] came across the border from neighbouring Burundi to try to oust Kayibanda. The invasion failed, as did a second attempt in December.

Soon after the first invasion the Kayibanda regime began a concerted and planned campaign to kill Tutsi, starting with the elimination of political opponents. Each prefecture was provided with a minister to supervise the killing. Bands of Hutu, accompanied by propagandists, organised expeditions in regions remote from their homes.[17] Rumours were spread of a plot by Tutsi against Hutu. There were roadblocks erected to prevent escape. The killing took place in the most atrocious fashion, in most cases carried out by the local population using whatever was available, mostly hoes and the *panga*, a long knife for cutting grass. Hutu peasants mutilated their Tutsi neighbours. Bodies and body parts were dumped in piles at the side of the road. The government version claimed that the Hutu population had run amok through fear of enslavement and that perhaps 400 civilians had been killed. The World Council of Churches estimated deaths in the region of 10,000–14,000.

One of the young army officers taking part was Théoneste Bagosora who, thirty years later in his cell in Arusha, would proudly proclaim on his curriculum vitae: "1963 Campaigns in the Bugesera against Inyenzi", using the word "cockroach" to describe Tutsi invaders,[18] a word they themselves used for their intention to infiltrate every part of Rwanda. Bagosora was fond of quoting a warning to these invaders, issued by President Kayibanda on 11 March, 1963: "Some of you are causing trouble for your brothers who live in peace in a democratic Rwanda … and suppose you take Kigali by force how will you measure the chaos of which you will be the first victims … it will be the total end of the Tutsi race."[19] A year later Kayibanda warned that if the Tutsi ever sought to obtain political power again they would find that "the whole Tutsi race will be wiped out".[20]

The 1963 killings brought Rwanda for a brief moment to international attention. When western journalists finally arrived in the country they had been so shocked at what they saw that they reported the organised slaughter as being reminiscent of the Holocaust in Europe. The British philosopher, Bertrand Russell, claimed that the killing had been the most horrible and systematic extermination of a people since the Nazi extermination of the Jews. Most of the Europeans living in Rwanda were indifferent, considering the massacres to be the result of the "savagery of the negro".[21]

The fact of genocide was never officially acknowledged. No one was punished. Rwanda slipped back into obscurity. The country increasingly came to be seen as a stable democracy with rule by the majority Hutu. The Tutsi, said to be nine per cent of the population, would be represented accordingly in all walks of life with vigilante groups ensuring that they were not acquiring more than their fixed quotas in schools and employment.

There was another genocide in 1972, this time in neighbouring Burundi. There the Tutsi had retained their power and in April, after an abortive coup by Hutu against their Tutsi rulers, there were massacres of unprecedented magnitude. An estimated 200,000 Hutu were systematically slaughtered. The US State Department estimated that an attempt had been made to kill every Hutu male over the age of fourteen; every Hutu member of the cabinet had been killed, all Hutu officers, half the country's school teachers and thousands of civil servants. In a special report produced by the Carnegie Endowment for International Peace, a congressional aide was quoted: "By the end of May we knew it was genocide from officially classified information from the State Department."[22] The Belgian government called it a "veritable genocide".[23] The reaction from the UN was muted. At its meeting in 1973 the sub-commission on the prevention of discrimination and protection of minorities forwarded to the Commission of Human Rights in Geneva a complaint against Burundi for gross violations of human rights. But when the commission met in 1974 the only action was a working party established to communicate with the government of Burundi. Then, just like Rwanda, after a few days in the headlines Burundi sank back into obscurity. The killings continued.

Kayibanda used the tragic events in Burundi to conduct a further crackdown against the Tutsi in Rwanda and started a campaign to "purify" the country. In Butare, Rwanda's second city, Hutu students toured the streets with megaphones warning Tutsi students to stay away from school. Jean Kambanda took part. "We requisitioned vehicles and toured schools telling Tutsi they must leave", he said.[24] He remembered how lists of Tutsi students were posted on walls and how tribunals were created to check the bloodlines of students to determine those who were "pure Hutu". President Kayibanda established "public safety committees" to control the ethnic quota system and many Tutsi were thrown out of their jobs. There was killing, violence and intimidation and the campaign was sufficient to cause another wave of Tutsi emigration.[25]

In the midst of all this violence, President Kayibanda was ousted in a coup. On 5 July, 1973 ten army officers, calling themselves the Committee for National Peace and Unity, seized power. They were led by a young, ambitious and brutal military leader, Juvénal Habyarimana. Habyarimana had been a soldier all his life and had been among the first officers to graduate from a newly created school for officers in Kigali. He had been in charge of Rwanda's police force as minister of the national guard and police. Just prior to the coup he was appointed minister of defence. His intention and that of the committee, he claimed, was to bring stability after the "events", the euphemism for the killing of Tutsi. Sure enough, on the day when Habyarimana seized power, the violence against the Tutsi suddenly ceased.

Jean Kambanda had marvelled at the new president's uncanny ability to control events. The Tutsi had welcomed Habyarimana as a saviour, he said, and Habyarimana had promised to unite the nation.[26]

Habyarimana went on to create one of the most rigidly controlled countries in the world. Rwanda became a one-party state. All other political parties were outlawed. His own party, the Mouvement Révolutionnaire National pour le Développement (MRND), was formed in 1974 and was represented on every hill and in every cell.[27] The party's national congress contained representatives from all 140 communes in Rwanda. Every Rwandan had to be a member of the MRND, even babies. No one could move house without permission from the party. No opposition to either Habyarimana or the party was allowed: long sentences were given for distributing "subversive" pamphlets and for "insulting" the president.

Rwanda's international reputation was of a boring, virtuous Christian country, in the mainstream of benign dictatorships.[28] The Rwandan government had a good track record for economic management and had moderate foreign policies. It had a working bureaucracy and a centralised system of administration, with executive, legislative and judicial branches of government. Habyarimana improved the infrastructure, the telephone system and the power supply network. What impressed foreign dignitaries was how overtly sober and simple the life of the president was. An ardent Catholic, his behaviour was compared favourably with the excesses of some other African despots.

The Habyarimana coup was described as bloodless but it was not.[29] An estimated fifty-five people, mostly officials, lawyers or businessmen close to the previous regime, were killed either by poison or by hammer blows after being arrested and thrown into prison. The families of these people were given sums of money to pay for their silence. Kayibanda and his wife were starved to death in a secret location.[30] A Rwandan journalist later estimated that during his rule Habyarimana killed some 700 soldiers in the army that he had helped to create.[31] These murders were perpetrated either in retribution or to eliminate witnesses or because of fears that someone would expose crimes committed by his coterie of officers.

The true nature of Rwanda's apartheid regime was overlooked. There were no Tutsi prefects or bourgmestres, only one Tutsi minister, two Tutsi members of parliament, out of 70, and one Tutsi officer in the army.[32] There were quotas established in schools and government service to limit the numbers of Tutsi to ten percent. There was only token Tutsi representation throughout government. Western donors interpreted this to mean that the government supported full integration of ethnic groups guaranteeing the Tutsi an equitable share of opportunities.[33] On the country's borders there was a festering refugee crisis. The stateless Rwandans in exile now realised that their plight might well last years. The refugee problem was not high on any agenda, although many western governments did help: Germany, Switzerland, Belgium and the US among them.

President Habyarimana reinforced the divisions between Hutu and Tutsi, and divided the country regionally. He came to rely increasingly on his kinsmen from the north: of the eleven officers who took power with him in 1973 all but one were from the prefecture of Gisenyi. The increasing power of northerners caused resentment in the south, especially among Kayibanda's former supporters.

Habyarimana's northern stronghold was Bushiru, a small agricultural region in Gisenyi on the periphery of the country. It included the communes of Karago, where the president came from, and the commune of Giciye, that of his wife. The Bushiru had always been fiercely independent. It had not been a part of Rwanda at all until the early years of the twentieth century when it was overrun by German and Rwandan troops from the south. It had taken several military expeditions by the German Schutztruppe between 1910 and 1912 to subdue the Bushiru and, in spite of their incorporation into the Rwandan state, the northern Hutu, the Bakiga, formed a distinct culture. They had a historical loathing of Tutsi and southern Hutu, blaming both of them for their subjugation.

Habyarimana was said to have a quiet charisma about him, while being somewhat aloof. He gave the impression of a man reluctant about power.[34] To perpetuate his rule Habyarimana relied for twenty years on regional and then later family politics. Agathe Kanziga, the president's wife, became particularly useful. Part of a well-established northern Hutu clan, she had relatives in key positions and built up her own network of associates and informers, at first called Clan de Madame and later known as the Akazu,[35] a word used during the monarchy to describe the group of courtiers surrounding the king. The members of the Akazu all came from the Bushiru, and it was this region that would benefit most from international aid and development money. An association called ADECOGIKA was created to develop their home communes and to share the spoils of power.

Later on, international investigators would try to unravel how this association had benefited and enriched Akazu members. In the trial the association ADECOGIKA was described by one of its Presidents, a colonel in the army called Théoneste Bagosora, as having been created solely to promote the social, economic, and cultural development of the northern *communes* of Giciye and Karago. Bagosora later described how ADECOGIKA was to benefit "a school, I would say a college, a group of schools or a school centre of Kibihekane, and that the school centre was also a private school subsidised by the state".[36]

For the overwhelming majority of poverty-striken Rwandans, in a heavily over-populated country, their situation only worsened. In 1989 a drastic fall in coffee prices – a main source of revenue for a country built like Rwanda on peasant subsistence agriculture – diminished foreign earnings by 50 percent. State enterprises were pushed into bankruptcy and health and education services collapsed. Child malnutrition rose dramatically. Corruption worsened as the spoils for the elite began to shrink. Opposition to the dictatorship was expressed. A member of parliament, Felecula Nyiramutarambirwa, publicly criticised the government for siphoning money from public funds destined for road construction – she suffered a fatal car crash. In November that year Father Silvio Sindambiwe, another critic of the regime and editor of a Catholic newspaper, was killed in a seemingly stage-managed traffic accident. Journalists Callizte Kalisa and Straton Byabagamba were killed and then their killers were themselves found dead in Kigali's central prison.[37]

At 2.30 p.m. on the afternoon of Monday 1 October, 1990, fifty armed men crossed the border from Uganda and shot dead the guards on the customs post. Within minutes hundreds more armed men poured into

Rwanda, wearing Ugandan army uniforms.[38] The invasion had begun. The rebel army, of the Rwandan Patriotic Front (RPF), was representing the refugees, all those Rwandans forcibly driven out of the country between 1959 and 1963. The UN High Commissioner for Refugees (UNHCR), estimated that in 1990 there were 900,000 Rwandans living in Uganda, Burundi, Zaire and Tanzania. This was Africa's largest refugee problem. The Rwandan government, arguing that the country suffered from over population, had refused any of these people the right of return. A Joint Ministerial Commission had been established by Uganda and Rwanda to discuss the refugee issue but there was slow progress. The RPF leadership apparently agreed that given the nature of the regime in Kigali, a return home could be achieved only through military pressure. The RPF demands included an end to the ethnic divide and the system of compulsory identity cards, a self-sustaining economy, a stop to the misuse of public offices, the establishment of social services, democratisation of the security force, and the elimination of a system that generated refugees. Internationally the RPF presented itself as a democratic and multi-ethnic movement seeking to depose a corrupt and incompetent regime.

The Rwandan elite panicked. The invading army was composed mostly of second-generation Rwandan refugees, over four thousand of them, who had joined Uganda's National Resistance Army (NRA) from their camps. The RPF invasion force consequently comprised well-trained troops with combat experience who had simply deserted their NRA positions and taken their weapons. They were under the leadership of a charismatic military commander, Major-General Fred Rwigyema. He was the most famous Rwandan refugee in the NRA. He had risen to become deputy commander of the army and deputy minister of defence. But then there had been growing resentment in Uganda towards the Rwandans and Rwigyema had been removed from office. Later it was decided that non-Ugandan nationals, including Rwandan refugees, were even to be precluded from owning land. It was this that was said to have prompted the invasion and the refugees' attempts to regain the right of citizenship in their country of origin.[39]

The RPF invasion was a failure, largely because both France and Zaire sent in forces to protect their ally. Zaire sent several hundred troops belonging to its crack unit, the Division Spéciale Présidentielle (DSP). France sent two parachute companies, ostensibly to ensure the safety of its own nationals. But France also set up a blocking position to prevent the invaders from advancing on the capital and its airport. Belgium did likewise but later withdrew because of a law forbidding the military to take part in a civil war. All military co-operation with Rwanda was cancelled by the Belgian government. In Kigali this was considered total abandonment. It was the French who saved the regime and who stayed on in Rwanda, providing financial and military guarantees not available from Belgium.

Fred Rwigyema was killed on the second day and more than half the invading force died in a humiliating retreat in the Virunga Mountains, a heavily forested mountain range in the north-west where many soldiers perished through cold and hunger. French spotter planes were used to locate those in retreat and many of them were killed by Rwandan army forces.[40] An estimated 10,000 people were arrested and a curfew imposed. Most of those who were arrested were detained in Kigali's Nyamirambo stadium, where they were told if the RPF got anywhere near the capital they would all be killed. In the main these people were educated Tutsi and Hutu, those who wanted an end to the regime. There were beatings and rapes and murders.

On 4 October, to heighten the fear of the RPF, the regime staged a fake attack on Kigali with gunfire and explosions all night long, intended to encourage citizens to make arrests of "Tutsi suspects". The Tutsi living in Rwanda, an estimated fourteen per cent of the population, were described as "accomplices" of the RPF invaders, or, in the Kinyarwanda word, *ibyitso*.[41] Amnesty International received numerous accounts of torture.[42] The army acted with extreme brutality. One prosecution witness later claimed that about fifty Tutsi had been brought to the Kanombe military camp run by Théoneste Bagosora and were summarily executed.[42] Others brought to the camp died of starvation. Some were tortured to death. All the Tutsi civilians working there were thrown out and many of the soldiers with Tutsi wives were dismissed from the army.[43]

The para-commandos, under Major Aloys Ntabakuze, were sent north from Kigali on 2 October to Umutara, where they were greeted the next day by a wave of terrified people fleeing the fighting. A witness later testified that Ntabakuze, using the information about ethnic grouping on the compulsory identity cards, had herded the people into two groups, Hutu and Tutsi, and then assembled the Tutsi in one place and killed them by throwing grenades at them. Later, on 10 October, another prosecution witness saw Ntabakuze order troops to eliminate all Tutsi living in a place called Bahima.[45]

Ten days after the invasion, in a commune halfway between Kigali and the prefecture of Gisenyi, meetings of local officials were called. People were told to burn the houses of the "inyenzi", referring to the Tutsis, and to kill them, because the Tutsi were coming to exterminate Hutu. Then the killing of Tutsi began, with the local authorities, teachers or local gendarmes directing attacks. One man witnessed his wife and six children killed by machete. At least 348 people were killed in forty-eight hours and some 550 houses burned. A total of 248 people were accused of these murders, their arrests prompted a visit of diplomats who had gone to Kibilira to see for themselves,[46] but none of those arrested spent any longer than four weeks in prison. On 19 December, 1990, in a report prepared in Kigali by the ambassadors of France, Belgium and Germany and the representative of the European Union in Rwanda, the following warning was issued: "The rapid deterioration of the relations between the two ethnic groups, the Hutu and the Tutsi, runs the imminent risk of terrible consequences for Rwanda and the entire region."

The French ambassador in Kigali, Georges Martre, wrote a cable to Paris: "… the Rwandan population of Tutsi origin … still count on a military victory … [which] … will enable it to escape genocide."[47] When the head of the French military cooperation mission to Rwanda, General Jean Varret, had arrived in Rwanda in 1990 he had been told by Colonel Pierre-Célestin Rwagafilita that the Tutsi were very few. "We will liquidate them", the colonel had said.[48]

It was Paul Kagame, the refugee from Gitarama who had left Rwanda as a child and grown up in Uganda, who rescued the RPF from collapse. Kagame, a secretive, sober, intelligent and determined man, took over the struggling remnants of the army. Within a matter of months he gave it direction, discipline and strategy. Kagame was reputedly a military tactician of enormous talent, a fact recognised during a military training course at the US Army Command and General Staff College at Fort Leavenworth.

Kagame, like Rwigyema, was an experienced guerrilla fighter. He had risen in the ranks of the Ugandan army to assistant director of military intelligence. Kagame was one of only twenty-seven recruits who had fought alongside the future Ugandan president, Yoweri Museveni, to oust Milton Obote. When Museveni took Kampala by force in January 1986 it was the first insurgent movement effectively to take power from an incumbent African government. Both Kagame and Rwigyema were instrumental in this success.

Kagame believed that only classic guerrilla warfare would destroy Kigali's rotting regime. He had little weaponry and manpower. His was a light infantry army having to re-supply by foot and he had to make the best use of all the RPF possessed.[49] Kagame was a truly impressive leader. He lived with his soldiers, shared their privations and knew that the war against the regime in Rwanda was likely to be protracted.

He did not wait long before attacking again, and this time he mounted a dramatic operation that successfully humiliated the regime. On the night of 22 January, 1991, RPF guerrillas attacked Rwanda's most notorious prison in the northern prefecture of Ruhengeri, known popularly as the Rwandan Bastille after the prison in pre-revolutionary France. The battle for the prison lasted most of the night and in the morning all the prisoners, some 1,500 people, including presumed and actual RPF supporters, were set free. It later emerged that when the attack happened, an order was sent from Kigali to a local army commander to kill all the prisoners. Captain Charles Uwihoreye had refused the order,[50] given to him in a telephone call with Colonel Elie Sagatwa, the president's personal secretary. Sagatwa called him twice and the second time told Uwihoreye that the order came directly from the president. Uwihoreye again refused to obey and was later thrown into prison in Kigali and saved only when a human rights group supported his case. The RPF held Ruhengeri for a day and withdrew before reinforcements arrived.[51] A large amount of military equipment was seized and the raid sent a shock wave through a government that had only a few months previously, albeit with French help, held the RPF at bay.

The regime reacted brutally. An organised campaign to kill the Bagogwe – pastoralists said to be of Tutsi descent who originated from the great forests covering the volcanic mountains in the north of Rwanda – was launched in January with the active help of local authorities, and lasted for three months. In one commune buses were sent round to collect up the victims, in another case a lorry. The Bagogwe were killed with spears, batons and even guns, and their houses were looted and destroyed. In Kinigi the order went out to "cut them to pieces". In some cases the killing was carried out by peasants who were told that this was special community work, and necessary to get rid of "enemies". In the prefecture of Gisenyi Bagogwe people disappeared into several army camps and were never seen again.

One woman lost five sons killed on the orders of the bourgmestre because, she was told, they might join the RPF. In some cases it was the *conseiller du secteur* who ordered the killing and members of the cell committee that helped to carry out the attacks. One burial site was discovered in the back garden of a bourgmestre. Some burial sites exposed the bodies of young men with multiple cranial fractures and amputation of limbs. Some prominent and powerful local personalities were seen to have been involved in the planning of these massacres and in some cases had taken part in carrying them out.

The exact figure of those killed will never be known. In many cases the communal authorities refused to issue death certificates. The names of some of the victims were published in a journal, the *Rwanda Rushya*, New Rwanda, and listed commune by commune some 300 names of people who were killed.[52] In response the minister of justice, Sylvestre Nsanzimana, promised an enquiry to catch the murderers but nothing ever came of apprehending those responsible.

These killings had started in the heart of the Bushiru, in the communes of Gaseke, Giciye and Karago, the most inaccessible region to outsiders. It was here that the practice of killing and the planning behind it – essentially the same methods used in the 1994 genocide – were rehearsed. Only a few days after the RPF prison raid a directive had been sent to the councillors in each sector, to organise collective work, or *umuganda*. The cell committees had carried out this directive. "It was our work to get rid of the accomplices of the inkotanyi", a killer said later. The Kinyarwanda word inkotanyi referred to RPF soldiers and the Tutsi in general. Any local authorities who refused to help were relieved of their functions.

The areas where the killing took place were sealed by roadblocks to prevent escape and entry was barred to human rights workers and journalists. But by August that year, when the evidence against his regime was mounting, Habyarimana was having to deny publicly his own responsibility in what had happened. A genocide of the Bagogwe some people were calling it:[53] the victims were killed for belonging to one particular ethnic group, and the intention had been to destroy them as a group. The number of Bagogwe and Tutsi people living in the Bushiru was seriously reduced; arrests, beatings and rapes continued with impunity. Six months after the attacks the region was finally opened up again and a great number of people fled to live in Kigali.

The Akazu was fearful. What its members dreaded more than anything was an alliance between the Tutsi, the southern Hutu and anyone else who was trying to create a democratic system of government.

2

CIVIL DEFENCE

By all accounts plans were being laid in Rwanda for mass murder on a countrywide scale towards the end of 1990 just after the RPF invaded. The idea that genocide of the Tutsi would solve all problems was spread in a series of secret meetings starting at the end of October, most of them taking place in Gisenyi prefecture.[1] It was clear to the planners that they would require many more people than just police and army personnel. The idea of mass mobilisation was not new. In the 1963 genocide there had been roadblocks and "self-defence" groups. But the militarisation of society which contributed to the speed of the killing in 1994 had its genesis in "civilian self-defence" (*auto-défense civile*) whereby peasants in each cell, the smallest of the administrative divisions, were armed.

The idea of a formal civilian defence force first emerged in 1989 when it was suggested as a way to protect the country from outside attack. The Rwandan ambassador to Zaire, in a confidential report to the Ministry of Foreign Affairs, had predicted such an attack: he claimed to have conducted an analysis of the Rwandan communities in Zaire, the Congo and Chad, the Central African Republic, Gabon and Cameroon, and had reached the conclusion that the country's enemies were to be found in communities where there was a majority of Tutsi. Some of these Tutsi, he warned, were receiving military training in Uganda. The ambassador worried about the weakness of the Rwandan army and he proposed that the Hutu youth of Rwanda should learn armed combat and that all civilians should eventually be organised in a programme of civil defence.[2]

After the 1990 RPF invasion weapons were distributed via communal officers to army reservists intended as the first line of defence. Each communal officer had to write a report about civil defence to the bourgmestre and a copy had to be sent to army command.[3]

The idea of creating a countrywide network of civil defence surfaced again in 1991. A part of the Rwanda government archive, seized when Kigali fell, reveals a detailed plan of nationwide civil defence first proposed by Colonel Augustin Ndindiliyimana, who at that time was minister for defence and security, responsible directly to President Habyarimana. In July Habyarimana was advised by Ndindiliyimana of the benefits of creating a trained militia in all of Rwanda's communes.[4] Ndindiliyimana told army officers that a lack of finance prevented compulsory military service. Nor were the means available to provide weapons to every person. But, Ndindiliyimana told officers, when finance permitted a civilian militia would be created to operate in tandem with the professional army. This was possible given Rwanda's young population, he said.[5]

At a meeting of prefects in September 1991, Ndindiliyimana explained how in the prefectures in the north, on the border with Uganda, the communal policemen living locally would be reinforced with army reservists. The salaries would be paid by the state.[6] Each prefect had to compile lists of the names of all the young men who had left to join the RPF. A more detailed plan was discussed in October in which all levels of public service were to be involved and it was to be organised by prefecture and commune.[7]

That same year each of the ten prefectures created a Council for Security, to examine the *auto-défense* of the population.[8] A law was drafted setting out a plan to protect the population, against RPF attacks, protect the infrastructure and obtain information on the presence and the actions of "the enemy" in the communes and cells and to denounce infiltrators. The ministers of defence and of the interior were to be responsible for preparing the lists of soldiers and gendarmes who were living in each commune. A national committee of civil defence was to be created that would bypass the government and receive orders from a National Security Council headed by the president.[9]

The Rwandan army grew rapidly, from 9,335 troops at the time of the 1990 RPF invasion to 27,913 by 1991. The vast majority of these recruits were uneducated peasants and there was a serious lack of discipline along with a problem of absenteeism. Two reports on the military were prepared by a group of French military advisers, the Détachement d'Assistance Militaire et d'Instruction (DAMI), who came initially from France's 11th paratroop division, from which the French secret service usually recruited its operatives.[10] Their reports noted serious deficiencies, including appalling maintenance of weapons and equipment. The report on the gendarmerie, written by the French Lt.-Col. Ruelle, revealed too few officers and insufficient training but he noted that French gendarmes were helping to rectify these deficiencies.[11] These DAMI assistants were in operational charge of the war against the RPF, firstly under Lt.-Col. Chollet and then, when news of his role leaked to a Belgian newspaper, under his deputy, Lt.-Col. Maurin. In the French army there was a widespread belief that any abandonment of the Habyarimana regime would be unacceptable.[12]

It was not only in the ranks that there were problems. In spite of a great deal of help from French experts a serious schism developed within the officer corps while moderates and extremists manoeuvred for position over how best to respond to the RPF threat and whether or not a peaceful settlement was possible. All army and gendarmerie officers were called to a meeting in Kigali on 4 December, 1991. More than 100 army officers assembled in the conference room of the École Supérieure Militaire (ESM), leaving their weapons in a side room to await the arrival of the president, their commander in chief. The atmosphere was tense and there was open disagreement. One of the officers later said that for him the day was a milestone. "A power vacuum suddenly opened up in front of us", he said. "Habyarimana had called the meeting but he did not know what to do. You could see his power eroding."[13] At the end of the day the face-saving compromise was the establishment of a military commission to investigate how to defeat the enemy "in the military, media and political domains".[14] It comprised hardliners and moderates who had to come up with a policy on how to win the war, a policy upon which all could agree. There were ten senior officers on the commission, including Colonels Théoneste Bagosora, Marcel Gatsinzi, Balthazaar Ndengeyinka, Léonidas Rusatira, Major Aloys Ntabakuze and Lt.-Col. Anatole Nsengiyumva.

A report was eventually produced but not all the members of the military commission members saw it and as far as can be ascertained a complete copy has never been found. Gatsinzi claimed that he did not attend all the military commission's meetings because he was not invited. The commission had been chaired by Colonel Bagosora, the commander of the Kanombe military camp where the meetings were held.[14] A key passage from the report was later circulated among senior army officers.[15] It was crucial because it identified the enemy in a particular way: "the principal enemy is the Tutsi inside or outside the country, extremist and nostalgic for power and who have never recognised and will never recognise the realities of the social revolution of 1959 and who want to take back their power by any means, including weapons. The accomplice of the enemy is anyone who supports the enemy."[16]

When some years later the genocide conspiracy was being considered by the investigators of the ICTR they set great store by this report and traced the conspiracy's roots to it. Those identified as extremists in the army had managed to legitimise their racist beliefs and a large part of the planning of the genocide was, the ICTR concluded, carried out in military offices.

One of these planning meetings, so a witness recalls, was chaired by Colonel Théoneste Bagosora. He claimed to have information that the RPF was secretly planning to kill the Hutu. In order to abort this plan, he said, the Tutsi should be exterminated. The witness was in an adjacent room, a radio transmission centre, listening to what was said and noting who was there. There was Jean-Bosco Barayagwiza, the director of political affairs in the Ministry of Foreign Affairs; Leon Mugesera, a political science professor and a stalwart of the MRND in Gisenyi; a bourgmestre, Juvénal Kajelijeli from Ruhengeri; Joseph Nzirorera, who was minister of public works, and Protais Zigiranyirazo. Among the army officers were Major Aloys Ntabakuze and Lt.-Col. Anatole Nsengiyumva, both of whom would have major roles in the events that were to follow.

After the meeting the conversation had continued in the nearby canteen and small groups started to discuss what was to be done. "They were calmly speaking about the extermination of Tutsi", said the witness. "The main subject was that you had to unwind – or undo the enemy action and stop the extermination of Hutu by Tutsi, and in order to do that the Tutsi had to be exterminated."[17]

Another witness reveals how Bagosora instructed the two general staffs of the army and the gendarmerie to establish lists of people identified as "the enemy and its accomplices". Lists were also prepared in the army's military intelligence department, G2, of "accomplices" of the RPF.[18] The weapons for the civil defence network came from the military.[19] The training of a youth militia was carried out by the military. In some places in the north there was overt distribution of weapons by the military, in order to achieve the one-armed-person-per-cell plan.

Steps towards democracy

While the secret plans were being laid there was pressure on the Rwanda government to change. The US State Department and the French Foreign Ministry were hoping to broker a settlement between the Rwandan government and the RPF, to contain and resolve the ongoing civil war. Inside Rwanda an emerging pro-democracy movement was growing. A group of thirty-three Rwandan intellectuals signed a manifesto which demanded immediate democratisation. Even the mass arrests after the RPF invasion in October 1990 did not deter the mood for change. Now, for the first time ever, there was a political opposition to Habyarimana's MRND. In March 1991 a group of 237 opponents of the regime publicly endorsed a new movement, the Mouvement Démocratique Républicain (MDR), that comprised supporters from Gitarama, the former President Kayibanda's home base. One prominent member was Jean Kambanda. The MDR also included personalities from the northern prefecture of Ruhengeri, prompting rumours that there must be a split in the northern mafia while infighting continued over decreasing spoils,[20] and people who had personal fights with Habyarimana. One of them, a former speaker of the national assembly, Thaddée Bagaragaza, was a former member of the MRND ruling elite and now he was trying to oust it from power. In a letter to the Interior Ministry in July 1991 he complained that the MRND was at a huge advantage over its rivals for it continued to use the offices of all the prefects and bourgmestres, and had the use of all official vehicles. He claimed that the MRND was issuing threats and extortion in order to keep its support.[21] Democratic politics in Rwanda was going to be a dirty business.

Gradually more parties were created. The Parti Social Démocrate (PSD), on the centre left, and then the Parti Libéral (PL), generally considered to be centre-right, were formed in 1991 with ambitions to bridge the Hutu and Tutsi divide. One of the leaders of the PL, Landoald Ndasingwa, once said: "I am a Tutsi, my wife is a white Canadian, several members of my family are married to Hutu, in fact we are all tired of this ethnic business."[22] Another party was the Parti Démocrate Chrétien (PDC), a Christian Democratic group, that had been difficult to establish because of the traditional support of the Catholic Church for the MRND.

In June 1991, when a new constitution was adopted that legalised the formation of political parties, the MRND quickly lost support; only in the north, in the strongholds where Habyarimana's people had benefited so well from his regime, did the MRND hold its power. A vibrant press came into being and much of it was pro-democracy, a development greeted with some concern. In a letter written by the president at the end of November 1991 he informed the army command that the enemy was financing some of Rwanda's newspapers to "poison the political atmosphere". The president provided a list of these papers and the names of the journalists who worked for them. He said he intended to enlist the Ministry of Justice to prevent the enemy hiding behind a free press.[23]

One of the papers listed was the openly pro-democratic *Rwanda Rushya*, New Rwanda, published by André Kameya. Kameya received a typed death threat on Ministry of Defence headed notepaper.[24] And so threatened did other journalists feel that the Executive Committee of the Association of Rwanda Journalists felt it necessary in December to issue a statement to say that the freedom of the press was essential in a democracy. The journalists condemned the lack of justice at a time when murders and disappearances were happening all over the country. The army and the legislature should be above politics.[25] There were five signatures on this statement but that of Vincent Rwabukwisi, the director of a paper called *Kanguka*, was missing. He had been thrown into prison after writing about human rights abuses. Another journalist, Noel Rugelinyange, had recently died in prison in mysterious circumstances.

The Interahamwe emerges

Each time there was a concession towards power sharing there was violence, and it was aimed not just at political opposition but against the Tutsi. Violence for political ends was now a part of political life in Rwanda. Youth gangs, who violently coerced support, were attached to each political party, and there was serious fighting among rival groups who tried to steal members from each other. It was almost impossible for the youth of the country, most of them unemployed, not to get involved. And most of the violence went unpunished. There was little law enforcement and the courts were under-funded and rarely operated as they should.[26]

President Habyarimana's MRND formed its own youth group at the end of 1991. It was called the Interahamwe. The name meant those who work closely together and who are united. It was better organised than the other groups and had a clearly defined structure, with various committees covering social and legal affairs, research and development, propaganda, evaluation and documentation. It was intended to be organised nationwide, in sectors, and a monthly contribution had to be paid by its members.[27] The treasurer of the Interahamwe, Dieudonne Niyitegka, would later claim that control of the Interahamwe rested with one man, a former ambassador and minister of justice, and then the president of the MRND, Mathieu Ngirumpatse.[28]

Members of the Interahamwe were given military training: witnesses from Camp Kigali, an army base in the heart of the city, saw government buses turning up at the barracks in 1992, carrying certain soldiers to secret places where they would train the unemployed.[29] The recruits were initially trained to handle weapons and use explosives and then later they were taught to kill, with the emphasis on killing at speed. Victims had first to be immobilised by having their Achilles heel cut. Two men are known to have taken part in the training. They were Colonel Leonard Nkundiye, a Belgian-trained Presidential Guard, and Colonel Innocent Nzabanita, known as Gisinda, wild animal.[30] One witness would later claim that the initial training of youth militia was started as early as January 1991 and was at first handled by French instructors.[31] There were several training places: of those known about, one was quite close to the international airport in Kigali, at the Bigogwe camp in Gisenyi, where Major François Uwimana of the para-commandos was in charge of training.[32]

The first time that the Interahamwe took part in organised killing may never be known but there are reports that in November 1991, some four months after Augustin Ndindiliyimana had suggested the creation of a civilian militia, they were involved in the killing of Tutsi in the commune of Murambi, east of Kigali.[33] Then in March 1992 there were more massacres, this time in the Bugesera, in the south-east corner of the country where there was a higher percentage of Tutsi than anywhere else. The killing saw the involvement of militia, local authorities and elements of the armed forces, together with the use of propaganda.

The Bugesera was flat, hot and dry and Tutsi had come to live there to escape the attacks against them in the 1960s. It was an inhospitable region with mosquitoes and tse-tse fly. It also contained the largest military camp in the country, the Gako camp. In October 1991 a group of 28 young Tutsi men had been taken there and badly beaten and eight of them never returned. In mid-February 1992 five more civilians were taken to the camp and they were released only after representations from human rights groups.

On 3 March, 1992 a news item was broadcast on Radio Rwanda that a Tutsi plot had been uncovered to kill prominent Hutu. Immediately afterwards, an order went out to the local authorities, who told people that there was going to be a special collective work session to "clear the bush"; everyone knew that this meant to kill the Tutsi. The killing of women and children was called "pulling out the bad weeds". Witnesses said that the killers came from neighbouring communes and that all the victims were Tutsi. "They said they had to kill Tutsi ... the proof of it was that they did not touch the Hutu ... they came with sacks to take our haricots, killed our goats and cows and even took our clothes", said a survivor.[34]

The killing began on the night of 4 March and lasted five days, during which time an estimated 300 people were murdered, most of them brutally. Pregnant women had babies gouged from them, the men had their penises cut. Some people were buried alive. Some victims bound hand and foot were thrown into the river Nyabarongo. There were photographs of some of the bodies published in the French magazine *Jeune Afrique* on 15 May, 1992. There were rapes and orgies, with soldiers, gendarmes and local authorities involved. Groups of soldiers were seen to fire their weapons on civilians. Some families were set alight in their homes. One of the victims, whose wife and four children were killed, said that there had never been any trouble with the neighbours before, not until the bourgmestre suggested it. The people who attacked his family came from another cell. An Italian nun, Antonia Locatelli, who had spent twenty years in the region, went to see her local bourgmestre, an MRND official called Fidele Rwambuka[35] who was widely believed to have been responsible for the violence, and told him it had to stop. She then launched accusations against the government on an international radio station. Two days later she was shot dead by soldiers.[36] While the killing continued terrified Tutsi fled to churches, clinics and schools and more than 15,000 sought sanctuary in communes elsewhere, in Nyamata, Rilima and Gashora.

The Interahamwe had travelled to the Bugesera from three sectors in Kigali, from Remera, Cyahafi and Bilyogo, and arrived in two minibuses and a lorry. There were Presidential Guard also present during the killing but they were wearing civilian clothes. A witness at the local Gako camp said that the commander there received a telegram to order him to put a company of his men at the disposal of the operation to "neutralise the enemy", which in the army was a term used to mean to kill Tutsi. The soldiers dressed in civilian clothes were taken by local people to the homes of their Tutsi neighbours.

The official response from the government was to describe what happened as "self-defence". The US and Canadian ambassadors in Kigali went to see President Habyarimana to express concern at the violence but the French ambassador, Georges Martre, refused to join them.[37] The Belgian ambassador, Johan Swinnen, cabled Brussels that the militia known as the Interahamwe had taken part in the killings in the Bugesera and that what had happened had been carefully planned. A commando group had been recruited from the national gendarmerie school, the École Nationale de la Gendarmerie in Ruhengeri.[38]

The real truth of what happened in the Bugesera would emerge later, when a group of Rwandan human rights activists held a press conference in Kigali to explain the role of propaganda and how the killings were directly linked to news broadcasts on Radio Rwanda, at peak times, warning the Hutu of attacks. The news bulletins were the work of a Hutu propagandist, Ferdinand Nahimana, a professor and historian who was in the president's inner circle.

In a desperate plea on 4 June, 1992, the director of Amnesty International in France, Michel Forte, said on Radio France International: "Those responsible for these massacres are soldiers with help from the civil authorities. No one at all has been punished. Not to punish these people will lead to a repetition of these horrors. An independent commission must be created to judge those civilians and soldiers responsible."[39]

In August that year a defector came forward from within the MRND. His name was Christophe Mfizi, and for fourteen years he had run the Rwandan information office, Office Rwandais d'Information, (ORINFOR). In an open letter, published in Paris, Mfizi claimed that Rwanda was being run by a secret group going by the name of Le Réseau Zéro, (Network Zero). These northern oligarchs were treating the country like a private company from which the maximum profit could be squeezed. Until this network was destroyed, then democracy in Rwanda stood no chance at all. These northerners had infiltrated all walks of life in Rwanda and in order to retain power this group was encouraging racism and regional division.[40]

The Zero Network

Similar concern came later in the year from regional experts. The existence of "a death squad" in Rwanda was announced in Brussels in December 1992 during a press conference held at the Senate. It was described as similar to those created in Latin America. The death squad had taken part in the Bugesera massacres in March and had helped to plan political killings, said a reputable source, Professor Filip Reyntjens from the University of Anvers. A lawyer, Johan Scheers, and a senator, Willy Kuypers, supported him. These accusations were not new. A year earlier, in November 1991, the RPF had issued a press release in Paris claiming the existence of a military commando unit led by a Captain Pascal Simbikangwa. It was supervised by Colonel Elie Sagatwa in the president's office, involved the president's brother-in-law Protais Zigiranyirazo, and was planning to eliminate political opponents.[41]

Now almost a year later the information was being publicly released in the Belgian Senate. It was detailed. It named names, thanks to three informers who claimed insider information. They accused the president's three brothers-in-law, Protais Zigiranyirazo, Séraphin Rwabukumba and Pierre-Célestin Rwagafilita, of being members of it. Others said to be involved were Colonel Elie Sagatwa, Pascal Simbikangwa, Alphonse Ntirivamunda, a nephew of the president, the commander of the Presidential Guard, Major Leonard Nkundiye, Anatole Nsengiyumva, the head of military intelligence, and Colonels Théoneste Bagosora and Laurent Serubuga. All of these people were members of the Akazu, and had a network of sympathisers in local authorities.[42] These claims were strenuously denied and a law suit was instigated by Rwabukumba which was halted only, according to Bagosora, because the civil war had resumed and when they lost, funds were no longer available.[43]

One of the informers was known as Janvier Africa. Little is known about how he fell out with the Akazu, but he claimed intimate knowledge of the activities of the extremists. Africa claimed to have worked for Rwanda's internal security services and to have been recruited to the death squad in 1989 whilst working in a Kigali hotel where he spied on guests. Africa said that he had obtained his job with the security services, Service Central de Renseignements, through Pascal Simibikangwa, who ran it. Africa also said that the preparation for the massacres of the Bagogwe and those of the Tutsi in Bugesera had taken place in the home of Simbikangwa – a villa in Remera, Kigali, which was nicknamed the Synagogue. According to Africa, this was where the plans for the Interahamwe were devised; one of the original ideas had been for senior members of the Interahamwe to be armed and trained by the Presidential Guard. Simbikangwa, who was paralysed and wheelchair bound after an accident, was ostensibly in charge of "criminology" but his reputation was as an expert torturer.

After the RPF invasion in 1990 Africa was recruited to work in the office of the president and became the press spokesman. He was ambitious and went on to create a journal, *Umurava*, financed by the president and the northern clique. But, in a series of statements made towards the end of 1992, Africa claimed that he had become sickened at the increasing violence demonstrated by those in power. Having once worked with them, he now believed that the country was run by a bunch of criminals committing more and more horrible crimes. Africa claimed that the massacre of the Bagogwe in January 1991 had been organised at a meeting at which both the president and his wife had been present. A "sorcerer" or soothsayer had been brought to the meeting by Elie Sagatwa and it was the soothsayer who had first suggested the idea of killing the Bagogwe people. Various senior members of the government had been at this meeting: Joseph Nzirorera, an MRND stalwart, Casimir Bizimungu who was the foreign minister, and Protais Zigiranyirazo.

Zigiranyirazo, the president's brother-in-law, was particularly notorious. Known as Mons Z, he was implicated in the murder of Dian Fossey in 1985. Fossey, an American ecologist with an international reputation, had a passion for the silver-back gorillas in northern Rwanda and had been found dead in her mountain research station, Karisoke, in the prefecture of Ruhengeri, with machete wounds to her face and neck. Key witnesses were eliminated: a certain Emmanuel Rwelekana was found dead in a prison cell, said to have committed suicide.[44] Nick Gordon, who wrote a book about Fossey's death, concluded that she was killed because she knew too much about the illegal trafficking by Rwanda's ruling clique and that she was trying to restrict tourism, which, given the presence of the gorillas, was a useful source of income for Rwanda.[45]

Zigiranyirazo was at the heart of the country's power structure and it is claimed that he was present when the decision was taken to kill the Bagogwe. The plan was to involve bourgmestres at a local level and to employ gendarmes to ensure that the operation went to plan. Africa explained that for months after the killing people had been unsure about what really happened because the entire region had been sealed off with strategically placed roadblocks. Witnesses were scared for their lives although some of them did later help human rights workers to locate mass graves.

Africa also claimed that Séraphin Rwabukumba, the youngest of Agathe's three brothers and a businessman, had provided a vehicle and machetes for the Interahamwe when its members took part in the killing of Tutsi in the Bugesera in March 1992. Rwabukumba strenuously denied this charge.

An arrogant man with a dominant personality, he worked in the foreign service department of the Banque Nationale de Rwanda,[46] as well as running an import-export trade company called La Centrale. There were plenty of other business concerns operated by those close to the president: the chef de cabinet, Enoch Ruhigira, ran the Office de Café (coffee export), and Michel Bagaragaza was the head of the Office du The (tea office). The president's family itself owned a hotel-restaurant, "Rebero-Horizon", and the night-club Kigali Nights,[47] and the president reputedly owned land in Zaire. There were also stories about a family business bringing cocaine from New York to Paris, but the details of these claims are unclear.[48]

These were by no means the extent of Africa's accusations. He claimed that a strategy of state terror had been devised and that the plan was to spread fear throughout the country by laying landmines. A curfew would be called and then landmines would be laid at night during the curfew hours by militia and soldiers. The opposition and the RPF would be blamed. The laying of mines had already begun, Africa claimed, and they had been put in taxis, in bus stations and anywhere where there was "a good concentration of Tutsi and opposition members".

Africa described how he personally had taken part in a terror campaign in the prefecture of Gikongoro during which forest fires were lit. Opposition politicians and the RPF had been blamed.[49] Africa claimed that he had driven to Gikongoro from Kigali with a military chauffeur in a vehicle that belonged to MINITRAP, the Ministère des Travaux Publics, de l'Énergie et des Mines (Ministry of Public Works, Energy and Mines). There were going to be "terrorist" attacks by the army organised on a nationwide scale and a state of emergency declared with a curfew. Later the president himself would ensure that calm was restored and he would be gloriously triumphant. In a last article, published in December 1992, Africa revealed how in October 1990, when the RPF invasion happened, there had been pretend attacks on Kigali in order to terrify the inhabitants. There were plans to infiltrate the opposition and ensure violence in those prefectures with a large number of Tutsi. A series of killings had been discussed and Colonel Laurent Serubuga was to be in charge of the operation. Those targeted included prominent and popular politicians and those army and gendarmerie officers who had taken part in the killing and were therefore witnesses to "state secrets".[50] Any candidate who stood in elections against the president would be killed.

Africa said that the plan was to have Interahamwe militia in every sector, at least ten who would be trained in all acts of terrorism; they would wear distinctive clothes and be equipped with cords, bayonets and be given shoes to wear. They would communicate with each other through the blowing of whistles, used to call for reinforcements. The best trained would carry hand grenades and guns and they would be given logistical support by the Presidential Guard. They would undertake what were called ten-minute raids in the neighbouring cells and these would create surprise and fear. Militia were already being trained outside the country in Zaire, at Kotakoli, and the first recruits was due back in Kigali in December 1992. The training, Africa claimed, was carried out by Israelis, and most notably in kidnap techniques and summary executions. He provided no further details of Israeli involvement.[51]

"I do not know why these recruits have not yet returned to Rwanda", Africa wrote in December 1992, "but I am warning you in advance. Do not be surprised by these attacks. I am fulfilling my duty in telling you about them."

Africa warned that a terrible and imminent danger awaited all Rwandans. The poison had been prepared, he wrote, and it was being administered to the country in small doses. Africa hoped that by exposing these plans something would be done to stop them.

Only much later would more details emerge of the death squads Africa had informed about. They had been part of something called Le Réseau Zéro (Zero Network) – a name chosen, some people speculated, to indicate the number of Tutsi the extremists intended to leave in Rwanda.

Zero Network was in fact a secret communications link, a radio network whose existence was known only to the extremists and which enabled them to keep in touch with each other. A witness for the ICTR, a communications expert, explained how the extremists trusted only each other. "They did not want their communications or their conversations or activities to be ... rather, they did not want the other members of government or officers or members of the army to be aware of their activities and communications".[52] The membership of Zero Network included Colonels Laurent Serubuga, Pierre-Célestin Rwagafilita, Augustin Ndindiliyimana and Déogratias Nsabimana, Major-General Augustin Bizimungu, Brigadier-General Gratien Kabiligi, Lt.-Col. Anatole Nsengiyumva and Major Ntabakuze. There were also 76 civilian members, among whom were Jean-Damascène Bizimana, Secretary-General of the Foreign Ministry, Joseph Nzirorera, Jean-Bosco Barayagwiza, Leon Mugesera, Protais Zigiranyirazo, the foreign minister Casimir Bizimungu, Mathieu Ngirumpatse and the businessman Félicien Kabuga.

The death squads were small groups of well-trained operatives in charge of executing the decisions taken by people called "dragons", the code used for those who issued the names of those targeted to be killed. "The dragons were supposed to be the names of the masterminds – I do not know whether this word is the appropriate word – the groups that were behind those activities, that is, anti-enemy activities, activities directed against the accomplices."

Another secret group was created in the military, called the Abakozi association. "That was a group of persons ... made up of soldiers and who worked with the commanders of the dragons ...". The Abakuzi, a Rwandan word which means the workers, was also used to describe death squads, but it was used mainly for those higher in rank and who were considered as good "workers". The witness explained: "To work meant to rid oneself of the inyenzi, of the enemy and its accomplices who were, based on what I knew, considered to be Tutsis and their accomplices."[53]

Political reform

Throughout 1991, the political reform process in Rwanda continued in fits and starts. The new constitution adopted in June of that year provided for a multi-party political system, the establishment of an office of prime minister, freedom of the press and the right of workers to withdraw their labour. The president continued to nominate and dismiss ministers and there was a series of unsuccessful attempts to negotiate a government. Finally, a year later, on 6 April, 1992, a coalition government was announced incorporating all the major opposition parties, the MDR, the PSD, the PL and the MRND. The cabinet was to be headed by Dismas Nsengiyaremye of the MDR. Later that month, to comply with the new constitutional prohibition of participation in the political process by the armed forces, Habyarimana relinquished his military title and functions. There seemed to be genuine progress towards change.

On 28 May, the RPF met Rwanda's opposition politicians in Belgium. A joint communiqué issued in Brussels by the RPF and the opposition parties declared they were fighting a corrupt regime that was in serious breach of human rights laws and that unless Habyarimana left office, there was no chance for peace. There was, they declared, no place in Rwanda for racism or for racist propaganda.

At the news of the alliance between the RPF and the internal opposition there was violence in Kigali and seven people were killed during street demonstrations. Journalists later discovered that the authorities had issued two permits for public assembly that day, one for the PSD and the other for the Interahamwe, and that the prefect of Kigali, Colonel Tharcisse Renzaho, had intended all along that street fighting should take place. Journalists witnessed gendarmes fire on PSD supporters and they noted that there were elements in the crowd that not even the MRND leadership could control – armed soldiers dressed in civilian clothes infiltrating the demonstrations and shooting at people. The journalists later discovered that these soldiers were Presidential Guards.[54]

There was an increasingly concerted opposition to the extremists and one of the first actions of the newly created government was to rid the army of the northern clique. As the new government was sworn to office in April 1992, it successfully ousted Colonels Théoneste Bagosora, Laurent Serubuga, Pierre-Célestin Rwagfilita and Pontien Hakizimana, who were "retired". The new army chief was Colonel Déogratias Nsabimana. The former presidential adviser on defence and security, Colonel Augustin Ndindiliyimana, from the south of the country, was given the command of the national gendarmerie.

One of these newly retired colonels was Théoneste Bagosora, who since

1990 had been the President of the ADECOGIKA association, a group dedicated to the financial benefit of the Bushiru region. Bagosora used the association to create for himself an effective political base. He was not widely considered to be a particularly good soldier, and Bagosora was known for his often violent and racist reactions towards Tutsi. Yet there was speculation that he considered himself to be the "dauphin".[55]

Later on, during his eventual trial, Bagosora would admit that in March 1991 he had tried to persuade Habyarimana to relinquish his role as commander-in-chief and that he had put himself forward for the job. On this occasion Bagosora had been accompanied by his brother, Pasteur Musabe, the director of the commercial bank, the Banque Continentale Africaine, also a man of influence, and a fellow northerner, Michel Bagaragaza, the head of the national tea export office.[56]

It was the MRND that rescued Bagosora's career after he was ousted from the army. He was nominated by the party as chef de cabinet in the ministry of defence. From this outer office Bagosora could have influence over policy and watch carefully the behaviour of the minister of defence in the new government, James Gasana. Gasana, although an MRND member, was not a part of the northern mafia. The senior civil servants in every ministry were always members of the MRND and they continually countermanded the orders of the opposition ministers. They ran a well-oiled bureaucracy which produced a great deal of documentation; reports, the minutes of meetings and letters typed neatly on headed notepaper and written in business French, carbon-copied, and filed carefully away in ring binders.

If the opposition in Rwanda thought that it had successfully neutralised the extremists in the army, however, it was to be disappointed. A study of some of the documents from the Rwanda military archive retrieved after the fall of Kigali shows how the G2 military intelligence department, headed by Lieutenant-Colonel Anatole Nsengiyumva, continually lobbied against negotiations with the RPF and was determined to resist political change.

As the country made its first tentative steps towards democracy, the more extreme and fantastic Nsengiyumva's voluminous reports to the president and to James Gasana became.[57] The word inyenzi ("cockroaches"), is used frequently to describe the RPF and the reports are full of claims that the army was damaged by the creation of a coalition government. In June 1992, just prior to the start of peace talks with the RPF, Nsengiyumva claimed that the PL, with the help of the MDR, had created a network throughout the country to carry out subversive activity. A pattern emerges in these documents of how terror tactics used by the extremists are often blamed on opposition parties.

Nsengiyumva subsequently informed on dozens of people, providing lists of names of soldiers and civilians he claimed had been secretly recruited by the RPF. These people had carried out terrorist attacks in Kigali, he alleged, using a secret cache of grenades. "[The] cockroaches who have infiltrated these teams want to attack the defences of the capital", he wrote. He also claimed that the "cockroaches had no intention of negotiating to end the war". His reports are littered with the names of people he calls "accomplices", both military personnel and civilians, and he claimed to have infiltrated a meeting of the PL where there were rumours of a coup against the president.[58] In a report dated 23 June, 1992 he claims proof of links between the "cockroaches" and members of the coalition government.[59] Then, on 2 July, Nsengiyumva provided a list of senior army officers who he claimed had met with members of the opposition.[60]

In July 1992, while internationally sponsored negotiations were being prepared between the RPF and the government, Nsengiyumva told the president that the real intention of the enemy was to take Kigali. The RPF was only pretending to negotiate.[61] Some weeks later he claimed that the progress towards democracy was demoralising the troops. "The men are beginning to think that the cockroaches are their kind brothers who want to return and that we will live together in peace", he wrote in a memorandum on 13 August, 1992. The army's war fighting capability was affected by such thoughts, he warned: the RPF was working through political parties to gain control of the country. Furthermore, he claimed that the general public was against a settlement with the RPF, and that certain officers were accusing the president of a failure to adequately defend the country.[62]

Just after this memorandum was written negotiations began in Arusha, Tanzania, between the RPF and the Rwandan government, sponsored by the Organization of African Unity (OAU), with Belgian, French and US observer delegations. Two days later there were killings in Kibuye of both Tutsi and opposition party members and once again local authorities and certain elements of the army took part.

Nsengiyumva and the secret agents who worked for him kept the closest watch on all aspects of Rwandan society. Opposition politicians were particular targets, and Nsengiyumva claimed to have discovered that the MRD was "inciting the population to civil disobedience". He accused the party of targeting Tutsi and then laying the blame on the MRND for the violence, and claimed that the new government wanted to get rid of Ferdinand Nahimana of the Office Rwandais d'Information (ORINFOR) which controlled Rwanda's press. It had been Nahimana who had so adeptly prepared the propaganda aired on Radio Rwanda to incite the Bugesera killings in 1992.

The terror attacks meanwhile had been steadily increasing for months. In April 1992, in the wake of the swearing-in of the new cabinet, there were explosions; a lorry blew apart in Gitarama killing seventeen people; a package exploded in a taxi in Kigali killing four people; a bomb exploded in a hotel in Butare, Rwanda's second city in the south, injuring thirty people. On 8 May, the minister of education, Agathe Uwilingiyimana, was attacked in her home and badly beaten by unknown aggressors.[63] An informer later revealed that the Interahamwe had been sent to kill her but they had baulked at the last minute and instead had beaten and robbed her and members of her family. Gendarmes had stood guard outside her house to ensure that her neighbours did not come to her aid.

Other reports from that time, some of them written by Laurent Serubuga, who had been with Habyarimana since the beginning, reveal a plan in October 1991 to mount a propaganda campaign within the army to ensure that soldiers were aware that the newly-created political parties were no more than a cover for the RPF.[64] In a March 1992 report Serubuga wrote to the minister of defence: "Tutsi students want to win the Hutu of the south to their cause … the Tutsi students have invented a story that the Hutu of the north want to massacre the Tutsi and southern Hutu."

Serubuga claimed that the vice-rector of the Nyakinama campus in Ruhengeri seemed to think that there was a plot to "clean" the country of Tutsi and that it would start with the killing of young boys. Serubuga told the minister of defence that he had no idea at all how this man could have come up with such an idea.[65]

Peace negotiations begin

The country was experiencing profound change. When in May 1992 a US official, ambassador Herman Cohen, assistant secretary of state for African affairs, visited Rwanda, he noticed organised demonstrations that were clearly anti-Habyarimana as he drove to meet the president. Then, in his meeting with Habyarimana, he found the president intransigent about the RPF. They were Ugandans, Habyarimana told him. Although he was willing to discuss the question of the return of Rwandan refugees, he was not willing to talk about the RPF because they were Ugandan army regulars and they should return home to Uganda.

Habyarimana assured Cohen of the progress to democracy in Rwanda, telling him that a government of national unity was in place with a prime minister and a foreign minister both chosen from the opposition. When Cohen met these ministers, who were indeed leaders of the MDR, they were unequivocal about their hatred of the repressive regime in Rwanda desperately clinging to power. But they were not enamoured of the RPF either.

The various opposition parties were multi-ethnic, Cohen reported to Washington, but massive military expenditures were ruining the economy.[66] The US was now actively involved in trying to find an end to the civil war and so were the French.

On 24 May, foreign minister Boniface Ngulinzira met representatives of the RPF in Kampala and afterwards the French government offered to host talks. A preliminary meeting was held in Paris in June and then official negotiations began in Arusha, Tanzania, on 12 July. The pressure for a settlement came from Belgium, the US, France and the OAU under its Secretary-General, Salim Ahmed Salim. It was hoped that protracted negotiations would give the two sides a chance to understand each other and allow for changing perceptions. This seemed to work: by September the two sides, the RPF and the Rwandan government, were discussing power-sharing and by October a timetable for a transition to a power-sharing democracy was being discussed.

There appears to have been popular support for the creation of democracy, when on 10 October, 1992, some 50,000 people came on to the streets of the capital to call for the resignation of President Habyarimana and denounce the militia – by now there were rumours of 400 militia in each commune. The prime minister wrote to Habyarimana to protest that the soldiers disguised in civilian clothes were members of the militia.[67] And then quite unexpectedly on 15 November, in a meeting in the north, the President had suddenly and publicly aligned himself with the militia. It seemed now as though the violence was sanctioned at a most senior level.[68]

The hardliners continued to preach hatred. On 21 November during an MRND meeting, the party's vice-president in Gisenyi, Leon Mugesera, addressed the party faithful at Kabaya and, speaking of Tutsi "accomplices" who had sent their children to the RPF, he said: "Why are we waiting to get rid of these families ... we have to wipe out these hoodlums. The fatal mistake we made in 1959 as to let them [the Tutsi] get out. They belong in Ethiopia and we are going to find them a shortcut to get there by throwing them into the Nyabarongo river .... We have to wipe them all out."[69]

The minister of justice, the PL politician Stanislas Mbonampeka, charged Mugesera with inciting racial hatred and issued a warrant for his arrest. Mugesera took refuge in an army camp. Mbonampeka resigned, unable to effect the arrest, and a successor was not found.

While the peace negotiations were in progress in Arusha there was secret planning within the army to continue to fight the RPF. With the help of French military advisers a new unit was created in the para-commandos, the Commando de Reconnaissance et d'Action en Profondeur (CRAP). Also trained by the French, the unit was intended to supply intelligence to identify RPF positions, to infiltrate the enemy and to eliminate certain members of it. It was an estimated forty-strong and comprised only soldiers from the north. Members of CRAP were later spotted during public demonstrations, wearing civilian clothes and taking part in terror tactics with the Interahamwe. Some of them were used in turn to train civilians. Colonel Déogratias Nsabimana, the army chief, told the minister of defence about this new group and made a special request for the provision of night vision equipment.[70]

According to several witnesses the commander of the para-commando battalion, Major Aloys Ntabakuze, held frequent meetings with his troops to persuade them not to accept a negotiated settlement. He said they must fight the Tutsi to the last. He told his troops that anyone who was not a member of the MRND was an accomplice of the enemy. Ntabakuze transferred all Tutsi NCOs out of his unit and he persecuted troops who came from the south. As the peace agreement neared completion Ntabakuze moved heavy weapons out of the camp to a secret location. There are witnesses who noted that when he later brought civilians into the camp it was members of CRAP who were responsible for their deaths.[71] Afterwards there would be fresh mounds of earth near the firing range.

The RPF attacks again

In a sudden and violent attack on 8 February, 1993, the RPF mounted a massive offensive and its troops reached within twenty-three kilometres north of Kigali. Were it not for the presence of French troops and advisers then the RPF could have taken the capital. The French sent reinforcements but in the Foreign Ministry in Paris the attack confirmed the view that the RPF could actually win the civil war. Paris announced that two more companies of French troops would be sent to Rwanda. The invasion showed how well the RPF had used the cease-fire time to build and train a disciplined force and it doubled the amount of territory under its control. So shocked was President Habyarimana that he personally called for a return to the Arusha negotiating table,[72] but not before he called for the reinforcement of the civil defence structures.[73]

Hundreds of people were killed and many thousands fled the RPF advance. The total number displaced by war in Rwanda reached one million – one seventh of the population. The aid agencies in Rwanda put their regular programmes on hold to help the displaced.[74] Huge camps were created where the children and the old were dying of starvation and dysentery. By late February there were an estimated 600,000 people on the move. In order to feed the displaced people in the north a massive airlift of food was organised by the UN and the World Food Programme.

The attack, according to the RPF, was launched to prevent further killing of Tutsi, murders that had taken place in a rampage with militia, local people and soldiers in Ruhengeri and Gisenyi between 22 and 31 January, when an estimated three hundred people were killed. In late February there was a ceasefire and in March peace negotiations were reconvened in Arusha.[75]

The diplomats taking part in the peace talks did not believe that the RPF had mounted an attack to prevent further killing. Instead there was speculation that it had done so in order to better dictate the terms of the next and most difficult phase of the negotiations, the merger of the two armies. On the table for the RPF was an offer of a fifteen per cent share in the new army, to reflect the percentage of Tutsi in Rwanda. In the end the RPF delegation managed to negotiate a forty per cent share with command level at fifty–fifty, down to field command positions. This was widely considered to be a tremendous victory for the RPF; so favourable, one of the US delegation argued, that it was bound to be rejected in Kigali. But in Arusha every effort went into obtaining a settlement, with little consideration of whether or not the eventual accords could really be implemented.[76] One US diplomat admitted to being "mesmerised" by the skilful tactics of the RPF in manipulating the government side.[77] In contrast the government delegation was divided, undisciplined and ineffective. President Habyarimana never once attended the talks and the government was represented by different political parties including the pre-democracy foreign minister Boniface Ngulinzira (MDR) and Landoald Ndasingwa, minister of labour and social affairs (MDR).[78]

The politicians had also insisted on the inclusion in the team of a hardliner, for without the presence of the extremists they could not be sure that any eventual agreement would be accepted back home. Colonel Théoneste Bagosora was the one chosen to join them, although it was clear from his attitude that he believed that they were all wasting their time. In turn the politicians thought Bagosora was crude and cynical and he told them that each time the power changed in Rwanda there was blood spilled. It was a Rwandan tradition.[79] Bagosora was a remote figure. He did not socialise with anyone during the talks, keeping mostly to his hotel bedroom, although he would use the public phone in the hotel lobby. After one particularly difficult session he had walked out in a fury and Patrick Mazimhaka, the vice-president of the RPF, spotted him later standing near the lift with his suitcases. Mazimhaka asked him where he thought he was going. Bagosora responded that he was returning to Kigali to prepare "apocalypse deux".[80] Mazimhaka described how Bagosora had looked directly at him and asked: "How did your people's blood get mixed with ours?" There had been a look of disgust on Bagosora's face. "He was always anti-Tutsi", one colonel remembers, "from the time when he took command of his very first unit." The same colonel said it was Bagosora's generation that had taken part in "the events" of 1963. "They were the ones who wanted to kill Tutsi", he said.

Bagosora would later write: "… the Hutu-Tutsi conflict was not mentioned during the negotiations in Arusha in spite of the fact that everyone knew that the war was launched by Tutsi who wanted to take back the power they had lost in the revolution of the Hutu people in 1959."[81] Nobody at the talks had much hope for their eventual success. Boniface Ngulinzira, who had found himself negotiating for the government on two fronts, first with the RPF and then with Bagosora the only link to President Habyarimana and the leadership of the MRND, said that the RPF was easier to work with than his own delegation.[82] Bagosora considered that Ngulinzira was an RPF accomplice.[83] Mazimhaka said that no one in the RPF team believed for one minute that President Habyarimana was sincere when he negotiated the accords. "But we put our faith in the international community", he said. A French delegation, in Arusha to help the government side, and in possession of intelligence that the RPF could win the war, believed that a negotiated settlement was the only way to preserve their influence. But the extremists never felt bound by the agreement concluded at the talks: Bagosora later claimed that they had been organised for the benefit of the RPF by the "great Anglophone powers".[84]

Back home in Kigali the army chief, Colonel Déogratias Nsabimana, was making strenuous efforts to prevent any possibility that the agreement would be implemented. He wrote to the minister of defence saying that soldiers needed "civic and psychological preparation", by which he meant history lessons about how evil the Tutsi monarchy had been. The teacher he proposed was Ferdinand Nahimana, the extremist ideologue who had recently been removed from running ORINFOR, and who had faked the news reports to incite the killing in the Bugesera in March 1992. Nahimana had been a professor at the Butare campus of the University of Rwanda and he was considered in some circles to be a talented historian.[85] Most notably he had written books and articles on the "Hutu nation". The army chief thought Nahimana could usefully write a syllabus for each battalion and then lessons could begin for the lower ranks.[86] Nsabimana told President Habyarimana: "The fact [is] that the Tutsi do not want to share power … this should be particularly underlined."

When confronted with evidence that there were soldiers in the ranks of the Interahamwe and that soldiers were handing out grenades to the militia Nsabimana denied all knowledge. In December 1992 he had sent a letter to the minister of defence to tell him that it was the job of the Ministry of Justice to conduct an inquiry into these accusations. But evidence of wrongdoing was growing.[87] A French journalist, Stephen Smith, reported in *Libération* on 9 February, 1993: "In the far hills of Rwanda … France is supporting a regime which for two years, with a militia and death squads, has been trying to organise the extermination of the minority Tutsi … the death squads, organised in a *Réseau Zéro* [Zero Network] by the

President's clan, are operating a genocide against the Tutsi as though it were a public service."[88]

The accusation did not apparently cause much concern for the French minister for cooperation, Marcel Debarge, who, during an official visit to Rwanda on 28 February, called on the opposition parties to "make a common front" with President Habyarimana against the RPF. Such a recommendation could be based only on the perceived ethnic divide in Rwanda and was, as the expert Gérard Prunier would later point out, almost a call to racial war.[89]

Further civil-defence plans

The February 1993 RPF attack had terrible consequences for the people of Rwanda. A fierce power struggle began in the political opposition which was split between those who favoured a negotiated settlement and those who did not. Suddenly it seemed as though all those who had warned that the RPF was not just acting for the refugees but was intent on seizing power had been right after all. All the Tutsi inside Rwanda were now labelled accomplices, "ibyitso", and Hutu members of opposition parties were called traitors to the nation.

There was also emerging evidence of human rights abuses by the RPF, making it easier to brand them as bloodthirsty feudalists. It was during the attack in Ruhengeri on 8 February for instance that RPF soldiers killed civil servants, one of them a bourgmestre and others responsible for ordering the killing of Bigogwe. Women and children had also been among the victims. The killings severely damaged the RPF's image among the liberal opposition in Kigali. In government, the prime minister, Dismas Nsengiyaremye, who had once considered the RPF to be quite moderate, now began to have his doubts.[90] He was one of those in attendance at a secretly convened four-day conference in March 1993, along with President Habyarimana, minister of defence James Gasana and the high command of the army and the national gendarmerie, to discuss what could be done about the RPF's actions.[91] The subject of civil defence was raised again and Nsengiyaremye said that he was not against the idea so long as the distribution of weapons was done in an orderly fashion. Discussion ensued on how to define the enemy and Nsengiyaremye resolutely stood his ground telling army officers that there was only one enemy attacking Rwanda with weapons, and that was the RPF.

It is clear that the February attack must have caused a renewed urgency to get on with the plans for "civil defence". A diary kept by Colonel Bagosora, pages from which were obtained by Human Rights Watch, contains the details of such a plan, although it is not clear if the ideas are his own for they bear a striking resemblance to those suggested in 1991 by Major-General Augustin Ndindiliyimana. The diary entries, written in a florid hand in French and on the pages for February, outline a plan for communal police or alternatively military reservists to give citizens military training. Bagosora had written that sixty men be trained for each commune, which would then be organised sector by sector with coordination between the military authorities and local administration. The diary mentions the ordering of 2,000 Kalashnikovs to bring to 5,000 the total numbers needed for the communes. Three to five weapons were to be delivered to each cell. Bagosora also notes that a propaganda campaign should be launched, aimed at human rights organisations and diplomats.[92] According to Bagosora this 1993 diary, produced later at his trial, was simply a notebook used for a series of notes taken in various meetings about the civil war that he had attended in Kigali.

He admitted that weapons were distributed to civilians, and in accordance with the plan outlined in the diary. But these weapons were only handed out in those communes that were near the war zone with the RPF. It was unfortunate that this distribution of weapons had been made public, he said, for in Arusha the RPF told him they would refuse to continue to negotiate unless the weapons were withdrawn. Bagosora complained that he was blamed for this entire episode, for distributing weapons without the knowledge of his minister. He had been made a scapegoat.[93]

A plan for civil defence was under active consideration in the prefecture in Kigali and promoted by the prefect, Lt.-Col. Tharcisse Renzaho, who wrote the following in a May 1993 letter to the minister of the interior: "We must continue to prepare the population for organised 'auto-défense' and to ensure command and control".[94] He later warned about a secret network of RPF personnel established in Kigali and provided a list of twenty names.[95] Renzaho had earlier worked in military intelligence and some of his surviving reports from the 1970s and 1980s seem consistent with his racism. He talks of the "corrosive action of Tutsi" and how they were poisoning people against the regime. In Kigali the Tutsi were "a permanent menace" and the Hutu were failing to exploit their victory over the Tutsi. Renzaho was also worried about how influential Tutsi exiles were on the international stage.[96] By this point, however, by March 1993, the central committee of the MRND was well on its way to consolidating the force of the Interahamwe. Among the most active in this endeavour was Joseph Nzirorera in Ruhengeri.[97] At some time in March, Colonel Bagosora had an audience with President Habyarimana, during which he had advised the president that his twenty year rule had lasted long enough, and that "as a friend" he was advising him to step down after the transitional period, provided for in the peace agreement. Bagosora said later that the president agreed to this honourable exit, but had later reneged on his promise.[98]

The role of the military

Lt.-Col. Anatole Nsengiyumva, the head of the G2 military intelligence department, claimed in a series of reports in June 1993 to be infiltrating what he called the "Tutsi milieu". He had learned much for his efforts: that a new RPF attack could be expected, that Gisenyi was the next target, and that the RPF was determined to conquer the Karago commune, the heartland of Hutu extremism, in the Bushiru. "This is a symbol for the enemy", Nsengiyumva wrote. The enemy would apparently seize a cache of weapons that they believed were hidden near a presidential villa at Rambura and would then begin "cleaning the region of elements close to the head of state". It would subsequently push into the communes of Giciye, Gaseke, Satinskyi and "the famous Kibilira, to avenge the Tutsi massacred in this region". It reckoned that it had the south of the country already in its pocket, wrote Nsengiyumva. It had smuggled weapons into the country and was hiding them near military camps. Nsengiyumva listed the names of Tutsi who were in possession, he claimed, of caches of weapons. He said that landmines had been distributed by Tutsi, and he warned of claims that landmines had been delivered to the minister Landoald Ndasingwa. "The Tutsi are leaving the capital because they know fighting is imminent."[99]

In June 1993, Nsengiyumva was given the job of operational commander for Gisenyi, which covered three prefectures, Gisenyi, Kibuye and part of Ruhengeri.[100] On his arrival he called together local Interahamwe leaders and told them that he too was Interahamwe. His reports to Kigali continually warned of another RPF attack which would oblige the government to sign a peace agreement "with its eyes closed". He warned that the RPF had won over public opinion. It had infiltrated the whole country, and had massive support from the Ugandan army, the NRA. He was frank in these reports; he believed the RPF was better prepared and more willing to fight than the Rwandan army. The RPF was determined to seize the capital, a strategy, Nsengiyumva recalled, used by Museveni, when in 1986, as peace negotiations were just coming to an end, he had suddenly seized Kampala. "This is the same phase that we are living through", Nsengiyumva warned. The RPF would take Kigali, ride out the ensuing international outcry and then everything would calm down and the takeover would be a fait accompli. The only way to fight the threat was a heartfelt appeal to national and international opinion.[101]

Similar fears were reflected at the Ministry of Defence where, in a series of secret reports, James Gasana indicated a hard-line stance and a lack of belief in the peace process. The language in these reports is intemperate and the views expressed are often extreme; Gasana stressed that the war must be fought on two fronts, both inside and outside the country, and he talked of fears about how the public could best identify the "accomplices". He claimed to have obtained a list of secret RPF instructions to their "accomplices" who had been ordered to throw their weight behind opposition parties. The "Hutu accomplices" of the RPF were being told "to sow chaos in Kigali, Ruhengeri and Gisenyi". The last RPF instruction on the list was apparently for these accomplices to tell the world, by written or broadcast means, "that the MRND wanted to exterminate the Tutsi and all the southern Hutu".[102]

Money and weapons

Throughout 1993 the violence in Rwanda increased. In those parts of the north where the war was fought there were parts of the army running amok with the soldiers living in ever-worse conditions and terrorising the local people. One victim said: "We are very poor. They have taken our cows ... everything. We are hungry. We have to cultivate for the soldiers. We have no other means of eating."[103] Soldiers in Kigali were killing civilians at the rate of four or five a day and one soldier even strangled a man in broad daylight in front of the post office and then walked away leaving the corpse.[104]

On 18 May, 1993 a politician called Emmanuel Gapyisi was assassinated. He had at one time been the president of the MDR party in Gikongoro but since the early 1990s was behind the creation of a new political party intended to be both anti-Habyarimana and anti-Tutsi. Gapyisi claimed that he was the true guardian of the "rubanda nyamwinshi", the majority people. For many he was the respectable face of extremism, and he attracted to his cause those who would never have joined the more lunatic fringe of Hutu Power. Gapyisi was shot just as he was beginning to attract considerable support and his death caused havoc: there was random violence and several bombs exploded in Kigali. In early July Prime Minister Nsengiyaremye wrote a public letter to President Habyarimana accusing him of trying to avoid any possibility of peace. The terrorist groups were trying to restart the civil war and this was a trick, said Nsengiyaremye.[105]

With the government's mandate due for renewal, and with Nsengiyaremye insisting that the RPF be represented, President Habyarimana manoeuvred once again, promptly concluding an agreement with a conciliatory group of MDR dissidents. On 17 July a new cabinet was sworn in with a mandate to sign a peace agreement with the RPF. The new prime minister was a former minister of education, Agathe Uwilingiyimana, the first woman to be appointed to the post.

James Gasana and Dismas Nsengiyaremye fled to Europe claiming that their lives were at risk. Elsewhere in Rwanda, in the countryside and in the urban communes, there were Tutsi people so afraid of night-time attacks that they regularly slept outdoors instead of at home.[106] In one overpopulated part of Kigali called Gikondo, the attacks against Tutsi residents and moderate Hutu were so terrible that in July 1993 people fled in terror to the neighbouring embassy of Burundi. An Interahamwe turned informer whose name was Felix Bandora later claimed that he had taken part in operations in Gikondo. He said that the violence had been ordered by the highest officials in the MRND and that the gang of Interahamwe that carried out the violence was about thirty strong. "We had to cut and burn everything in our path, men, women and children. We had to instil terror. We wore red armbands to know each other." Bandora said that some of the Interahamwe did not want to take part but were frightened in case they were killed, and some Interahamwe thought they were under surveillance for any sign of weakness. A year earlier, in July 1992, the people of Gikondo had noticed the presence of Presidential Guards among the gangs of youths in their neighbourhood.[107] Bandora also said that he was part of an armed escort that was provided to a Presidential Guard by the Interahamwe. The name for the Interahamwe in Gikondo was the 64th battalion Zoulou, he said, and their chief was Séraphin Rwabukumba, a brother of the president's wife. Rwabukumba took a delight in terrorising and killing people.[108]

The Gisenyi Interahamwe leaders met Nsengiyumva again in December 1993 at the Hôtel Méridien. This time Nsengiyumva was accompanied by Joseph Nzirorera, who was then minister of public works, one of the government portfolios retained by the MRND. Nzirorera, largely responsible for financing the Interahamwe, sang the praises of Nsengiyumva and said they were very lucky to have him as an Interahamwe because he was a very important person. Nsengiyumva promised them weapons to use "in order to eliminate Tutsi and Hutu who were opposed to President Habyarimana". Nzirorera was one of the most important people in the MRND because he provided party finance. At this meeting he gave 20,000 Rwandan francs to each Interahamwe.[109] Nzirorera also took part in the distribution of weapons at the national level. Twenty Kalashnikovs were provided at the meeting; they were to be used, Nzirorera said, "to eliminate the Tutsis when things exploded in Gisenyi".[110] Nsengiyumva also wrote to the minister of defence to request 150 weapons and 9000 bullets for each commune in the Bushiru region. He would handle the distribution and the training of civilians and would report back, he said.[111]

There is testimony that detailed documents were drawn up for the national civil-defence programme together with the numbers of weapons and amount of ammunition required. A secret government commission was established to organise it. Kigali was to receive the best protection but apparently under the plan nothing had been provided for the parts of the country where the war with the RPF was not expected to take place.[112]

3

A PROGRAMME OF HATRED

The campaign against the Tutsi, which began after the RPF invasion in October 1990 and which ultimately became relentless in its incitement to ethnic hatred and violence, began in earnest in the pages of a journal called *Kangura*. *Kangura*, a word in Kinyarwanda meaning "wake others up", promoted the cause of a Hutu nation. Over the three years from 1990 to 1993 the journal devoted many column inches to inter-ethnic hatred and was an integral part of a campaign to denigrate Tutsi. Witnesses testify that it was financed by military officers, MRND members and an intelligence agency of the government.[1] One of its well-placed patrons was Lt.-Col. Anatole Nsengiyumva. Between 1,500 and 3,000 copies were printed twice a month – there were two editions, one in Kinyarwanda and one in French – and some of the early editions were printed on a government printing press.[2] Although Rwanda's literacy rate was less than thirty per cent, the news in *Kangura* was sensational and spread like wildfire. "Everyone spoke of *Kangura*",[3] a witness said. Copies of the journal were read aloud at public meetings and eventually during the rallies of the Interahamwe. To be mentioned in its pages invariably meant imprisonment or death.[4]

Because of its intimate links with the army *Kangura* sometimes appeared to be extremely well informed. It came to be regarded as a platform for President Habyarimana to prepare the ground for his decisions although *Kangura* did not hesitate to criticise him over concessions he was considered to have made in Arusha. *Kangura* appealed to the Hutu population to be vigilant against "the enemy and his accomplices" and its denigration of Tutsi was quite overt. One of its most infamous issues was number six containing what were called the Hutu ten commandments. These amounted to a manifesto against Tutsi, which was not only an outright call to show contempt and hatred for the Tutsi minority, but also to slander and prosecute Tutsi women. "A traitor is anyone who befriends, employs or marries a Tutsi."[5] On the back of this issue six there was a large picture of President François Mitterrand with the caption: "It is during the hard times that one comes to know one's true friends".[6]

One of *Kangura's* editorials in the 9 February, 1991 issue advised: "Let us learn about the inkotanyi [RPF supporters] plans and let us exterminate every last one of them." *Kangura* promised the "defence of the majority people", and it warned: "you understand that when the majority people is divided [then] the minority becomes the majority".[7] In another issue, in March 1993, *Kangura* published an article that included the words: "A cockroach gives birth to a cockroach … the history of Rwanda shows us clearly that a Tutsi stays always exactly the same, that he has never changed … the inyenzi who attacked in October 1990 and those of the 1960s are all linked … their evilness is the same."[8] At one point *Kangura* claimed that 70 per cent of the rich in Rwanda were Tutsi and that they monopolised the banking system. They occupied jobs that Hutu failed to get. There were warnings in Kangura that if Tutsi men failed to infiltrate Rwandan life then they sent in their women to seduce the Hutu. It reported that many people who said they were Hutu were in fact Tutsi and that the real Hutu should keep an eye out for such people, who were recognisable because they "lacked commitment to the Hutu cause". The propaganda taught that the RPF had launched its invasion of Rwanda to re-establish the Tutsi monarchy and enslave the Hutu.

The owner, accountant and editor-in-chief of *Kangura* was a man called Hassan Ngeze, a northerner and relatively uneducated man from the Nyakabungo cell in Gisenyi's Rubavu commune. His lack of formal training did not stop him from pursuing his ambitions to be a political leader of some influence and he was aware of the power that lay with the press. Witnesses remember seeing him with Colonel Nsengiyumva and Colonel Laurent Serubuga while in his home commune. Some years later when Ngeze was called to account for his crimes he was described as "a venomous vulgarian and purveyor of racial libel and slander".[9] There were always hints and suggestions in the articles he wrote about final plans and extermination.

Kangura issue number 54, published in March 1994, for example, contained a piece about what Ngeze claimed was going to happen to the Tutsis and their accomplices if fighting with the RPF was ever to resume: "Presently the accomplices of the inyenzi have compiled a list of 1600 persons who fought them most and these people must [be] killed during this transitional period ... thus the population feels threatened and prefers to follow them. The plan has been named the Final Plan. We know the number of those who are going to die but we are still looking for their names with a view to informing you .... Moreover, the accomplices of the enemy are well known. Therefore the inyenzi should have the courage to understand that they are making a slight error, they shall be exterminated. They should realise that if they strike again, none of the accomplices will survive."[10]

The CDR party

Kangura was central to the growth of extremism and it became the mouthpiece for a new political party created in February 1992 called the Coalition pour la Défense de la République (CDR). The CDR was an offshoot of the MRND. It promoted the most anti-Tutsi policies and banned from its membership anyone with Tutsi grandparents. It campaigned for a "pure Hutu" nation that was ruled by the majority. Its members rejected the idea that Rwandans were one people and considered the whole idea a Tutsi trick designed to weaken the majority Hutu. Article 2 of the Statute of the CDR clearly spelled out its objective: "the CDR's purpose is to defend the Republican institutions that emanated from the social revolution of 1959, and to ensure the respect of the sacred principles of democracy and the defence of Rwanda."

At first the CDR was used to advance positions that neither President Habyarimana nor the MRND could publicly endorse. But it soon developed its own momentum and in March 1993 the CDR issued a communiqué accusing President Habyarimana of ceasing to care about the interests of the nation and stating that, in agreeing a ceasefire with the RPF, he had "capitulated".[11] In time the CDR created its own militia; its name was Impuzamugambi which means "those with a single purpose". Ngeze, the editor-in-chief, led the Impuzamugambi in Gisenyi.

Another key figure in the CDR was Jean-Bosco Barayagwiza. Barayagwiza was a powerful public speaker and he used this talent to promote the extremist policies of the CDR. Once described by the RPF as a "fascist thug", he had a gift for manipulating the truth that meant in time he became the international propagandist for the génocidaires. Barayagwiza literally helped to prepare Rwandan public opinion to support genocide, and once the genocide began he was part of the plan to hoodwink the international community about what was really going on.

Barayagwiza was born in 1959 in the Mutara commune of the Gisenyi prefecture. A northerner, he was the Secretary-General of the CDR. (The president of the party, Martin Bucyana, was a southerner, and had been appointed to show that the party was not run exclusively by northerners; Bucyana was however, the only southerner on the CDR's ruling committee.) Barayagwiza had earlier joined the civil service, eventually becoming the director of political affairs at the Ministry of Foreign Affairs. He was at this post throughout the planning of genocide and then for the three months that the genocide lasted. Barayagwiza had had children by a Tutsi mistress, but to show that the CDR had to be one hundred per cent Hutu he deserted her.[12]

Barayagwiza had given a speech at the first ever rally by the CDR in Kigali in March 1992. It was at this rally, in the stadium in Nyamirambo, that Barayagwiza had used the phrase "tubatsembasembe", which means "we shall exterminate them"; it was taken up as a chant of the Impuzamugamgi who would sing it to a catchy tune.[13] One witness later described how the CDR was essentially a platform "to incite people to understand the evil within the Tutsi". For Colonel Bagosora, who was with the government team negotiating with the RPF in Arusha, one of the major flaws in the eventual peace agreement was the failure to include the CDR as a political party. While hastening to add that he was not a CDR supporter, Bagosora thought that the CDR should have been allowed into government as a matter of principle. "The CDR had met all the requisite conditions defined under Rwandan law in order to be approved or accepted as a political party operating in Rwanda", he said afterwards.[14]

The birth of hate radio

Further anti-Tutsi propaganda was stirred up by a new radio station which burst upon Rwanda just as the Arusha talks were being successfully concluded. It was a station that was to revolutionise the country's broadcasting and eventually its whole society. Up until then there had been one national broadcaster, Radio Rwanda, which was staid and solemn. This new station was called Radio-Télévision Libre des Mille Collines (RTLM) and had been created by a so-called free and independent broadcasting company set up, according to its documents of incorporation, "to create harmonious development in Rwandese society". In the street markets hundreds of cheap portable radios suddenly became available and the new station was immediately popular. It appealed to the young people with its disc-jockeys, pop music, and phone-ins. The announcers, unlike those who worked for Radio Rwanda, used street language. Using the FM frequency, RTLM carried no factual reports but there were commentaries and lengthy interviews and it soon became obvious that the new radio station was part of a campaign to promote extremist Hutu propaganda.

RTLM had been devised in November 1992 when Ferdinand Nahimana and Joseph Serugendo, a technician responsible for Radio Rwanda and a member of the Interahamwe,[15] had travelled to Brussels to purchase broadcasting equipment. Nahimana, it will be remembered, was the ideologue behind a faked news item broadcast on Radio Rwanda and intended to incite the Bugesera killings. He had turned down a job as adviser at a new ministry of information, into which ORINFOR was absorbed, saying that he had plans to create a new radio station. He had already collected funds at Ruhengeri University to help to finance it.[16]

The station would eventually have a transmitter that could reach the whole of Kigali, part of the Bugesera to the south and Kibungo to the east. Another transmitter was installed towards the end of January 1994 on Mount Muhe, in Gisenyi prefecture, which allowed broadcasts to the north, to Ruhengeri. The only place where it was difficult to hear RTLM was in Butare in the south and in Gisenyi town in the north. The leadership of RTLM wanted to place the transmitter in a secure area where there was a strong membership of MRND. They also had to avoid using any of the existing Radio Rwanda installations because that would have entailed depending on the goodwill of the government, which could at any time have prohibited RTLM programmes with respect to equipment that did not belong to it.[17]

The new transmitter was installed with great ceremony. Jean-Bosco Barayagwiza had come from Kigali in a motorcade, with one of the vehicles broadcasting songs by Simon Bikindi, Rwanda's best-known singer, via megaphone. Bikindi came from Gisenyi and had organised a music and dance display for the visit of the Pope to Rwanda in September 1990. The antenna itself was carried in a military truck and escorted by soldiers. A holiday was declared by the local authorities.[18]

As the radio station was being established and shares were being sold there was a huge rally in the Amahoro hotel, with more than 1,000 people in attendance. This was in early 1993. On the podium were Ferdinand Nahimana, Barayagwiza, Ephrem Nkezabera, Joseph Serugendo, Phocas Habimana and Félicien Kabuga. Kabuga, a rich businessman and one of the station's major shareholders, opened the meeting by thanking Nahimana for having had the idea of creating RTLM.[19] It was agreed that those present on the podium could manage the station, with Ephrem Nkezabera responsible for finance. There was a possibility that a loan might be given to RTLM by the bank BACAR, whose director-general was Pasteur Musabe, the younger brother of Théoneste Bagosora, the director in the office of the minister of defence.[20]

Nahimana would later serve on RTLM's twelve-member Comité d'Initiative which constituted a de facto board of directors because, as far as is known, the general assembly of shareholders never met to elect a board. Nahimana assumed the role of manager of the station and all the journalists of RTLM were recruited by him either directly or under his authority.[21] Ferdinand Nahimana and Jean-Bosco Barayagwiza were the two persons authorised to sign cheques on the RTLM bank accounts.

Félicien Kabuga became RTLM's president and Phocas Habimana the office manager. Below Habimana were the RTLM staff divided into three groups: the editorial staff headed by editor-in-chief Gaspard Gahigi, a member of the central committee of the MRND, who had worked for Radio Rwanda. The administrative staff and the technical services staff worked under Joseph Serugendo.

RTLM's broadcasts began in the morning in Kinyarwanda and most journalists were expected to be there by 8.30 a.m. While the broadcasts continued in Kinyarwanda, Gahigi would hold an editorial meeting at which he distributed work to the staff. Some people were sent to do interviews, while others were asked to gather information, and some of them remained at the RTLM offices to continue to operate the station. At midday the broadcasts closed down and work at RTLM stopped. At about

5 p.m. broadcasts were resumed, starting with Kinyarwanda programmes, and then from around 8 p.m there were broadcasts in French, until the station closed at 10 p.m. There were also weekly editorial meetings to explain policy. Phocas Habimana was usually there, and Ferdinand Nahimana occasionally attended, as did Jean-Bosco Barayagwiza.

That false information was broadcast on RTLM to instil fear and incite violence was confirmed some years later by witnesses who testified at the International Criminal Tribunal for Rwanda. One notable example was the broadcasting of a news item claiming that a secret RPF list had been found containing the names of all those people that the RPF was intending to kill. This particular broadcast went out on 14 January, 1994, just three months before the genocide began, and claimed that Félicien Gatabazi, a government minister from the PSD party, and Martin Bucyana, the president of the CDR, were on the hit list. Some weeks later Gatabazi and Bucyana were assassinated. This witness later testified that he had been shown a copy of the "RPF list" before it was broadcast and that news items of this type were prepared for RTLM by a special and secret group whose members included Ferdinand Nahimana, Pasteur Musabe, Michel Bagaragaza, Juvénal Uwilingiyimana and Théoneste Bagosora.[22]

There was some opposition to the exploits of the extremists. The government of Rwanda and RTLM had signed an agreement on 30 September, 1993, which authorised RTLM to operate a broadcasting station on the condition that the radio station would not broadcast programmes inciting hatred, violence or any form of division. On 26 November, 1993, barely two months later, Nahimana, Barayagwiza and Kabuga were called before the minister of information for being in breach of this undertaking. They were called in again early the following year, on 10 February, 1994, because of broadcasts failing the requirement. The station was also in breach of law number 54191 of 15 November, 1991 that permitted the creation of a radio station for the purpose of a free press in Rwanda and that also included provisions to punish persons who used the press to commit offences against individuals or groups, such as defamation and public slander.

No one was ever formally accused. The radio station had some very powerful patrons. A complete list of shareholders of RTLM, some twenty-five pages long, starts with the major shareholder, President Habyarimana. It goes on to list all the members of his inner circle, the Akazu: businessmen, bank managers, journalists, army officers and government officials. The singer Simon Bikindi was a shareholder as was Théoneste Bagosora. He had more shares in the station than anyone else in either the army or the ministry of defence.

RTLM was an immensely successful creation. Once, when diplomats asked President Habyarimana to take it off the air, he had responded that since the West had pressured him to move towards democracy, he no longer had the power to control the airwaves; democracies guaranteed free speech.[23]

Arming the country

It was during 1993, in the year that the Arusha Accords were negotiated, that a project began to import into Rwanda a huge number of machetes and other agricultural tools. The purchase of these tools took place in eighteen separate deals, and by companies not usually associated with agriculture; the same companies had made no such imports in either 1991 or 1992. As well as machetes they imported razor blades, nails, hoes and axes, screwdrivers, scythes, saws, spades, knives, pliers, pincers, scissors, hammers, and shears. These tools came into the country under government import licences headed "eligible imports". The overwhelming majority of the tools were imported from China. As an illustration of the sheer volume involved, the total number of machetes imported in 1993 weighed 581.175 kilos and cost US$725.669: there was an estimated one new machete for every third male in the country. According to bank records, a total of US$4.6 million was spent on agricultural tools in 1993 alone. One of the companies involved in these purchases belonged to Félicien Kabuga, the businessman who had helped to finance RTLM – he quite openly used it to purchase huge amounts of machetes from a company called Oriental Machinery Incorporated in Beijing. By the end of 1993 there were hidden stockpiles of brand-new tools in most communes. While Rwanda's economy was in collapse, the militia was expanding with thousands of new recruits from a rising number of unemployed. The training and arming of the communal police had begun.[24]

Assault rifles, guns and grenades were distributed throughout 1993. Some militia leaders were issued with AK 47s, for which they had to fill in requisition forms; the distribution of grenades required no such paperwork. By the time the genocide began, some 85 tons of munitions are thought to have been distributed throughout the country.[25] One early estimate, part of a civil-defence programme prepared in November 1991, was a requirement for 87,000 weapons for the population and 6,250 weapons for the communal police.[26]

In the three years from October 1990 Rwanda, one of the poorest countries in the world, became the third largest importer of weapons in Africa, spending an estimated US$100 million. How could it afford to do this? The answer is straightforward. The money to pay for the arming of Rwanda came from international funding. While in the country at large the public services collapsed, money was found, largely through quick disbursing loans, to pay for armaments, tons of agricultural tools, the armed forces, and the militia. Rwanda was the subject of a Structural Adjustment Programme (SAP), an agreement with the government dating from October 1990, which meant that its economy was in the hands of the world's most powerful international institutions, the World Bank and the International Monetary Fund. Some US$216 million were earmarked for Rwanda through the SAP, some of it from the European Union and with sizeable contributions from France, Germany, Belgium and the US.

A SAP is intended to prevent economic chaos and provide reform in order to create a sound, efficient financial system with low inflation. When Kigali was finally abandoned in July 1994 records recovered from the banks showed that there had been flagrant misappropriation of funds, sometimes with the same invoices used two or three times. Experts who studied this paper trail estimate that in the three years leading to the genocide a total $US112 million were spent on weapons and tools.[27] It is a mystery why five missions sent by the World Bank to follow and supervise the SAP between June 1991 and October 1993 apparently failed to notice all this frenzied activity, although in April 1992 the World Bank's president, Lewis Preston, had written to President Habyarimana to raise the question of military spending at a time when there was famine in the south and warnings that health and welfare provisions were collapsing. President Habyarimana had responded that the increase in military spending was necessary because of the war with the RPF and the need to defend the country from aggression from Uganda.[28]

Most of Rwanda's arms deals were negotiated through the Rwandan embassy in Paris, a seven-floor building in the 17th arrondissement, on orders from the Ministry of Defence in Kigali. When the genocide was over, extensive records were found in these embassy offices but not one of them concerned Rwanda's relationship with France. All the documents relating to this crucial aspect of the genocide had been destroyed by Colonel Sébastien Ntahobari with the help of his secretary. Ntahobari, a trained pilot, was the military attaché in Paris, appointed at the end of 1992. He was responsible for the administration of all arms purchases and had kept thorough accounting records. The ambassador, Jean-Marie Vianney Ndagijimana, had known what was going on because he jointly managed two bank accounts held by Rwanda in the Banque Nationale de Paris. But Ndagijimana, who had resigned from the MRND and joined the MDR, fell under more and more suspicion and eventually he was relieved of his post.[29] There were leaks about the arms deals negotiated in Paris and the RPF was particularly well informed about them. After that Ntahobari had control of the two BNP bank accounts and was the main middle-man between the government in Rwanda and the arms dealers, both government and independent traders.

Another important link in the arms trading business was the Rwanda embassy in Cairo where a first deal had been concluded only weeks after the October 1990 invasion with the help of Egypt's deputy foreign minister, Dr Boutros Boutros-Ghali. For years the Rwanda government had wanted to purchase weapons from Egypt but had had no money to do so. Once the SAP was in the pipeline the Egyptian government had been persuaded by Boutros-Ghali to change its mind. The initial deal with Egypt was for a total of $US5.8 million and included 60,000 grenades, weighed in kilos, some two million rounds of ammunition, mortar bombs, 4,200 assault rifles, rockets and rocket launchers.[30] These items were flown to Rwanda's international airport by the Egyptian airline ZAS. A series of other deals followed, with thousands of landmines, grenades and Kalashnikov assault rifles sent from Cairo to Kigali over the years 1990 to 1993. There is at least one witness who can testify that it was Colonel Théoneste Bagosora who sent the requests for weaponry to the second secretary in the embassy in Cairo, a relation of President Habyarimana whose name was Zikamabahali.

France was also involved in providing Rwanda with arms. It is estimated that between 1991 and 1992 it sent weapons worth at least US$6 million and that by 1993 Rwanda was receiving US$4 million worth of weapons annually from France. There was also a massive arms deal with an independent French company, DYL, in May 1993, with the government ordering US$12 million worth of weapons. The contract was signed by the minister of defence, James Gasana, and, for DYL, Dominique Lemonnier. Soon after the deal was agreed a bank official in Kigali, Jean Birara, took the risky and exceptional step of warning diplomats from western embassies in Kigali about it. The deal turned out badly for the Rwandans; they paid for the military equipment – some US$4,528 million into a DYL bank account at the Banque Internationale du Commerce in Geneva – but the weapons never arrived.

By the end of 1993 the country was awash with arms. So openly distributed were the weapons that a bishop from Nyundo, in north-west Rwanda, issued a press release asking the government to explain why arms were being handed out to civilians. The government's response was to claim that local people had to learn to defend themselves because Rwanda did not have enough troops.

The Arusha Accords signed

The peace agreement was signed in Arusha on 4 August, 1993. It was a comprehensive settlement between the RPF and the government in Kigali and was hailed as a triumph of diplomacy. It provided for a new Rwanda, a system of governance that was parliamentary rather than presidential and meant that in future the power in Rwanda was to reside not with a president but with a council of ministers. The president was reduced to a figure-head, with not even the authority to nominate ministers, his power secondary to that of the prime minister. A government of national unity was to be created, based on the rule of law, political pluralism and human rights. Under the terms of the accords a transition period would see the creation of a transitional government and a transitional national assembly. The transitional government was to contain twenty-one ministers, with the ministries shared between the main parties. The MRND would have five portfolios, the RPF five, and the other parties would share the rest. The prime minister of this transitional government was named as Faustin Twagiramungu, who was the president of the MDR party. The MRND, the formerly all-powerful one party, was transformed by Arusha into a minority.

The peace agreement also provided for the merger of the armies, with the creation of a 19,000-strong new army of national unity which was made up of 60 per cent from the government side and 40 from the RPF, with the command positions split evenly. Both parties to Arusha pledged to promote security and the accords upheld a ceasefire agreement made on 16 September, 1991 that included the "suspension of supplies of ammunition and weaponry to the field" and a ban on the movement of shipments of arms from abroad.

Further provisions of the ambitious agreement were the result of an attempt at a human rights agenda. It incorporated the right of return for all Rwandan refugees, along with provisions for the ethnic designation to be removed from identity cards and for there to be no amnesty for previous wrong-doing or human rights abuses; anyone, including President Habyarimana, could be investigated and charged.

Some diplomats considered Arusha to be "almost perfect preventive diplomacy", and the best agreement that could possibly have been reached.[31] Others believed it was a recipe for disaster because it took no account of the serious human rights abuses already underway in Rwanda. In reality the sceptics failed to make their voices heard effectively, and events would prove that the agreement was little more than a short-lived truce between two long-standing enemies.

The conspirators in Kigali considered the agreement a sell-out imposed by outsiders, a victory deal for the RPF. From now on they would use it only as a way of buying time until alternative plans were laid. In the human rights community, and betraying far more realism than the diplomats, one expert said of the peace deal: "The human rights workers … were not fooled. We did not think that someone capable of organising massacres would suddenly turn into a democrat. We saw what was happening. We kept telling the Belgian authorities."[32]

The abuse of human rights in Rwanda had been a cause for concern for years, even before the October 1990 RPF invasion. Here was a country with a tradition of impunity for wrong-doing in which the judiciary was denied independence and citizens were subject to control over their residence and movement. One illustration of the problem, was provided by Dr Greg Stanton, an academic specialist for the United States Information Service, which runs the libraries and cultural centres at American embassies around the world. In 1989 Stanton made a study of the administration of the Rwandan judicial system. He organised a meeting of Rwandan judges and prosecutors to discuss recommended reforms, and also planned a conference in Kigali on enforcing human rights in Central Africa with representatives from Rwanda, Burundi, Zaire, Uganda, Kenya, and Tanzania.[33] Stanton was concerned at the ethnic divide and the quota system for Tutsi and he spoke with the President of Rwanda's Court of Cassation, Joseph Kavaruganda. Stanton found Kavaruganda a warm, humane man. The two men agreed that the potential for genocide in Rwanda was very real and that the danger was present in the national identification cards that noted each person's Tutsi, Hutu or Twa ethnic identity. Stanton asked if the cards could be declared unconstitutional on the grounds that they could be used to facilitate genocide, but Kavaruganda told him there was no power of judicial review of the laws in Rwanda. Kavaruganda suggested that Stanton talk directly to President Habyarimana to raise the matter. At a reception at the president's house in 1989 Stanton did ask the president to take ethnicity off the ID cards, but the president was impassive. The eventual peace agreement in 1993 called again for the deletion of the mention of ethnicity on identity cards and new cards were once more ordered. This time they were delivered, but not until the first week of April 1994 just as the genocide began. The delay has never been explained.[34] The mention of ethnicity on identity cards was legally abolished in November 1990 and new cards were ordered from French companies but none arrived.

With the attempts to create a democratic system of government in Rwanda, society had gradually opened up and a vigorous human rights community began to develop. This community included volunteers, the newly created independent press and all those human rights groups which had tried to document the torture and killing that had taken place during the RPF invasion of October 1990.[35] In 1992 one of them, the Association for the Defence of Human Rights and Civil Liberties, had used the word genocide in a report on the massacres of Tutsi in the northern prefectures of Gisenyi and Ruhengeri.[36] Another group had drawn up and published a list of all the people who had disappeared, sometimes as many as ten a week.[37]

It was because of this work and at the insistence of local human rights groups that an international commission of inquiry was created, a group of outside western experts to investigate human rights in Rwanda and to name those responsible for the abuses. The ten members of the commission visited Rwanda in January 1993 and their report was produced in March. It ran to 100 pages and was extremely detailed. With witness testimony it described the massacres that had taken place in the previous two years and claimed that people had been tortured or badly beaten and that some had been held incommunicado in military camps. The Tutsi victims were attacked for the sole reason that they were Tutsi, the report concluded, and authorities at the highest level, including President Habyarimana, were responsible. The Rwandan army and the national gendarmerie were also implicated; the militia had operated with impunity and the courts were paralysed, the report found.[38] The RPF was not immune: the report detailed human rights abuses on its part which ranged from attacking a displacement camp and a small hospital to forcing peasants to carry pillaged goods for soldiers.

The report did not accuse the Rwandan government directly of genocide because some of the authors thought the word was "too politically charged". But the word was used in the report's accompanying press release in the headline: "Genocide and war crimes in Rwanda". The press release was written by William Schabas, a Canadian human rights lawyer who was convinced that the presence of genocide in Rwanda was indisputable. The intent to destroy the Tutsi as a people was obvious, the press release stated; there was a pervasive racial ideology and propaganda, essential ingredients for genocide.

The government's response to the international commission's report was to send Ferdinand Nahimana to Brussels to claim that the commission was linked to the RPF. President Habyarimana took on a Belgian lawyer, Luc de Temmerman, to represent the government, and he threatened to initiate a case against his accusers.[39] In June 1993, Africa Watch reported that there were official lists of "accomplices" being prepared along with an increasing distribution of weapons.[40]

The work of the international commission was however taken seriously enough in the UN Commission on Human Rights for a Special Rapporteur to be sent to Rwanda in April 1993. Bacre Waly Ndiaye, whose full official title was the Special Rapporteur for the Commission on Human Rights for Extrajudiciary, Summary or Arbitrary Executions, visited Rwanda for ten days, between 8 and 18 April. His report was published in August. It described how in the past two years some two thousand people in Rwanda had been murdered and in the overwhelming majority of cases they were Tutsi. In view if this it was decided that the word genocide was appropriate and that the Convention on the Prevention and Punishment of the Crime of Genocide of 1948 was applicable.[41] When Ndiaye had returned from Rwanda to his office in Geneva he had been warned against the use of the word genocide, for this was the most serious accusation to level at any government. "It was a serious matter. I was accusing them of going beyond ethnic killing. Everyone wanted to be sure that I had enough evidence." Ndiaye was told to be cautious but he reported to his superiors at the UN Commission on Human Rights that he had sufficient prima facie evidence and that for two years there had been active monitoring of human rights abuses in Rwanda. Since 1990, from the time of the mass arrests after the first RPF attack, there had been a total of seven international human rights reports on Rwanda and each contained detailed information about the regime and the violence that it meted out to its own citizens.[42] The information had often been hard to obtain and sometimes it had come from courageous informants who had put themselves at great personal risk. Ndiaye had no doubt about the fact of genocide. The government was using propaganda to create a situation in which all Tutsi inside the country were collectively labelled accomplices, he reported. The massacres were planned and prepared with targets identified in speeches by representatives of the authorities. Those who carried out the massacres were under organised leadership and local government officials had played a leading role.

Ndiaye believed that one spark was all that would be needed for the situation to degenerate. His previous experience in Bosnia had taught him the benefits of community policing and this was precisely what was required in Rwanda. The gendarmes in Rwanda, he said, should be given the means to adequately police the streets. He also thought that a national reconciliation campaign should be organised to attempt to eliminate "the negative effects in people's minds of the odious disinformation advocating ethnic and political intolerance, hatred and violence". The militia should be disbanded, he recommended, the distribution of arms should cease, propaganda had to stop and impunity for killers had to end.[43]

"It was clear that for the Rwandan army the enemy was the Tutsi", Ndiaye said some years later. "The Tutsi were the human shield and target." When he was in Rwanda he had met people who had escaped massacres.

He had been dismayed to discover that civilians were being killed in army barracks located in central Kigali. He was given detailed evidence about the torture and beatings carried out by the army. These killings had nothing to do with the war with the RPF. He was surprised that such a thing was allowed in Rwanda for he had believed it to be a well-structured and organised country.[44] He noted the existence of death squads and was told about Zero Network, which he understood was made up of powerful individuals who were attempting to discredit the peace agreement.

Although widely and publicly available, Ndiaye said later that he might just as well have put the report in a bottle and thrown it into the sea. "In those days most of the human rights reports did not attract a great deal of interest, not even in the rest of the UN system", Ndiaye said. The protection of civilians was not on the agenda. "In a sense I think they used to see us as amateurs", he said of the diplomats and officials in the Secretariat building in New York.

The human rights reports put the abuses in Rwanda squarely before the international community. President François Mitterrand of France ordered that an official protest be made but there was no public criticism.[45] Belgium recalled its ambassador for consultations for a short time. The US redirected part of its financial aid from the government to aid agencies.

Perhaps it was considered that the human rights abuses had been due to the tensions of war time. Perhaps it was hoped that the massacres would not be repeated. In any case once the peace agreement was signed in August 1993 attention turned to other issues. When President Habyarimana visited Washington in October 1993 the assistant secretary of state, George Moose, was urged to raise human rights questions and especially the issue of accountability for past abuses which Africa Watch had detailed. But no one wanted to spoil the positive atmosphere surrounding the peace agreement.[46] The danger to the Tutsi civilians and the pro-democracy Hutu of Rwanda was not a priority issue. There began a headlong rush to implement the Arusha Accords. Plans were already being made to devise a United Nations peacekeeping mission for Rwanda to monitor the transition from dictatorship to a democracy. There was a growing and optimistic assumption that the extremists in Rwanda could be subdued and that they would eventually come to accept that peace was their only option.

4

MISSION IMPOSSIBLE

There was criticism after the genocide that the commander of the United Nations peacekeeping mission for Rwanda, a Canadian soldier, Major-General Roméo Dallaire, was inadequately briefed. Some years later Dallaire said that, had he known about the human rights reports produced in 1993, he would have insisted on a much larger peacekeeping force from the start. Others said that nothing could have prepared him, or anyone else, for what was to come. Afterwards he speculated on this, his words suggesting the nature of a Greek tragedy: "You sort of wonder … when you look back at the whole thing … whether or not we were set up … whether or not the UN and myself fell into something that was beyond our ability to manage."[1]

Major-General Dallaire was involved with the mission for Rwanda from the start. He had been appointed the chief of the UN Observer Mission Uganda-Rwanda (UNOMUR) established in May 1993 to strengthen a shaky ceasefire between the Rwandan army and the RPF and as one of 81 observers had been responsible for patrolling a buffer zone between them on the Rwanda and Uganda border. At the end of August 1993 Dallaire was asked to travel to UN headquarters in New York where he was invited to head a reconnaissance mission for a proposed peacekeeping operation for Rwanda. No briefing documents had been prepared for him in New York and when he arrived in Rwanda all he had was an encyclopaedic summary of Rwandan history, which his executive assistant, Major Brent Beardsley, had photocopied in a local library.[2]

Dallaire's first visit to Kigali came a few weeks after the Arusha Accords were signed and everyone he met told him of their confidence in the peace agreement and of their belief that with the help of the UN the agreement could be implemented. There were some warnings about the dangers to come – the head of the gendarmerie, Major-General Augustin Ndindiliyimana, pointed out that there was no control over the distribution of weapons to civilians and he was told of the "hostile public information campaigns" aired by a privately owned radio station that was not supportive of the peace agreement – but by and large the mood was upbeat.[3]

Consequently the initial report that Dallaire prepared about the peacekeeping mission achieving its goals was positive. He took part in the back-room deliberations to discuss it with officials at UN headquarters and diplomats recall his optimism.[4] A determined soldier, Dallaire quite obviously enjoyed solving the problems that arise with a complex challenge; detail fascinated him and he developed a passionate commitment to the mission. Dallaire was an internationalist who had risen through the ranks and had waited his entire military career for a peacekeeping command.

On the face of it the assignment was unambiguous. A three-year civil war had ended in peace, with a handshake between the government and invading rebels. There was to be reform of the corrupt regime and the creation of a power-sharing government. A timetable was agreed that would lead to multi-party democracy. This was a classic, text-book peacekeeping mission.

It was France that had first suggested the idea of peacekeepers for Rwanda and her diplomats had aggressively lobbied members of the Security Council to agree to a mission. The French gave confidential assurances that the parties in Rwanda were truly committed to seeing the democratic process through to the end.[5] There was not much enthusiasm from other permanent Council members, though. Two of them, the US and the UK, argued against help for Rwanda for reasons of economy. There were already seventeen UN operations and 80,000 peacekeepers worldwide and the US was liable for a third of the peacekeeping bill. Congress was increasingly hostile towards the UN, and had been withholding its dues for years, almost bankrupting the organisation. The legislators in Washington were reluctant to appropriate any money at all, particularly for more UN peacekeeping, which was considered an abomination among some senior military in the Pentagon.[6]

The Council itself was overwhelmed with problems in the UN missions in Cambodia, Somalia and the former Yugoslavia. Rwanda, in comparison, was quiet. There was not much time devoted to it.

The arguments in favour of UN help for Rwanda in the Security Council were persuasive, first from France and then most particularly from the Nigerian ambassador Ibrahim Gambari, who described Rwanda as a pathetic country, one of the poorest in the world. How could the West encourage this country to democratise, as the US had done, and then turn its back? Gambari, one of the ten non-permanent members on the Council, said that there was a moral duty to help with the transition to democracy in Rwanda. There were complaints from the African group at the UN that resources were being monopolised in Europe to maintain the large and costly operation in the former Yugoslavia.

And yet each time the mission for Rwanda was discussed there was insistence from the US and the UK that any mission must be small and economical. This insistence had a decisive effect on the eventual mission. Dallaire had originally devised the operation for an estimated 8,000 troops. Reluctantly, he agreed that a responsible minimum was 4,500. This figure was pared down yet further by officials in the Secretariat even before it was put before the Council because the US had hoped for no more than a symbolic presence of between 100 and 300 peacekeepers. Eventually a compromise total of 2,548 was agreed.

The report given to the Security Council by the UN Secretary-General Dr Boutros Boutros-Ghali on 24 September, 1993, requesting the creation of the mission for Rwanda, was optimistic.[7] France, the one Council member with an intimate knowledge of Rwanda, had mounted a diplomatic campaign to convince its fellow members of the viability of the Arusha Accords. When the time came to discuss Rwanda there was no mention of the human rights reports in the Council and nothing about a pattern of violence against the minority Tutsi. The author of the reports produced by the UN Commission on Human Rights, Bacre Waly Ndiaye, later said that had anyone asked his advice he would have told the Council that the priority in Rwanda was the immediate protection of civilians at risk. The peacekeeping mission that the Council proposed for Rwanda was too small to make a difference.

Peacekeeping after Mogadishu

For more than forty years the UN peacekeepers had represented a pragmatic response to the Cold War. Peacekeeping, appropriately used, was an enormously useful device. It depended not on war-fighting soldiers but on troops trained in mediation and conciliation. A single peacekeeper at a check-point flying a UN flag was a symbol. The peacekeeper's weapon was not the rifle slung over the shoulder but his credibility; he represented a world community of states and the Security Council's will for peace. These UN troops were not expected to solve conflict but to monitor compliance with already agreed ceasefires; the operations were solely dependent on the co-operation of the relevant parties for their effectiveness.[8] The range of operations throughout those first forty years – among them the UN Special Committee on the Balkans in 1946–49, that monitored and investigated border violations between Greece and its neighbours; the UN Truce Supervision Organisation, sent to monitor the partition of Palestine in 1948; the 1956 UN Emergency Force, established to serve as a buffer between Egypt and Israel in Gaza and the Sinai Peninsula; and the 1960–64 operation for the Congo, known by its French name, the Organisation des Nations Unies au Congo – was enormous.

With the end of the Cold War a second phase of UN peacekeeping began. The UN force sent to Namibia to help its decolonisation from South Africa, for example, had a wider range of tasks than previous missions. The frequency of UN operations also grew steadily; between 1989 and 1994 there were eighteen new missions, more than had been dispatched in the UN's first forty-five years. This evolution into high-cost, large-scale and open-ended missions found the Council soon overwhelmed in crises. The blizzard of mandates, often ambiguous, inadequate and written with scant consideration of the realities on the ground was impossible to respond to effectively; in Bosnia and Somalia, for instance, peacekeepers found they needed to rely on the use of limited but gradually intensifying armed force. And there were tragic mistakes, when the Council sent peacekeepers into situations with orders they could not follow, and which the Council refused to change.

One of the ambassadors who was in the Council at that difficult time remembers: "We were a bunch of diplomatic amateurs." New Zealander

Colin Keating said: "The UN … it's not ready to deal with all this."[9] No one knew how to handle the new demands and complexities of the post Cold War world.

The UN's nemesis came in Mogadishu, Somalia, where the pitfalls of combining force with peacekeeping were finally and fully exposed. Somalia had been in a state of anarchy since 1992, with heavily armed gangs preventing the delivery of food aid and millions starving. Classified as the single worst humanitarian crisis in the world, President George Bush Snr. had sent thousands of US troops there on a mission of humanitarianism as he was about to leave office in December 1992. President Bill Clinton had come to office in January 1993 committed to UN peacekeeping and promising to upgrade the size and professionalism of the UN headquarters staff, and he said he was willing for US troops to come under UN command. In March 1993 the US operation in Somalia was duly transferred to the UN and the mission immediately became more ambitious: its intention was to restore law and order and to compel the Somali militia to disarm. It was given all the powers of the Charter, Chapter VII, the enforcement powers. The US ambassador to the UN, Madeleine Albright, was enthusiastic about the mission and she told the Council how in Somalia the UN was embarking on an unprecedented enterprise aimed at "nothing less than the restoration of an entire country".[10]

But the operation went disastrously wrong. In June 1993, twenty-three Pakistani peacekeepers were hacked to pieces by rampaging mobs whilst trying to inspect weapons that were under UN supervision. Fifty more were seriously injured because of a lack of adequate equipment. After that the Council mandated the UN troops, in Resolution 837, to arrest the warlord accused of having been responsible for inciting the crowds. The resolution emphasised the crucial importance of disarming the warlords and neutralising a radio station that was spreading anti-UN propaganda. From then on and throughout the summer months an untold number of Somalis were killed as elite US troops in raid after raid tried to find the warlord under suspicion for the Pakistani deaths. "It became a rogue operation", a UN lawyer said in New York.[11] The high civilian casualty count was blamed partly on the Somali fighters' use of women and children as active participants and at one point the US shelled a hospital accusing the militia of using it as a vantage point. Although these US operations were outside the command and control of the UN it was the

UN that was widely blamed and accused of flouting human rights with impunity. There were objections from other countries providing troops for Somalia; Italy threatened to pull out her 800 soldiers unless the US stopped their "Rambo-like" raids. The Italian and Nigerian troops had almost come to blows at a roadblock about the interpretation of the mandate. The mission was a mess.

Worse was to come. On 3 October, 1993, in a hail of bullets and missile fire, elite US troops who were attempting to arrest the warlord thought to be responsible for the Pakistani deaths ended up in a street battle with Somali fighters. A total of eighteen American servicemen lost their lives and eighty-four more were wounded. The US troops had parachuted and driven into a residential area and had been pinned down by Somali fighters and trapped in a maze of tiny streets. In a terrifying night-time fire-fight the US troops had to be rescued by a UN peacekeeping force of soldiers from Malaya and Turkey driving Pakistani tanks. The battle in Mogadishu was the worst US military humiliation since Vietnam and the US immediately announced, to the jubilation of the Somali warlords, that US troops were pulling out of Somalia and urged all western nations to do the same.

There remained the image, broadcast around the world, of the body of a US serviceman dragged through the streets to a jeering and jubilant crowd. The Clinton administration distanced itself quickly and maintained correctly that the doomed mission had been "under the authority" of the UN, failing to mention that the attempt to arrest the warlord had been a US operation. The Secretary-General, Boutros Boutros-Ghali, tried to distance the UN and blamed the US. The deaths had come in a failed US operation, which had been conducted by US troops without the UN either on the ground or in New York even being told, he said. Within days the Clinton administration was accused in Congress of turning US foreign policy over to feckless UN bureaucrats, and Boutros-Ghali was accused of Napoleon-like ambitions.[12] A Peace Powers Act was immediately prepared to make it impossible for the president to commit any more troops to UN operations. The battle in Mogadishu had strengthened the hand of those in the US Defense Department who had always wanted to distance the US from UN missions.[13]

The Security Council subsequently commissioned its own report on what had happened in Somalia and, after reading it, suppressed it. It outlined in graphic detail a UN mission completely out of control, with a patchwork command structure as unstable as it was dangerous and contingents refusing orders from UN commanders. One of the most serious weaknesses identified was a false assessment of the capability of the Somali fighters and the UN's lack of intelligence-gathering capability.[14] The report recommended that the UN must return to peacekeeping, to the principles of consent, neutrality, and impartiality. Impartiality was of paramount importance: peacekeeping only worked with a clear mandate and a will on the part of the people to achieve peace. The Council report recommended that never again should the UN undertake enforcement action. A peacekeeping official said: "The international community will be very careful in future. We've learned that [troop contributing] states don't want to take casualties ... you can't do coercive disarmament."[15]

It was two days after the deaths of the US soldiers in the battle of Mogadishu that the Council was due to vote on whether or not to create a mission for Rwanda. So sudden and determined was the retreat from UN operations by the US that many people thought that Rwanda would be lucky to get anything at all. In the end the Council reached a compromise decision and on 5 October, 1993, the UN Assistance Mission for Rwanda (UNAMIR) was created under Resolution 872.[16] The mission was intended to be small, it had the weakest possible mandate and it was to run on a shoe-string.[17] The persuading arguments had been that this was traditional peacekeeping and that the two most important ingredients were present – a ceasefire and a peace agreement. There was speculation that a deal was probably struck whereby French support in maintaining UN sanctions against Iraq helped to persuade a reluctant US to vote for UNAMIR.[18] However the vote came about, one thing was certain: from this moment on, the Security Council would play a central role in the future of this tiny African country.

Burundi's president assassinated

When Major-General Dallaire's plane touched down at Kigali's international airport on 22 October, 1993 for the start of the mission, the timing could not have been worse. The day before there had been a catastrophic turn of events in neighbouring Burundi with the assassination of the president, Melchoir Ndadaye, in an attempted coup. This utterly destroyed Burundi's gradual but brave and determined progress towards democracy and power sharing. Ndadaye was the first elected Hutu president, an astonishing achievement in a country traditionally ruled by Tutsi and with a Tutsi army. He was a moderate who had chosen to work alongside a Tutsi prime minister. And he was killed by officers in the army, an army that he had left untouched.

In Rwanda the assassination of Ndadaye had immediate effect, with the Hutu extremists using it as a huge propaganda coup and blaming the death on "progressive politics" and on "reconciliation with the Tutsi". The news was broadcast on RTLM that the assassination was part of a plot to "eliminate the Hutu" so that the Tutsi could control the entire region. The vast crowd at an extremists rally held in Kigali two days after the assassination was told that the RPF was responsible for President Ndadaye's death. They were also told that the RPF had no intention of abiding by the peace agreement but that instead it was going to conquer Rwanda and re-establish the Tutsi monarchy. A politician called Froduald Karamira brought the crowd to fever pitch with a warning that "the enemy" was everywhere, among them all. Everyone knew he meant Tutsi. "We cannot sit down and think that what happened in Burundi will not happen here", Karamira said. He shouted, "All Hutu are one power … pawa, pawa". The word *pawa* was shouted over and over again.

At that moment the extremist movement coalesced.[19] Karamira was from Gitarama, not a part of the ruling clique but a member of the MDR, the party that had once been the greatest threat to the MRND. It was a threat no longer. Karamira, it was claimed later, was successfully used by Habyarimana to split the MDR party.[20] At the rally Karamira had reviled the MDR president, Faustin Twagiramungu, who had been named in the Arusha Accords as the prime minister in the transitional government. Karamira called Twagiramungu and other MDR moderates inyenzi (cockroaches) and puppets of the RPF. Karamira was also critical of President Habyarimana for having conceded too much to the RPF.[21] The speech was a turning point: "All Hutu are one power", Karamira intoned.

In Burundi the assassination destroyed a fragile five-month-old experiment in democratic power-sharing, a process that made the Habyarimana regime look anachronistic and untenable. Much still remains to be explained about the events in Burundi. Prior to his death Ndadaye had entered into talks with the French about a military presence in Burundi and Tutsi army officers had apparently become suspicious of the links that

Ndadaye might forge with France, particularly in the light of the active support France was giving the Hutu extremists in neighbouring Rwanda. The rebellious troops had killed not only the president but his constitutional successor and other politicians, stripping the democratic movement of its entire leadership.[22] In the countryside the Hutu, who thought of Ndadaye as their president, were encouraged to take revenge on their Tutsi neighbours. Thousands were killed. In revenge the army retaliated and began to kill Hutu in the name of "pacification". In total more than 50,000 people are thought to have lost their lives. And many more thousands fled to Rwanda: an estimated 375,000 refugees arrived in the country spreading stories of terror and massacre at the hands of the Tutsi army.

This refugee crisis came as Major-General Dallaire was establishing a nascent UNAMIR headquarters in Kigali. The disaster created an extra responsibility for the UN mission: a requirement to monitor the southern flank, the border with Burundi, which had never been anticipated when Dallaire had made his initial recommendation for the force structure. There was now a string of refugee camps all along the border, additional to those in the north which housed the 371,000 people made homeless after the February 1993 RPF attack, and in the months to come these camps would become fertile recruiting grounds for young and able-bodied men who would later join the Hutu Power cause.

The events in Burundi received little attention in the outside world. The international press was not interested and at the UN, where an appeal was made for help for Burundi, the response from the Security Council was one of stony silence.[23] Naturally, this was greeted with relief in the Department of Peacekeeping Operations (DPKO), where they were trying to cope with too many missions, too few resources.

A difficult start for UNAMIR

In peacekeeping the transition period is always the most dangerous. It is the time when extremists can make the most of a vacuum. Any delay or any hint of a lack of commitment serves only to encourage the hardliners who do not want peace. The original peace deals tend to unravel as the parties learn to exploit the UN for their own advantage.

At the best of times it took the UN ninety days to get a mission in place. The troops also needed equipment for which the average procurement time was four months. In Rwanda things were much worse than average. The mission was slow to establish and from the start was desperately understaffed and ill-equipped. The peacekeeping department had proposed setting up a stock of basic equipment but the member states refused to pay US$15 million to fund it.[24] At one point Dallaire was so short of resources that he was obliged to borrow money from the United Nations Development Programme (UNDP) to pay his staff and to fund accommodation and meals, rental of vehicles and premises.

It was plain to see just how half-hearted the United Nations effort for Rwanda really was. The force structure given to the peacekeepers, and in particular the equipment, bore no relationship to what was really needed. There were to be twenty-two armoured personnel carriers (APCs) and eight military helicopters to allow for a quick reaction ability. No helicopters arrived and only eight APCs were provided, of which five were serviceable. They did not arrive until March 1994 and they came direct from the UN mission in Mozambique without tools, spare parts or manuals. Most of the troops, some 942 soldiers, came from Bangladesh, but they had hardly any training. Dallaire tried to train them to create a quick reaction force but they were well below acceptable operational standard. Bangladesh was supposed to have provided a composite force of a medical company, an engineer squadron, a half-battalion of infantry and a movement control platoon.

The headquarters of UNAMIR was in a motel on the edge of eastern Kigali and on the road to the airport. It was a bleak and ugly concrete block building whose tiny rooms each had a balcony looking over a desolate expanse of bare earth with a football stadium in the far distance. The stadium was to be used as transit accommodation for UN troops. Dallaire was followed by an advance team of twenty-one military personnel on 27 October. They spent their time sorting out a nightmare of logistics, steering a course through the bureaucratic UN labyrinth. They lacked everything, from telephones to desks and chairs. When the first troops arrived from Bangladesh they had no bottled water or food; instructions issued by the Secretariat in New York that all contingents should be self-supporting had simply been ignored.

Although by 17 November, 1993 only a handful of peacekeepers had arrived, the headquarters was officially opened by President Juvénal Habyarimana who with his entourage, including members of his Presidential

Guard, came to the hotel for a small ceremony. President Habyarimana expressed his gratitude for all the UN was doing: "Welcome to Rwanda, soldiers of the United Nations, soldiers of peace, soldiers of hope."[25] The local press took lots of photographs.[26]

But even while President Habyarimana and Dallaire exchanged pleasantries, that same night in northern Rwanda a series of grotesque massacres was taking place. There were five altogether, between the hours of 11 p.m. and 2 a.m. in the demilitarised zone north of Ruhengeri. A total of thirty-seven people, including women and children, were killed; the fathers and husbands were well known because they had just been successfully elected in their home communes. The spread of the killing, over a distance of more than 50 kilometres, gave the impression that they were carefully co-ordinated. In each case there was the same efficient elimination of witnesses, and no interest in stealing or destroying houses or furniture. Dallaire reported the news to UN headquarters in New York: "The swiftness, the callous efficiency and the ruthless number of men, women and children murdered principally by machetes and bayonets was obvious in this well orchestrated operation", he wrote. The news of the killings was broadcast early the next day, in great detail by RTLM.

There was another massacre at the end of November in Kabatwa in the north, near the Volcanoes National Park, when eighteen people were killed with knives and firearms. Again Dallaire reported back: "Examples of the atrocities include hands cut off, eyes pulled out, skulls crushed in, and pregnant women cut open." The day before, 29 November, six children and an adult had disappeared while collecting water in the national park. They were later found tied and killed. Dallaire's military assistant, Brent Beardsley, was sent from the Kigali headquarters to investigate. After a long mountainous walk he and his team found the bodies of the missing children. Each of them had been strangled by a rope and had a red burn mark round the neck. The girls had been gang raped. Some of the children had been hit on the head with a blunt instrument.

It was Beardsley's first week in Rwanda. He thought that it could not get any worse than this. He asked his translator who would do such terrible things. The translator, a Rwandan attached to the UN mission, told him it was the rebels because a glove had been found at the scene of the crime similar to those worn by RPF rebels. The local people, speaking to Beardsley through this translator, also said that the rebels had been the perpetrators. Beardsley was suspicious of the way in which the man translated his questions and was even more suspicious later when, on the way home, the translator gave a long speech about the evils of the rebels. Afterwards they had gone to the local hospital to see one of the survivors who had earlier been carried down from the mountain. She was six years old. She had been raped. She was in a coma suffering spasms from brain damage, and was under UN guard. The doctor said that she would die if she was not evacuated to Europe but she died the next day anyway, without being able to give any information at all about the attackers.

When he returned to Kigali Beardsley told Dallaire of his suspicions that para-commandos from the government side might have been responsible for the killings. There was a para-commando training camp only a short distance away. The rebels were nowhere near the place in question and would have been obliged to travel almost 100 kilometres over some of the roughest terrain in the world, through thick forest. At the base of the mountain Beardsley had met a government patrol led by a lieutenant-colonel who said that he was the local commander. Beardsley told Dallaire that each of the victims had been strangled and that he had noticed how the para-commandos wore a red cord around their waist which may have accounted for the marks around the children's necks. The para-commandos also carried knives with round metal bases which would explain the indentations on the skulls of the children.

The next day Beardsley returned to the mountain with the father of one of the victims. As they retraced their steps the man stepped on a landmine and was killed. Beardsley said that the landmine was identified as one of those used by the government and that the mine may have been set to deter the UN investigation. Dallaire measured the risks and cancelled all further investigation of the site. His report to UN headquarters was as follows: "The terms indiscriminate and ruthless are certainly not exaggerated as in these circumstances … the manner in which they were conducted in their execution, in their co-ordination, in their cover-up, and in their political motives lead us to firmly believe that the perpetrators of these evil deeds were well organised, well informed, well motivated and prepared to conduct pre-meditated murder. We have no reason to believe that such occurrences could not and will not be repeated again in any part of this country where arms are prolific and political and ethnic tensions are prevalent."[27]

There was something else that marked these events. The local media leapt on the story, exaggerating the death toll and accusing the RPF of carrying out the murders. On RTLM the announcers denigrated the UN peacekeepers for failing to make any immediate arrests. Accordingly, Dallaire received demands from the minister of defence, Augustin Bizimana, calling for the UN to immediately arrest these "rebel culprits". Dallaire asked if the minister would provide information of his own. These murders had after all taken place in the minister's home region, the northern prefecture of Ruhengeri. No information was forthcoming. The culprits were never found. From that point on, and every day for the next four months, Rwanda's popular new RTLM radio station broadcast a stinging rebuke to Dallaire and the UN. Every day, just before the French programmes began, an announcer would say: "We are still awaiting the results of the UNAMIR enquiry into the killings .... Either Major-General Dallaire comes up with something or he should leave the country."[28] UNAMIR would be portrayed as biased towards the RPF.

Dallaire did not know of the rebukes in these broadcasts because there was not enough money available to pay for the monitoring of the media. He instead speculated that, given the location of the murders in the north-west presidential stronghold, they were probably intended to destabilise the de-militarised zone (DMZ), a strip of land 120 kilometres long and 20 kilometres wide in the mountainous, heavily forested terrain with few dirt roads. This land stood between the two rival armies, that of the Rwandan government and that of the RPF whose headquarters were in a former tea plantation on the border with Uganda. There were peacekeepers monitoring the DMZ but with severe limitations in resources – they had only ten vehicles, two radios and no night-vision equipment. Two totally ill-equipped Tunisian platoons were responsible for the entire area. Dallaire told UN headquarters that it was critical for armed and tactically deployed troops to be available throughout the DMZ to provide security for a large population of displaced people. A constant presence of troops was needed to man checkpoints, mount observation posts and conduct search operations for illegal arms, he said, because the emergence of the unexpected terrorist group had created the need for continual investigation.

Dallaire knew that the killings were an immediate challenge to UNAMIR.[29] He also thought they were a well planned effort to divert his attention away from the capital. Whoever was responsible wanted to deter countries from providing troops for his mission. He concluded that a "very sophisticated and subversive group" was intending to scupper the peace agreement. And he told New York that the race was now on between the peacekeeping mission and "negative elements".[30]

Dallaire identified another force to be reckoned with – the reservists, those who were retired from Rwanda's police force, the gendarmes and the army, but who could be called upon at a moment's notice to destabilise Rwanda, should the politicians wish them to do so. "They would do this and have done this in co-operation with youth-wingers", Dallaire wrote. The term "youth wingers" was initially used by Dallaire to describe the gangs of youths attached to the various political parties. The security situation was difficult because the communal police was weak and inefficient.[31]

Whilst aware of a "small but vocal and influential minority which continues to undermine the peace process", Dallaire maintained his fiery determination to succeed. He wrote in one cable in December 1993: "Rwanda is on the way of becoming another success story for the UN peacekeeping operations."[32] But in reality the mission was in serious trouble. At the end of the same month he reported to New York that the mission was no more than "a minimum viable force" as long as no significant threats emerged. Command and control were precarious due to the noted deficiencies of communications equipment. The emergence of an armed and ruthless third force determined to abort the peace would require a change in the force structure and a significant increase in resources.

The Arusha Accords undermined

On 3 December, 1993 Dallaire was sent an anonymous letter purportedly from a group of officers in the Rwandan army. It was neatly typed and it began by telling him that in the main the Rwandan government army had welcomed the creation of UNAMIR to help with the application of the Arusha Accords. The letter went on: "But some soldiers, essentially from the same region as the President … remain firmly hostile to the Accords …. These soldiers have always been looked after by the regime of President Habyarimana and they are resistant to the political evolution." The letter claimed that in spite of the president's fine speeches in support of the accords he was in reality "the instigator of diabolical manoeuvres to sow disorder and desolation in the population". The letter pointed to the murders of civilians in the north in November, the murders that had so shocked UNAMIR at the outset of the mission and that Dallaire had promised to investigate. The letter also told Dallaire that the regime was to blame for these massacres and that more massacres were planned. They would spread throughout the whole country especially where there were large concentrations of Tutsi, most notably in the Bugesera, Kibuye and Kibungo areas. This was a strategy designed to convince public opinion that the problems of Rwanda were ethnic in nature and that they had been incited by the RPF. The massacres would in effect serve as a pretext to re-start the civil war. Opposition politicians including Faustin Twagiramungu, Landoald Ndasingwa, Félicien Gatabazi, Dismas Nsengiyaremye and Boniface Ngulinzira, all of them having played some sort of role in the peace talks, were going to be assassinated. The authors maintained that they had written the letter to Dallaire and to all the diplomatic missions in Rwanda because of "revulsion against these filthy tactics".[33] Army chief Nsabimana's reaction to the letter was to call it a "tract" and to claim that it had been written "by the enemy". He said that it was intended to sow discord in the Rwandan army.[34]

There was a more public warning later that month when on 13 December a Rwandan human rights group reported that the increasing violence against the Tutsi was part of a "Machiavellian plan" that was being organised by civil and military authorities and that the "lying, fascistic propaganda … was orchestrated". It was time for Habyarimana to assume responsibility and put an end to the "extermination of a people in which an organisation of killers is protected by certain authorities". The international community should stand up to the "banalisation" of crime in Rwanda.[35]

There were more revelations in a local paper. On 17 December a chilling article in the journal *Le Flambeau* reported information about a "fatal day" to fall on 20 December or perhaps 23 December. Reminding readers of the phrase that the Nazi Germans had used to describe the operation to exterminate those they considered their enemies, "most notably the Jews", the article said: "Rwandese fascists and their chief have decided to apply the final solution to their fellow citizens judged enemies of the regime." The newspaper claimed that the plan for Rwanda's final solution had been denounced in a speech by an opposition minister,

Félicien Gatabazi, the head of the PSD, and that details of it had been contained in an anonymous letter written to the UN force commander. The newspaper also claimed that some 8,000 Interahamwe had been trained by the French army. Two men were named as having the job of identifying the households of the future victims – Joseph Nzirorera, Secretary-General of the MRND, and Noel Mbonabaryi, a close ally of Habyarimana and a long-term civil servant. In a desperate plea at the end the article warned: "The lone voice of Gatabazi is not sufficient." The international community must "denounce vigorously and without any ambiguity the mafia that finds itself at the head of Rwanda which today dissatisfied with its people has decided to dissolve them". The article pointed out that there had been a lack of firmness in dealing with the Nazi menace while their crimes against humanity were being planned.[36]

It seemed as though no one believed in the accords any more. On 15 November, 1993 Habyarimana had made a speech in which he described the agreement as a mere piece of paper. In private he told the American ambassador Bruce Flaten that the government negotiators at Arusha had exceeded their authority and that one of the major sticking points was the composition of a transitional government and the distribution of cabinet posts.[37] Five days later President Habyarimana was to be found in the Hôtel Rebero in Gisenyi, a hotel he owned. It was at a meeting there that the methods by which grenades, guns and machetes could be distributed to the Interahamwe were decided.[38]

The opposition was also disenchanted with the peace process. Jean Kambanda, at this point the president of the MDR in Butare, later claimed that no one had ever believed in the accords.[39] Kambanda was from the Hutu Power wing of the MDR and, like Karamira, so effective at the rally, had been used to undermine the party's president, Faustin Twagiramungu. In his genocide confession some years later Kambanda claimed that in October 1993 he had a private meeting with Habyarimana, organised through a friend, Emile Nyungura, who was the president's nephew. Nyungura warned Kambanda to be very careful about talking while the president's wife was in the room and also, Kambanda claimed, told him that the people surrounding the president were dangerous. Kambanda saw the president alone. He says that he spoke frankly with him, asking him how on earth he thought the country could be saved when he was quite clearly no longer in control. Nothing was working any more. Kambanda claims that Habyarimana told him that power sharing was no solution at all. The Arusha Accords had not been accepted, no matter what people said.

Some sections of the Rwandan army were by this stage making quite serious and obvious efforts to undermine the Accords. There are witnesses who can testify that Major Aloys Ntabakuze, commander of the para-commandos, held a meeting as UN troops began to arrive in November 1993 to tell his soldiers that the RPF had no intention of abiding by the peace agreement. This was a "stand-by" period. "Your duty is to serve the nation … by waiting", he told them.[40] Others were planning to hide archives and destroy the more compromising documents. There were plans for the security services to go underground and for an ultra-secret and informal intelligence cell to spy on "the enemy". The secret services were concentrated in Kigali and there were suggestions to make them more decentralised; there needed to be rapid training of personnel and approaches were made to try to get France or South Africa to help. "Our President founded our army and he knows that all officers will help with this problem", a report prepared in the Ministry of Defence noted.[41]

There was also more public involvement between the military and the Interahamwe militia. One month into his mission, at the end of November, Major-General Dallaire became aware of the military training being given to the youth groups he had called the "youth-wingers". In the first week of November Dallaire had watched an MRND-organised demonstration, at which the Interahamwe had driven around the capital in their particular and colourful uniforms making lots of noise, but, he noted, they did not appear to have any weapons. This opinion was gradually revised. By the end of the month in an internal memo Dallaire shows how early he knew that the "youth-wingers" had illegally secured arms including hand grenades and rifles.

"Blind and deaf in the field"

The commander of the Kigali sector of UNAMIR was a determined and hard working Belgian officer, Colonel Luc Marchal. Marchal had been *chef de cabinet* in the office of the Belgian minister of defence. He had served in the army for thirty years, fifteen of them as a para-commando, and he had spent five years in Zaire. Dallaire liked him immediately. "Unlike many of his countrymen, Luc carried no colonial baggage", Dallaire wrote later.[42] Marchal was the most senior soldier in the Belgian contingent of UNAMIR, which had a total of 440 troops and, being the best trained and the best equipped, formed the backbone of the mission. Marchal was given the command in October 1993 and he was wary from the start. Before he left Brussels he had complained at operations headquarters about the lack of firepower available to his troops in the event of evacuation. He was told not to worry. "You're going to Club Med", was the answer to his qualms.

Belgian Prime Minister Jean-Luc Dehaene's government had always been enthusiastic about UN help for Rwanda, recognising publicly how important it was to end the civil war and bring peace to the former colony. The Belgian foreign minister, Willy Claes, had written personally to his counterpart in Washington, the secretary of state Warren Christopher, to try to relieve US fears about the establishment of another mission in Africa at a time when Somalia was proving so difficult. Then, in October 1993, the Belgian army sent a reconnaissance team to Rwanda under the command of Colonel Jacques Flament. Flament's report was alarming: the extremist Hutu faction was dangerous and there was a possible negative impact of the Hutu radio station. There were weapons hidden in secret caches, a lack of discipline in the army and increasing banditry. There was also hostility towards Belgium. In spite of this the Belgian government remained keen to have troops serving in UNAMIR and wanted to protect the large Belgian community in Rwanda. Only later would it emerge that one other reason for Belgium enthusiasm was that their contribution of troops for Rwanda could be used as an excuse to withdraw a Belgian contingent from Somalia.[43]

No one worked harder than Colonel Marchal to make UNAMIR a success. He was relentless. He believed that the transition was achievable. But Marchal was also a realist. He knew the difficulties were immense. "I felt in the uncomfortable position of a fireman who when called to a fire can't get near it because there are too many obstacles diverting him from his principal task", he wrote later.[44]

Marchal was responsible for one of the cornerstones of the UNAMIR mandate, the creation in Kigali of a weapons-free zone in a ten kilometre radius from the centre within which military units would be required to store their weapons and ammunition. Weapons and troops could only be moved in this area with UNAMIR permission and with a UNAMIR escort. Such a zone, eventually to be called the Kigali Weapons Secure Area, would make the capital city secure for the swearing-in and functioning of the transitional government. Marchal's first impressions of Kigali did not bode well for the future however. He found an "omnipresence" of the forces of order. In the book he wrote later he described: "... gendarmes and police patrolling, soldiers everywhere, tanks at certain key roundabouts, anti aircraft guns surrounding the airport".[45] For the next few months his main preoccupation was to change that reality.

The procedure by which a weapons-free zone could be achieved, through roadblocks, control centres and patrolling, was discussed at length with the commanders of the Rwandan gendarmerie and the Rwandan army. The operational procedure was agreed only after long weeks of negotiation and it was finally signed on 24 December, 1993. It was during these long negotiations that Marchal first met Colonel Théoneste Bagosora.[46] Marchal noticed how Bagosora, the chef de cabinet in the ministry of defence, held sway at these talks, even when the minister of defence, Major-General Augustin Bizimana, and the army chief of staff, Colonel Déogratias Nsabimana, were present. Dallaire also attended some of these meetings with his assistant Brent Beardsley. Beardsley recalled that Bagosora was not regularly prominent at these meetings and at some of them sat at the back taking notes. At other times he assumed a higher profile, Beardsley noted.

Bagosora was a graduate of the most prestigious military academy in France, the École de Guerre Française in Paris, and was the first Rwandan to be accorded the honour. He had also taken part in training exercises with the Belgian army. Marchal said he did not trust him. Bagosora had bad manners and he would rudely jab with his finger to make a point. He had a quick and nervous temper and his face would tremble with anger when he thought he was being thwarted. One particular incident Marchal remembered from those early days was a routine patrol near the villa in Kigali where Bagosora lived. Peacekeepers had become suspicious of a large gathering of soldiers in his garden and had got out of their jeeps. As they approached, Bagosora had ordered his soldiers to aim their weapons at them to stop them coming any closer.[47] The peacekeepers had quickly withdrawn to avoid any confrontation.

Colonel Marchal had arrived in Rwanda with very little information. Several times he had asked Brussels for operational directives but no single document had ever been provided. He did not even receive any Rules of Engagement which governed what the soldiers could and could not do.[48] He wondered why no information was ever passed to him about those with whom he had to negotiate. Neither the French nor the Belgian government, intimately involved in the affairs of Rwanda, gave the UNAMIR officers any help at all.

"We were blind and deaf in the field", Dallaire would complain bitterly after it was all over.[49] There existed a wealth of material about Rwanda but none of it was ever made available to his mission. The UN was expected to operate in an information void. His request to UN headquarters for an intelligence-gathering capability was rejected because this would have been contrary to peacekeeping policy. Instead Dallaire had circumvented UN headquarters and asked Colonel Marchal to appeal directly to Belgian military intelligence, the Service Général du Renseignement de l'Armée (SRG). As a result, a two-person cell was finally created in Kigali to gather and analyse intelligence material. A small amount of money was provided to pay for informers, several of whom were found. But ultimately the intelligence this network of informers provided went straight to Brussels and even Dallaire was not privy to all of it, for reasons which remain obscure to this day.

Dallaire in turn, using his own money, set up his own small intelligence unit, led by Captain Frank Claeys from Belgium and a Senegalese captain called Amadou Deme. The first thing that these two discovered was that the killings in the north in November were the work of Rwanda para-commandos from Camp Bagogwe.[50]

5

MORNING PRAYERS

Peacekeeping requires ceaseless political direction. For each mission it is the job of the Secretary-General to give leadership, operational guidance and political control, and to prepare and issue the terms of reference to which each mission must adhere.

When it came to the question of Rwanda, the Secretary-General Dr Boutros Boutros-Ghali had more experience of the country than almost anyone else on his senior staff. Few were better placed to understand the risks inherent in Rwanda's divided society. Boutros-Ghali, who had been a deputy foreign minister of Egypt, had first visited Kigali in 1983 and the high-level Egyptian-Rwandan diplomatic traffic went through him. Boutros-Ghali visited Rwanda again in 1988 and the following year had negotiated a co-operation agreement between Rwanda and Egypt, dealing with the then foreign minister, Casimir Bizimungu. Boutros-Ghali also knew President Juvénal Habyarimana, for in 1990 he had helped to oversee Habyarimana's state visit to Cairo and was the head of the delegation which accompanied him. After the RPF invasion in October 1990 Boutros-Ghali had been the catalyst in a secret arms deal between Cairo and the regime in Kigali to buy Egyptian weapons worth US$5.889 million.[1]

Boutros-Ghali was a French-educated academic who had received a doctorate in international law from the Sorbonne in 1949. He had been brought into government as an international relations expert when working as a professor at Cairo University but he never lost his love of

France and was instrumental in facilitating Egypt's entry into la Francophonie, the world-wide association of nations sharing the French language.

When Boutros-Ghali ran for the office of Secretary-General of the United Nations, a campaign lasting two years, France was the only permanent member of the Council to support his candidacy. And when, on 21 November, 1991, he learned of his selection by the Council he immediately telephoned President Mitterrand to tell him. "He seemed to feel a personal victory in my election", Boutros-Ghali wrote later.[2] At the time France was looking for an influential role in the newly revitalised post-Cold War Security Council.

Never had a Secretary-General taken over the UN at a more propitious time. For most of its history the Security Council had been paralysed by Cold War divisions but in January 1992, when Boutros-Ghali took office, it was unified at last. Boutros-Ghali claimed that if he had been offered the job five years before, he would have turned it down because the UN had been "a dead horse".[3]

Boutros-Ghali was an advocate for human rights in the developing world. He had been one of the leading advocates of an African Charter of Human Rights in 1978, a proposal adopted with the specific inclusion of the rights of peoples as well as of individuals, and he had declared when he took office that it was time for the UN to shift from its emphasis on world development to human rights. Boutros-Ghali was, if nothing else, a man well versed in the political rhetoric of the west.

The UN special representative meets Dallaire

In November 1993 Boutros-Ghali appointed a special representative for Rwanda. This is a vital role in all peacekeeping missions because the person entrusted to it provides political guidance in any peace process. In Rwanda, where murder and terror were a part of the political system, it was never going to be easy. Plots and intrigues were difficult to follow and the parties were riddled with unscrupulous people for whom politics was the only way to enrichment.

Boutros-Ghali's appointment for the difficult posting to Rwanda was controversial. Jacques-Roger Booh-Booh, a former foreign minister of Cameroon, was immediately considered to be a biased choice because

Cameroon was part of la Francophonie. Boutros-Ghali shrugged off the criticism. He was a forthright, outspoken and confrontational Secretary-General. He was also described as an old fashioned diplomat who could see nothing unless it was through a Francophone prism.[4] What was undeniable was that Booh-Booh and Boutros-Ghali were friends and that both had strong links with the Cameroonian elite.

The special representative arrived in Kigali on 23 November, 1993. Almost immediately there was antagonism between Major-General Dallaire and Booh-Booh. Booh-Booh proclaimed openly that all his efforts were short-circuited by Dallaire who refused to stick to his military brief.[5] He said that the mission had arrived too late and that this, he claimed, was being used as a pretext not to create the transitional institutions. Later Booh-Booh would claim that he realised at once that neither party was abiding by the peace agreement. He knew this because some of those on the "government side" were personal friends of his, particularly Casimir Bizimungu, the foreign minister. They had served their respective countries at the same time.[6] He told Dallaire that only a direct appeal from Boutros-Ghali had brought him out of retirement; he would sooner have been busy with his extensive banana production at home.[7]

For his part Dallaire accused Booh-Booh of having undermined him and said Booh-Booh had called for his resignation. Booh-Booh had gathered around him a group of Franco-African advisers, who were hostile to Dallaire.[8] France itself, Dallaire learned later, had written to the Canadian government to request his removal as force commander. Booh-Booh would complain that Dallaire had failed to make as many efforts carrying out more rigorous searches on the side of the RPF. Booh-Booh said it was a problem of fairness and equity. And there were apparently objections to references that Dallaire made in reports to the presence of French officers among the Presidential Guard.[9]

Gradually Dallaire lost credibility at UN headquarters, for which he blamed Booh-Booh,[10] and gained a reputation as an interfering maverick who failed to understand political matters that were none of his concern. So difficult was the relationship between force commander and special representative that an independent inquiry set up subsequently by the UN to investigate what happened described it as a contributing factor to the overall failure of the mission.[11]

Tension in the Security Council

The regular morning meetings in the Department of Peacekeeping Operations (DPKO) were known as "morning prayers". It was at these, on the 37th floor of the Secretariat building in New York, that reports were given of the latest news from the various missions around the world.[12] In the last few years there had been nothing but bad news. The senior UN bureaucrats whose job it was to turn Security Council mandates into actions were beset with problems as they tried to manage several problematic missions with ever-changing Council instructions. It is the job of the civil servants to coordinate policy, decide the concept of UN missions and handle the operational procedures. It was up to the bureaucrats in New York to manage and administer field missions, in much the same way that a public service responds when a government entrusts responsibility to it. More time recently had been spent either trying to scrounge soldiers and military equipment from exceedingly reluctant governments or facing fierce criticism from the field for the inability to provide sufficient means and material to fulfil mandates.

The DPKO had been created in 1992 after a major restructuring of the Secretariat. But it was understaffed and starved of funds. It was clear to everyone in the field that at headquarters there were simply not the resources to cope with the responsibilities imposed by an ambitious Security Council.[13] In spite of the new workload at the UN Secretariat the number of staff committed to peacekeeping operations had not changed since 1987.

The creation of the UN Mission for Rwanda (UNAMIR) in October 1993 was greeted with relief at DPKO, and the operation seen as a welcome departure from the more difficult enforcement missions of the past few years. This was probably the reason why it was endowed with so much hope at the UN. Both diplomats and officials were convinced that Rwanda would be a winner, a mission to redeem the UN's battered reputation so severely damaged by disastrous failures, particularly in Bosnia and Somalia. The UN was badly in need of a success. It needed to excel at what it did best – managing transitions through traditional peacekeeping.

Most peacekeeping missions are established for six months with mandates due for renewal by the Security Council at regular intervals. In the case of UNAMIR there was stricter oversight, with the provision of a review after ninety days to determine whether or not substantive progress was being made towards implementation of the Arusha Accords. On 30 December, 1993 Boutros Boutros-Ghali duly submitted a report to the Council on the progress of the mission. This report was based on information provided daily from the field by Dallaire and Booh-Booh. The standard operating procedure was to route all communications between a force commander and DPKO through the civilian hierarchy, in this case through Booh-Booh and his staff. The DPKO then sent all reports from all missions to the Secretary-General's office on the 38th floor. Dallaire's sections of the cables were particularly detailed: "The recent split in the Liberal Party along ethnic lines and the ever present CDR party of Hutu hardliners make for a level of concern that will require a pro-active defusing by UNAMIR in order to deflate the inflammatory rhetoric and extensive disinformation", he reported to New York. The CDR party, the extremist pro-Hutu anti-Tutsi group, was, he said, "in the shadows".[14]

But this fine detail was not what the Council was told. Nor was Dallaire's long list of his most urgent requirements, or his view that the operation was a logistical nightmare, reported to the Council. Boutros-Ghali forbade this. He detested what he called "micro-management" by member states in the Council and wanted to manage operations himself with no transparency or accountability to the Council, preferring to deal selectively with a few permanent members on difficult or contentious issues. His period of office was consequently marked by constant tension between himself and the Council about the appropriate level of Council involvement in decision-making. He even went so far as to issue an edict that the head of the DPKO, Under Secretary-General Kofi Annan, was not to appear in the Council; the Secretariat's advice was to be filtered through Boutros-Ghali's personal representative.[15]

Annan was not unaware of Dallaire's problems. There was not a UN commander in the field without complaints, and Annan told Dallaire that while UN headquarters understood the difficulties, the Security Council would not be expecting to receive a "catalogue of these problems". All the Council would be discussing was the substantive progress regarding the implementation of the peace agreement.[16]

Annan was a veteran UN official from Ghana with a master's degree in management from the Massachusetts Institute of Technology. Ever since his appointment to DPKO on 1 March, 1993, eight months before, he had ridden the storm of peacekeeping chaos. He had experienced the nightmare mission in Somalia, though only later would he be critical of the speed with which the US withdrew its troops after the deaths of eighteen of its soldiers there. A dangerous impression had been given, he believed, that the easiest way to disrupt a UN mission was to kill peacekeepers.

Annan began his professional life as a budget officer and administrator but he was a quiet, steady and thoughtful man and had managed to make the often difficult transition from finance and management to international diplomacy. He was dedicated to the founding principles of the UN, that peace rested upon economic and social stability and that a fairer world could be created through international cooperation. He had direct experience of working in the field and had managed some complex tasks including negotiating the release of 900 international staff from Iraq following that country's invasion of Kuwait in 1990. And he had led the first UN team to Iraq after the war to organise the sale of Iraqi oil with which the purchase of humanitarian aid was funded.

Annan was well acquainted with the UN's constant crisis-management situation, its inherent weaknesses, its institutional complexity, and its serious and damaging lack of co-ordination between organisations and programmes. Dallaire thought Annan tireless in his efforts to try to save the UN in such troubled times.[17] It was not easy with a Secretary-General who worked very much to his own agenda.[18]

Accordingly the report submitted to the Council by Boutros Boutros-Ghali in December 1993 was essentially optimistic in tone: the two sides were showing goodwill and cooperation in their contacts with each other and with the UN.[19] The report did however mention the existence of a "well-armed and reportedly ruthless group" operating in the area of the de-militarised zone (DMZ) "with a view to disrupting or even derailing the peace process". To deal with that, the report proposed that a second infantry battalion be deployed, originally envisaged following the installation of transitional institutions.[20]

In the Security Council's discussion of the report the US continued to seek economies and expressed worries about how much the mission was costing, proposing the withdrawal of some UN personnel from Rwanda. The Secretary-General promised to make economies in the mission. On

6 January, 1994, the Council adopted Resolution 893, in which it agreed early deployment of additional forces but stressed that continued support for UNAMIR would depend on the full and prompt fulfilment of the peace accords.

The US delegation asked for more information about the terrorist group that had murdered civilians in the DMZ in November. The information was readily provided by Dallaire who sent a cable to UN headquarters in which he described the massacres that had taken place. He had no proof of who was responsible but wrote that the "manner in which they were conducted in their execution, in their coordination, in their cover-up, and in their political motives lead us to firmly believe that the perpetrators of these evil deeds were well organised, well informed, well motivated and prepared to conduct premeditated murder. We have no reason to believe that such occurrences could not and will not be repeated again in any part of this country where arms are prolific and political and ethnic tensions are prevalent."[21]

RPF troops in Kigali

In compliance with the Arusha Accords, the RPF was to send a battalion to Kigali to ensure the protection of its political leaders in the transitional government. The battalion was to be transported from the RPF's northern base in Mulindi to Kigali, a journey of some sixty kilometers, with a UN escort. Once in Kigali the troops were to be billeted in the centre of town where their security would be the responsibility of the peacekeepers; their movements would be restricted and there would be UN observers watching them. Their compound was a large and dominant government building, the Conseil National pour le Développement (CND), a national symbol. It was close to the barracks of the Presidential Guard.

At dawn on the morning the troops were to be moved Colonel Luc Marchal, the commander of the Kigali battalion of UNAMIR who had planned the transfer operation, met Jacques Bihozagara, an RPF politician who had been chosen as the deputy prime minister in the transitional government. Bihozagara told Marchal that he feared a trap and asked him to cancel the operation. Marchal assured Bihozagara that the supervision of the movement of RPF troops to Kigali was one of the main reasons why the UN was in their country, to provide security for their battalion.

Marchal said that the UN wanted to ensure that the peace agreement would go ahead. In private he considered this to be the first real test of the peace process. Bihozagara remained pessimistic.

Bihozagara was one of Marchal's important contacts as he had been the RPF European representative in Brussels; the other was Charles Kayonga, the commander of the RPF troops who were to come to Kigali. Kayonga was also fearful of the move. He did not trust the peace process and told Marchal that the transfer was the moment of truth. Marchal told neither man that he had earlier received dire warnings from Belgian military intelligence headquarters in Evere, Brussels, and that their advice was to postpone the operation. Dallaire and Marchal had discussed the possible risks and both agreed that the operation must go ahead. Continued delay would further weaken an already fragile peace process.

The operation took place on 27 December, 1993 in a convoy of ninety buses, lorries, coaches and jeeps. It stretched four kilometres, winding its way towards the capital with UN peacekeepers from Belgium keeping closest to the RPF troops. Marchal admired the RPF troops for their discipline. While possessing nothing like the manpower of the Rwandan army, they were determined and able fighters. From the moment they were safely installed in the CND building later that day, however, they lost his trust. In clear violation of the Kigali Weapons Secure Area, each of the 600 soldiers was carrying a loaded weapon. Kayonga, when confronted with this information, had told Marchal that the UN had no jurisdiction within the confines of the parliament building.

Marchal initially thought that the rebels were just testing the UN, but incidents between the RPF and the UN observers responsible for monitoring their movements increased on a daily basis.[22] The rebel soldiers left the confines of the CND without the required UN escort. A week or so after their arrival they had toured the centre of town in several vehicles, a demonstration to show their presence to their supporters. On the same day RTLM broadcast that "the cockroaches have invaded the capital".[23]

There were rumours that the RPF had infiltrated men and weapons into Kigali and the UN noted a series of convoys, lorries that came from the rebel headquarters in Mulindi which were loaded with firewood for the troops to keep warm in the CND compound. These convoys were kept under the watchful eye of UN peacekeepers but once in Mulindi they often disappeared into the compound. On the return journey, when ostensibly loaded with wood, they should have been searched as they reached the limits of the Kigali Weapons Secure Area but there was never the manpower for the searches.[24]

The Arusha Accords also required that the French troops in Kigali would withdraw once the RPF battalion arrived. The event was marked in an official ceremony filmed for French television news. A not so public policy was to leave some French soldiers behind, the members of a small military assistance mission known as the Détachement d'Assistance Militaire et d'Instruction, or DAMI. The Rwandan army also retained its French military assistants who were listed with Rwandan officers on official army records.[25]

There were others too by now, and they were more shadowy figures – rogue elements of French mercenaries present in Rwanda who had manipulated and schemed their way into the hearts and minds of the country's elite. These French operatives adhered to a belief that this part of Africa was an essential and a traditional part of la Francophonie and should forever remain so. One of them, Paul Barril, insisted on telling everyone he met that he was an adviser to President Habyarimana.[26] Barril had probably been involved with Rwanda for some time because he once claimed that he knew of a member of the French secret service who had single-handedly stopped an RPF advance in 1992. In the autumn of 1993 Barril was to be found in Burundi as "security adviser" to President Melchoir Ndadaye. The day before Ndadaye's assassination on 21 October, 1993 Barril had left Burundi for Kigali where he made contact with Hutu extremist ministers from Burundi who were broadcasting appeals on RTLM to their supporters to take reprisals for the assassination of a Hutu president.[27]

For Hutu Power the very idea of RPF troops in Kigali was an appalling prospect. The army commander, Colonel Déogratias Nsabimana, considered that the RPF presence would be a "Trojan horse".[28] Accordingly, the government was prompted to strengthen the civil defence network. The country was being prepared for war and it was decided to divide it into zones: two war zones – one centred on Kigali and its environs (Ruhengeri and Byumba), and the other centred on Kibungo and Gisenyi – and a peace zone, made up of Gitarama, Butare, Gikongoro, Cyangugu and Kibuye. Kigali was believed to be the location most coveted by the RPF and consequently the civil defence system there was the strongest. The government was told in reports from army officers that Kigali had been infiltrated by the RPF and that there were two lines of defence in the city, first the military officers who lived at home and second the reservists.[29] At the end of December reports were received by Belgian military intelligence that Bagosora and Séraphin Rwabukumba had recently discussed the best way to orchestrate a campaign of violence by the Interahamwe that would torpedo the Arusha Accords. The campaign would begin in areas where MRND sympathisers were thin on the ground.[30]

Intelligence gathered

On 5 January, 1994, President Habyarimana took his oath of office amid much pomp. But the afternoon's ceremony, the inaugural meeting of the transitional National Assembly, had to be cancelled because of a violent demonstration during which Presidential Guard in civilian clothes and members of the Interahamwe militia had terrorised politicians trying to reach the building. The list of ministers for the transitional government had been controversial from the start: it included several members of the Hutu Power wings of the parties involved and omitted several of the moderates' names. Booh-Booh however saw the swearing-in of the President as a major step forward and considered the failure to install the transitional government a minor blip. The President, he calculated, would be able to broker a deal.[31]

Two days later, on 7 January, a meeting was held between the MRND president, Mathieu Ngirumpatse, the minister of defence, Augustin Bizimana, the commander of the gendarmerie nationale, Major-General Augustin Ndindiliyimana, and the army chief, General Déogratias Nsabimana. They were planning tactics to hide weapons stocks from the prying eyes of the peacekeepers.[32]

The following day there was the first real show of the militia's strength when an angry machete-waving mob suddenly materialised from nowhere. It was a Saturday morning, at around 8 a.m., and it was the first time that the peacekeepers saw the terrifying power of the Interahamwe and Impuzamugambi militia. Hundreds of youths converged on two roundabouts adjacent to the CND where the RPF was housed. The mob blocked the two roundabouts and in so doing cut the city's east-west axis.

Colonel Marchal realised with shock that his options that day were severely limited, as indeed they would continue to be throughout the whole operation. The Belgian peacekeepers, the strongest in the mission, were suddenly cut off from his headquarters because they were located in fourteen different positions around the city. Marchal pulled back from the demonstration and provided for Rwandan gendarmes to stand by. His men were not trained in crowd control. Abuse was hurled at the peacekeepers. This was a turning point for everyone because the element of planning and control involved showed how the power of the militia could be switched on and off at will.

It was two days later that Marchal met an informer called Jean-Pierre. Dallaire had told Marchal that a man had come forward, claiming to have important information for the UN. The man had been highly recommended by Faustin Twagiramungu, the politician chosen as the future prime minister in the forthcoming transitional government. Even so, there was such a cloak-and-dagger feel about the whole business that it crossed their minds that it could be a set-up.

Marchal met the man alone. It was late at night on 10 January. There had been a power cut and a candle was placed on the table between them. The man had taken out a weapon and put it next to the candle. Jean-Pierre claimed to be a senior member of the Interahamwe. He said he was responsible for the security of the MRND headquarters and alleged that his orders came from the very top, from the party's president, Ngirumpatse, and the army commander, Nsabimana. He warned that UNAMIR was infiltrated and that a stream of information about UNAMIR decision-making at the highest level was being passed to Ngirumpatse.[33] And he proposed a deal whereby he would reveal all he knew about what was going on at a press conference if the UN would help him escape Rwanda with his wife and four children. He claimed that his own military training had taken place in Israel.

Jean-Pierre also alleged that careful planning had gone into the demonstration two days before and that government buses had been used to ferry in militia from all over Kigali. There were guns and grenades hidden nearby. The crowd had included some fifty Hutu hard-liners, soldiers and gendarmes in civilian dress. Hidden in the crowd was an MRND minister together with the sous-prefect of Kigali. If the Belgian peacekeepers had tried to disperse the crowd then some of them would have been killed. This was part of a plan to get the Belgian soldiers withdrawn from Rwanda, he said.

Jean-Pierre claimed to be responsible for the provision of weapons to members of the militia and he said that he oversaw the military training of new recruits, which included discipline, arms and explosives training and close combat. He said that each of the twenty to thirty cells that he controlled could kill one thousand people every twenty minutes.[34] His job was to systematically arm all cells in the capital. In every single cell, there were militia armed with weapons who had a basic military training. The reason he had decided to reveal all of this, he said, was because he had recently been asked to list every Tutsi in each cell and he had been told it was for their extermination. His mother was a Tutsi. The defence of the country was one thing, but killing Tutsi was where he drew the line.

The meeting over, Marchal went straight to see Dallaire. It was two months into the mission. The peace process had stalled. Both men agreed that there was only one option: they must put Jean-Pierre's claims to the test. They must immediately conduct an operation to seize the hidden weapons. They must challenge the veracity of the informer and send a loud and clear signal of their determination to secure Kigali's Weapons Secure Area. A weapons seizure would expose the duplicity of the Rwandan government and consequently would either galvanise the political process or reveal it as a sham.[35]

During the night of 10–11 January Dallaire wrote a fax to UN headquarters in New York. Instead of sending it though the normal route however, via the office of Booh-Booh, he sent it to the Secretary-General's military adviser, a Canadian General called Maurice Baril. Dallaire was being cautious. He thought that Booh-Booh's office might be infiltrated.

The cable Dallaire sent that night relayed information about the informer and provided specific details of Jean-Pierre's claims that he had been told to register Tutsi people with a view to their eventual extermination. Dallaire asked New York for guidance on how best to protect the informant. And he told headquarters that he intended to make plans to seize the weapons.

Marchal privately thought that he and Dallaire had uncovered a monstrous Hydra and he wondered how they would be able to fight it without unleashing an apocalypse. The following night, 11 January, he met the informer again and this time Jean-Pierre claimed that the hidden weapons were about to be distributed, a decision due to be announced at a meeting in the MRND offices at 3 p.m. the following day. Marchal meanwhile continued to hold his usual meetings with the army chiefs and gendarmes about how the Kigali Weapons Secure Area was to be monitored.

The next day Dallaire received a cable from New York. It refused permission for arms seizures and spelled out in detail the limits placed on his mission. Both he and Marchal were stunned at the news. Dallaire says that his failure to persuade New York to act on Jean-Pierre's information haunts him still. The tone of the cable, he remembers, suggested a total disconnect between him and New York, as though they no longer trusted his judgment to conduct an operation. Dallaire said that the operation that he proposed, reasonable and carefully explained, was nowhere near as dangerous as that which had brought the RPF contingent to the capital.[36]

The cable also instructed Dallaire to tell the president of the MRND and President Habyarimana of the informant's claims. Marchal's reaction to this was to try to further prove the informant's credibility and he arranged another meeting with Jean-Pierre, who this time alleged that conspirators were actively preventing the creation of the transitional government. Jean-Pierre claimed it was the commander of the Presidential Guard, Major Protais Mpiranya, who had successfully barred access to opposition politicians trying to get to the inaugural national assembly meeting on 5 January.

Marchal told Jean-Pierre that he wanted some proof of the weapons cache. Jean-Pierre agreed to accompany a Senegalese peacekeeper, Captain Amadouh Deme, to the headquarters of the MRND and in the basement there Deme saw a large quantity of ammunition and boxes of Kalashnikov assault rifles. For the next two hours Jean-Pierre and Deme toured Kigali while Jean-Pierre pointed out more than a dozen hiding places for weapons in false ceilings, buried boxes, septic tanks and under bushes at strategic roundabouts.

Marchal believed that the MRND weapons should be seized immediately because of Jean-Pierre's claim that they were about to be distributed to civilians. The ideal time for a raid, he thought, was three days later, when everyone was due to attend an MRND rally at the Nyamirambo stadium. Strongly worded though his and Dallaire's pleas were for an agreement to a raid, no approval came from New York. Marchal would later blame the

"Mogadishu syndrome", the name given to the reluctance on the part of the Security Council to take "offensive" action and put at risk the lives of peacekeepers all because of the disastrous US operation in Somalia.

Dallaire and Booh-Booh told President Habyarimana about Jean Pierre's allegations when they went to see him on 13 January.[37] They protested about the violence that had taken place on 8 January, and said that it had been directed "at one ethnic group" by the militia of the MRND. President Habyarimana seemed alarmed at this, they told New York, and had denied all knowledge of the alleged activities of the militia and promised to investigate.[38] Dallaire and Booh-Booh also told Habyarimana that if further violence occurred then they would immediately inform the Security Council of the information they had received about the militia, they would investigate who was responsible and make appropriate recommendations to the Council. It was an idle threat. Although there was a great deal of violence in the weeks to come, Jean-Pierre's information never did reach the ambassadors in the Council in New York.[39]

There was a flurry of cables back and forth between Kigali and New York as Dallaire tried to find a formula for a weapons-seizing operation that would meet the concerns of the officials at UN headquarters. "Force Commander is prepared to pursue this operation in accordance with military doctrine with reconnaissance, rehearsal, and implementation using concentrated overwhelming force should at any time during reconnaissance, planning or preparation … an undue risky scenario present itself then the operation will be called off", Booh-Booh assured to Under-Secretary-General Annan.[40] Dallaire himself tried to involve the Rwandan gendarmerie in planning an operation but this proved difficult: the gendarmerie was infiltrated with Interahamwe.

Other informants came forward in the following weeks to give information to a small intelligence unit created in the Belgian battalion under Lieutenant Marc Nees. Marchal was suspicious of the Nees network, however, and could not discount the fact that it may have been infiltrated. Marchal's suspicions were vindicated later when it transpired that one of Nees' network, a Captain Gaspard Hategekimana with the nickname "Power", a member of the Presidential Guard turned informer, had played a decisive role when the genocide began in the murder of the prime minister and her husband and that he had led the hunt across town to track down and kill her four children.[41] In the welter of documents he received from Nees there was a distinct lack of commentary, analysis and recommendations. The information collected was of no practical use to him in conducting daily UN patrols and there never were any answers to the most basic questions.[42] No one would tell him, for instance, why on the night of 30 January grenades had exploded all over Kigali. No one could tell him who was behind the assassinations and the sudden explosion of violence at the end of February. No one could tell him why the month of March was so eerily uneventful. No one could tell him whether or not this was a calm before the storm or whether it was part of an evolving struggle towards democracy. Marchal likened his position to sitting atop a powder keg while watching a lit fuse coming closer.

A narrow mandate

There would be many accusations in the press later on that the cable Major-General Dallaire sent to UN headquarters on 11 January was treated routinely.[43] This is untrue. There was consternation when the cable arrived. But the consternation was not caused by the allegation of a conspiracy to murder the Tutsi; it was the result of Dallaire's declared intention to raid a weapons cache, an operation that he was planning to undertake in the next thirty-six hours. Such an operation was considered in New York to be outside the bounds of the mission mandated by the Security Council in October 1993. The mission was fundamentally weak: the demands of the US and the UK for a short and inexpensive mission, born out of public humiliation at the Somali debacle, had been largely agreed to, and the US particularly was determined that it should stay that way. Rwanda would have no more than a peacekeeping mandate. Officials in the Secretariat, and under the guidance of the Secretary-General, had anticipated the reluctance of the US, and had therefore recommended, when it came to devising the mission for Rwanda, a much narrower mandate than was envisaged in the Arusha Accords. There were no provisions in the mandate for protecting civilians, collecting illegal arms, or taking action against armed gangs. Security of "the country" was limited to securing Kigali. These critical points were left out of the mission largely because of an unwillingness to spend any money and to take any risks. It would have been useless to argue against the US, officials were later to claim, for a stronger mandate more in line with the Arusha Accords was just not on the cards.[44]

And so, at the meeting held at UN headquarters after the arrival of Dallaire's cable – a meeting attended by Assistant Secretary-General Iqbal Riza, the Director of the Africa Division, Hedi Annabi and the Canadian military adviser to whom the cable had been sent, Maurice Baril – it was agreed that on no account was Dallaire to try to seize any weapons.[45] While the peacekeepers were allowed to assist the parties in establishing a weapons-free zone, and consequently to help the Rwandan authorities to confiscate any arms within it, they could not recover the weapons themselves.

After the genocide was over Dallaire's 11 January cable came to be known in the press as the "genocide fax". But, in reality, it was only the first of many warnings that would be issued in the weeks to come.

6

ON THE EDGE

In early 1994 the hate radio station Radio-Télévision Libre des Mille Collines stepped up its broadcasts against the Arusha Accords, against opposition pro-democracy politicians, against the Tutsi and against the UN mission. In fact the Arusha Accords were never explained to the people of Rwanda. The validity of the UN mission in Rwanda was increasingly challenged. It seemed as though peace never stood a chance.

In order to try to explain the UN role in the country, Major-General Roméo Dallaire organised a press conference. No one came. Most of the local press was hostile to the UN, viewed peacekeepers with suspicion, and boycotted their briefings. The international press, at a time when exposing what was going on might have made a decisive difference, was simply not interested. What little international coverage there was on Rwanda described a tribal conflict between the "majority Hutu and minority Tutsi".[1] Dallaire bemoaned the lack of international coverage not only of events but also of what the UN was trying to achieve in Rwanda.

The grave problems that Rwanda faced were hardly a secret. Two of the most important aid agencies in Rwanda were clearly expecting a large number of casualties should the peace process collapse. The International Committee of the Red Cross (ICRC) and Médecins Sans Frontières (France) began to stockpile medicines and water, and four huge tents were put up in the courtyard of the Centre Hospitalier de Kigali (CHK), the central hospital, to increase its capacity. The ICRC and MSF (Belgium) discussed how in the event of large numbers of casualties they would collect the wounded from the streets and which agency would provide emergency medical care. An expert logistician, Eric Bertin, who headed the MSF mission in Kigali, assessed the capacity of local clinics. In Geneva the ICRC kept a medical team in reserve for Kigali.

The hostility towards Belgian troops was getting worse. In one incident members of the Interahamwe militia surrounded a minibus full of soldiers and chanted at them, calling them "Tutsi". A grenade was thrown into the headquarters of Colonel Luc Marchal. The commander of UNAMIR's Kigali battalion thought that the virulent anti-Belgian campaign might have been triggered by an incident when a group of Belgian soldiers in civilian dress had badly beaten Jean-Bosco Barayagwiza on his own doorstep and in front of his family. One of the Belgians had put a gun to his head, and told the Secretary-General of the extremist CDR that if he or his party or the local media ever insulted or threatened Belgians again they would kill him. Barayagwiza went public.[2] On another occasion Belgian soldiers roughed up Colonel Théoneste Bagosora.[3]

Many of the soldiers in the 450-man half-battalion provided by Belgium were para-commandos. They had completed a tour in Somalia which had been an enforcement mission. In Rwanda their behaviour was aggressive, destructive and racist; they had critical deficiencies in training and discipline, and Dallaire once considered recommending to New York that the Belgians be pulled from the mission.[4]

At the end of January, in one of his regular reports to Operational Command in Brussels, Colonel Marchal said that this was now an impossible mission; the peacekeepers of UNAMIR had undertaken 924 mobile patrols, 320 foot patrols and established 306 control points. They had collected nine weapons. On 15 January, the Belgian ambassador in Kigali, Johan Swinnen, had written to his Foreign Ministry that the UN possessed proof of the existence of at least four secret arms dumps. He told the ministry that Dallaire had appealed to New York for new instructions concerning the mandate, and that UNAMIR must either be allowed to enforce the ban on arms in Kigali or be withdrawn.[5] A way must be found, he told the ministry, to stop the continuing weapons distribution. "It just cannot go on like this", he quoted Marchal as saying.[6]

Dallaire continued to try to get approval for more forceful action and tried to enlist the support of the UN Secretary-General's special representative, Jacques-Roger Booh-Booh. In a memo to Booh-Booh on 31 January, Dallaire warned "The present security situation is deteriorating on a daily basis. Many groups seem to be directing their activities to violent attacks on ethnic and political opponents." A determined propaganda campaign was being waged against UNAMIR and the local media was "being used by a faction to incite ethnic, partisan and anti-UNAMIR activities". Dallaire pleaded for "determined and selective deterrent operations", which he argued were in accordance with peacekeeping doctrine,[7] and the only way to gain the respect of the local population. In February, however, a cable from Kofi Annan reminded Dallaire that his mandate was modest and only authorised him "to contribute to the security of the city of Kigali ... established by the parties": "We wish to stress that UNAMIR cannot and probably does not have the capacity to take over the maintenance of law and order in or outside Kigali. Public security and the maintenance of law and order is the responsibility of the authorities. It must remain their responsibility as is the case with all peacekeeping operations."[8]

Hate radio flourishes

One of the peacekeeping mission's great weaknesses, Dallaire believed, was its lack of a radio station.[9] On several occasions Dallaire had asked New York for a broadcasting capability, but without success. In his reconnaissance report dated 11 September, 1993, Dallaire had requested finance for this, having decided that it was not a good idea to rent air time on the government-run radio station or RTLM. Without it the UN would be cut off from the people,[10] who seemed to have no idea why the UN was in their country. "It is a critical operational and welfare requirement that we obtain such a station", he wrote. It was important to educate the local people in human rights and democracy and to respond to unfounded accusations against the UN by politicians.[11] He believed it was a grave error that the mission was unable to disseminate information to the local people in French and Kinyarwanda and to stop it being filtered by the local media.[12]

On 27 January, Dallaire expressed fears to Booh-Booh about his inability to monitor the media and formally requested a small monitoring and translation centre. Dallaire stressed the urgency of this request. "This country is glued to the radio and UNAMIR has borne the brunt of a lot of misinformation". He described how a recent inflammatory broadcast had been made by the prefect of Kigali, Colonel Tharcisse Renzaho, accusing the rebels of sheltering killers in the battalion stationed at the CND.[13]

Colonel Marchal agreed that something had to be done about the hate radio which he was sure was clearly organised by "disinformation specialists". Day after day the announcers denigrated the UN. Rwandans were hardly in a position to sort out fact from fiction. The Belgian ambassador in Kigali, Johan Swinnen, sent numerous messages telling Brussels that the hate radio's broadcasts were vitriolic. A Belgian national called Georges Ruggiu who was living in Rwanda and who had been recruited to work as a so-called journalist at RTLM, was accusing Belgium over the airwaves of being in league with the RPF. Swinnen reported to the Ministry of Foreign Affairs in Brussels that the radio was broadcasting calls for the extermination of the Tutsi.[14] Swinnen told Brussels that the anti-Belgian campaign was orchestrated at the highest levels and that he doubted the assurances he had received from President Habyarimana that it would stop. The hate radio was used to tremendous effect to denigrate the Belgian peacekeepers, and it broadcast plenty of material about their drunken and violent exploits. Eighteen Belgian para-commandos were sent home from Rwanda in disgrace and many more were reprimanded for their behaviour. Marchal imposed a night-time curfew on this contingent.

Rwandans too made attempts to stop the hatred spewing out over the airwaves. François-Xavier Nsanzuwera, who was the state prosecutor for Kigali City and Kigali Rural Prefecture, had growing concerns about the inflammatory broadcasts. In February 1994 he called a meeting with the RTLM director Noel Nahimana, and the information minister Faustin Rucogoza at which both the minister and the prosecutor expressed their concerns about radio and newspaper incitements to ethnic hatred. Rucogoza reiterated his belief in media freedom but he called for restraint. The meeting ended on the understanding that the campaign of denigration would stop. Towards the end of March, however, Nsanzuwera heard people were bribing RTLM journalists to stop their names being broadcast: being named on air as an "accomplice" of the RPF meant certain death. RTLM broadcasts were so inflammatory that Nsanzuwera recommended that the station be totally shut down, but this did not happen. Rucogoza had warned him that if he tried to do anything against RTLM, he would be killed, so powerful were its backers.

One broadcast alleged that the then attorney general, Alphonse Nkubito, was involved in a plot to assassinate the president. Nkubito wanted charges filed against the journalist who broadcast the story, Kantano Habimana. Nsanzuwera saw this as an opportunity to summon Habimana and another journalist, Noël Hitimana, whose broadcasts were racist and inflammatory. Nsanzuwera said, "When I interrogated Habimana he said that the only thing that he did was to read out a telegram given to him by his superior [Ferdinand] Nahimana." When Nsanzuwera told the attorney-general this, he was warned that Nahimana's involvement meant the Akazu was behind the allegation against Nkubito. Nsanzuwera was told that he "would be killed if he pursued it."[15] The office of the prosecutor had already been repeatedly physically attacked by both the Interahamwe and the Impuzamugambi militias.

On 21 February, the office of Joseph Kavaruganda, the president of the constitutional court, was broken into in broad daylight and important files were stolen. The culprits, he said, were members of the extremist CDR. Kavaruganda wrote pleading with the President to do something about the CDR and the Presidential Guard. Kavaruganda claimed that Presidential Guard were involved in the recent murder of a clerk of the court, Christian Munyameza, whose body had been dumped on the main road to Gisozi. Kavaruganda said he was himself being harassed and threatened. On one occasion, Captain Pascal Simbikangwa, who ran the secret intelligence services, came to the court to tell Kavaruganda's security detail that they were guarding "a cockroach" and that the group that would kill him had already been chosen: he would be killed during the daytime and his escort would be powerless to prevent it. Two weeks before the genocide began, on 23 March, an Interahamwe called Enoch Kayonde, had shouted at Kavaruganda that they could take him out at any moment they chose.[16]

The Arusha Accords

It was planned that the Arusha Accords would be implemented in accordance with a timetable that provided for the establishment of a broad-based transitional government by September 1993, but this timetable was based on the unrealistic assumption that the UN mission would already be deployed. UNAMIR was not created until 5 October, however, and so it was hoped instead that the transitional government would be in place by the end of 1993.[17] But there were continual delays and towards the end of January 1994 Dallaire met the RPF leadership in Mulindi, some sixty kilometres north of Kigali. The headquarters of the RPF was located in a large abandoned tea plantation with extensive buildings, including a charming old house and a formal garden going to seed.

Dallaire was sure how impatient Major-General Paul Kagame was, but as usual Kagame appeared calm and confident, though he was clearly annoyed at the delays. Kagame said his concern was for the refugees who were returning to Rwanda from Uganda. These people were desperate and ready to take up arms in order to get home. Kagame reminded Dallaire that the RPF had been created for these refugees and they were the reason why there had been a war. It was too much to expect them to continue to be patient. Soon they would face the situation that "someone is going to be a winner".[18] Dallaire believed that the RPF troops who were stationed in Kigali were showing a "siege or prison mentality" caused by their claustrophobic confinement to the CND complex.

Colonel Marchal was concerned at evidence of a lack of faith in the peace process. Jacques Bihozagara, a senior RPF politician, had told him of a belief that the regime in Kigali was actively preventing implementation of the agreement. Bihozagara warned that if there were further killings of Tutsi, the RPF would take revenge. Bihozagara, who despaired at the weakness of the UN mission, claimed that President Habyarimana was the cause of the delays and should be replaced by Joseph Kavaruganda, the president of the constitutional court.[19] Bihozagara said President Habyarimana had successfully connived to divide the opposition,[20] and confided that given the experiences elsewhere in Africa the attempt to create democracy was probably nothing more than a ruse to retain power.

As the peace agreement faltered, the RPF became increasingly bellicose. Dallaire reported low-level intelligence about RPF preparations for war. There were more movements of food and people across the border between Rwanda and Uganda but not massive amounts. Nothing could be confirmed however. The UN monitoring of the Rwandan border with Uganda was hampered by a lack of equipment, and especially helicopters which were crucial in monitoring such an extensive area.[21]

Then they heard an RPF strategy meeting had been held in Mulindi; afterwards there were a number of incursions in and on the edges of the demilitarised zone. Dallaire believed that preparations could be under way for an offensive and that the RPF might be preparing to put pressure on the eastern and western flanks of the DMZ to block any moves by the government army. If so, they would then march on Kigali to link up with their battalion there, but this would only be possible if they had enough forces and logistics to break out of their zone and march to Kigali. Dallaire doubted it; the RPF did not possess such an offensive capability and their advertised strength was an exaggeration. Their "blatant incursions into the demilitarised zone" were possibly a ploy to intimidate the government and to pressurise it to abide by the peace agreement. Another possibility was that the incursions had been carried out by government soldiers disguised as RPF soldiers. As a precaution Dallaire moved more UN military observers into the RPF sector. Later, he claimed that there was information that the RPF was receiving shipments of weapons and ammunition from the Ugandan state's National Resistance Army.[22]

A feeling of impending doom

Towards the end of January the violence worsened; there were grenade attacks, assassinations, and in Kigali automatic weapons were fired into the CND where the RPF battalion was housed. All the Tutsi who lived near the CND fled for safety elsewhere. An armed RPF escort found itself faced with hundreds of militia hurling anti-Tutsi abuse. On 24 January Dallaire told New York that UNAMIR could no longer meet the increasing security demands and that there were going to be larger and more aggressive demonstrations possibly aimed against the peacekeepers. He had already outlined nine alternative courses of action, including a return to Mulindi of the RPF battalion and an evacuation of UNAMIR.[23]

There were ominous signs from the Rwandan army. The troops in the north had not been paid for weeks and the soldiers were short of food. There was looting. There had been a noticeable movement of troops from south to north and reinforcement of positions north of Kigali.[24] The army high command wanted to move a commando battalion from the north into Kigali, but Dallaire refused permission and immediately posted UN observers at the Rwandan para-commando camp. The observers noted that some 200 recruits had been moved from southern refugee camps to a place in the north-east called Gabiro where there was suspected militia training. They had travelled in requisitioned government buses.

During a long evening meal with the minister of transport, André Ntagerura, at a Kigali restaurant called the Péché Mignon, Dallaire was told that President Habyarimana had lost his power and that his political party, the MRND, had become a law unto itself. Ntagerura was in a position to know. He had been in the government for thirteen years and he was known as "the dean of the MRND". Ntagerura confided in Dallaire that anyone hoping that President Habyarimana would come up with a solution to the current impasse was "knocking at the wrong door".

Ntagerura gave Dallaire a long list of grievances about the RPF, accusing them of infiltrating men and weapons into Kigali and claiming their sole aim was a return to the pre-1959 feudal system. Ntagerura said the UN was weak. He complained about the aggressive and womanising Belgian contingent, and said that Dallaire had lost credibility because there had been no arrests after the November massacres of Hutu officials in the north. Ntagerura said that it had not gone unnoticed how quickly Dallaire had condemned the MRND militia for the recent killings of Tutsi in Kigali.

Dallaire told Ntagerura that, as far as he could ascertain, the victims of the recent violence in Kigali had all been Tutsi and that all witnesses had accused the Interahamwe militia of these murders. At the mention of the Interahamwe the minister showed genuine concern and warned Dallaire that this militia would react to any provocation because of a belief that President Habyarimana had "given away the farm" to the RPF. After the supper was over Dallaire wrote a long report to New York, telling UN headquarters of his belief that the tide had turned against the old regime and that the pro-democracy Hutu and the RPF were "rubbing their noses in it". His report ended with the words, "I am getting the impression that both sides have us spinning around. I believe that we must gain the initiative...".[25] Afterward Dallaire was told by headquarters that it was not his job to write such reports.[26]

An increasing number of people were coming forward with information. Donat Murego, the secretary of the MDR party, who had recently been identified with the Hutu Power faction of this party, told the Belgian ambassador, Johan Swinnen, in confidence that the Interahamwe was going to launch a civil war and that it would exploit anti-Belgian hostility. Murego claimed that the anti-Belgian campaign waged over the airwaves by the RTLM radio station was orchestrated by Félicien Kabuga, the MRND financier, together with the president of the MRND, Mathieu Ngirumpatse and Ferdinand Nahimana. Later on the Banque de Kigali records would show a bank account, "Funds for National Defense" whose signatory was Félicien Kabuga.[27]

Rumours were circulating in Rwanda every day about what was going to happen, about plans, plots and intrigue. In Washington, in the State Department's Africa Bureau, officials did not take the stories at all seriously. Similar tales had been circulating for some time, it said.[28]

A public debate

In the first days of February an uneasy calm settled on the city; the violence ceased. Then a public debate was announced, to be held in the prefecture of Kigali. Given full media coverage, it was attended by several ministers, as well as army officers, senior civil servants, the bourgmestres and members of the public. It lasted six hours and there were many frank exchanges. Colonel Tharcisse Renzaho, the prefect of Kigali, was conciliatory, saying he wanted an end to the violence. This was in the presence of the UN force commander and the head of UNAMIR's civilian police, an Austrian, Colonel Manfred Bliem, both of whom had been invited. Bliem had arrived in December to take command of UNAMIR's sixty-strong Civilian Police component (CIVPOL).

The debate was a strange event, with the minister of defence Augustin Bizimana talking about the need for the Rwandan gendarmerie to help the peacekeepers to collect up all the illegal arms and grenades that were circulating. Dallaire immediately seized on this opportunity and told New York that he must respond to requests from the government to conduct operations to recover illegal arms. These would not be "deterrent" operations but "joint operations".[29]

The gendarmes were now more in evidence in the streets. A meeting was organised between the leaders of the Interahamwe and peacekeepers so that the militia could show its "good faith". Dallaire was confident enough to request that Renzaho be issued a visitor's pass for UN headquarters: the prefect had committed himself to assisting the mission of UNAMIR.[30] On 4 February, at a meeting with Bizimana at the Ministry of Defence, Dallaire was promised a list of civilians authorised to carry weapons. He had requested this list some time previously. Bizimana told Dallaire he was sorry that too little had been done to help the peacekeepers, and he said that a propaganda campaign would be organised to help promote the work of the UN.[31]

There seemed to have been a change of heart in the army leadership, among the leaders of the MRND and in the Ministry of Defence. Everyone seemed to want to put a stop to the violence.

An informal party was held on 9 February at the home of the head of the army, Colonel Déogratias Nsabimana. There, minister of defence Bizimana, in a conversation with the Belgian ambassador, Johan Swinnen, suggested a visit to the Belgian battalion to meet its officers. President Habyarimana, in his fluent French, waxed lyrical about the strong links that existed between Rwanda and Belgium. Marchal had a tête-à-tête with Habyarimana who told him how much he hoped that Belgium would play a major role in the peace process.

Marchal remained doubtful and suspicious. The following day, 10 February, he went to the army command for a more formal reception, also given by Colonel Nsabimana, where he was told by some of the officers that the Arusha Accords would never work. That same day Marchal met leaders of the Interahamwe in Kigali who warned him that large numbers of Tutsi were going to be killed. And in mid-February, a prosecution witness later recalled, a meeting was held of junior officers chaired by Colonel Kabiligi. He told them that the war would resume on 23 February, when the enemy, the "Tutsi and the Hutu who are on the same side of the divide" would have to be eliminated: Kabiligi used the French word, "déraciner" – to uproot – to describe what had to happen to these people. The junior officers were told their job now was to distribute weapons to civilians.[32] There seems to be some evidence to suggest that the plotters were not able to agree a start date.[33]

Then as suddenly as it had arrived, the uneasy calm was gone, put to an end by a number of ugly incidents between peacekeepers and militia. Dallaire received information that two people were targeted for assassination: Landoald Ndasingwa, a linguist and former professor, now vice-president of the Parti Libéral (PL), and the president of the constitutional court, Joseph Kavaruganda. Dallaire sent peacekeepers to protect them. On 20 February a national rally was held in support of the peace agreement with people from all over the country coming to Kigali. But there was a counterdemonstration, with stone throwing and tyre-burning. Faustin Twagiramungu, who was to be the prime minister in the transitional government, the current prime minister, Agathe Uwilingiyimana, and other opposition leaders wanted to march together to support peace and democracy, but it was only with the help of UNAMIR and the Rwandan gendarmerie that they were able to do so and the rally could take place. At one point a platoon of Belgian peacekeepers was surrounded by an angry crowd throwing stones. The platoon had to fire 65 shots in order to extricate themselves.

The next day, in a carefully planned operation, the militia sealed the centre of Kigali with roadblocks and then stormed the foreign ministry, holding officials hostage for several hours. Militia rampaged through the constitutional court and stole documents. That night, just as he was getting out of his car, Félicien Gatabazi, the minister of public works, was shot dead: three bullets tore into his back. Gatabazi was head of the Parti Social Démocrate (PSD), the second-largest opposition party, a Hutu and a moderate. There was immediate suspicion that his death was linked to a dossier he had compiled that was said to contain proof of corrupt deals entered into by President Habyarimana.[34] Gatabazi had recently publicly revealed the names of all the camps where training of militia was taking place, and had accused the Presidential Guard of training militia at the Kanombe barracks in Kigali. His death, which was widely believed to be the work of a professional killer, had been predicted in the anonymous letter sent to Dallaire in early December purportedly from disaffected army officers warning of a "Machiavellian plan".

The following day, 22 February, Kigali was a ghost town. The only people outdoors were groups armed with machetes standing at all the main road junctions. They were watched over by peacekeepers and gendarmes. On the road south to Butare, roadblocks were in place. There were grenade attacks and killings, and in the afternoon the president of the extremist CDR party, Martin Bucyana, who was returning home to Kigali from Butare, was lynched by a mob.

The news of Bucyana's death spread quickly and when it reached Jean-Bosco Barayagwiza, the Secretary-General of the CDR, he immediately sent a fax to Gisenyi in the north, to the editor-in-chief of *Kangura*, Hassan Ngeze, to tell him that the Tutsi must be hunted down and killed, even if some were hiding in churches. Ngeze subsequently toured the town with a megaphone to encourage a hunt for "accomplices". The Impuzamgambi, the CDR youth militia, immediately sprang into action to take revenge.[35] At UN headquarters at the Amahoro Stadium, information was received that a terror campaign was about to erupt, and Dallaire ordered his peacekeeping troops to red alert.

In Gikondo, a poverty-stricken, industrial and over-populated part of Gisenyi, Tutsi families became trapped in their homes by jeering mobs containing *Karani*, strong-arm market porters. "They surrounded our café and our house", a witness recalls. "They were screaming and shouting that they were going to kill us ... to kill all the Tutsi in Gikondo." The mob had knives and machetes. The witness could see Interahamwe wearing their army boots, some with grenades. Someone in the crowd that night, an Interahamwe who knew this family, decided to protect them, telling the mob they would leave them till later. So the crowd went on to another house. The bar and café next to it were completely looted. One of the neighbours, a young lawyer called Jean de Die Mucyo, later brought to the bar a woman who had been raped. That night more than forty Tutsi were killed in Gikondo and eighteen children were orphaned. There was similar violence against Tutsi in Nyamirambo.[36]

After this, many Tutsi left their homes in Gikondo and 130 people went to stay with a man who sold foam mattresses. They felt they would be safe in his compound because he told them that he had a friend in the army. They left their homes sure they would be looted, but at least their departure brought to an end months of constant threats and harassment from gangs of youths. "We knew it wasn't over", someone said some years later. "But at least it was quiet. There were so many killers in Gikondo."

That day, 22 February, the situation had never been more tense. Just north of Kigali, there had been an ambush on a convoy of buses that was to have brought the RPF political leadership to the capital from their base in Mulindi; they were to take part in the inauguration of the National Assembly, another attempt to install the transitional administration. But the RPF military leader, Major-General Paul Kagame, had sent the buses back empty. He said he had received intelligence about movements of government troops and he had become suspicious.

The ambush began with automatic weapons and grenades, and the convoy's UN escort had simply fled, its Belgian soldiers speeding away in their two vehicles. The RPF soldiers who accompanied the buses had to be rescued from the ambush by their colleagues barracked in the CND building. One of them was killed.[37] Kagame said that from this moment he realised how little his soldiers could rely on UN protection.[38] Dallaire said the shame that this incident brought UNAMIR forces was never expunged.[39]

As night fell on 22 February Dallaire cancelled all joint patrols. There were fewer and fewer gendarmes to take part in them.

The resumption of the civil war, as predicted by Colonel Kabiligi to junior officers earlier that month, did not take place the following day, 23 February. The reason for this delay, if a later prosecution witness is to be believed, was because someone had realised that the children would be at school and the students would be at university. There would be a postponement until Easter, when the children would be at home. A telegram was sent to the military commanders in the north that "operations" were suspended and a new date would shortly be disclosed. This witness indicated that the president was now in on the plot.[40]

Another witness would later testify that it had been President Habyarimana who had prevented further escalation. He had warned extremists that to continue to kill Tutsi meant to fall into the "enemy snare".[41] On 26 February, the members of the RPF political leadership that had arrived with the battalion in the CND, left for their headquarters in Mulindi, never to return.[42] When Jacques Roger Booh-Booh went to visit the RPF headquarters in Mulindi on March 1, he said that he had returned to Kigali extremely pessimistic. The RPF leadership told him that they had left Kigali because the cease-fire had been violated by President Habyarimana, and that Habyarimana was waging war.

A stronger mandate needed

So concerned was the Belgian government at the deteriorating situation that on 21 February the Belgian foreign minister Willy Claes arrived in Kigali. In his later testimony to the Belgian Senate, Claes claimed that by then he had written to Boutros-Ghali to tell him that unless the peacekeepers took firmer action then UNAMIR might soon find itself unable to continue at all. Claes was being warned by foreign office officials that the peace process in Rwanda was being sabotaged.[43] On receipt of the letter Boutros-Ghali had asked to see Belgium's UN ambassador, Paul Noterdaeme, and told him he was perplexed. Dallaire had been given permission to seize weapons but told that he had to achieve this with the active participation of the Rwandan authorities.

The US and the UK were against the provision of a larger force for Rwanda. These two permanent Council members stressed that the mission in Rwanda fell under chapter VI of the UN Charter and this did not provide for enforcement action.[44] Both the US and UK ambassadors told Noterdaeme that it was up to Dallaire to help the Rwandan authorities plan and execute operations in order to eliminate the stocks of weapons.[45] On several occasions the Belgian ambassador tried to get a change in the mandate for UNAMIR but with no success. The only concession was to take away UNAMIR peacekeepers stationed in the demilitarised zone in the north and move them to Kigali.

The Belgian army would later conduct its own investigation into what happened and the eventual report was classified secret. It concluded that the threats in Rwanda had been so serious that peacekeeping had been completely inappropriate. The enquiry accused the officers of UNAMIR of having placed too much trust in the Rwandans. They blamed Dallaire and his officers for having underestimated the dangers to the UN force.[46]

During his visit Claes noted with some shock that the regime did not even try to disguise the stockpiling of weapons. He had seen for himself how armaments were openly distributed to civilians. Claes says that the special representative, Jacques Roger Booh-Booh, told him in a private conversation that he no longer believed that the peace agreement stood a chance. In a meeting with Claes, Dallaire told him that the mission could not stay indefinitely and that the lack of resources was causing serious concern. Dallaire told him that UNAMIR had to get tougher and more active.[47]

On 25 February, a telex was sent from the Ministry of Foreign Affairs in Brussels to Noterdaeme at the UN to tell him urgently to seek a more robust mandate for the UN peacekeepers in Rwanda. The telex warned: "Political assassinations and deterioration in security could lead to a new bloodbath. In case of deterioration, if the order of UNAMIR remained unchanged, it would be unacceptable for public opinion if Belgian blue helmets found themselves in Rwanda as passive witnesses to genocide."[48]

In testimony to the Belgian Senate some years later Claes said he warned Boutros-Ghali that Dallaire was achieving nothing at all because he continually had to await instructions from New York. Claes says he also warned the US administration that President Habyarimana could be playing a double game.

Seeking sanctuary

By now some Tutsi were trying to plan an escape route, while others had left the country. At the end of February two reception centres were opened, one of them near the UN headquarters at the Amahoro Stadium, in order to shelter Tutsi who were too terrified to sleep at home.[49] Some people thought that with the UN in their country they would be safe. Some thought that the political assassinations in February were intended to restart the civil war.[50]

There was an arrest in the Gatabazi murder case. The state prosecutor for Kigali city and Kigali rural prefecture, François-Xavier Nsanzuwera, had experienced many problems with his own investigations department and much interference from the ministries of justice and defence.[51] In the case of Gatabazi he asked for help from UNAMIR's civilian police force CIVPOL. This had been set up with a mandate to establish law and order and to conduct special investigations in cooperation with the local authorities in cases involving ethnic or politically motivated crime. It was Nsanzuwera who made the arrest of the suspect in the Gatabazi killing with UN civilian police standing by. The suspect was a local leader of the Interahamwe[52] and owned a large café where the Interahamwe and the Impuzamugambi would eat at lunchtime. The café, called Las Vegas, doubled as a brothel.[53] A UNAMIR situation report described how after the suspect was arrested pressure was put on Nsanzuwera to release the man but the prosecutor refused "because the arrest is legal". For the first time, Nsanzuwera was threatened over the airwaves of RTLM.[54] He requested UN protection which was granted.[55]

Dallaire was increasingly troubled. In an internal memo written on 23 February containing information he was receiving about continuing weapons distribution, the activities of death squads, target lists, and the planning of civil unrest and demonstrations, he had writtten: "Time seems to be running out as any spark on the security side could have catastrophic consequences".[56] A few days later, 27 February, a cable addressed to Annan suggests that Dallaire was increasingly desperate: "We are rapidly depleting and exhausting our resources in Kigali and may in the near future be unable to secure the weapons secure area ...". It had dawned on Dallaire that the terror tactics were being controlled by someone. "Last week it was very active and hostile in Kigali and this week it appears to be at an easy calm." This "faction" was exploiting the fear of the population and claiming that the violence was the fault of the RPF and their "supporters". The gendarmerie was stretched thin and exhausted, and its members were unwilling or unable to stem the violence. Dallaire was unsure of its targets. "The present terrorist campaign in part appears to be aimed at their supporters in Kigali and possibly (unconfirmed) members of their ethnic groups."[57]

An account to headquarters written by the Secretary-General's special representative for Rwanda, Jacques-Roger Booh-Booh, of a meeting of the diplomatic corps, states that Dallaire told ambassadors that he did not think that the killing in Kigali in February was "ethnically motivated" and solely directed against the Tutsi minority. At this point, the French ambassador had said that Dallaire's views should be made as widely available as possible in order to prevent the RPF from claiming there were "anti-Tutsi massacres" as an excuse for resuming the civil war.[58]

Booh-Booh himself did not believe that the problems were "ethnically motivated". In a three-page cable sent to New York in the last week of February he wrote: "In view of Rwanda's long and tragic history of ethnic conflict, the possibility of ethnically motivated incidents is a constant threat ... however we do not have conclusive or compelling evidence that the events of the past two days were either ethnically motivated or provoked ethnic consequences." There was no recognition in the cable that the Tutsi and anyone who protected them were the targets of an orchestrated campaign of hate. Booh-Booh reported that twenty-five people had been killed and one hundred injured as a result of "incidents" at the end of February.[59] He acknowledged that some people were seeking shelter in churches, and in a later report he did reveal that in Cyangugu all the victims of the February violence were Tutsi.[60] However in another cable to the office of the UN Secretary-General at the end of February his language was entirely different and described how political parties were split into "Hutu and Tutsi factions".[61]

At the end of February a peace group in Kigali calling itself the Association des Volontaires de la Paix issued a press release to "denounce the genocide of the Tutsi in a programme organised by the extremists in the CDR and the MRND". A UN military observer in a remote part of the country reported to UNAMIR that he had noticed that in some schools teachers were registering the ethnic identity of their pupils and seating them according to who was Tutsi and who was Hutu.[62]

Belgian and French activity

Increasingly disturbing information was being collected by Belgian intelligence. In late February a secret report on the Interahamwe militia was produced within the Service Générala du Renseignement de l'Armée (SGR) in Brussels. The report, for internal Belgian use only, described how the militia was organised by members of the old but still-powerful regime that was clinging to power during a political transition; the old regime was doing all it could to oppose the concessions already given. The intelligence report contained a detailed list of all the murders and violence in which the Interahamwe had taken part. It showed how the Interahamwe was helped by government departments, travelling the country in lorries provided by Onatracom, the country's public transport company, and using the communications equipment provided by the army. The report described how five buses left Kigali every day to take young men to a camp in the Akagera national park for basic military training. The names and locations of other training camps were provided. The report described how members of the Interahamwe were allowed to kill with almost total impunity. It gave the names of powerful people who supported the militia, all of them close to President Habyarimana and the MRND.

The people of Rwanda, the report said, lived in fear of the Interahamwe whose victims, in the main, were political opponents. "It is difficult to investigate among a population secretive and hypocritical by nature", the report stated. It did not mention the racist campaign against the Tutsi and in one paragraph only was there mention of the fact that the Interahamwe had been asked to "localise" the Tutsi families in each cell, and the conclusion that there would be massacres of Tutsi. The report recommended; "One must not exaggerate the importance of the Interahamwe", adding the truism, "it would be an exaggeration to claim that the whole population was in line with its philosophy." It described the Interahamwe as young, disaffected men with no future and little discipline. The report contained one paragraph about this death squad, describing it as a well-trained group that specialised in assassinations and brutal acts of intimidation with close links to the Presidential Guard.[63]

In fact, there was nothing new in the Belgian report on the Interahamwe. A report by the MDR opposition party in May 1992 had already revealed how the Interahamwe was the idea of two people, Charles Nyandwi and Mathieu Ngirumpatse, and that its creation had been approved by every member of the MRND national committee. Ngirumpatse, a former Minister of Justice, had been Rwanda's ambassador to Ethiopia and Germany. He was known as a scholar and musician. The first Interahamwe recruits came from a Sunday morning football club called Loisirs (Leisure): that was how Jerry Robert Kajuga, a Tutsi, had become involved, for he was the football club president and in exchange for the use of his players he had been named president of Interahamwe. The Interahamwe was recruited from the youth of Rwanda and among its advisers were familiar names: Protais Zigiranyirazo, Séraphin Rwabukumba, Joseph Nzirorera, Mathieu Ngirumpatse, and Pasteur Musabe. There were links with certain army colonels too, including Théoneste Bagosora, Anatole Nsengiyumva, Tharcisse Renzaho, Pierre-Célestin Rwagafilita, Elie Sagatwa and Laurent Serubuga. Some recruits came from the Presidential Guard and from the state intelligence services run by Captain Pascal Simbikangwa. Sometimes the Interahamwe appeared in public in a uniform consisting of MRND colours, but they always wore military boots, provided from army stocks, and they were generally armed with machetes, clubs and stones. The Interahamwe was spread nationwide and some prefects were keen to create groups of Interahamwe in their own localities.[64]

Colonel Luc Marchal was becoming increasingly alarmed at the situation. The Interahamwe was only one of many problems confronting the mission. They were becoming more aware of a determined policy to target Belgian troops and in early February Marchal had reported to Brussels that members of the Zero Network[65] were provoking trouble and that the stockpiling of weapons continued. He said Mathieu Ngirumpatse, the president of the MRND, was said to have given orders to change the locations of the arms caches: in future weapons were to be stored at the homes of army officers. The intelligence network run by Lieutenant Marc Nees was receiving increasingly alarming information.

At first Nees had given oral reports to Marchal but from 15 January he had produced written reports, twenty-nine in total, all of which were attached to the daily situation reports and sent to the Belgian army operations centre. An informer from the Nees network claimed in early February that huge quantities of weapons were stored in houses owned by President Habyarimana in Gisenyi, Ruhengeri and Kanombe camp; weapons had been distributed to militia in Gikondo. Nees warned that he had heard that the Presidential Guard was training youth in Kigali in the technique of rounding up people. The army was giving paramilitary training to refugees from the camps in the south who had fled Burundi.

The Belgian ambassador, Johan Swinnen, was told in March by the prime minister, Agathe Uwilingiyimana, about the training of militia. Uwilingiyimana had given him the details during a reception and while she was standing close to a minister from the MRND: there were people who thought she was naïve.[66] Swinnen told his foreign ministry that his own estimate was that three hundred youths had received military training since the UN arrived. He reported that UNAMIR officers estimated that the total number of Interahamwe was in the region of fifteen hundred. Tutsi families were continuing to leave their homes and seek safety in churches or anywhere they saw the UN flag.[67]

Nees also received information provided by the prime minister and it included a claim that in the prefecture of Gitarama there was not one cell or sector left without an Interahamwe present.[68] In nine places in Kigali the Tutsi residents were sleeping in churches at night.[69] On 2 March Lieutenant Marc Nees told Marchal about an informer from the MRND who was claiming that in the event of an RPF attack a plan had been prepared to exterminate all the Tutsi in Kigali.

Undoubtedly influenced by these reports, when the Belgian minister of defence, Leo Delcroix visited Rwanda in March, with twelve members of the Senate and House of Representatives, he publicly called for UN officers to take the initiative themselves. In spite of what New York was saying they should simply order immediate weapons seizures.

Although the Belgians were exceedingly well informed, the French too had crucial links with the Rwandan regime at this time. As Dallaire later observed, "The French, the Belgians and the Germans had military advisers numbering in the dozens at all levels of the military and gendarmerie command and training structures in Rwanda."[70] There were known to be six Belgian nationals advising the Rwandan army as part of military technical cooperation. Some of them were attached to a commando training centre. A French military co-operation team that was openly acknowledged to be in Rwanda is thought to have included not the twenty personnel officially claimed but of forty-seven. These people were attached to key units in the army and in the gendarmerie as "advisers" or "technical assistants". A list of Rwandan army officers prepared within the Rwandan Ministry of Defence and dated 5 March, 1994, shows three French nationals working as "technical assistants" in the reconnaissance battalion. In the Rwandan air corps there were two French flying instructors, a navigator, an air traffic controller and a mechanic. In the para-commandos, under Colonel Aloys Ntabakuze, there were four French nationals including a major in the French army. In the commando training centre there was a French national.[71] One can safely assume that in the course of their work they passed on a considerable amount of information to Paris.

Belgian intelligence records show that two Frenchmen had installed a listening system on Rwanda's telephone network, and were particularly interested in the communications of the local embassies.[72] Also according to Belgian intelligence sources, French diplomats in Rwanda were advising opposition politicians that if they wanted to stop the RPF they had to give their support to President Habyarimana. Swinnen told his foreign ministry that France was continuing to send weapons to Rwanda.

But while spying on each other, Belgium and France were now cooperating on plans for an emergency evacuation. Colonel Marchal had prepared plans for the Belgian contingent of UNAMIR and on 24 March he went to the French embassy to meet Colonel Cussac, the defence attaché, and Colonel Maurin, the head of French military cooperation. They discussed possible joint plans to evacuate French and Belgian nationals living in Rwanda. Marchal sent his evacuation plan to Belgium army headquarters for comment. Several times Marchal asked Belgian army headquarters to provide him with heavy weapons to defend the airport in the case of an emergency evacuation. Marchal informed Brussels that the Bangladeshi troops responsible for UNAMIR's Quick Reaction Force were barely trained and equipped with Russian armoured personnel carriers, APCs left over from the UN mission in Mozambique, which rapidly broke down. Marchal never did receive a response to his urgent requests for weapons and operational directives, or a response to his evacuation plans.

Everyone duped

By March, the transitional government, the cornerstone of the Arusha Accords, was still nowhere in sight. After several vain attempts to install it, the process was still blocked because the opposition was so badly split about which candidates should have ministerial positions. President Habyarimana was widely blamed for these disagreements, and during his March visit the Belgian minister of defence Leo Delcroix urged Habyarimana to take a few initiatives so that he could no longer be blamed for holding up the peace process.[73] After delays and arguments, Habyarimana suddenly outmanoeuvred everyone by insisting that the extremist and blatantly anti-Tutsi CDR be given a place in the transitional government.

The CDR had consistently opposed the Arusha Accords but now it wanted a part in the process. The RPF was bound to reject the idea categorically: it had described the CDR as a "fascist" organisation, an "above ground incarnation of underground forces who were murdering Tutsi". Hitherto the leadership of the CDR had steadfastly refused to sign the National Assembly Code of Ethics for politicians, an integral part of the Arusha Accords, but now the CDR leadership announced that it wanted to sign it.

The inclusion of extremists during peace negotiations is a problem that bedevils all peace agreements. The inclusion or not of the CDR had caused serious rifts during the talks in Arusha because the RPF had steadfastly refused to negotiate if the CDR took part, describing it as an extremist wing of government and therefore ineligible as a political party. US diplomats and officials had made desperate attempts to persuade Major-General Paul Kagame to change its mind about the CDR. One US delegate was heard to say that it was better to have the extremists "on the inside of the tent pissing out, than on the outside of the tent pissing in".[74] According to the State Department desk officer for Rwanda, an inter-agency meeting to discuss Rwanda had agreed as early as March 1992 that the CDR had to be included.[75] The French too lobbied hard for the inclusion of the CDR. But the RPF prevailed.

By mid-March, the CDR issue was back on the agenda. It was widely seen as the final stumbling block to peace and there was renewed pressure on the RPF to allow the CDR into the transitional government or be seen as holding up the peace process. On 28 March, a statement issued by the diplomatic corps in Kigali urging the RPF to accept a CDR role in the transitional government was signed by the Secretary-General's special representative, Jacques-Roger Booh-Booh, the Tanzanian facilitator to the Arusha Accords, the ambassadors of Belgium, France, Germany, the US, Burundi, Uganda and Zaire, and the dean of the diplomatic corps, the Papal Nuncio, Giuseppe Bertello. President Habyarimana announced that he would refuse any transfer of power unless the CDR was involved.

Booh-Booh wrote a cable to Kofi Annan at the end of March to say that the blockage in the peace process was due to the intransigence of the RPF.[76] Booh-Booh had complained of the same intransigence in February when Habyarimana had proposed that as part of the National Assembly Code of Ethics for the political parties, a requirement should be added to provide a "general amnesty" for wrongdoing. The RPF had dismissed this idea outright.[77]

Dallaire was aghast when told about the pressure on the RPF to accept the CDR, and he said that everyone had been duped by Habyarimana: "the entire political and diplomatic community fell into his trap ... we caused the demise of Arusha the day all our diplomats, with the UN Secretary-General's special representative in the lead, accepted the President's gambit." He wondered, not for the first time, whether anyone was paying real attention to Rwanda.[78]

Nevertheless, in March the security situation seemed much less dangerous than in February, and an uneasy calm settled over the city. But the Hutu extremists seemed to grow in confidence about their planning. Perhaps they believed the maxim that to keep a secret one needed to broadcast it: at the end of March a Belgian soldier in Kigali overheard Colonel Gratien Kabiligi and the army commander Colonel Déogratias Nsabimana, talking about how if the Arusha Accords were implemented they would be able to eliminate the RPF and the Tutsi in no more than fifteen days. The soldier reported these remarks to his senior officer.[79]

Later on, Luc Marchal recalled how Nsabimana told him that he feared that the RPF would trigger war in the coming days and that the RPF had been building up stocks of weapons and equipment to support military operations.[80]

While there was less violence there was increasing fear caused by rumour and speculation. Some opposition politicians believed that a programme of mass political assassination was planned for Wednesday 23 March but then they heard that this had been called off.[81]

Two days later, on 25 March, a further attempt was made to install the transitional government, but at the last minute President Habyarimana came up with his own list of candidates for office which omitted the name of Hamidou Omar, who was due to take the seat allotted to the Islamic Democratic Party (PDI). The ceremony was cancelled. Hamidou Omar fled.

In the prefecture of Kigali, lists were being neatly typed of all the people in the city, listed cell by cell, who were responsible for "defense populaire". These lists were sent to the army chief Nsabimana on 31 March, with a covering letter from the prefect Colonel Tharcisse Renzaho.[82] Renzaho had by now been co-opted into the army's State Security Department.[83] An exceptionally powerful personality in the city, he had control over the bourgmestres, councillors, and the leaders of the civil defence network. He had contacts in the gendarmerie and was in close contact with the city's Interahamwe. Renzaho had grown rich by seizing property from those Tutsi whom the Interahamwe had forced to flee, and his office in the prefecture was a useful meeting place for hardliners to plan and organise strategy.[84]

On 29 March, at a meeting in the army command headquarters, the details of the "civil defence" plans were discussed. The meeting, chaired by the army chief Major General Déogratias Nsabimana, also included his staff, the Préfet of Kigali, Renzaho, and the operations commander of the city. Weapons were to be made available for distribution "to selected civilian personnel", reported Nsabimana in a later report. Bagosora denied attending this meeting, and denied seeing Nsabimana's report about it. Bagosora explained that as Directeur du Cabinet of the Minister of Defence he was not allowed to open secret and confidential letters.[85]

April 1994

On Friday 1 April, Colonel Luc Marchal gave a briefing at the Belgian embassy in Kigali about his plans for evacuation should civil war resume.[86] Marchal knew that if it did, his units could defend neither themselves nor foreign nationals. He had a pitifully small amount of ammunition: enough to sustain only a one-to-three-minute fight.

An evacuation plan for UN civilians was already in preparation in the Secretariat building in New York.[87] It was expected that UNAMIR would assist in this evacuation.

Major-General Dallaire had gone on leave in March. Passing through New York for meetings at the UN Secretariat, he had met the Belgian ambassador to the UN, telling him of his doubts that a "master plan" existed in Rwanda designed to create confrontation.

Once back in Kigali Dallaire immediately began to finalise plans to seize hidden stockpiles of weapons: he had obtained agreement from officials in the Department of Peacekeeping Operations for an "operational directive" to mount a raid involving the Rwandan gendarmerie. Legal sanction from Kigali's public prosecutor was obtained and on Friday 1 April a raid took place early in the morning near the Kanombe camp in Kigali. One rifle, some military documents and marijuana plants were found. The gendarmes had proved to be inept and the news of the raid was leaked. Dallaire immediately instigated a plan for another raid.

On RTLM there were broadcasts all that day claiming that the opposition was planning a coup d'état and that it was being led by the prime minister, Agathe Uwilingiyimana, a southerner, together with other politicians from the south.[88] The news item stressed that the prime minister ought to know that if the President of the Republic was ousted then all the Tutsis would be exterminated.

Some years later a witness testified that President Habyarimana had by now lost power: the *de facto* head of the country was Protais Zigiranyirazo, and no one was ever appointed to office without his approval.[89] The witness said that it was Zigiranyirazo who financed *Kangura*, which had been criticising the president since the very beginning of party politics. *Kangura* had carried an item in December 1993 that the President might soon be killed by a militant Hutu soldier who felt let down by the Arusha Accords.[90] A January 1994 issue of *Kangura* contained a claim that the President would be killed in March.[91] *Kangura* had warned: "If they [the Tutsi] commit even the slightest mistake they will perish and if they make the mistake of attacking again all accomplices will perish in Rwanda."[92] A witness would later testify that *Kangura*'s editor-in-chief, Hassan Ngeze predicted that President Habyarimana was going to die sometime in April.

A Rwandan soldier from Camp Kigali would later testify that he heard a rumour that President Habyarimana was going to be killed. He had heard Bagosora say several times that "an apocalypse" was necessary to ensure that all Tutsi would perish.[93]

On Easter Saturday, 2 April, Dallaire met with the Minister of Defence, Major-General Augustin Bizimana, and they discussed why the Joint Military Commission to plan demobilisation was stalled. Dallaire recalls that it was not a good meeting. Bizimana told Dallaire that the country was on the verge of war.

Dallaire then flew by helicopter to meet with Major-General Paul Kagame at the RPF headquarters in Mulindi whom he recalls as distant and withdrawn. Dallaire complained to Kigali about recent ceasefire violations in the east of the demilitarized zone. Kagame wanted to know how acceptance of the CDR by the diplomatic community had come about. Kagame's face was as sombre as Dallaire had ever seen it. "Something cataclysmic is coming", Dallaire remembers Kagame saying. Kagame told Dallaire: "once it starts, no one will be able to control it". Kagame wanted some 450 RPF supporters to be allowed to travel to Mulindi to celebrate the Easter holiday, but Dallaire told Kagame that there were only enough UN peacekeepers to provide escorts for 60 people.

On his way back to the UNAMIR headquarters, Dallaire remembers how at that moment he thought the entire political process "had gone ethnic" and that the Arusha Accords had failed.

That Saturday Booh-Booh passed an agreeable and informal day at the presidential residence in Gisenyi, on the banks of Lake Kivu, with President Habyarimana, his wife Agathe, and Colonels Bagosora and Nsengiyumva. Joseph Nzirorera, Higaniro, and Pasteur Musabe were also there. At some stage during the day, according to Rwandan journalist Venuste Nshimiyimana, Habyarimana told Booh-Booh to let the UN Secretary-General know that he would arrange the swearing in of the transitional government for Friday, 8 April. It is reported that Nzirorera had immediately retorted, "We won't let it happen, Monsieur le President." Nzirorera, the minister of public works and a former Secretary-General of the MRND, had been at Habyarimana's side since he had come to power in 1973.[94] He had managed to build a close relationship with the president's wife and was an associate of her brother Zigiranyirazo.[95] Early that morning, Nshimiyimana had conducted an interview with Booh-Booh for Radio Rwanda in which Booh-Booh said that because of the delays in the peace process it was likely that the Security Council would decide in a few days' time to pull out UNAMIR completely. Booh-Booh himself remembers telling the guests at the villa that day that the UN Secretary-General was worried about the renewal of the UNAMIR mandate.[96] Habyarimana denied the delays were his fault and complained that Uganda and the "international community" were placing too much pressure on him and doing nothing about the RPF. Habyarimana said it was vital for the CDR to be given a place in government. Booh-Booh would recall how he had warned Habyarimana that day of the rumours that his life was in danger. "The rumour was rife", said Booh-Booh. He said that the President had already heard these rumours.

On Sunday, Easter Day, 3 April RTLM broadcast the following announcement: "On the 3rd, the 4th, and the 5th there will be a little something here in Kigali. And also on the 6th, 7th and 8th you will hear the sound of bullets and grenades but I hope that the Rwandan armed forces are on the alert." Years later this broadcast was replayed in an ICTR courtroom in Arusha. The journalist Noël Hitimana is heard to speak of "something that would happen" starting between 3 and 5 April. (Easter holidays.) He said there would be an outbreak of violence with "bullets flying and grenades exploding".[97]

That night the daily situation report sent to New York by UNAMIR contained the words, "Fear among the Tutsi population is limited and few Tutsi take shelter in churches and other public places during the night".[98]

Inadequate briefing at the Security Council

On Monday, 4 April, Habyarimana went to Zaire to see his neighbour President Mobutu at his home in Gbadolite. Mobutu was his most faithful ally in the region.[99] In Kigali the plans continued for an operation to seize weapons, and together Dallaire and the head of the gendarmerie, Major-General Augustin Ndindiliyimana, decided that it would take place at Nyakabanda in a few days' time.

That evening, Colonel Luc Marchal attended a reception at the Hôtel Méridien for the national day of Senegal. There were thirty-five peacekeepers from Senegal in UNAMIR. Sitting at the same table as Marchal was Colonel Bagosora and his wife Isabelle Uzanyinzoga.

Marchal remembers that Bagosora gave them a history lesson on the "ethnic divide", claiming that it was "ancestral". Bagosora told Marchal that the RPF had no intention of sharing power and that its only motivation was to take power by force. For Rwanda to enjoy even one day of peace it was necessary "to eliminate the Tutsi". That Bagosora should say such a thing did not surprise Marchal: what did surprise him was that Bagosora should express such views in the presence of the force commander, Major-General Dallaire, who was also sitting at the same table.[100] In a confidential report written a year later Marchal wrote: "Everyone knew, even in Belgium, what was going to happen for the plan of genocide was in place for a long time."[101]

The next day, Tuesday 5 April, a Belgian soldier patrolling the Kanombe Camp noticed that guards had restricted access so that the UN observers could no longer get near the perimeter fence. A machine gun had been mounted at the main gate.[102] The prime minister, Agathe Uwilingiyimana, told Dallaire that she had heard the Interahamwe militia was planning to attack political opponents in Kigali.

The official refusal of the RPF to countenance the inclusion of the CDR in government came that day, in a detailed four-page letter sent to the UN Secretary-General. It described the CDR as a "terrorist and fascist formation". The letter raised the issue of human rights in Rwanda, quoting a paragraph from the International Federation of Human Rights report of March 1993 using the word "genocide" to describe the killing of Tutsi in Rwanda. The RPF letter pointed out that both the MRND and the CDR stood accused of massacres and that investigators for human rights organisations had described how the militia of the CDR was so omnipresent in Gisenyi that it was suicidal for a Tutsi or a Hutu without an MRND membership card to go out at night. The letter pointed out that the security situation had worsened since then because of a continuing distribution of weapons.

The letter went on to quote the CDR manifesto: "The majority, (Hutu) have nothing in common with the minority (Tutsi and Twa); the three ethnicities should live in peaceful co-existence, each defending his proper interests...". It quoted words spoken by Jean-Bosco Barayagwiza on the hate radio: "the cockroaches only ever give birth to cockroaches". The CDR's only role, the letter maintained, was to defend the Habyarimana dictatorship through violence. The RPF wanted the CDR outlawed through the Rwandan courts. The letter was copied to Kofi Annan and to the President of the Security Council, and it made an official complaint about Jacques-Roger Booh-Booh on the grounds that by insisting on the inclusion of the CDR he had failed to adhere to the Arusha Accords, since the agreement specifically provided that the CDR be excluded.[103] The RPF accused Booh-Booh of being in league with President Habyarimana. The letter was signed by the president of the RPF, Colonel Alexis Kanyarengwe.[104]

The day the RPF letter was distributed Rwanda was due for discussion in the Security Council.[105] UN peacekeeping missions are given six-month operating periods and after that the Security Council has to decide the conditions for extending or ending the mandate. The US was determined that UNAMIR should close: that unless the transitional government was not immediately created, then UNAMIR would pull out. The Clinton administration, post-Somalia, was determined to demonstrate a tough policy towards peacekeeping to show that the UN could be selective in the use of its resources. For weeks, and to no avail, there had been pressure to force the creation of the transitional government and a failure to do so was considered to be the cause of an increase in violence. At the US embassy in Kigali the creation of the transitional government was considered the only possible solution to the deadlock. One insider remembers how the creation of the transitional government was viewed by the Security Council too as "a miracle cure".[106]

In the first week of March the Secretary-General, Dr Boutros-Ghali, had used his own pressure to force progress and he had already threatened that the mission would withdraw. He met with André Ntagerura, the Rwanda minister of transport, who had been sent as a special envoy to New York by Habyarimana. Boutros-Ghali told this envoy, "I have achieved the impossible for you .... You don't want peace ... you don't deserve the help that has been given to you." Boutros-Ghali told Ntagerura that plenty of other places in the world needing aid were more worthy of UN help.[107]

By now the US was in possession of enough information to indicate the simmering volcano that Rwanda really was. As the Security Council meeting was taking place that day a US defence attaché based in the Cameroon turned up in Kigali with a noncombatant evacuation order, or NEO, to ensure that all 257 US citizens were safely rescued from

Rwanda.[108] A CIA report had circulated in January, a desk level analysis that if the peace process failed in Rwanda then up to half a million people would die. The US was also in possession of a report from a recent visit to Kigali by Prudence Bushnell, the deputy assistant secretary of the Africa Bureau of the US State Department, and the director of the Office of Central Africa, ambassador Arlene Render. They had been briefed by Booh-Booh who, in response to a question from Bushnell, said that the trouble in Rwanda was the result of "common banditry", with criminals taking advantage of the unsettled political climate and resulting tensions.[109]

The UK government was also in possession of information about the dangers existing in Rwanda. A report detailing the risks had been sent to London by the High Commissioner in Kampala, Edward Clay, who after a visit to Kigali had provided the Foreign and Commonwealth Office with details of what was happening.[110] It has since been acknowledged that the UK government was also reading Dallaire's increasingly desperate cables warning of an impending calamity, although it remains unclear how the British government managed to obtain what were strictly internal UN documents.[111]

No information was shared with the Security Council. France, intimate with the regime, provided nothing at all other than proposing that UNAMIR be given a six-month mandate, disagreeing with the US that the mission should close.[112] The information given to the Council consisted of a written report that had been initially prepared in Kigali by special representative Booh-Booh with input from Dallaire, and then read by officials in the UN Secretariat. The report had then been discussed with the Secretary-General who made his own changes. It was submitted to the Council, as is customary, under his name. This report was optimistic in tone and stressed that both sides were respecting the ceasefire. Missing from Boutros-Ghali's report were details of a ten-page military assessment prepared by Dallaire which highlighted his serious deficiencies in capability and equipment.

Some of the non-permanent members of the Council would later complain that they were inadequately briefed. Whilst the permanent five, the US, UK, China, Russia and France, had their own worldwide intelligence-gathering capabilities, this was hardly the case with the non-permanent Council members. They largely relied on officials in the UN Secretariat for their information.

"We were kept in the dark", the New Zealand ambassador, Colin Keating, would later claim. Keating, who sat through all the briefings on Rwanda and read all the reports presented to the council about Rwanda by Boutros Boutros-Ghali, believed that everyone was very "discreet" with their information. "Perhaps they felt their hands were tied", he said. In the Council the non-permanent members came to see Rwanda not as the smouldering volcano it really was, but rather as a small civil war. The situation was much more complex and dangerous than was ever officially revealed to the Council, whose members were won over by the Arusha process and even more convinced by a joint Rwandan government-RPF delegation that came to New York to plead for help.

When asked some years later why the Security Council was so inadequately briefed about the realities in Rwanda, the Secretary-General Dr Boutros-Ghali replied: "Everybody knew that the people coming from Uganda were Tutsi and the people in power were Hutu and that it was a war between Hutu and Tutsi. We did not need to tell them that, it was evident. What was not evident was that there was a plan of genocide."[113] The error had been that the Council followed "the US lead", he believed.[114]

The US view that UNAMIR should close did not go unopposed. Nigeria argued that Rwanda should be given sufficient time to achieve democracy and receive the resources and attention given by the UN elsewhere, particularly in the former Yugoslavia where there were currently more peacekeepers stationed than anywhere else in the world. Five days earlier the Council had extended the mandate of this UN mission for another six months and decided to increase its strength to 3,500 troops.

The last to speak in favour of keeping the Rwandan mission was Rwanda's UN ambassador, Jean-Damascène Bizimana; in January 1994, Rwanda had taken a seat as one of the non-permanent members, and it was now a privileged insider in the Council.

The debate centred on how long to keep the mission going and in the end a compromise was reached. At 7.10 p.m. the ambassadors filed from a small room at the back of the Council chamber where the private discussions are held and proceeded to a formal and open meeting. In the Security Council chamber they voted for resolution 909 extending the UNAMIR mandate for three months until the end of July. This was subject to a review in six weeks' time. If by then the transitional government was not up and running, the UN would pull out.

A regional meeting

In Kigali Dallaire and Colonel Marchal were undeterred at this new and dramatic deadline. The next day, Wednesday, 6 April, they pushed ahead with plans for another arms seizure, this time in Nyakabanda, an area within the city. That morning there was a meeting at the headquarters of the gendarmerie where it was decided that peacekeepers from the Kigali sector would throw a cordon around the area. UNAMIR would also help with personnel and logistics. Marchal liaised with a gendarmerie officer, Colonel Paul Rwarakabije. The operation was to take place at 4.30 a.m. the following day, Thursday. Marchal was optimistic. "I felt we had learned our mistakes from the failed operation several days before", he wrote.[115]

President Habyarimana spent time travelling that week. On Monday he had visited neighbouring Zaire and its President, Sese Seko Mobutu. Now he was leaving Kigali again from the international airport to fly in his personal jet the short distance to Dar es Salaam for a regional summit meeting. This summit had been originally planned for 29 March. Habyarimana was due to return to Kigali at 5 p.m. that same day and had asked that a meeting be arranged for the heads of all the political parties upon his return.[116] The UN special representative, Jacques-Roger Booh-Booh, personally invited to attend, chose not to go. Accompanying the president was an unusually large delegation, including the army chief, Major-General Déogratias Nsabimana and the commander of the Presidential Guard, Major Bagaragaza. Some said later that he took these two men with him on the journey for his own security. He was scared, one of his officers recalled.[117] According to Faustin Twagiramungu, before the President left Rwanda he gave instructions that arrangements be made for a swearing-in ceremony of the transitional government in accordance with the Arusha Accords on Friday, 8 April. Twagiramungu thought how tired and worn down the president looked.

Habyarimana was delayed in Dar es Salaam because President Museveni had arrived late at the summit.[118] Present at the meeting were the host, the President of Tanzania Ali Hassan Mwinyi, Habyarimana, the President of

Burundi Cyprien Ntariyamira, the vice-president of Kenya Professor George Saitoti, the President of Uganda Yoweri Museveni, and the Secretary-General of the Organization of African Unity, Salim Ahmed Salim.[119] The four-page communiqué issued after the summit included a plea for reconciliation in Burundi to help the ailing peace process. One paragraph urged the creation of the transitional institutions in Rwanda in accordance with the Arusha Accords, but the communiqué did not reflect the reality of the meeting. Habyarimana had been told in no uncertain terms to stop playing a dangerous game with the security of the region and implement the peace agreement. Habyarimana had accepted politely and told them he would proceed with the accords. There was little enthusiasm in his voice, someone remembered.

The 6 April communiqué was a rushed affair. Habyarimana had to sign a French version of it at the airport.[120] He then offered a lift in his jet to his Burundian counterpart, President Ntariyamira. By then it was so late that he cancelled the meeting with politicians arranged for that evening in Kigali. Only then was he able to climb into his Mystère Falcon jet for the one-hour journey home. After greeting his three French crew he sank his heavy frame wearily into one of the jet's leather armchairs.

7

CRASH

Shortly before 8.20 p.m. the presidential jet circled once in the clear night sky above Kigali International Airport.[1] On its final approach a ground-to-air missile was fired, hitting one of the wings. A second missile hit the tail. The plane became a ball of fire in the sky. There was a huge explosion as the wreckage hit the ground. It landed in the garden of the presidential palace.

Several people at the airport saw what happened, as did two Belgian officers in the garden of a house in Kanombe, the district where the airport is situated. One of these officers saw the exact trajectory of the first missile. He heard the whoosh as it was launched and saw a red-orange flash in the sky, then heard an aircraft motor cutting out. The sky lit up as another missile was fired. The aircraft fell to the ground and immediately he heard the sound of heavy weapons' fire. This officer straightaway telephoned a colleague, Major Grégoire de Saint-Quentin, a French gendarme and a part of a French team attached to the para-commando battalion. The French officer told him that it would be wise to organise immediate protection for Belgian colleagues.

A Belgian soldier stationed in a disused control tower at the airport saw the runway lights illuminated, he thought in anticipation of the arrival of a weekly Belgian Hercules carrying troops returning from leave. The soldier saw the lights of an aircraft, then a light travelled upwards from the ground. The lights of the aircraft went out. Several seconds later another light left the ground from the same place as the first and the plane turned into a ball of fire falling towards the ground. A loud explosion followed. This officer immediately radioed his company commander, who later confirmed with the operational control tower that this plane was the presidential Mystère Falcon.[2] Other witnesses testified that as the plane approached the airport, the runway lights were extinguished.[3]

A Rwandan student officer at the airport who was listening to the radio station RTLM heard the announcer say the presidential jet was coming in to land. Then, suddenly and surprisingly, the broadcast stopped and classical music was played.[4]

In the large airport building there was panic among Rwandan soldiers. The Presidential Guard, there to escort President Habyarimana the short distance to his home, threatened people with their weapons.[5] The director of the office of the president, Enoch Ruhigira, was waiting in the airport's VIP lounge to receive the President. He was said to be carrying a protocol signed by the prime minister, Agathe Uwilingiyima, and other politicians that was a final agreement on the creation of a government to see the country through its transition to democracy.[6]

Only later would a UN peacekeeper, a Belgian officer, realise that the Presidential Guard had completely surrounded the airport.

There were twenty peacekeepers, all Belgian soldiers, on the airport perimeter. A short time after the crash they found themselves surrounded by members of the Presidential Guard. Two, perhaps three of them were disarmed.[7] One witness claimed that gunfire was heard in Kanombe about an hour after the plane crashed.[8] Initial reports spoke of an explosion of munitions at Camp Kanombe. The UN Special Representative, Jacques Roger Booh-Booh said that he heard the noise of an explosion. "I believe the entire town of Kigali heard that noise", he said later. "It sounded like weapons". Some five to ten minutes after that the director of cabinet of the president, Enoch Ruhigira, had telephoned.

"Mr. Special Representative, the presidential plane has been attacked. Please come and help us. Come and help save the president." Booh-Booh said that he had sensed this was serious but he had no idea whether or not the president was dead.

The news that the presidential jet had crashed reached the offices of the Ministry of Defence in a telephone call from a senior officer who commanded the Kigali operational zone. The minister of defence, Augustin Bizimana, was out of the country, and the officer who took the call immediately tried to reach Colonel Théoneste Bagosora, the director of the office of the minister of defence. He failed to do so. Bagosora was apparently at a reception being given by the officers of UNAMIR's Bangladeshi contingent.

According to a UNAMIR report, at 9.18 p.m. a roadblock was established on the outskirts of Kigali, near the Hôtel Méridien, by Presidential Guards who were described as "nervous and dangerous".[9] Further from the city centre and on the airport road there were already roadblocks manned by the Presidential Guard as part of the security detail for Habyarimana's homecoming.

One of the first orders from UNAMIR headquarters given that night was for peacekeepers to go immediately to the crash site. A group of Belgian soldiers set out, but they were stopped at 9.35 p.m., disarmed and taken to the airport by Presidential Guards. The roadblock contained elements of a French-created unit in the para-commando brigade Commando de Reconnaissance et d'Action en Profondeur (CRAP). The rumour was that they were trained by a French officer called de Saint-Quentin, a gendarme from the French military assistance team, known as the Détachement d'Assistance Militaire et d'Instruction (DAMI). One witness said that this French gendarme lived inside the Kanombe military camp.[10]

After the crash, the air traffic controllers closed the airport under orders from the Presidential Guard. The Belgian Hercules was diverted to Nairobi.[11]

Shortly after the crash a section of CRAP, whose barracks were at Camp Kanombe, was ordered to the Presidential villa, a few minutes away where the wreckage of the plane lay smouldering in the garden. They were instructed to collect the bodies from the crash site.

Camp Kanombe, with an estimated 4,000 troops, was under the flight path of the Kigali airport and several soldiers, alerted by the sound of the plane's engines, had spotted it in the night sky and witnessed the missile attack. One Rwandan soldier stationed there, said he thought the missile had come from Cumi n'cyenda, some 19 kilometres away in the Nyarugunga Valley. He was ordered to stay at the camp.[12]

Another remembered: "You know, its engine sound was different from other planes; that is, the president's engine's sound .... We were looking towards where the plane was coming from, and we saw a projectile and we saw a ball of flame or flash and we saw the plane go down; and I saw it. I was the leader of the bloc so I asked soldiers to get up and I told them, 'Get up because Kinani has been shot down.' They told me, 'You are lying.' I said, 'It's true.' So I opened my wardrobe, I put on my uniform and I heard the bugle sound".[13] "Kinani", the Kinyarwanda word used with affection to describe President Habyarimana, means someone who is very famous, who is invincible, who has been able to resist all his enemies.

The bugle was sounded and on hearing it, the witnesses said the soldiers thought the RPF had attacked the camp. Every soldier went to his unit's armoury. Soldiers from the para-commando battalion gathered on the parade ground, while other units congregated elsewhere in the extensive camp grounds.

As the para-commandos collected their weapons at around 9 p.m., their commander Major Aloys Ntabakuze appeared briefly and told them, "There is information circulating to the effect that the president's plane has been brought down. We have not yet confirmed this information, but soldiers should stay together, and we are going to the crash site, so stay where you are." Between 9.30 and 10 p.m. he came back. According to a witness, "Ntabakuze said that the news was true and that the president's plane had been brought down and that all the people who were with the president had also been killed."[14] Ntabakuze told the troops, "You must have heard it on the radio." Another prosecution witness, who says he was on the other side of town in Camp Kigali, and who was a soldier with the reconnaissance battalion, claimed that the battalion assembled after a bugle call to be told by its commander, François-Xavier Nzuwonemeye, that the death of the president was something that "the Prime Minister" would have to answer for and the soldiers were ordered to block roads leading to her house with vehicles.[15]

Bagosora intervenes

The operations room at army headquarters in central Kigali was in chaos. A Rwandan colonel telephoned army command about forty minutes after the plane had crashed and was told that the Presidential Guard had not yet officially confirmed that President Habyarimana was dead. When the colonel arrived some half-hour later no one seemed to know what had happened, only that the presidential jet had exploded and that it had probably been hit by missile fire. Then news came in that the army chief of staff, Major-General Déogratias Nsabimana, had been on board. The officers who were present realised at once that they would have to appoint a new chief of staff immediately. Quietly they filed into an adjacent meeting room in order to decide whom to choose.[16]

Colonel Théoneste Bagosora joined them soon afterwards. He said that when summoned to the meeting he was initially suspicious and had gone first to the Ministry of Defence: he was afraid of a trap, thinking that there might have been a coup.[17] It had struck him what a fateful day this was for Rwanda. The power vacuum that had opened up was enormous. Everyone responsible for the country's security was dead.[18] President Habyarimana, his political counsellor Juvénal Renzaho, Colonel Elie Sagatwa, the head of presidential security, and army chief Nsabimana had all perished in the plane. The minister of defence, Augustin Bizimana, was attending a meeting in Cameroon along with Colonel Aloys Ntiwiragabo, the head of army intelligence, G2.

Bagosora wanted to chair the meeting. He said it was his duty to assume responsibility, claiming superiority as the director of the office of the minister of defence. It was true that the position did traditionally carry some considerable power. Before the formation of political parties, President Habyarimana had occupied the positions of both president and minister of defence while the director of the office of the minister had run the ministry. Bagosora had been appointed as director thanks to his strong links with the MRND – he had been officially retired from the army in 1993 – and by April 1994 the ministry was controlled by him. But that night he did not have strong support: he had never had operational control of troops and his reputation as a soldier was not good.[19] One of the colonels suggested that it would be more appropriate for Major-General Augustin Ndindiliyimana, chief of staff of the National Gendarmerie, to chair the meeting, but he did not want to. "We could not understand it", one of the officers recalled. "How could someone with the rank of general refuse and leave the way open to someone like Bagosora?"[20] Throughout the meeting there were several telephone calls for Bagosora. Each caller was told that he would call back, and he left the meeting room several times to use a telephone in private in an adjacent room.

There was fear at the meeting that night about the power vacuum.[21] Most of them believed that the prime minister, Agathe Uwilingiyimana, was incapable of governing. They talked about the possibility of continuing to abide by the Arusha Accords, but this would mean involving the RPF. Bagosora adamantly dismissed any suggestion that the prime minister should assume any powers. She had proved incapable of uniting her government and, he told them, only two days earlier she had tried to mount a coup using southern politicians and army officers.

Bagosora suggested that the military should take over, but only one officer, Lt.-Col. Cyprien Kayumba, who was the director of financial services in the Ministry of Defence, supported him. Someone replied, "Not at the end of the twentieth century ... not like this." They were desperate to avoid the impression of a coup.

The United Nations was in the country, someone said, and the Arusha Accords were still valid. They agreed to call the UN mission to show that this was not a coup and to invite the Force Commander to join the meeting. Some of them were relieved when they heard that Major-General Dallaire had accepted; he arrived immediately at around 11 p.m. He was welcomed by Bagosora, who told him that it was suspected, but not confirmed, that the aircraft had been shot down.

"We told him of our problem", a Colonel said. Dallaire told them bluntly that if the army took power, then the UN would leave. "We were happy he said that", a Colonel remembered.

Bagosora told Dallaire that he did not want the Arusha Accords to be jeopardised, but the military needed to take control. This would only be for a short time, after which they would hand the situation over to the politicians. He wanted to keep the peace with the RPF. He acknowledged that the Presidential Guard was out of control but said every effort would be made to return them to their barracks.

"I didn't trust him for a minute", Dallaire later wrote.[22]

Dallaire told them that it was important that the Rwandan army remain in barracks. The Presidential Guard should return to barracks immediately. It was the job of the National Gendarmerie to maintain order. UNAMIR would be closely monitoring the RPF. It was critical that UNAMIR should be allowed to investigate the crash site, he said.

Order had to be maintained that night, replied Bagosora, and UNAMIR assistance would be crucial. What the country needed was a transitional authority to hand over power to politicians when they were prepared to govern. Bagosora added that the military would speak with the RPF "when the political situation is clearer".

Colonel Luc Marchal arrived. He had crossed the city from east to west, and remarked on how calm it was, much calmer than some other recent evenings. He was delayed because he had encountered a roadblock in the centre of town manned by the Reconnaissance battalion. It had taken him an hour with the help of a gendarme to negotiate his way through it.

Marchal thought the officers there at the meeting that night were genuinely trying to come to grips with what had happened.[23] Bagosora seemed to be chairing the meeting and Marchal was struck by his demeanour. It was out of character for him to defer, and yet at one stage he tried to persuade Ndindiliyimana, the head of the gendarmes, to assume the chair. Bagosora appeared genuinely shocked by the death of the President. Years later Marchal said this historic moment had remained clear in his mind, and that he thought these army officers were overwhelmed with what had happened. "Their conduct, their intonation, doubts that were expressed, their facial expressions, these … are signs which are not misleading. Without any hesitation, I would like to include in that assessment Colonel Bagosora, at least for the hours immediately following the attack on the presidential plane."

Dallaire suggested that they must contact the prime minister. "Bagosora stood up then", Dallaire recalled, "and leaned toward me, his knuckles pressed hard on the table." Bagosora insisted that she had no authority. Not one officer in the room was in favour of the prime minister. Although Dallaire mentioned it several times, no one agreed. Marchal advised that the prime minister should appeal for calm over the radio. To no avail.

They tried to agree on a temporary chief of staff. Bagosora suggested Colonel Augustin Bizimungu, the commander of military operations in the north, in Ruhengeri. Bizimungu was a hardliner who had helped to organise the training of the Interahamwe in the region. Bagosora denied later that he had ever suggested such a thing. He said that the name Bizimungu had not been mentioned that night.[24] Bizimungu was not at the meeting, and a soldier had been ordered to drive to Ruhengeri to tell him of the president's death.[25]

The longest-serving army officer was Colonel Léonidas Rusatira who had been the director of the office of the minister of defence before Bagosora was appointed. Rusatira was now the director of the École Supérieure Militaire, the military school, but he had never held operational command. Bagosora had always considered Rusatira to be a rival, and would not allow him to become chief of staff. With his suggestion rejected, Bagosora agreed to the appointment of a moderate officer, Colonel Marcel Gatsinzi, who was in Butare in the south of the country. He was the head of the École des Sous-Officiers, the officer school. He would have to come to Kigali at once.

Several times Bagosora assured Dallaire of his cooperation. He gave a guarantee that the army and gendarmerie would be strictly controlled and would collaborate with the work of the UN mission. Major-General Augustin Ndindiliyimana agreed to strengthen the joint gendarmerie-UNAMIR patrols, but it is now known that he subsequently gave no orders to that effect.[26] Ndindiliyimana asked Dallaire to convince the international community that this was not a coup.

Dallaire said it was important that the peacekeepers who were detained at the airport be released immediately by the Presidential Guard. He stated that there must be "saturated patrolling" by joint National Gendarmerie and UNAMIR patrols, and he offered to stay with them at headquarters until the Kigali Sector Commander could arrive to take over.

Dallaire gave a guarantee that there would be an international inquiry into the death of the president. He said that UNAMIR headquarters had issued red alert, the highest level possible, just before 10 p.m. It was the third time it had done so since January.

At midnight, as Dallaire was consulting on the telephone with the UN Secretary-General's special representative, Jacques-Roger Booh-Booh, Bagosora said that he wanted a meeting with him. Dallaire, before he left to accompany Bagosora to Booh-Booh's residence, asked once again for the officers to reconsider speaking to the prime minister. "We thought Bagosora might come back with the wrong message so we suggested that Colonel Ephrem Rwabalinda go as well", an officer recalled. There would be a meeting of all the army commanders the following day.

It was well after midnight when Dallaire, Bagosora and Rwabalinda held a brief meeting with Booh-Booh at his residence. Booh-Booh asked at once whether or not this was a coup. Bagosora assured him it was not. He advised that they continue to try to implement the Arusha Accords, and said the MRND national committee should meet in order to name a new president. The ambassadors of those countries who were observers to the Arusha Accords would meet at 9 a.m. Bagosora agreed to contact the MRND but once again he rejected any role for the prime minister, telling

Booh-Booh that she had been rejected by her own party and by the people of Rwanda. Dallaire said that at the end of the meeting he suggested to Booh-Booh that the prime minister should appeal for calm on the radio. Booh-Booh had agreed.

Afterwards Booh-Booh talked by phone with the prime minister who asked him to help her to deliver a radio message to Rwanda. He promised to do all he could to help.[27] A Rwandan gendarme at her home also spoke with her: she told him that the situation was very dangerous but that she felt protected by UNAMIR.[28]

At dead of night armoured vehicles from section B of the reconnaissance battalion were driven out of Camp Kigali,[29] in clear breach of the Kigali Weapons Secure Area. They slowly trundled to the prime minister's house only a short distance away.

After the meeting with Booh-Booh, Bagosora and Dallaire returned to the Military School where Bagosora was due to report to waiting officers on his meeting with Booh-Booh.

Marchal travelled back to his headquarters at 2 a.m. and was again surprised at how calm the city was. He encountered no roadblocks, and thought the situation was under control. Dallaire later briefed him by telephone about the meeting with Booh-Booh, telling him that the prime minister was to address the nation and that the MRND were going to choose a new President. Dallaire wanted Marchal to send peacekeepers to ensure the security of Radio Rwanda and to provide an armed escort for the prime minister to the studio. Marchal gave the order to one of his officers at 3 a.m., and four jeeps carrying nine soldiers and one officer from the Belgian contingent were sent to her house. Marchal was told that there were roadblocks in the centre of town. There could be no guarantee of success.

That night at 11 p.m., a witness later testified, a telegram was sent to Rwandan army officers to the effect that Belgian soldiers were suspected of shooting down the president's plane.[30]

Only later would it emerge in an international courtroom that Bagosora instructed the reconnaissance battalion to stop anyone going to Radio Rwanda. The witness testifying against him was a former member of the reconnaissance battalion who received and filed the military communications cables.[31]

Evacuations begin

On that Wednesday evening the president of the constitutional court, Joseph Kavaruganda, had had a family supper at home in Kimihurura, about twelve kilometres from the airport, and watched a video. The family was protected by five Ghanaian UN peacekeepers who slept in his garage. At 11 p.m. the phone rang. It was his eldest son in Brussels, Jean-Marcel, ringing to tell him of Habyarimana's death in a plane crash, which had just been announced in Belgium.[32]

Many ministers lived in Kimihurura, a residential area of detached villas set in large gardens with doormen on the gates of the individual compounds. At midnight Kavaruganda received a telephone call from his neighbour, Frederic Nzamurambago, the minister of agriculture and president of the PSD Party. Nzamurambago told him that everyone in their neighbourhood who was a member of the MRND was being evacuated by Presidential Guards. He had noticed a lot of military activity starting at about 10 p.m. Their gateman had been told that the Presidential Guard wanted to know who was in the house because government ministers had to go to the camp of the Presidential Guard. Nzamurambago had refused to go. Instead he had called the UN.

The evacuation was of serious concern to Colonel Innocent Bavugamenshi, the National Gendarmerie officer in charge of VIP protection. When he had heard about the death of the president he had immediately telephoned the gendarmes protecting the prime minister and those with Faustin Twagiramungu, the prime minister designate in the transitional government. Bavugamenshi ordered reinforcements for both units. He then spoke with gendarmes on duty in Kimihurura and Bavugamenshi learned that there were Presidential Guard there and that they had begun to escort MRND ministers out of the area for their protection. Bavugamenshi was immediately fearful and tried to reach the head of the National Gendarmerie but he could not find him and instead telephoned National Gendarmerie headquarters and spoke with a duty officer there, Colonel Paul Rwarakabije, to tell him to send a unit to Kimihurura. Rwarakabije advised him to call army headquarters; the gendarmes could not take on the Presidential Guard. By 3.30 a.m. Bavugamenshi had been informed that three opposition ministers had been killed. The dead included Déo Havugimana, a director of the office of the minister of foreign affairs and a member of the MDR.[33]

Twagiramungu, the prime minister designate, was told about the death of the president by a friend who telephoned his home. He tried to confirm the news but no one responded to his calls. Then he heard from Paris, from the Rwandan ambassador there. He was told the president of Burundi, Cyprien Ntaryamira, had also been on the plane – because his own plane was slower than that belonging to President Habyarimana, a gift from the French government. On board the plane there had also been two Burundian government ministers, Bernard Ciza and Cyiaque Simbizi. Twagiramungu remembers how incredible it all sounded. Soon afterwards he learned that one of President Habyarimana's sons had appeared on TV news in Paris to confirm his father's death. At around 1 a.m. Twagiramungu contacted Booh-Booh, who told him that Uwilingiyimana should take up the reins of government.

Kavaruganda was called again from Brussels at 3 a.m. Jean-Marcel told him that the news in Belgium was that Rwanda had fallen into a political void. Kavaruganda told his son that he was going to wait for official confirmation of the death of Habyarimana from the government. It was up to the MRND to choose a new president.

Kavaruganda's neighbour Nzamurambago telephoned at 4.30 a.m. He was extremely agitated. He said they were trapped. The neighbourhood had been sealed by the Presidential Guard and all the MRND dignitaries who lived there had gone. At 6 a.m. Nzamurambago saw the Presidential Guard approach Kavaruganda's house.[34]

The Abakigas meet

Major Aloys Ntabakuze, the commander of the para-commando battalion, returned to his office at Camp Kanombe from the crash site at around 11 p.m. He went straight into a meeting with certain senior officers, a group drawn from all over the camp, not just officers of his own battalion. Someone was there from the camp's Medical Social Centre. A witness at Camp Kanombe later explained that these people were a northern clique, known as Abakigas, from Kiga, the stronghold of Hutu extremism: "You had to be a member of the Akazu in order for you to take part in the meeting. Yes, he could have been at the Medical Social Centre, but he knew Ntabakuze .... The important thing here was that [the people at the meeting] had a common scheme. It was not necessary for him to be a member of the para-commando battalion for him to be able to participate at that meeting .... I'm talking about the Kigas [sic]; that is the Abakigas, members of the Akazu. They had a common goal; they had a common objective. I am talking about high-ranking officers from the Abakiga, from the Kiga region. They had the same plan. They didn't hide anything from one another; in other words, there was no secret between them. The [officer] orderlies were Abakigas, natives of Kiga. They didn't have secrets for [sic] the Abakiga orderlies, but what the orderlies or the aides could not do was to sit around the tables with senior officers. There is hierarchical respect in the army. You have to respect an officer, but the orderlies, the aides, were there by the door, waiting to be called in order for them to do errands. But there was no secret between them. They were all Abakigas."[35]

Sometime that night, this witness remembers, Colonel Bagosora came to the camp to join those in Ntabakuze's office.[36]

That night, soldiers from CRAP were ordered to help the Presidential Guard evacuate the bodies from the crash site. There may also have been another mission. One witness claims that it was soldiers from the para-commando battalion who were ordered to help to eliminate MRND opponents and that Ntabakuze had a list of people that had already been prepared. This witness claimed that Ntabakuze murdered some of his own men that night.[37]

In the early hours Ntabakuze came out of his office. He summoned all the companies of the para-commando battalion present in the camp. There were an estimated 700 soldiers on the parade ground. According to several witnesses he told them he had no doubt it was the "inyenzi-inkotanyi" who had shot down President Habayarima's plane.

According to one soldier, Ntabukuze told them that "All soldiers should get out and start killing people who were against the government, including Tutsis". The witness added, "We were told ... that the enemy who had downed Habyarimana's plane were Tutsis. And next to the camp there were Tutsis living so we started with this neighbourhood."[38]

Another witness tried to explain Ntabakuze's use of the words "inyenzi-inkotanyi" (cockroach-warfighter): "With regard to the distinction between the inyenzi-inkotanyi and the Tutsis, such a distinction did not exist because it was said that the inyenzi-inkotanyi was within the Tutsis, so inyenzi-inkotanyi was the same thing as Tutsis. And the inyenzi-inkotanyi were fighting using weapons, whereas the Tutsis were their accomplices."

One para-commando company was already out of barracks, having been ordered out before the plane had crashed. It was company two, under the command of Lieutenant Jean de Dieu Gahutu, and was now in Kimihurura where it had been assigned to reinforce the Presidential Guard near the CND building where the RPF was barracked. The third company was now ordered to go to Kabeza and the fourth company was sent by Ntabakuze to Remera. Both these places were residential and close to the airport. The first company was sent to Kajagali, a market area with many shops, the nearest area to the military camp and with many residential houses.[39]

A witness recalled the orders given to these troops: "Before leaving the camp, we were ordered to kill anyone who had an identity card bearing the Tutsi ethnic group reference and anyone who was opposed to the government. So any soldier could kill anyone with an identity card, an identity card bearing that reference to the Tutsi ethnic group." They left the camp at around 6 a.m. on Thursday, 7 April.[40]

A soldier from the first company recalled what happened when they got to Kajagali: "They started forcing people out of their houses, asking them for identity documents. If on your ID card you had the word Tutsi, then you would be killed." For each house there were two or three soldiers, with no more than five soldiers per house.

"Company one worked in the houses which were in the Kajagali centre, alongside the Interahamwes. By the end of that day, all the houses had been visited .... The soldiers shot their victims, but Interahamwe used machetes."

Some of the Interahamwe were afraid of killing, but when they saw the soldiers killing people, they did the same. The soldier said that it was mostly troops from outside Kigali – from Gisenyi and Ruhengeri from the northern heartland of Hutu Power, who did the killing. Others did not. "Some of them did not obey the orders. I mean, they had ... they were aware of the value of the human being. They carried ... when they were given orders, they took along their guns and they held it in a sling, but they didn't kill, because some of those people that had to be killed were related to them, you know, members of their families."[41] The bodies were gathered and loaded on trucks. "They had to be removed from the centre so as to avoid a stench", said the witness.

One para-commando later testified that during this operation his company must have killed about 500 people and that the first company finally left the area at 3.30 p.m. on Thursday, 7 April.[42] This witness recalled that in 1993 his company had been told by Major Ntabakuze during a military assembly that if the "inkotanyi" were to resume hostilities, they were "going to start" with the Tutsis living close to the camp. "Instead of going to fight the inkotanyi who were too far in the forest, they would start with the enemy, the Tutsis who were living close to the camp", he said.[43] In the centre of town, according to one eyewitness account, the Mayor of Kigali, Tharcisse Renzaho had begun to distribute weapons through the Interahamwe representative in each sector of the city.[44]

The early hours

Just before dawn on Thursday, armoured personnel carriers appeared on the streets in central Kigali. They had been recalled by the reconnaissance battalion from the president's residence, Rambura, in the north where they had been kept in the garden in order to evade UNAMIR control.[45] They were sent to Radio Rwanda, the president's home and the Hôtel des Mille Collines.[46]

At the Radio Rwanda building the peacekeepers sent to ensure access to the studios had found their way blocked by twenty-five soldiers and two armoured vehicles. One of the Belgian peacekeepers talked to a Presidential Guard who told him that the prime minister was not working for them any more: she was "unemployed".

During the night these peacekeepers had heard gunshots and screams and had seen a lot of movement of soldiers. In the early hours a Rwandan soldier, hearing gunshots, had telephoned the duty officer at headquarters. He spoke with Lt.-Col. Cyprien Kayumba and told him that the gunfire was near the prime minister's residence. Kayumba told the soldier, "It is us trying to prevent the prime minister from going to the radio station." When the soldier asked why, the phone went dead.[47]

Another army officer, worried that he could hear almost constant gunfire, said that he telephoned army headquarters at around 5 a.m. and was told that an order had been issued to prevent the prime minister from getting to the radio station. At that same hour in the Ministry of Defence, someone on the late shift heard gunfire and called both Bagosora and

Ndindiliyimana to tell them.

The sound of automatic gunfire could be heard from 5.30 a.m. that morning coming from the National Gendarmerie camp at Kacyiru and the Presidential Guard camp at Kimihurura. Colonel Marchal wanted to carry out a reconnaissance by helicopter to get a better idea of what was going on, but his pilot, Major Norbert de Loeker, could not get to the airport because of roadblocks. At his force headquarters at 5.30 a.m., Major-General Dallaire heard sporadic machine-gun fire and rocket and grenade explosions in various areas of the city. On at least one occasion the RPF returned fire aimed at them.[48]

As the sun came up Colonel Théoneste Bagosora was to be found addressing a crowd of Interahamwe in Remera, an area close to the airport where there was a notorious militia group with the name Inyange. He was urging them to start killing "the enemy", and someone hiding nearby heard him telling the crowd they must erect roadblocks and "hunt the Tutsi … house after house", one prosecution witness later recalled.[49]

In densely populated Gikondo many people had been awake all night. One resident said that when she heard that the president had been killed in a mysterious plane crash she knew how catastrophic this was for all Tutsi. Her parents managed to sleep. At dawn she saw them sitting together in bed quietly drinking cups of tea. What were they doing? They must flee. But they told her it was over. There was no point going anywhere any more, and there was nothing anyone could do. "They will kill us progressively", her mother gently told her.[50]

At 6 a.m. it was reported through the UNAMIR radio communications network that rumours had been planted that Belgian soldiers had shot down the plane.[51] The Belgian peacekeepers were scattered at isolated posts throughout the city, and at first light in Kimihurura a small group cantoned in a house code-named Viking saw soldiers walking down the street. They wore the black berets of Presidential Guards. The peacekeepers began to hear the sound of breaking glass, screams and gunshots. Nearby, three Belgian peacekeepers were guarding the house of the lawyer Félicien Ngango, the first vice-president of the PSD. He was set to become the president of the transitional national assembly, and was the vice-president of the human rights organisation ARDHO. Twenty Presidential Guard arrived at the house and told the peacekeepers to get out. Four peacekeepers set out from Viking to help take Ngango's family into their compound, but were stopped at a roadblock. When all the peacekeepers eventually obeyed the Presidential Guards and returned to Viking they heard screams and gunshots. They watched as a woman ran out of a nearby house naked and was shot by a Presidential Guard. A woman was raped by a soldier in front of their perimeter fence. When the soldier realised that peacekeepers could see him he shot the woman in the head. At one point that morning they heard a baby cry and then a gunshot, after which the crying stopped. Some people managed to reach the peacekeepers' compound but the Presidential Guard stuck their weapons through the hedge and threatened to fire on everyone. The peacekeepers asked those people sheltering to leave. The people in terror walked out to their certain death.

At 6 a.m. in another nearby house, the president of the constitutional court, Joseph Kavaruganda, heard a knock at the front door. A UN peacekeeper, the captain of Kavaruganda's UNAMIR escort, was standing on the doorstep with a Presidential Guard. "This man has come to take you to where you will be safe", the peacekeeper told Kavaruganda.

The Presidential Guard said: "I am Captain Kabera of the Presidential Guard. I am Officier d'ordonnance du President.[52] Normally, I accompany the President everywhere he goes but this time I was not with him because I was on leave."

Kavaruganda had received death threats from Presidential Guard officers and in September 1991 when a new constitution was legalised an attempt had been made on his life. In the previous few weeks he had been described on RTLM as "one of the most important RPF accomplices". Now there were soldiers in the garden carrying weapons. "Give me the time to dress and I will come back. Wait for me outside", Kavaruganda said. He shut the door and locked it. He telephoned the headquarters of the Bangladeshi UN peacekeepers who were in charge of his daily security, and they told him they were on their way. His children Julitha, twenty, and Julian, thirteen, took shelter in the bathroom.

At 6.55 a.m. there was another telephone call from a desperate Jean-Marcel in Brussels who told his father to flee while there was still time. "It is too late", his father said. "They are already here. The whole area has been sealed since last night and the MRND ministers have been evacuated with their families."

"And the UN?" his son asked.

"The Presidential Guard is surrounding the house, about forty of them with Captain Kabera. They have disarmed the UN soldiers." Kavaruganda told his son he had telephoned UNAMIR headquarters and the command headquarters of each of the different UNAMIR contingents. They had told him to stay clear of stray bullets and wait for reinforcements to arrive.

Jean-Marcel heard gunfire and the sound of a door breaking inwards. His father said: "For us it is finished. You three on the outside ... be brave in life. I was never disappointed in any of you. They have come to the bedroom ... adieu." It was 7.05 a.m. when Captain Kabera and Presidential Guard burst in. A soldier was holding Julitha.

Kabera saluted Kavaruganda. "Monsieur le President, you will come with us by free will or by force but we are going to keep you safe and put you with the others so that the RPF doesn't take over, so that you can install the institutions for the transition. We already have the minister of information, Faustin Rucogoza."

"I'm not mad," said Kavaruganda. "You can't put in place any of the institutions if the President is dead." He asked to dress. Kabera said it would not be necessary. Kavaruganda dressed anyway. His wife Annonciata handed Kavaruganda his identity card.

"That won't be necessary", said Kabera.

Kavaruganda walked from the house and was put into a small red lorry parked on the road that belonged to the Ministry of Public Works.[53]

In the house next door Presidential Guards were looking for the president of the PSD, Frederic Nzamurambago, the minister for agriculture, who had managed to hide. The Presidential Guards had forced his wife, children and domestics to lie on the floor and wanted to know who was a Tutsi. Some of the children tried to put up their hands but their mother stopped them. One of the soldiers then hit a maid with an axe and then all of the soldiers started beating everyone. They took out their guns and started shooting. One boy, Nzamurambago's son, survived because he was protected from the bullets between two armchairs. Afterwards he hid in the roofspace. About an hour later he heard the voice of his father who had been found by the soldiers. His father was refusing to hand over money and the soldiers killed him. After the soldiers left, the boy fled next door where he found Kavaruganda's widow Annonciata and her two children.[54]

The fate of the prime minister

Dallaire spoke with Radio Rwanda's station manager and was told that Presidential Guards were blocking the entrance. He called the prime minister and she told him she would stay at home. She had heard that two ministers had been kidnapped. Dallaire tried to make arrangements to make a broadcast himself but his request was rejected by RTLM. Someone there told him that UNAMIR was killing Rwandans, which Dallaire told them was totally untrue. Radio Rwanda technicians said they had been warned not to allow any address from their studios.[55]

Nevertheless at 6.30 a.m. an official communiqué announcing the death of President Juvénal Habyarimana was broadcast on Radio Rwanda. The communiqué was the first official confirmation of the death of the president. It explained that he had died in mysterious circumstances, adding that the minister of defence was asking the armed forces to stay vigilant and assure the security of the people of Rwanda. The population should stay at home and wait for new directives. The communiqué, written by Lt.-Col. Cyprien Kayumba, was signed by Bagosora.[56]

Some of those who heard this communiqué were immediately fearful, remembering how a curfew had been imposed during the mass arrests that followed the RPF invasion in October 1990. This had served to trap people in their homes. "I kept quiet", a survivor said when she heard about the communiqué from her husband. "I realised it was over for the Tutsi."[57]

There were no civilian cars on the streets, only military vehicles. Some of the militia were circulating before dawn, and at daybreak others began to dig up buried weapons.[58] People made desperate telephone calls to friends to relay news about who had been killed that night or taken away by soldiers or gendarmes. At every UN location the phones constantly rang for hours with desperate calls for rescue.

The killings by para-commando companies continued in residential areas around the airport. Meanwhile, just outside Remera, a Jesuit community called the Christus Centre was targeted by Presidential Guards. The Centre, a religious retreat, was in a large compound. Several hundred people from Gikondo had fled there in February in the wake of the murder of the CDR president, Martin Bucyana. These Tutsi families had eventually been driven home after Interahamwe had encircled the centre and the local authorities had ordered the priests to send the people away.

On the morning after the crash, shortly after 6.30 a.m., as mass was being held in the chapel, three Presidential Guards burst in.[59] They ordered the sister in charge to get the register to enable them to see who was staying there. The soldiers separated the Rwandans from the Europeans staying at the centre. After carefully scrutinising identity cards, the soldiers directed all the Rwandans into room 28. An officer arrived and told his men to lock the door of the room. A survivor hiding in the library heard two loud explosions and automatic weapons fire. When the door was opened later that day everyone inside was dead.[60] The seventeen dead included priests, seminarians and visitors, as well as the Superior of the centre, a 67-year-old Jesuit priest, Chrysologue Mahame, who had been instrumental in creating the human rights organisation Association des Volontaires de la Paix.

For others that Thursday morning, life continued as normal; the civil servants in the various ministries went to work,[61] as did the office staff working in army headquarters. A soldier collecting documents from the military transmission centre met a friend, a sergeant in the Presidential Guard. The sergeant was pleased with himself. He had come from Kimihurura, he said, where he had made a lot of money. They were searching for and arresting people on the orders of Bagosora, he said. Some people gave money because they thought if they did so they would be spared. At that moment a mini-bus went past travelling towards the Presidential Guard camp and they saw the minister of information, Faustin Rucogoza, sitting in the back seat.[62] Rucogoza was later shot in the head at the Kimihurura Presidential Guard Camp.[63]

Not far away, the UN peacekeepers who were to provide the escort for the prime minister had arrived at her house. It was 7 a.m. and it had taken four hours to get through the roadblocks to reach her. At the last roadblock they had been accused by Rwandan soldiers of trying to kill her. As they arrived at her house, their commander, Lieutenant Thierry Lotin, radioed to say they had been shot at. They could hear heavy firing. Fifteen minutes later they realised that the house was surrounded by Rwandan soldiers. At home with her husband Ignace Barahira, a lecturer at the University of Butare, and her five children, Agathe Uwilingiyimana had given an interview to a French journalist, Monique Mas of Radio France Internationale. "There is shooting, people are being terrorised, people are inside their homes lying on the floor. We are suffering the consequences of the death of the head of state", Uwilingiyamana said.[64] She spoke by telephone with Marc Rugenera, the minister of finance. They agreed that a Council of Ministers should be organised, but Rugenera remembers pointing to the difficulties given the curfew and roadblocks. She said she had heard that Rucogoza and his family had been taken away by Presidential Guards.[65]

The prime minister spoke over the telephone with prime minister designate Twagiramungu at about 8.30 and told him there were Presidential Guards outside her house but they had not yet entered the compound. Two ministers had been kidnapped. Twagiramungu later said that this was the moment when he realised he was now a target too. A short time later he fled to the home of an American friend. He knew then that there would be no government left, only the army high command: all this time there had been a power struggle at the heart of everything and now it was finally exposed. The elimination of the political opposition was under way, "starting with their leaders, from the top to down – I mean, to the [base] of the pyramid, people were killed", he said later.

There was a sudden explosion and the prime minister took flight with her five children, the youngest of whom was just three years old. The prime minister's neighbour was the councillor of the US embassy, Joyce Leader. Uwilingiyimana had already made a desperate phone call to Leader, pleading for help. Now she tried to climb the fence into Leader's compound but it was too high and a peacekeeper tried to help her. There were shots. Leader urged the peacekeeper to abandon the effort.[66]

Unable to shelter with the US diplomat, the family managed to climb into a compound run by the UN Development Programme. The five children, all in their pyjamas, were taken into the home of a UN employee.[67] "We heard her screaming", Leader would remember. "Suddenly after the gunfire, the screaming stopped and we heard people cheering."

The UN peacekeeper in charge of the prime minister's escort, Lieutenant Lotin, wanted to follow the prime minister and he radioed his commanding officer. He was told that if he did so he would lose radio contact for the only communications equipment was in their four jeeps.[68] Suddenly, to the sound of screeching tyres, the prime minister's escort of ten Belgian peacekeepers and the five Ghanaians of her routine nightly guard were surrounded by Presidential Guard. Lotin was told by a Presidential Guard officer that he must give up all weapons and they would be escorted to a UN location. Lotin was twenty-nine years old. He radioed again from the jeep at 8.49 a.m. to say there was "high tension" with the Presidential Guard and asked, would it be "OK to surrender". He was told to negotiate.[69] He said four of his men were already disarmed and on the ground. Lotin had the capacity to resist – each of the Belgian peacekeepers had an automatic rifle, half of them had revolvers and there were two semi-automatics in the jeeps. But he was told to relinquish his weapons if he thought it necessary. It was up to him to judge the situation. Lotin, receiving an assurance that the peacekeepers would be safe, and adhering to peacekeeping doctrine, told them to voluntarily disarm, although one of them secretly kept a pistol hidden inside his jacket. They were taken in a minibus driven by Major Bernard Ntuyahaga, of headquarters staff, to Camp Kigali, the home of the reconnaissance battalion.

They got out of the minibus and were approaching the UN military observers posted at the camp entrance when they were set upon by Rwandan soldiers. There had been a parade in progress; soldiers were in formation on the parade ground, and the rumour went round that this was the group of Belgians who had shot down the president's plane. The peacekeepers were beaten with iron bars, rifles, sticks and stones; six of them managed to take shelter in the gatehouse. Some Rwandan officers in the camp tried vainly to disperse the soldiers to stop the beatings but to no avail. The five Ghanaian peacekeepers managed to escape.[70]

The Crisis Committee

Colonel Théoneste Bagosora spent the morning of Thursday, 7 April in a series of meetings. At around 7 a.m. he was at the Ministry of Defence with senior members of the MRND Executive Committee including Mathieu Ngirumpatse. The stated purpose of this meeting was to appoint a new President of the Republic but apparently it was agreed that this was impossible because under the circumstances they could not convene the party's national congress. Ngirumpatse refused to take the presidency, saying that it was too risky for him. He did not want to jeopardize his political future; instead he apparently began to prepare a contingency plan for when the crisis was over, the details of which have never emerged.[71] From now on Ngirumpatse would ostensibly take a back seat.

Then, as had been prearranged the night before, Bagosora drove in his Audi 1000 to the residence of the US ambassador to Rwanda, David

Rawson. Both Major-General Ndindiliyimana and Colonel Rwabalinda were also at this meeting but the ambassadors from France, Belgium and Germany, who were supposed to arrive, failed to turn up because there were not enough peacekeepers to provide them with an escort. Rawson asked Bagosora why there were the sounds of gunfire and Bagosora told him that the Presidential Guard were firing in the air to express their anger at the death of President Habyarimana. When Rawson asked Bagosora why the prime minister was prevented from getting to the radio station, Bagosora made no reply.[72]

An hour later Bagosora was back at the Military School where he was met by Colonel Léonidas Rusatira, its commander. All Rwandan Government Force (RGF) commanders and all senior officers from the National Gendarmerie were present at the meeting, about one hundred officers. There were commanding officers of the operational sectors, the commanders of the military camps and officers of the general staffs of the army and the gendarmerie. Mostly they were northerners, since traditionally more young men from the north joined the army. On the podium were Colonel Bagosora and General Augustin Ndindiliyimana; a third chair remained empty for General Dallaire who had not yet arrived. Bagosora opened the meeting by saying he was speaking in his capacity as the director of the office of the minister of defence, as Augustin Bizimana was at an international meeting in Yaoundé, Cameroon.[73] He told them that the president and his fellow passengers had died in mysterious circumstances. There had already been a meeting of senior army commanders, he said, and a temporary chief of staff had been chosen, Colonel Marcel Gatsinzi, who was now on his way to Kigali. The commander of UNAMIR, Major-General Roméo Dallaire, was due to arrive. The special representative, Jacques-Roger Booh-Booh had also been informed of these events.

Bagosora explained that none of the transitional institutions provided for under the Arusha Accords had been created. Without these transitional institutions in place there was no provision for the loss of the head of state. The MRND officials he had met with earlier could not find an acceptable candidate for president, and it was impossible to convene the party congress. Any candidate for president would also need approval from the RPF with whom the Arusha Accords provided for power-sharing.

The only solution, he said, was for the military to find an answer. The military could take interim power. There was general disagreement. This was inappropriate at a time when the country was moving towards democracy. It would lead to a renewed civil war with the RPF. What about the prime minister? Bagosora dismissed any role for her. He added that he did not even know if she was still alive.[74]

Many officers were dismayed at the killings that had already taken place and said that the reconnaissance battalion should go to town and "recuperate the Presidential Guard", which was said to be furious at the death of the president. Most of the officers agreed that Bagosora should continue to liaise with the MRND. They suggested that contact be made with members of other political parties with a view to creating a provisional government. This was a priority and no attempt at discussion with the RPF could take place without it, nor would there be any hope of a return to the Arusha Accords. It was decided that the military should create a Crisis Committee to include a range of senior officers: there were a mixture of hardliners and moderates.[75] The Crisis Committee was intended as a way to coordinate the country's security and defence until such time as a provisional government could be created. There were assurances that the Crisis Committee would work with the politicians.

The sound of automatic fire and exploding grenades interrupted their deliberations. At one point the firing became so loud that some of the officers thought the military school was under attack. In fact, the noise was coming from Camp Kigali not more than 100 metres away. The door of the conference room opened and the commander of the camp, Lt.-Col. Laurent Nubaha, came in and spoke with Bagosora. Bagosora would later say that Nubaha told him that there were UN peacekeepers in trouble at Camp Kigali. In his trial Bagosora changed his story and was adamant that Nubaha had told him about "trouble" in the camp.[76]

Major-General Dallaire arrived with a Rwandan army escort and his Belgian senior operations officer, Major Peter Maggen. Dallaire had been forced out of his jeep at a roadblock. On his way to the military school, as he passed the entrance to Camp Kigali he noticed several UNAMIR soldiers lying on the ground. He knew then that his mission had started to take casualties. He was by now in a Rwandan army vehicle and he ordered the driver to stop, but the driver refused telling him it was too dangerous. When they arrived at the Military School the atmosphere tensed as Rwandan soldiers realised that Maggen was a Belgian, and

Dallaire realised this officer was in some danger. He would later testify to Maggen's bravery that day.[77]

Bagosora, who was in mid-speech when Dallaire entered the meeting room, was shocked to see him, but soon recovered his composure.[78] Dallaire told the assembled officers that they had to stop the crimes of the Presidential Guard. UNAMIR was staying put and he would assist them in preventing another civil war. All units must return to barracks. His mission was still the implementation of the Arusha Accords. There was scattered applause.[79] The officers asked him to be their intermediary with the RPF and to ask the RPF leadership to show moderation in an effort to overcome this sudden crisis. The meeting ended at midday.

Bagosora had stood in a group of officers afterwards. There was Colonel Kundiye, who was then the commander of military operations in the Mutura region, a former commander of the Presidential Guard; Major Nzuwonemeye, who was a commander of the reconnaissance battalion, and Major Ntabakuze, the commander of the para-commandos battalion. One witness would later recall that Bagosora said to these officers in Kinyarwanda, "*Muhere aruhande*". This phrase translates, "Go about it systematically from one place to another," like tilling a field, for instance, or clearing bush, systematically from one place to another.[80]

Afterwards, and under Rwandan army escort, Dallaire returned to the Ministry of Defence to find the building almost deserted. He was told that everyone was at lunch. When Bagosora returned, Dallaire, concerned about the peacekeepers, repeatedly and insistently asked Bagosora to allow him to go to Camp Kigali. Bagosora told him it was unsafe. Bagosora promised Dallaire that he would ensure the camp was secure and would obtain the release of the peacekeepers.

Dallaire would later explain that precipitous action in that tense and uncertain security environment could have been the spark that would ignite a wider conflict and place UNAMIR in an adversarial role. Their only reasonably available solution was to continue to negotiate as a neutral force. Dallaire remembers Bagosora briefing a senior officer about the release of the peacekeepers.

Bagosora suggested to Dallaire that it was an urgent necessity to withdraw Belgian troops from Rwanda because of the rumours circulating that they were to blame for the death of the president. Bagosora said the situation was difficult because he was not in command of all the elements in the army.

Dallaire also enlisted the help of Ndindiliyimana in order to get to Camp Kigali, to no avail. Ndindiliyimana told him that Bagosora would take charge of the problem but Bagosora adamantly refused permission for the force commander to enter the camp.[81] According to one senior officer, Ndindiliyimana was by now busy warning certain of his own officers of a list that had been prepared of moderate officers who were to be killed.[82]

Bagosora that afternoon was seemingly taken up with administrative affairs in his office, working on reports and letters. Dallaire said later that it was incredible to witness. He had never found anyone so calm and so at ease with what was going on. Bagosora received a few phone calls and met with one or two senior officers. He shuffled papers and signed some documents in a very slow methodical fashion. Ndindiliyimana, at times, was falling asleep. Dallaire said that it was as though they were totally completely out of step with what was going on. "I mean totally on another planet, or something was operating as per plan; that in fact, what was going on they were conversant with and it's just doing its thing". Dallaire said that by now there were killings everywhere. "There were reports coming from everywhere. I was telling him I had problems. The gendarmerie was practically immobile in a defensive position. There were phone calls to the effect that people were being killed, wounded. Ambassadors could not move about to meet people. Bagosora talked about the situation as simply an "excess".

By now, said Dallaire, he had concluded that whatever it was that was going on, then Bagosora was the "kingpin". Bagosora had not lost the position of authority that had been created the previous night. Dallaire believed that the plan that they had previously heard so much about from a variety of informers, this singular scenario that was to throw the country into crisis, well then all fingers pointed to the hardline elements of the government, particularly the MRND party and the CDR.[83]

The Presidential Guard moves in

Outside in the street that morning a gendarme who was trying to reach the prime minister's house was told to go no further by Presidential Guards who had mounted a roadblock at the corner of the Military School and the Avenue Paul VI. The gendarme was told not to worry for gendarmes were already looking after the prime minister. The Presidential Guard told the gendarme that the prime minister was in hiding in a UN compound near her house.

Dallaire spoke by telephone with an official in the Department of Peacekeeping Operations in New York to inform him that the peacekeepers might have to use force to save the prime minister. He was told that there would be no change in mandate; UNAMIR could fire only in self-defence.[84]

Colonel Marchal was thinking by now that the crisis was so serious that it was becoming likely that some of his men would pay with their lives.[85] The gendarme responsible for VIP protection, Colonel Innocent Bavugamenshi, had arrived in Marchal's office at 7.30 a.m. desperate for help. Bavugamenshi told Marchal that ministers who did not belong to the MRND were being "neutralised" by the army. He thought a systematic search-and-kill operation was being aimed at opposition politicians.

Marchal could offer no words of comfort. He did not tell Bavugamenshi he already knew what was happening at Kimihurura. There were too few peacekeepers in Kimihurura to make any difference.

"But what could we do? How far could we go without going too far?" he wrote some years later. Either they tried to fulfil the mission, step by step and with inadequate resources, or they took account of the state of their force.

From 9 a.m. that morning the Presidential Guard went house to house; some Presidential Guards complained because the Interahamwe had not already carried out "the work". One witness saw a Presidential Guard kill one of his colleagues, a Hutu adjutant, because he had hidden Tutsi in his house. The Presidential Guard brought people to the tarmac road to kill them in order to make it more convenient for the military authorities to pick up the bodies.[86]

The newsroom blackboard

Sometime between 11 a.m. and noon, seven heavily armed Presidential Guards clattered into the offices of RTLM. Their officer demanded to see the journalist on duty. The Belgian announcer Georges Ruggiu came out to see them, and they told him that the prime minister was dead. They said it with some pride: they went on to admit that they had just killed her. They had been in a detachment sent to her house, and the Belgians protecting her had been "sent off somewhere else".

After this, Ruggiu wrote a list of names of politicians on the newsroom blackboard: those people he thought would be the next to be killed. Ruggiu later explained, "We knew that opponents ... the opposition to Habyarimana was under threat." Twenty names were written in chalk including those of the president of the constitutional court, Joseph Kavaruganda, and Boniface Ngulinzira, the foreign minister who had negotiated the Arusha Accords. Also on the list was the minister of information, Faustin Rucogoza, who had tried to do something about RTLM's campaign of racism and hate.

Three of the names on Ruggiu's initial list were already dead. Félicien Ngango of the PSD, the politician set in place to take over as the president of the transitional national assembly under the Arusha Accords, had been murdered. Minister Landoald Ndasingwa, the vice-president of the Liberal Party and minister for labour and social affairs, was also dead: the Presidential Guard had turned up at his house and shot him together with his Canadian wife Helene, their two children and his mother. The order to kill Ndasingwa had apparently come from a captain in the Presidential Guard. The minister of information, Faustin Rucogoza, and his family had been taken to an army camp and killed at its entrance. The bodies of the ten members of this family had been left on the ground at the entrance to the camp. A sergeant had given the final order for their deaths.

Ruggiu said of the list, "I put them on the list of people threatened. I didn't know that they had been killed. Some people we were told had been killed. We knew that some people who were members of particular political parties, who were opposed to MRND, were under threat, and so we put them on those lists."

Across the city, by the late morning Colonel Luc Marchal was appraising the appalling situation. Belgian peacekeepers were being held hostage by Presidential Guards at the airport. The joint patrols were not happening because the Rwandan gendarmes were ineffective. There was still no access to the crash site. At the airport, according to UN military observers, the stocks of bombs and anti-aircraft cannon under UN supervision had been seized and were being put in position around the runway.

There were roadblocks in the centre of town manned by the reconnaissance battalion; some of the roadblocks were reinforced with tanks. From first light there had been endless calls for help; an estimated 100 an hour into the UN headquarters.[87] To his shock and consternation, as Marchal was taking a call for help from Landoald Ndasingwa, he heard gunfire and screams. Marchal knew that the attacks were not improvised. The Kimihurura area where most ministers lived was cordoned by soldiers and gendarmes, and people were being eliminated. Marchal was unsure whether other forces had by now seized power. The situation was similar to the one in February when there had been a sudden deterioration in security. UNAMIR could not be indifferent, but neither could it suddenly turn itself into an intervention force. Now it had failed to protect the VIPs at Kimihurura, failed to assure the prime minister's access to the airwaves to calm the people. The first victims were those very people whom the UN had a duty to protect, those who had put their faith in the UN peacekeepers. Marchal hoped that the meeting that had been arranged with the diplomatic corps would allow them to discuss the various political options. He did not yet know that, for lack of a UN escort, the diplomats had been too scared to leave their homes.

The impotence of UNAMIR was more obvious than ever before, as had been demonstrated graphically that morning at around 9 a.m. when its Quick Reaction Force comprising Bangladeshi soldiers and three armoured personnel carriers had been turned back from a roadblock after being threatened with anti-tank weapons. From now on, the Bangladeshi contingent would obey no orders unless from their own commanders. The sixty-strong Tunisian company, which was well led, well trained and disciplined, had no vehicles of its own, communications equipment or logistics. The Belgians were scattered throughout the city in fourteen different places.[88] They did not have enough Motorola radios.

The only good news was that the peacekeepers at the airport had been released, although they were immediately detained at a roadblock.

The deaths of peacekeepers

At the Ministry of Defence early that afternoon, Major-General Augustin Ndindiliyimana spoke with Seth Sendashonga, an RPF representative. Sendashonga said that if the massacres of their supporters did not stop, the RPF company would break out of their barracks in the CND and stop the killing themselves. All around the CND, people were being killed, sometimes in clear view of RPF soldiers. Ndindiliyimana said he could not control all the units who were in a panic over the death of President Habyarimana.[89] No one in the ministry seemed to want to do anything, though Dallaire had offered to mediate between the Rwandan army and the RPF.

At around 4.15 p.m. the soldiers of the RPF broke out of their barracks and dismantled the fence of the CND. They launched an immediate attack on the Presidential Guard barracks at Kimihurura and a gendarmerie base in Remera.

The RPF soldiers went to areas where the militia was operating. In Remera they killed a large number of civilians: there were reports of more than 120 people having been killed in what appeared to be an organised operation. Marchal was told of this killing by witnesses. The RPF soldiers then quickly moved to other parts of the city in an attempt to provide protection for civilians who were known to be their supporters.[90]

Another communiqué from the armed forces, written by Bagosora, was broadcast at 5.20 p.m. It purported to come from the Crisis Committee and it cynically called on "the government in place" to assume its responsibilities and create the transitional institutions in accordance with the Arusha peace agreement. It announced the formation of a Crisis Committee to ensure security and to give support to the politicians.

The population was invited to stay calm and not be drawn into hate and violence. The young should refrain from "vandalism". The authorities in all prefectures were to examine the security situation. The communiqué was signed by Bagosora.[91]

While the RPF was dismantling the fence at the CND at 4.15 that afternoon, a convoy of cars and military vehicles entered the outskirts of the city bringing the new army chief, Colonel Marcel Gatsinzi, to the capital from Butare. The convoy included Dr Theodore Sindikubwabo, the president of the parliament, who was in an official Mercedes. The convoy was shot at as it arrived at the main roundabout on the approach to the centre of Kigali. Some officers laughed at Gatsinzi when he had asked who was responsible. They would not tell him. He had been suspicious and he had not travelled in his official military vehicle and was uninjured. In the convoy was President Habyarimana's brother, Dr Seraphim Bararengana.

The Crisis Committee met at 7 p.m. Bagosora wanted to preside over the meeting and when this was refused he became insulting. The chief of staff, Colonel Marcel Gatsinzi, remembers that Bagosora wanted to become the president of the Crisis Committee. Bagosora was told that this was impossible. It was a military committee and he was retired.[92] When Colonel Rusatira questioned the powers of the Crisis Committee, Bagosora, near the end of his tether, stormed out of the meeting accusing them of preventing him having a role in something he had created.[93]

For the second time the officers agreed that the Presidential Guard must return to barracks. They would issue another communiqué for calm to be restored.

On the night of 7 April, Major-General Paul Kagame of the RPF sent a message to UN headquarters in Kigali that he was ready to send a battalion to assist government forces in preventing further civilian killings by renegade forces. In an interview, Kagame claimed he suggested that they secure some areas, creating safe havens. He said he told Dallaire that there was no mandate in the world that could stop their combined forces ending the bloodshed. Dallaire did not trust the RPF offer. By now both sides were killing non-combatants.

"I needed troops from a third party", he said. He believed a strong UN force to stop the killing was absolutely essential. To have cooperated with Kagame would have guaranteed losses among his thinly spread-out force. Major-General Kagame had announced from his headquarters in Mulindi that an RPF battalion was moving towards Kigali to stop the killing. The purpose was to "assist government forces" in keeping "renegade forces from killing innocent people".

Only later would it be established that all that day there had been requests to Bagosora and to Ndindiliyimana from army officers and from the RPF to control the military, and most notably the Presidential Guard, who were murdering civilians. These requests were ignored and Bagosora, according to his ICTR indictment, ordered Ntabakuze, the commander of the para-commando unit, Major François-Xavier Nzuwonemeye, the commander of the reconnaissance battalion, and Lt.-Col. Leonard Nkundiye, former commander of the Presidential Guard, to proceed with massacres.[94]

The indicment claimed that Nzuwonemeye ordered some of his soldiers to help the Presidential Guard to assassinate the prime minister, and also ordered his soldiers to "get rid of the enemy and its accomplices", meaning opposition politicians whether Hutu or Tutsi and all Tutsi.[95] A prosecution witness claimed that the order to prevent the prime minister from going to Radio Rwanda came from the deputy commander of the reconnaissance battalion, Colonel Innocent Sagahutu, as did the order to prevent her leaving her house. When the members of the reconnaissance battalion arrived at her house, the Presidential Guard were already there with an armoured vehicle. Sagahutu, claimed the witness, had been sent an order to kill the prime minister.[96]

All that day, according to his eventual indictment at the International Criminal Tribunal for Rwanda, Bagosora ordered groups of soldiers, including elements of the Presidential Guard and of the para-commando battalion, to carry out selective assassinations.[97]

At 9 p.m. that night at Camp Kanombe, Major Aloys Ntabakuze was trying to find suitable coffins for the victims of the plane crash. He was tired and angry. One witness recalls him saying: "They have killed him ... but many will die because of it."[98] He told a group of soldiers to go to collect Tutsis resident in Kanombe and bring them to the camp.[99]

The bodies of the prime minister and her husband were taken to the morgue at the Camp Kanombe by members of the reconnaissance battalion. The prime minister's children had been smuggled to the Hôtel des Mille Collines by UN peacekeepers. Presidential Guards were still searching for them.[100]

That night, according to a later witness, there was a private party at the Hôtel des Diplomates. While drinking champagne, certain army colonels toasted the future. Bagosora spoke openly of eliminating Tutsi, something that could be achieved by mounting roadblocks all over the country.[101]

Across the road, in the morgue next to Kigali's central hospital, the bodies were piling up. And it was here, in a side room, that Dallaire found the bodies of the ten Belgian peacekeepers who had been sent that morning to escort the prime minister to Radio Rwanda to appeal for calm. The dead peacekeepers were found piled in a heap. Their boots were gone; some of the corpses still had flak jackets, but they were opened. Most had bullet wounds to the chest and head and some had been bayoneted. They had died in a firefight one by one, the last soldier looking for shelter behind the bodies of fallen comrades.

Dallaire said he concluded that the implementation of the plan was moving ahead, as the informer had warned them; they were killing Belgians to get rid of UNAMIR. "There was no way I was leaving", Dallaire said later.

On the way back to headquarters that night, Dallaires's UN vehicle, clearly marked with a blue flag in front on the right fender, and with a blue flag on the back, was fired on at a roadblock. This particular roadblock, the one on the road from central Kigali to the airport, would become familiar in the weeks ahead. It was manned by para-commandos.[102]

8

ZERO NETWORK

The news of the death of President Juvénal Habyarimana reached the north of Rwanda quickly and according to several witnesses there were killings of civilians that same evening. On the evening of Wednesday, 6 April, in the north of Rwanda, Lt.-Col. Anatole Nsengiyumva was having supper. When he heard the news of the plane crash he immediately returned to barracks,[1] and went straight to his office, followed by a gendarmerie officer who was his well-known right-hand man, Lieutenant Bizumuremyi.

Nsengiyumva, the military commander of the Gisenyi operations, was responsible for the prefectures of Gisenyi, Kibuye and part of Ruhengeri. A former head of Military Intelligence, G2, he had been appointed to this command three months earlier. He had brought Bizumuremyi with him from Kigali where Bizumuremyi had worked under the alias Mutoko as a Zero Network operative.

There are witnesses who have described what happened at the camp that night. They have described how Nsengiyumva and Bizumuremyi conferred for about an hour; during that time there was a telephone call from Colonel Théoneste Bagosora who was in the capital Kigali, some 160 kilometres away.[2]

Afterwards Bizumuremyi ordered company commanders to assemble their men, and when they were assembled Bizumuremyi told them the news of President Habyarimana's death at the hands of "unknown perpetrators". There was no news of any survivors in the presidential jet.

"Everybody seemed depressed. We were wondering what was going to happen", a soldier recalled. Shortly afterwards Nsengiyumva arrived on the parade ground and confirmed the news. "He said there was no specific information about this. He seemed very depressed. He didn't say much". But he did tell Lieutenant Bizumuremyi that "work" had to be done to "finish off the inyenzi". Then he went back to his office with Bizumuremyi.

A leader of the Gisenyi Interahamwe, Barnabé Samvura, arrived soon afterwards. By then a large crowd had gathered at the camp entrance, possibly as many as two hundred people with militia among them. Nsengiyumva had summoned to the camp certain militia and local authority leaders.[3]

According to the witnesses present that night, Bizumuremyi addressed the crowd: "The soldiers have gone to do their work, their normal work", he told them. "As for you, you are going to also begin your work. Go everywhere, spare no one, even – not even babies. Do it quickly so that in the morning, we will have finished." Weapons and grenades were handed out, and the crowd went towards the town. It was late at night. Bizumuremyi went back into the camp for a while, and then he also left to go towards Gisenyi.

At some stage Nsengiyumva telephoned army headquarters in Kigali and left a message to say that a radio operator in Gisenyi had intercepted an RPF message which said, "Our friends Belgium [sic] shot the plane."[4]

That night some of Nsengiyumva's conversations were overheard by a military intelligence operative who would testify against him. "The colonel was talking about the evilness of Tutsis", this anonymous and protected witness told a court at the International Criminal Tribunal for Rwanda (ICTR). In one call Nsengiyumva was heard to say that the apocalypse had come but "we now have to wait". Nsengiyumva complained that Bizumuremyi was late returning from the town. When the lieutenant did eventually arrive he told his commander that the "Rubavu" operations were completed and that people would continue to "work" in the rural areas. Colonel Théoneste Bagosora called on the "cell phone". Nsengiyumva told Bagosora that the operations in Rubavu had been completed and they were now ongoing in the rural areas.

There were orders that night to organise an "evacuation system": vehicles would be sent to patrol the streets and the rural areas to "evacuate" the bodies.

The witness said: "There was mistrust of the international community because there were observers and foreigners who could come by. So this was all very well organised. The vehicles went everywhere around to pick up bodies." On Thursday, 7 April, the day after the plane crash, Nsengiyumva went into Gisenyi to see "the operations" for himself, going to Rubavu. It would soon become a habit for Nsengiyumva to go through town to "assess the situation on the ground".[5] One day Nsengiyumva would be called by a witness at his trial "the Supreme Commander of Genocide in Gisenyi".[6]

Gisenyi prefecture was the heartland of Hutu extremism. It was here that the liaison between the military, the civilian authorities and the militia was the closest.

The coordination between the military and militia groups in Gisenyi was largely the work of Bizumuremyi. Witnesses have described how he was responsible for running a special group of operatives, recruited among soldiers and gendarmes, and known as the "detractors". They wore civilian clothes and worked with military intelligence and army security officers. The job of the "detractors" was to inform on the activities of soldiers while they were outside military camps and file reports on individuals to Nsengiyumva. These spies were in charge of disciplining soldiers, and they also participated in militia activities, and helped to train militia. Every day Bizumuremyi gave Nsengiyumva, who loved paperwork, a daily account of militia activity in the prefecture.[7] In early 1994 the militia leaders of the Interahamwe and the Impuzamugambi had been given portable transmitter-receivers by Bizumuremyi to enable him to pass orders to them. There was also a private radio communications system which was independent of the others and situated in Nsengiyumva's office. This was his probable link to Zero Network, the communication system exclusive to the conspirators.

The Gisenyi massacres

The killing in Gisenyi started within hours of the plane crash. It was systematic and well-organised with soldiers and militia taking part. The militia drove around in vehicles provided for the purpose and were armed to the teeth. Whole families were taken away on lorries, told they would be safe but instead taken to the public cemetery, known to the extremists as the "commune rouge" (red commune), where they were killed. Those people who tried to flee to neighbouring Zaire were shot at the border.[8]

In some sectors no one was left alive to bear witness. In the commune of Rubavu, where the militia went "to work" on the night of 6 April, one woman, released by an Interahamwe she knew, was the only person who lived to recount what happened. She said people had been taken to the local stadium to be killed.

"They came into houses and asked people for their identity cards. They took away people whose ID said Tutsi and anyone they decided looked Tutsi ... there were people at the stadium who were sorting out people ...".[9] It was in the commune of Rubavu that the "commune rouge" was situated.

On the morning of Thursday, 7 April, the head of each cell told Hutu residents that an important meeting was to take place near the Gisenyi bus station. Between 7 and 8 a.m. Interahamwe were collected from all parts of town in commandeered vehicles. The crowd that congregated at the bus station was addressed by Nsengiyumva. They referred to him as "Colonel Anatole" and he told them that they must implement the instructions he had issued. Roadblocks needed to be reinforced, and Tutsis "would be exterminated because they had just killed the president". Weapons were distributed, including grenades and Kalashnikov assault rifles.

Later that morning, a group of Interahamwe arrived at the military camp and after a meeting Nsengiyumva gave them weapons.[10] This group of militia then made its way to a residential area in the centre of Gisenyi town. Their driver later recalled: "They killed people. I personally remember that I went to the Bugoyi *cellule* [cell], and there they killed a teacher – a lecturer – and his daughter." He said they had been given a list by Nsengiyumva of people to kill. "We came out of the meeting with the list. Four soldiers from Gisenyi camp accompanied our group. We boarded the Daihatsu vehicle that I drove. On the way we picked up several Interahamwe to join those who attended the meeting. I can estimate there were about sixty Interahamwe on board my vehicle."[11]

This prosecution witness testifying at the ICTR said that Nsengiyumva had told them to organise night patrols, and set up roadblocks in the cell. He told them the enemy was the Tutsi.

At 5 p.m. Colonel Anatole Nsengiyumva organised another meeting. People were summoned to it through a megaphone mounted on top of a van that toured the streets. People were told that the enemy had launched an attack. "They asked us to be vigilant", said a witness. "They said they were going to send equipment."[12] Without further delay, there appeared in each cell a carton of Chinese-made grenades. That night, said the witness, the massacres started. Weapons were distributed at the office of the commune and then off-loaded to the sectors. These weapons came from the military camp.

"I saw a large group of youths, which I believed were Interahamwe, assembled at a car wash near my home and the main Gisenyi market. Immediately, I saw Colonel Anatole Nsengiyumva come in his military jeep with some soldiers and start unloading some boxes from the jeep. They were arms. Guns and grenades were in the boxes, as I realised later. The soldiers started distributing the guns and grenades to the Interahamwe who were there. I got scared, and quickly ran back to my house. I was still curious, and I looked through one of the windows of my house to see what was going on outside."[13]

A house located behind the Palm Beach hotel in Gisenyi was owned by a militia leader called Bernard Munyagishari, who worked in the Ministry of Youth in Kigali until the Interahamwe was created. Then he had moved to Gisenyi, where his house became the headquarters of the Interahamwe. On the night the president was shot a meeting was held at Munyagishari's house, with perhaps more than a thousand people present. The next day Nsengiyumva was seen at Munyagishari's house. One witness saw green crates of weapons unloaded from his jeep.

The plans for genocide in Gisenyi were more advanced than anywhere else, evidenced some years later by the testimony of prosecution witness Omar Serushago, a militia leader, in an ICTR courtroom. Serushago was described by one witness as having been "virtually the son of Anatole", but in exile he had turned informer. Serushago revealed there were six groups of Interahamwe and Impumnganzi in Gisenyi, and each night they would meet together to report on the Tutsi who had been killed that day.[14] Serushago told the court: "Tutsis and Hutus know each other very well. One can easily identify a Tutsi by his attitude, his bearing, and a Tutsi can recognise a Hutu by his attitude, his bearing and his physique. I would like to inform the Chamber that this hatred existed for a very long time, since 1959 in particular, until the time when the genocide took place in 1994."

On Thursday, 7 April, Nsengiyumva told Bizumuremyi that in the nearby Nyundo diocese the priests, nuns and monks had to be displaced, and everyone else who was there too, because soldiers were going to occupy that position. Nyundo diocese was in Kanama commune, next to the commune of Rubavu. The bishop of Nyundo's residence was there, as well as a seminary and several schools.

The bishop, Monseigneur Wenceslas Kalibushi, was having an Easter meeting with priests from the diocese, and on Wednesday some of the priests had stayed the night at Nyundo. By Thursday morning, following the announcement of the death of President Habyarimana, the families of Tutsi teachers from the various schools in the area started to arrive, coming for safety as they had done before at times of crisis.

But by Thursday afternoon a large crowd had arrived at Nyundo carrying machetes, daggers, bayonets, and rifles. Two priests were killed. The women and children were put in the chapel but the armed mob came back a few hours later and killed them all.[15] Afterwards soldiers were ordered to requisition disinfectant from the hospital in order to clean the chapel and the surrounding areas.[16]

The militia took Monseigneur Kalibushi to the "commune rouge" in Gisenyi town, but he was released by Colonel Nsengiyumva because Bagosora had said that to kill him would provoke diplomatic incidents and go against international opinion. The bishop was taken to the Hôtel Méridien in Gisenyi where he was placed under the protection of a small group of soldiers. The Holy See intervened and he was later released.[17]

The UN presence in Gisenyi consisted of a group of military observers. They lost contact with Kigali hours after President Habyarimana's plane was downed. Contact with the military observers was resumed on 10 April when they managed to communicate with colleagues in Butare. They said that Gisenyi was in "total chaos". There were massacres everywhere. They estimated that tens of thousands of Tutsi had been killed. They had watched on Thursday, 7 April as militia entered the Hôtel Méridien and started to kill people in front of them. The militia threatened the military observers and stole their possessions. These observers eventually managed to escape Rwanda via Ruhengeri.[18] One of them prepared a report that finally reached Kigali on 19 April. It described how a priest had assembled 200 children in a church for protection but they had all been massacred.[19]

The killings spread

In the prefectures of Ruhengeri, Gisenyi in the north, Kigali in central Rwanda, Kibuye in the west, Kibungo in the south-east, Cyangugu in the south-east, and Gikongoro in the south, there was killing that first day, Thursday, 7 April. The violence was often preceded by a rumour, spread by local officials and soldiers, that the RPF and its "accomplices" had shot down President Habyarimana's plane.

In the south-eastern prefecture of Kibungo the killing began within hours of the president's death. In Sake, near the border with Burundi, rich Tutsi families were targeted by Interahamwe.[20] There was killing in that prefecture from early Thursday morning involving local authorities and Rwanda soldiers. In the prefecture of Gikongoro, immediately the news of the president's death was announced the houses of Tutsi were set on fire and Tutsi began to flee for their lives to churches and to schools.[21] In the prefecture of Kibuye there was a higher percentage of Tutsi than anywhere else in the country and one survivor recalled how a few hours before the death of President Habyarimana, a bus full of young men had arrived from Kigali. After the announcement of the president's death the young men had started to whip up the population, telling everyone that the Tutsi had killed the president.[22]

In Mabanza in Kibuye a teacher recalled: "Because of my activities in the Liberal Party, I was one of the first people that the bourgmestre and his deputy wanted to kill. The other Tutsi tried to protect me. Already on the seventh the homes of some Tutsi began to be demolished." He described how his home was attacked by people from the neighbouring prefecture of Gisenyi. Four people died trying to protect him.[23]

In Cyangugu, the prefect, Emmanuel Bagambiki, whose previous job was prefect of Kigali, sealed the border with Zaire early on Thursday. Early that morning local authorities were telling people in the prefecture that Tutsi had killed President Habyarimana.[24] In some parts of the prefecture the killing started that afternoon; Tutsi houses were burned and thousands of Tutsi began to flee their homes.[25] In the prefecture of Greater Kigali there was killing of Tutsi that day. Only two prefectures were calm, Butare and Gitarama.

In Gikondo within Kigali, the militia poured into the streets on Thursday, 7 April, and moved from house to house killing with machetes, clubs and sometimes firearms. The hunt for Tutsi extended to searching the houses of Hutu to see if anyone was being hidden. The Gikondo orphans, eighteen children, whose parents had been killed by militia in February and who were being cared for in a school, were all slaughtered. The man responsible for this would later commit suicide after learning that his own mother denounced him.[26] In another area of the city, in Nyamirambo, the militia arrived from elsewhere and took control of the streets. Anyone found to be sheltering a Tutsi was killed. Thousands of people who were sheltering in the St. André School in Nyamirambo, were attacked by the Interahamwe that day, Thursday, 7 April.[27]

In Kigali the hunt continued to eliminate Rwanda's political opposition. Journalists were among the first targets and it was later estimated that forty-eight were eventually killed.[28] André Kameya, the editor of *Rwanda Rushya* (New Rwanda) was hunted the first day when fifteen soldiers went to his home, but he had already gone to hide in a nearby church.[29] Also targeted were people from the human rights community and certain prominent lawyers on lists already prepared, because they had defended political detainees or simply because they were Tutsi. Still others, both Hutu and Tutsi, were targeted for having worked towards democracy. Some others were killed because they were prominent southern Hutu.

An interim government announced

The military Crisis Committee reconvened on the morning of Friday, 8 April, at the Military School. The new army chief of staff, Colonel Marcel Gatsinzi, began the meeting by expressing official condolences from the Rwandan Government Forces (RGF), to the UN and to UNAMIR for the deaths of the ten peacekeepers. Gatsinzi promised an enquiry into their deaths. Gatsinzi announced that those gendarmes not involved in fighting the RPF would help the International Committee of the Red Cross (ICRC), to identify and bury the dead.

That morning Bagosora was at the Ministry of Defence and at 9.30 a.m. Dallaire noticed him there, presiding over a meeting of politicians. Bagosora seemed embarrassed at the presence of the politicians. All that morning military escorts were sent from Bagosora's office in the Ministry of Defence to find certain ministers. And perhaps more intriguing, the evidence from one eyewitness that Bagosora had been advised by General Ndindiliyimana that unless a head of state was chosen, it would look just like a coup d'état. It was for this reason that Bagosora was told he could not possibly take control and that ministers had to be chosen for an interim government.[30]

One of them was Jean Kambanda, of the MDR, an economist and banker from Butare. Kambanda claimed that when he heard about the death of President Habyarimana, he had taken refuge with his family at a gendarmerie base in Kigali. It was by chance, he claimed later, that just as he was returning home to collect some clothes, he had met fellow MDR member Froduald Karamira.[31] The next day, Friday, 8 April, Karamira came to find him and escorted him to the Military School. There, said Kambanda, he learned to his great surprise that he was to be Rwanda's new prime minister.[32]

Gathered at 2 p.m. in the lecture hall were the officers of the military Crisis Committee together with politicians representing all the main political parties. All the political parties who had signed the agreement for the first multiparty government in April 1992 were present. The meeting was opened by the chief of staff of the Nationale Gendarmerie, Major-General Augustin Ndindiliyimana and he gave the floor to Colonel Théoneste Bagosora. Bagosora explained that because of the deaths of the president and the prime minister a political void had opened up. They had been called together because their party leaders had put them forward for membership of a new government.

The MRND was represented at the meeting by its president Mathieu Ngirumpatse, its first vice-president Edouard Karemera, and its national secretary Joseph Nzirorera. Bagosora gave the floor to Ngirumpatse, who explained to the assembled politicians that the procedure for choosing a new president would comply with the 1991 constitution because no agreement could be reached on the Arusha Accords. The 1991 constitution provided that in the case of the death of the Head of State, the President of the Parliament would be appointed as an interim president for sixty days.

The current president of the Parliament was Dr Theodore Sindikubwabo, an MRND member from Butare who had just arrived in Kigali. Sindikubwabo was a paediatrician and was described as "docile".[33] He was nominated as President of Rwanda and approved. Ngirumpatse then called on the parties to nominate their candidates for government.

The MDR representative, Froduald Karamira, put forward Jean Kambanda as prime minister. "No one asked me if I would be prime minister", he said later. "No one asked me if I would accept or not. I knew and I presume all the other ministers knew that outside people were dying … were being killed."

The meeting ended at 4 p.m. with the signing of a protocol for an official agreement between the parties. The preamble pointed to the death of the president and the "unexpected" death of the prime minister and members of her government. The protocol provided for a prime minister who would be put forward for approval to the interim president. An interim government would be installed to handle the affairs of state, particularly a rapid return to order and security. The protocol provided that the interim government would pursue negotiations with the RPF with a view to establishing transitional institutions.

After these solemn declarations, an official from the French embassy in Kigali contacted Jérôme Bicamumpaka, the man chosen as minister of foreign affairs in the interim government. The French wanted official government permission for their troops to land at Kigali International Airport in order to evacuate their nationals. The French had already stressed to Bicamumpaka that a recognised government needed to be in place as soon as possible. The membership of the interim government should be announced immediately, advised the French ambassador, even before a swearing-in ceremony.[34]

The prime minister in the interim government, Jean Kambanda, would later claim in his ICTR interrogation that it was Bagosora and Ngirumpatse who had decided on the idea of an interim government. Kambanda understood that the initial intention of the Crisis Committee was for it to take power with Bagosora taking the presidency. The political opposition would have been represented in the Crisis Committee by Major-General Ndindiliyimana and Colonel Rusatira. Instead, claimed Kambanda, what happened was that the French ambassador, Jean-Philippe Marlaud, and the UN special representative, Jacques-Roger Booh-Booh, had counselled that they must adhere to the Arusha Accords. A military committee was not provided for in the accords.

Kambanda was told that a meeting had been organised between Bagosora, representing the Crisis Committee, and the president of the MRND, Mathieu Ngirumpatse. The first vice-president was there,

Edouard Karemera, and the national secretary, Joseph Nzirorera. They had discussed the situation with Bagosora and some other members of the Crisis Committee. The military was against Faustin Twagiramungu, the prime minister designate under the Arusha Accords. He was considered to be pro-RPF. It was at this meeting, held in the early hours of Friday, that the decision was taken to choose a new government. One witness said that Ngirumpatse and other politicians, such as Frodauld Karamira, Joseph Nzirorera, Edouard Karemera, Justin Mugenzi, and Donat Murego, all helped devise the interim government, but at the request of Bagosora.[35]

The first cabinet meeting of the interim government was held at 8 p.m. on Friday even though the swearing-in ceremony was not to take place until the next day. The meeting, at which the military was present, was purportedly to ensure continuous administration of the country and to renew contact with the RPF in order to put in place the transitional government and also to try to do something about the displaced people.

It was ambassador Marlaud who later that day made a call to the Belgian ambassador, Johan Swinnen, to tell him about the new government. Swinnen quickly realised that all the ministers came from the Hutu Power factions of their parties, yet Marlaud was claiming that the interim government could prevent a coup.[36]

That night the ministers were forbidden by military officers from going home for security reasons and they all stayed at the Hôtel des Diplomates. Many of the MRND politicians who had been moved and protected during the night were now in this hotel, where they were guarded by members of the reconnaissance battalion.

That evening the names of the members of the interim government were read over the radio by Valérie Bemeriki and Noël Hitimana. After Bemeriki read out the names of the ministers she began to giggle and told her listeners the opposition members in the previous government could not be found.[37]

In Kigali hundreds of people were sheltering in churches, hospitals and hotels. People were seeking safety in the large redbrick Église St Famille, and in the pastoral centre, St Paul. There were people in the Sabena-owned five-star Hôtel des Mille Collines, in the French Lycée Notre Dames Des Citeaux, in the Hôtel Kiyovu, and in the offices of the International Committee of the Red Cross. Near the UN headquarters there were people in the Hôtel Méridien, in the King Faisal Hospital and in the Amahoro stadium.

Not even the hospitals were safe. On Friday, 8 April at the central hospital, the CHK, situated in the heart of the town and a short distance from the Hôtel des Diplomates and Camp Kigali, nurses watched in horror as a group of Interahamwe marched people to the hospital mortuary where they killed them, leaving the bodies where they fell. Another group of militia was in the hospital killing the injured and sick. All the victims were Tutsi. Most of the dead bodies in the morgue and stacked up outside it were naked because their clothes had been looted. A military officer known as Lieutenant Pierre was recording all the names of the Tutsi on the hospital staff. Soldiers turned up at the hospital to find girls who were hiding in the laundry room.[38] The daily number of Tutsi killed in the CHK would from now on be reported on a daily basis to military authorities.

The control of large parts of the city of Kigali was now firmly in the hands of its prefect, Colonel Tharcisse Renzaho. Renzaho had been appointed prefect in 1990, four days after the October RPF invasion. The appointment of a prefect was usually reserved for a civilian candidate but Renzaho had taken over at a time of crisis when thousands of people had been arrested as "accomplices".

While the members of the interim government were being chosen on Friday morning, Renzaho had called together the city's local authorities from the communes and from the sectors for a meeting of the so-called Prefectoral Security Council, a committee that had been established as part of the civil defence structure. Renzaho painted a bleak picture. He told them that the situation was "catastrophic". There was fighting in the city between the army and the RPF, whom he claimed had smuggled into Kigali hundreds of men and weapons. Some local officials had not been able to get to the meeting, he claimed, because they had been "systematically eliminated" by the RPF. He described how refugees were seeking shelter everywhere. Public order was threatened and war was creeping into every part of town. Infiltrators were causing "inter-ethnic confrontation". Food was becoming scarce. In some sectors local authority had disappeared; two out of every three bourgmestres were themselves having to shelter in the prefecture. The gendarmerie camp in Remera had been lost to the RPF: "We must remain vigilant against the common enemy who has resumed hostilities". He urged the local authorities to arrest all "trouble makers". There would be a meeting twice a week from now on to evaluate what was happening.[39] An ICTR prosecution witness would later testify how Renzaho ordered that a total of thirty roadblocks be erected in Nyamirambo. This meant roadblocks were established in each cellule at places where there were junctions at roads and footpaths.[40]

Bagosora communicated by radio, presumably through Zero Network, with Renzaho that day. He wanted to make sure that one of their targets, the manager of the Banque Rwandaise de Développement, had been "liquidated".[41] While Renzaho confirmed the man's death, there was an interruption on the same frequency from the MRND Secretary-General, Joseph Nzirorera, who wanted to make absolutely sure that this killing had taken place.[42] Several witnesses, including the new army chief, Colonel Marcel Gatsinzi, noticed that the radio receiver in Bagosora's office bore a sticker indicating the call signs of the commanders of the reconnaissance battalion, the Presidential Guard and the para-commando battalion, the army's strongest units and all of them stationed in Kigali. The call signs were linked to Bagosora's office in the Ministry of Defence. With the death in the president's plane of Colonel Elie Sagatwa, who had been Habyarimana's private secretary as well as head of the Presidential Guard, it was speculated that the command of the latter had passed to Bagosora who worked through their commander Major Protais Mpiranya.[43]

Terror in Kigali

Major-General Dallaire kept some convoys patrolling but, after finding the bodies of the peacekeepers on Thursday night, he had pulled back and increased the size of the contingent at the airport. It was their only lifeline. His priorities were the protection of his ill-equipped and poorly trained contingents, his civilian staff and the people sheltering with them.

The UN mission in Rwanda was in chaos. A peacekeeper remembers pandemonium. There was fear and panic. The UN civilian staff congregated in the Hôtel Méridien, the nearest modern hotel to UNAMIR headquarters. The headquarters of the Kigali battalion of UNAMIR was shelled and the staff moved to the hotel. Some Belgian peacekeepers were in shock and locked themselves in their hotel bedrooms. Other soldiers sat in corridors with their suitcases at their sides. No security had been organised for the hotel. The special representative Jacques-Roger Booh-Booh, in fear for his own safety, also moved into the hotel.

A report sent that Friday from UNAMIR to New York contained a description of the terror that was gripping Kigali. The report described a "well-planned, organised, deliberate and conducted campaign of terror initiated principally by the Presidential Guard". It reported the massacres of Tutsi in Remera, and described how aggressive actions had been taken against the opposition leadership, the RPF, against particular ethnic groups, against the civilian population and against UNAMIR. "Is the mandate of UNAMIR still valid?" was the plea in the report.

Not all the calls to UNAMIR for assistance could be answered because of roadblocks. There was no water or electricity supply, and toilets and showers had ceased to function. All UNAMIR camps were now sheltering civilians terrified for their lives.

Because their stores were inaccessible, most peacekeeping units had minimal water and food. Rationing of food had begun, although attempts were being made to share food and water with the terrified people. "The greatest contribution we make to refugees is providing them with a sense of security within the chaos of Kigali. Civilian casualties were impossible to estimate but they were heavy and primarily 'ethnic in nature'".

The peacekeepers of UNAMIR were isolated in many different locations; it would take Major-General Dallaire two weeks to find out where all his troops were and to gain access to them. Kigali was not being monitored, patrolled or secured. They were managing no more than a "defensive survival exercise". Fuel was going to be the biggest difficulty; because of the electricity blackout their generators were critical to power their radios. The local phone network was not functioning and UNAMIR's only link with the outside world was one satellite phone with a fax at force headquarters. There was a critical shortage of weaponry which meant that UNAMIR would be able to defend itself for only a limited period. Their medical supplies were already depleted.

The airport was not under UN control. The runway was blocked and Presidential Guards and a large force of "uncertain" government troops had secured the perimeter. The UN evacuation plan devised by Colonel Luc Marchal had been based on an assumption that UNAMIR had a functional and secure airport and immunity from attack. "It must be understood that the city of Kigali is in a state of war", New York was told in a faxed cable. They were attempting to secure the force HQ and the Amahoro stadium, but fighting had started in this area between the RPF and the Rwandan government forces (FAR), and this was making the task difficult.

The Security Council had met in New York on Thursday night, to discuss the crisis. The French were inclined to suggest withdrawal of UNAMIR but made no move to propose this. The priority was for the safety of all the foreign nationals and the question was posed whether UNAMIR could extend protection to foreigners and then assist in evacuating them.[44]

Secretary-General Boutros Boutros-Ghali was in Europe. In a cable Annan told him that if an interim authority was established and signs of a semblance of stability returned, the continued presence of UNAMIR would become an important factor in restoring order. "If, on the other hand, the situation continues to deteriorate there may be no option but to recommend withdrawal of UNAMIR to the Council."[45]

In Washington the first decision, taken within a matter of hours of the president's death, was the immediate closure of the US embassy in Kigali. The US State Department contacted the Belgian ambassador to the US to discuss the emergency evacuation of all the US citizens in Rwanda and to find out whether or not there could be a modification of the rules of engagement to allow the Belgian contingent of UNAMIR to take care of foreigners in Rwanda and help to evacuate them. Even before the plane crashed, US evacuation plans were under way. A US defence attaché based in the Cameroon was already in Kigali: he had arrived at the Hôtel des Mille Collines on the afternoon of Wednesday, 6 April, carrying a satellite telephone and a noncombatant evacuation order, known as an NEO, to ensure that all 257 US citizens were safely evacuated. Within twenty-four hours of the crash, US satellites and other intelligence gathering capabilities were prioritising Rwanda as part of the evacuation order to ensure the safety of the US nationals.

As soon as the news of the president's death had reached Washington, Prudence Bushnell, the deputy assistant secretary of the Africa bureau in the State Department, wrote a memo to secretary of state Warren Christopher to suggest an appeal for calm. Bushnell, who had recently visited Rwanda, warned that there was a strong likelihood that widespread violence would break out in either Rwanda or Burundi, particularly if it turned out that both presidents had been assassinated.[46]

Other countries soon followed Washington's lead. The speed of the decision to evacuate the estimated 4,000 foreigners from Rwanda was unprecedented.

On the first day of the crisis, Thursday, the Belgian ambassador to the UN, Paul Noterdaeme, went to see Kofi Annan, the Under Secretary-General in charge of the Department of Peacekeeping Operations (DPKO). There were 1,520 Belgians in Rwanda, and Noterdaeme said that his priority was for their safety: he wanted to know if peacekeepers could offer these people protection. The Belgians wanted UNAMIR to have a more forceful mandate. Annan's response was to tell him that Dallaire's first duty was to his soldiers. A more forceful mandate would require UNAMIR to be re-equipped and reinforced. Nothing was more dangerous than asking a peacekeeping mission to use force when it was ill-equipped to do so. Annan told Noterdaeme that three permanent members of the Security Council, the US, the UK and Russia, were already reluctant about UNAMIR. Noterdaeme said that if Belgians were going to be massacred then Brussels had not ruled out flying in another battalion. Noterdaeme recalls that after seeing Annan he went directly to talk with British and American diplomats, who told him that they were considering pulling out UNAMIR completely.[47]

The Belgian foreign minister, Willy Claes, thought that there had been a coup d'état and there were going to be widespread massacres, yet according to a later Belgian Senate enquiry, only once in one cabinet meeting of the government, was a plan discussed to stop the massacres. The idea was dismissed as it was deemed to constitute interference in Rwanda's internal affairs.[48] There were claims later from a French general, Christian Quesnot, who was the head of military affairs during the Presidency of François Mitterrand, that help to stop massacres was discussed with Belgium and Italy but the idea "came to nothing".[49]

Willy Claes spoke on the telephone with UN Secretary-General, Boutros Boutros-Ghali, and asked him for an immediate change in the mandate to allow for enforcement action to avoid more Belgian deaths. Claes claims that Boutros-Ghali said he needed time to "consult with experts". Claes said he telephoned Boutros-Ghali the following day to be told that the mandate could not be changed immediately because no one knew if the members of the Security Council would agree to it.[50] Claes said afterwards that following the deaths of the Belgian peacekeepers the preoccupation was to avoid any more Belgian deaths. "You could say that this is inadmissible", Claes later told a Belgian Senate inquiry.[51]

Noterdaeme claimed to have been approached by a French diplomat whom he did not name but who apparently warned him that on no account should the Belgians think of reinforcing their contingent in Rwanda for whatever reason. It would be too dangerous for them because in Rwanda they were blamed for the death of the President. This French diplomat said he had just spoken with Rwanda's UN ambassador, Jean Damascène Bizimana, who thought that the Rwandans would adopt a more lenient attitude should the French wish to intervene for "humanitarian reasons".[52]

That first day the French UN ambassador, Jean-Bernard Merimée, went to Annan and said that the French were drafting a statement for the Security Council to call on the Rwandan army to cooperate with UNAMIR to restore stability and order.[53]

The evacuation

A cable from UNAMIR to New York on Friday explained that UNAMIR was actively supporting a military Crisis Committee, created to stabilise the security situation which had called on the political parties in the current transitional government to meet and establish legal authority.

The military leader of the RPF, Major-General Paul Kagame, had told UNAMIR he was dispatching a battalion to Kigali to stop the killing. Dallaire's immediate reaction was to advise Kagame that new forces in Kigali would be counter-productive, but they had welcomed a suggestion from Kagame that he would be willing to attend a meeting in Kigali to further the peace process.[54] At midday on Friday, 8 April, UNAMIR headquarters was told that an RPF battalion had begun to move towards Kigali.[55]

Despite Dallaire's focus on trying to get Kagame to come to Kigali to negotiate a ceasefire, Kagame remained sceptical about the proposal to enter into talks. He said later, "I told him that I thought that that was not a good proposal at all. I said it's not the right time and the place for me to come. I kept in touch the whole day ... then I got more information from our people, I learned that [the militias] had taken different leaders in Kigali, some were being killed and so on ... and when it came to 1 p.m. I asked him 'what do you expect us to do? ... what is the UN doing about it?'"[56]

Kagame said Dallaire been insistent that he go to Kigali and meet with Bagosora, Gatsinzi and other leaders. Dallaire even offered to escort Kagame to Kigali, but Kagame said, "some of those people may not care if it's the UN, they can still shoot you down." He told Dallaire it did not make sense to keep listening to him and arguing while people were being killed.

Kagame launched his offensive that day. Before it began there was time for all peacekeepers in the demilitarised zone to withdraw. It was a three-pronged attack: fighting broke out in Ruhengeri in the northwest, Byumba in the centre and Gabiro in the east. When news came of the RPF attack, the remainder of the Rwandan governmental forces under the moderate General Gatsinzi could no longer resist the call of the extremists.

Dallaire wrote to New York that he needed to know what the major countries were planning to do regarding evacuation of the expatriates or UNAMIR. The cable ended with the words: "Kigali would have been in a worse situation without UNAMIR." They were trying all they could to get the parties to a ceasefire. That was the best assistance they could give.[57]

In his book written some years later Dallaire claims that in a satellite phone conversation that night with officials in New York, including Kofi Annan, he said he urgently needed two battalions and logistics support.[58]

But the priority remained the evacuation of ex-pats. Secretary-General Dr Boutros Boutros-Ghali wrote a letter to the President of the Security Council on Friday to point out that if an evacuation of foreign nationals became unavoidable, under its present mandate UNAMIR would be hindered in providing assistance. He reported if UNAMIR was required to help with an evacuation, the force commander had estimated that he would need two to three additional battalions for that purpose.[59]

A late-night meeting of the Security Council discussed the strengthening of UNAMIR to enable it to secure the evacuation of UN civilian personnel and foreign nationals should the situation deteriorate further. Iqbal Riza told ambassadors that the force commander hoped for progress on interim political authority.[60] The news of the appointment of an interim government in Rwanda reached New York at around 6 p.m. on Friday. It was considered a hopeful sign that the situation would stabilise in the next few days.[61]

In the early hours of Saturday, 9 April, at 3.45 a.m., a French C-160 landed at Kigali International Airport and French soldiers disembarked. The runway, which previously had been blocked, had been cleared for the landing.

An astonished UN peacekeeper watched as boxes of ammunition were unloaded from the plane and transferred in perfect co-ordination with the Rwandan army to trucks to transport them to Camp Kanombe. The French then took control of the airport, installing artillery and anti-aircraft weapons. The French secured the airport road and the road to the French embassy.

The force commander of UNAMIR, Major-General Dallaire, had been told that the French were landing forty-five minutes before they did so. Dallaire was not to know that this landing was a part of Operation Amaryllis, the French operation to rescue its nationals from Rwanda. Colonel Luc Marchal was told by Brussels to put his Belgian peacekeepers at the airport under the control of Colonel Jean-Jacques Maurin, the French military attaché at the embassy. UN vehicles were to be used by the French for their mission and were simply driven away by French parachutists.

The French were joined later by troops who flew into Rwanda from Belgium and Italy for a joint rescue operation. This began on Saturday, 9 April. Dallaire was told by UN headquarters to cooperate and instructed that only for the rescue of foreigners could he exceed his mandate and use force.[62]

The first people evacuated from the French embassy were Rwandan VIPs who had been sheltering there.[63] On the first French evacuation flight were President Habyarimana's widow, Agathe, and members of her family. Later that day some sixty children were evacuated from the Sainte-Agathe orphanage which she patronised; they were accompanied by thirty-four helpers, all of them said to be Hutu extremists. The French evacuated a total 394 Rwandans.

On this first plane were the bodies of six French nationals, including those of the crew members from the Presidential jet, and three others. Two French communications experts, who had been living in Kigali, Adjudant-Chef, Alain Didot, his wife Gilda, and Adjudant-Chef René Maier were murdered on the afternoon of 7 April. According to French military accounts these murders were committed by RPF operatives who subsequently buried the bodies in Didot's garden. The house was ransacked and communications equipment and documents destroyed.[64]

The Gikondo massacres

As far as can be ascertained, the first time the word "genocide" was used to describe what was happening in Rwanda was on the day the evacuation of foreigners began, on Saturday, 9 April, in Gikondo.[65]

The Catholic church in Gikondo, an imposing building of red brick, built on the crest of a hill, was one of the largest in the city with room for a congregation of 2,000 people. The church was set in lush and well-tended gardens. In the complex, run by the Pallotine Missionary Order of the Catholic Church, were a dozen Polish priests and nuns. It was an extensive campus with a small chapel, community centre, and print shop with an adjoining warehouse and separate housing quarters. For two days, terrified people had fled to the church, and by Saturday morning about 500 men, women and children were sheltering there. Some people were so frightened they were hiding beneath floors or roofs.

A mass was organised that morning and people gathered in the church. During the mass there was a commotion outside: those inside could hear shooting and grenades exploding. The door of the church was opened and two soldiers of the Presidential Guard and two gendarmes entered. They began to check identity cards and told the few Hutu in the church to leave.[66]

One of the priests protested but he was told by gendarmes that the church was harbouring "inkotanyi". The priest told the soldier that the people were Christian worshippers, the members of his congregation. But the gendarmes insisted and continued to examine identity cards. A Presidential Guard officer arrived and told the soldiers not to waste their bullets because the Interahamwe would soon come with machetes. Then the militia came in, one hundred of them, and threatening the priests they began to kill people, slashing with their machetes and clubs, hacking arms, legs, genitals and the faces of the terrified people who tried to protect the children under the pews. Some people were dragged outside the church and attacked in the courtyard. The killing continued for two hours as the whole compound was searched.[67] Only two people are believed to have survived the killing at the church.[68] Not even babies were spared. That day in

Gikondo there was a street littered with corpses the length of a kilometre.[69]

There were UN witnesses to the killing in Gikondo. Major Jerzy Maczka and Major Chudy Ryszard, both from Poland, were among the unarmed UN military observers (UNMOs) from sixteen countries, spread throughout Rwanda and living in local communities to ensure compliance with the peace agreement. The observers were an integral part of UNAMIR. When the attack on the church began, the two Polish majors had been in the gardens. With rifle barrels held at their throats by gendarmes, the two were forced to watch as the militia pulled people out of the church and killed them. They saw whole families run for their lives. Maczka tried to contact UNAMIR headquarters but the channels on the Motorola system were jammed with calls for help, and he could not get through. Afterwards he helped the priests with the wounded and took photographs of the dead. What he had witnessed was clear cooperation and a division of labour between the police and the army on the one hand, and the militia on the other. He knew they were looking for Tutsi. There was a pile of identity cards, charred as though in an effort to burn them to erase any evidence that these people existed.

That afternoon, ambulances from the International Committee of the Red Cross (ICRC), drove up the hill to Gikondo church with medical teams. The chief delegate of the ICRC in Rwanda, a Swiss called Philippe Gaillard, was with them. They were looking for survivors. Gaillard estimated that the death toll in the city was in the region of 10,000 people killed in barely two days.[70]

But it was not the scale of the killing that told Gaillard what was happening in Rwanda. He had spent years as a medieval scholar, and he realised at once that what was happening was not peculiar to Africa as many people later supposed. This apocalypse existed in the works of Bruegel, in the cast of monsters descending into the hell of Dante. Gaillard had seen similar killings in Burundi in October 1993. The same methods were used.[71]

That day in Gikondo, Gaillard turned to a French journalist, Jean-Philippe Ceppi, who had accompanied the ICRC to Gikondo. It was genocide, said Gaillard. The intent of this killing was to destroy a human group.[72]

In Gikondo there was evidence and proof of genocide. What was demonstrated so terribly was the determination of the perpetrators to eliminate the targeted group. These were not political killings. People had fled to the church in Gikondo to escape the house-to-house search for Tutsi, thinking they would be safe, believing that the killing would pass after a few days as had so often happened in the past. Formerly the church had been a sanctuary. Now once they were in the church people were trapped. What was also evident was that the mob carrying out the killings was organised, working in concert with and guided by both Presidential Guards and national gendarmes.

The killing in Gikondo was done in broad daylight with no attempt to disguise the identity of the killers, who were convinced that there would be no punishment for their actions. The killing took place in full view of UN representatives and priests. The killers were not dissuaded by pleas from anyone for them to stop.

Later that Saturday, Ceppi wrote a story for his newspaper, the Paris-based *Libération*: "The streets of Gikondo, like all other working-class places in the city ... are filled with assassins, with gunfire and screams of terror." Ceppi described gangs of youths, including children, carrying machetes and knives. "The Rwandan army seals the exits and takes part in looting." In front of the French embassy Ceppi had seen bodies in the streets being eaten by dogs.

"The hunt for Tutsi goes from house to house ... they are denounced by neighbours and police." Ceppi described how the assailants checked people's ethnic grouping on their identity cards. At other times a sign of wealth or a nose too long was reason enough to kill an individual. Ceppi wrote that many southern Hutu had been killed by neighbours who were northerners. The RPF army was said to be within fifteen kilometres of the capital. "But before they get here the genocide of the Tutsi will be over", he predicted. That afternoon garbage trucks pulled up outside the church, and prisoners from the jail loaded the bodies inside.

There were UN peacekeepers in Gikondo that afternoon. They came in an armoured personnel carrier that pulled up in the road outside the complex. A Canadian, Major Brent Beardsley, and two Polish soldiers from Poland, Major Stefan Stec and Major Marek Pazik, walked up the path to the church to speak with the priests who were in the porch tending to people so badly injured they were unlikely to survive.[73]

All over the gardens of the church, dead bodies were lying in pools of blood. Whole families had been cut down with machetes, terribly mutilated and left to bleed to death.

Within a few days the priests and nuns of Gikondo were evacuated from Rwanda. In the days to come the militia returned repeatedly to the church at Gikondo to make sure that no Tutsi was left alive.

Another French journalist, Jean Hélène of *Le Monde,* was at Gikondo that Saturday. He had spoken with one of the priests, who was shocked that his own parishioners had carried out the killing. The priest had whispered to Hélène: "What have we managed to do in this country all these years?"[74]

The interim government created

The interim government had been sworn into office at the Hôtel des Diplomates, a short distance from Gikondo, in a ceremony that Saturday morning. The interim government comprised seventeen ministers representing all political parties and was presented to the world as a "coalition". The low-key ceremony lasted barely an hour and afterwards there was a party. Only twenty people turned up for the ceremony in the hotel, which had been commandeered by the army.

It was explained that they were living through an "interim period" and that all other solutions for the country had been judged inappropriate. The Crisis Committee never met again.

The new President of the Republic of Rwanda, Dr Theodore Sindikubwabo, signed an address to the people of Rwanda, prepared for him in advance, telling them that the crisis they faced called for exceptional measures. There were urgent matters of state to attend to, particularly the restoration of law and order. There had to be contact with the RPF "to put in place the transitional government as rapidly as possible", particularly in the light of the decision in the Security Council to impose a six week deadline on the UN mission. The declaration promised help for "the displaced", and announced that a prime minister, Jean Kambanda, had been "nominated" and that "we have accepted the list of ministers of his government".

The declaration presented the interim government as legitimate, and no one questioned who the "we" might be who had created it. The declaration ended with a plea to the international community for dynamic support for Rwanda, adding it was badly needed in such difficult times.[75]

Those in control were beginning to worry about the increasing number of dead bodies in the streets. In secret, Mathieu Ngirumpatse and Joseph Nzirorera, convened a meeting of the national committee of the Interahamwe at the Hôtel des Diplomates, where militia leaders were directed to go out and stop the killings at the roadblocks and to limit killing to the side roads. The bodies should be moved into piles for collection. They told the militia that the "international community" was present in Kigali.[76]

But international attention was elsewhere, focused on the evacuation of the foreigners. That morning the assistant secretary of state for African affairs, George Moose, put the final touches on the plan to evacuate US citizens by telephoning Burundi and speaking to the UN Special Envoy there, Ahmedou Ould-Abdallah. Moose told him that the US government needed authorisation from the government of Burundi to land in the capital, Bujumbura. Some three to five C-130 cargo planes were needed for the evacuation of Americans trapped in Rwanda. Ould-Abdallah was delighted to assist and told Moose that there would be no problem.

On Sunday, 10 April, a convoy of nearly 100 cars left Kigali travelling south. The cars were full of Canadians, Germans, Americans and other foreigners. They reached the Burundian capital Bujumbura later that day.

That day Dallaire received a telephone call from one of the UN Secretary-General's senior advisers, Under-Secretary-General Chinmaya Gharekhan. Gharekhan told Dallaire that he must plan a withdrawal of UNAMIR. Dallaire said that withdrawal was out of the question because of the number of people who were being protected, and that he needed a new mandate and a modest reinforcement. Writing in a cable to New York that day he pointed out that if UNAMIR was to remain in place, it would have to be supported with logistics. The force was equipped for peacekeeping, not peace enforcement.[77]

The peacekeepers of UNAMIR helped with the evacuation of ex-pats, providing transport and escorts for the convoys that went to Kigali International Airport. One group of Belgian peacekeepers, a platoon of Belgian soldiers, was ordered to abandon 2,000 people they were protecting at a school in Kicukiro in order to help the evacuation. At the school, the École Technique Officielle (ETO), a large complex of classrooms and houses run by Salesian Fathers, families were camped in the classrooms or huddled together on the playing field. The compound was surrounded by jeering Interahamwe threatening them at the perimeter fence.[78]

The commander of the ninety peacekeepers at the ETO was Lieutenant Luc Lemaire. He tried to get food for the people and tried to persuade a senior officer in the Rwandan army to protect them. Lemaire's final evacuation order came on Monday, 11 April, and he faltered. "I did not want to leave", he said later. He wanted his order confirmed to be sure that his commanders knew the consequences.

The peacekeepers sneaked away but some of the people, realising what was happening, tried to hang on to the departing UN lorries. As soon as the peacekeepers were gone the militia started firing at the people and threw grenades into the crowd.

"We had no weapons … not even a stick", one survivor said.[79] The people were herded along a road by militia and soldiers, who beat and insulted them for being Tutsi. One observer saw Théoneste Bagosora watching this agonising march.[80]

Bagosora would later be accused of coordinating the ETO massacre with Ntabakuze, who was further up the road blocking an intersection with his jeep and escort. This massacre, according to witnesses, was supervised by soldiers.[81]

The people eventually reached a gravel pit at Nyanza, near a primary school and it was here that they were killed, the Presidential Guard helping the militia. The next day the militia came back to make sure that no one was left alive.

Rwanda abandoned

A total of 3,900 people of 22 nationalities were evacuated from Rwanda. In Kigali, one by one all embassies but the Chinese closed their doors. For the French it was a hurried departure. Left behind in their embassy was a staggering pile of shredded paper, enough to fill a room. This was the paper trail of a secret episode and it was successfully destroyed. In a report on lessons to be learned from this hurried six-day evacuation by France, the military analysts would later conclude that too much time had been lost shredding documents. A quicker way in future should be found to destroy them.[82] The story of the French links with the extremists is in all probability lost to history.

Eric Bertin, who was the head of Médecins Sans Frontières (France), made the decision to pull out his agency after hearing that at the central hospital the killers had thanked MSF for providing "a collection point for Tutsi".

During the evacuation Bertin noted that the French troops drove freely around Rwanda. He still wants to know why the French evacuation force did not prevent the slaughter. Bertin was taken to the airport in a Rwandan army truck driven by Rwandan soldiers but with an escort of French soldiers.[83]

The US embassy was the first to close. In Washington officials were letting it be known, off the record to journalists, that expectations should be kept as low as possible, blaming the appalling experience of the UN mission in Somalia. On Monday, 11 April, when asked by a journalist about whether the US could lead an international effort to restore order in Rwanda, Michael McCurry, the spokesman for the US State Department, answered that the situation would be under review at the UN, the appropriate place for such a discussion.

At the Defence Intelligence Agency there were satellite photographs of Rwanda showing massacre sites, including images of Kigali. In this agency officials were working out the number of people already killed, regularly updating their estimates. It is claimed that the key agencies in Washington failed to absorb the information, whose source could not be revealed. Other agencies disagreed with the worst-case assessments of the DIA.[84]

In the US Department of Defense the killing in Rwanda was considered inevitable. A third-ranking official, under-secretary Frank Wisner, was sent a memorandum about Rwanda on Monday, April 11, in which he was told that unless both sides could be convinced to return to the peace process, "a massive (hundreds of thousands of deaths) bloodbath will ensue that would likely spill over into Burundi". In a dire prediction the memorandum described how the entire region could be destabilised with millions of refugees fleeing to Uganda, Tanzania and Zaire, their numbers far exceeding the capacity of these nations to cope.[85] But no amount of information seemed likely to rescind an almost total retreat from Rwanda.

Only the Organization of African Unity spoke for the people of Rwanda. In a press release issued in New York it urged the Security Council to help to protect the lives of civilians in Rwanda and increase the size and the mandate of UNAMIR.

The Chinese embassy was the only diplomatic mission left in Kigali. Left behind were all the Rwandans who had worked for the Europeans, a source of great bitterness to this day. Rwandans who managed to board evacuation lorries were taken off at roadblocks and killed, with French and Belgian soldiers looking on.[86]

The evacuation was devastating for Rwanda. It sent a signal to the extremists that their well-laid plans could now be implemented without fear of too many prying western eyes. All that remained were a few foreigners who refused to leave, the peacekeepers of UNAMIR and the ICRC. This agency quickly created an emergency hospital in Kigali under the leadership of the Chief Delegate Philippe Gaillard, whose own presence in Rwanda was the deciding factor in the decision of the ICRC to stay.

The officers of UNAMIR believe to this day that had the European troops that came to rescue the expats stayed on in Rwanda, the killing could have been stopped there and then. Colonel Luc Marchal is convinced of this. Together with the moderates in the Rwandan army and with the peacekeepers there would have been ample troops to restore calm. There were already 2,500 peacekeepers with UNAMIR, there were 500 Belgian para-commandos, part of the evacuation force, together with 450 French and 80 Italian soldiers from parachute regiments. In neighbouring Kenya there were 500 Belgian para-commandos, also a part of the evacuation operation. In Burundi there were 250 US Rangers, elite troops, who had come to evacuate the US nationals. There were 800 more French troops on standby.

The peacekeepers of UNAMIR considered the eventual pull-out of the evacuation troops an affront to their mission.

The force commander, Major-General Roméo Dallaire, said it was "inexcusable apathy ... that is completely beyond comprehension and moral acceptability". He said his mission was left to fend for itself, with neither mandate or supplies. He had sent a blizzard of reports to New York and received nothing in return. "There was a void of leadership", he recalled. "No supplies, no reinforcement, no decisions."[87]

The "work" continues

The much-needed legitimacy that the interim government lacked was provided by the Catholic bishops of Rwanda on Monday, 11 April, when they issued a statement supporting the interim government and praising the Rwandan army who were "taking to heart the country's security". The bishops appealed to the people of Rwanda to support the interim government and appealed for an end to war.

The bishops expressed their shock at the killing of "political leaders and the innocent". They condemned the authors of this killing whom they believed were prompted by "sadness and pity" at the death of the president. The communiqué noted that priests and nuns had been killed and that the assassins had even pursued "refugees" into religious buildings, and remarked that this was unprecedented. The communiqué was signed by a bishop, Monseigneur Thaddée Nsengiyumva.

For years the Church in Rwanda had tolerated a racist society, and in some Rwandan churches the so-called differences between the Hutu and the Tutsi people were preached from the pulpit. The Church had considerable influence over the people of Rwanda. The system of education in Rwanda had been established by the Churches, and according to a 1991 census, 90 per cent of all Rwandans were Christians, 62 per cent were Catholic, 18 per cent were Protestant and 8 per cent Adventists.[88] Next to the government, the Church was the largest employer running social, educational and medical institutions. The Catholic Archbishop, Monseigneur Vincent Nsengiumva, had been a member of the central committee of the MRND for years. The churches were closely associated with Habyarimana's dictatorial regime. For the interim government, obtaining the support of the bishops was a large step along the road to general acceptance.

The prime minister in the interim government, Jean Kambanda, later said that the only person who ever talked to him about the intensity of the massacres was Philippe Gaillard of the ICRC. Gaillard had come to see him and, stressing the neutrality of the ICRC, had told him that for public health reasons action needed to be taken about the number of bodies in the streets.

Kambanda said later that not one person in the country denounced the massacres. No one had the courage to do it. "I did not see a civil authority do it or a moral or religious authority, even an expat … no one spoke out publicly." Kambanda says that he regrets not speaking out but claims he had no choice as it would have led to certain death. He claims that all he could do was to try to stop or restrain the atrocities. "I looked to convince rather than confront", he claimed later.[89]

Kambanda assured Gaillard that something would be done about the bodies. He organised an announcement on the RTLM radio station for lorry drivers to come to see the minister of works at the prefecture of Kigali. Kambanda said that the "responsibility" lay with the ICRC, and that all the minister had organised was "evacuation".

The drivers were met at the prefecture by the prefect, Colonel Tharcisse Renzaho, and by Dr Casimir Bizimungu, the minister of health in the interim government. The drivers were told that mass graves must be dug in order to bury the dead. Bizimungu said that a priority was to clear the bodies at the central hospital (CHK) "before whites come and photograph them". Many bodies had been unloaded at the hospital, brought in trucks. Sometimes the nurses had noticed that not all of these people were dead; the survivors they found were treated by hospital staff.[90]

A large pit was dug by mechanical diggers in Nyamirambo where lorries full of bodies started to arrive. The interim government minister who was largely responsible for organising the disposal of many of the bodies was Hyacinthe Nsengiyumva Rafiki, the minister of public works and energy.

The transformation of Rwandan society by the interim government started immediately. On Monday, 11 April, it summoned Rwanda's prefects to Kigali to discuss a policy of killing Tutsi. Kambanda remembers how frank and honest the prefects were when talking about the killing, although no one actually called it that. The word "activities" was used instead. Each prefect reported on the "security situation".

The meeting with the prefects took place in the Hôtel des Diplomates. The prefect of Ruhengeri had been killed, and the prefects of Gitarama and Butare were absent, their prefectures classed as "inactive". This inactivity was why, Kambanda later explained, these prefects were eventually "eliminated". The prefect of Kibuye sent a detailed report, commune by commune, and went so far as to accuse the gendarmes of not supporting them adequately in their "activities". The prefect of Kibungo gave a verbal report. In Byumba almost the whole prefecture had been taken over by the RPF. The prefect of Gisenyi gave a report on the progression of the massacres in his area.

The foreign affairs minister, Jérôme Bicamumpaka, told the interim government that they could not win; the international community was against them. They thought him alarmist, said Kambanda later.

Kambanda remembered that Colonel Tharcisse Renzaho, prefect of Kigali, had given his own report on the "activities" in the form of "directives". Renzaho explained the importance of keeping the massacre sites secret. He told them that ministers must make every effort to portray the country in a good light. Renzaho said he would be speaking on the radio as often as necessary as a government spokesman.

It would have been customary after such a meeting for a report to be issued to each prefect. "We did not produce a report on this criminal activity", said Kambanda afterwards, as though apologising for the lack of minutes. "It was more subtle than that." Kambanda was counselled against producing a report when the minister of defence, Augustin Bizimana, told him to issue a directive instead. There would soon be a government directive to allow them "to secure the country" and to continue to "work".

When questioned some years later about the use of the word "work", Kambanda had the following exchange with his interrogators:

"What was the definition of 'work' at that moment ... was there any definition other than to kill people?"

"There were two meanings."

"Two meanings?"

"That is to say that during this period people weren't working at all. People just got together in the morning and listened to the radio to see what was happening. So 'work' could mean making one's living."

"Yes?"

"Yes ... but in the historic context in the past 'work' meant 'kill Tutsi'. In 1959 when people said that they were going to 'work' this meant we are going to massacre ... going to eliminate the Tutsi ... so there was a confusion."

Kambanda explained that the real problem in Rwanda and the origin of the massacres was the thought of power-sharing between the Hutu and the Tutsi. "This question was never discussed", he said. "The question never came up. Everyone knew that this was the issue. No one wanted to bring it up." In the next three months the information that the prefects gave the interim government was more nuanced as though some had realised the reality of what was happening, claimed Kambanda.

In the next three months the victims were not only Tutsi. Thousands of Hutu rejected the policy of killing Tutsi and they lost their lives because of it. Thousands of Hutu who were thought to be too sympathetic to the RPF were killed. Many Hutu acted with tremendous courage to save their Tutsi neighbours.[91]

One notable Kigali man managed for the next three months of genocide to protect an orphanage in Nyamirambo. Dismas Mutezintare Gisimba risked his life on several occasions to save the 400 children and adults sheltering there. Afterwards he said, "The education I got from my parents really helped to ward off the evil during the genocide. If parents had really made their children understand that Tutsi have the same flesh as them and that their blood is the same as them, they wouldn't have dared to kill their fellow men in such a cruel manner. The people who took part in the genocide had learned from their parents that Tutsi are bad by nature and were created to die."[92]

9

APOCALYPSE TWO

The fleeing of the interim government from Kigali on Tuesday, 12 April was a miserable spectacle. The ministers' flight from the capital began in an unseemly scramble from the foyer of the Hôtel des Diplomates. The ministers were carrying their own suitcases and hastily piled into cars lined up outside. One minister was almost left behind and had to ask a colleague for a lift. One of the cars ran out of petrol.

The sound of heavy artillery fire could be heard from the distant hills. RPF troops were in the north-eastern part of the city, arriving faster than anyone could have anticipated to join their beleaguered battalion in Kigali. They had covered a distance of sixty kilometres by foot in a few days, carrying packs and weapons. Their bombardments focused now on the barracks of the Presidential Guard.

And so there began a three-month battle for Kigali.

The Hôtel des Diplomates emptied that morning. The families of the MRND ministers who were staying there were evacuated by French soldiers and taken to the airport where French planes were waiting to fly them to France.[1] The evacuation of foreigners was by now well under way.

For some ministers that morning it was the first time they had ventured from the hotel since they had been brought there by Presidential Guard in the hours after the death of President Habyarimana. To their utter astonishment their convoy was stopped at roadblocks.

Just before they crossed the narrow Nyabarongo bridge above the wide riverbed on the outskirts of the city, they were stopped at a roadblock surrounded by corpses. Kambanda described people "completely out of control", and he had seen looting and killing. In some places there were two roadblocks, one manned by militia and the other by soldiers. Some of the "uncontrolled roadblocks" were manned by both military and civilians. Even Kambanda's head of intelligence was looted at a roadblock. Kambanda soon received so many complaints about them that he determined to do something about them.

Some years later an interrogator for the International Criminal Tribunal for Rwanda (ICTR) asked Kambanda about the roadblocks and the origin of the people who complained to him about them.

"They were Hutu."

"They were Hutu. Did any Tutsi come to complain to you?"

"I did not have any."

"You did not have any. Do you have any information about what happened to these people whose ethnic origin was Tutsi?"

"They killed them."

"They killed them?"

"They killed them."

"It was the norm, wasn't it? They looted the Hutu and killed the Tutsi."

"Yes."

When asked the purpose of the roadblocks, Kambanda said they were to "control the Rwandan population ... to look for enemies, associates of the RPF and collaborators – the Tutsi."

Kambanda said some roadblocks were established before the interim government was created, a number of them on 6 April. Some roadblocks were manned by Interahamwe who were wearing army uniform, he said, and on 7 April he had seen armed civilians at roadblocks with army officers. The creation of roadblocks was portrayed as spontaneous, he said, but in fact it was MRND officials who were responsible.[2]

After some of his ministers complained to him that some of the roadblocks were "anarchic", the interim government held numerous discussions. One suggestion was that the roadblocks be placed strategically all over the country but with only the military operating them. There were complaints that there were not enough soldiers for this and it was suggested the Interahamwe, who after all had military training, should help with the roadblocks.

Kambanda thought that the only person who could control the Interahamwe was Mathieu Ngirumpatse, chairman of the MRND. Kambanda was once asked by a politician to tell Ngirumpatse to stop the Interahamwe from killing civilians. Kambanda said he did not dare summon Ngirumpatse into his office, but he did later mention to Ngirumpatse that the military, not the Interahamwe, should control the roadblocks. Ngirumpatse told him that this was the very role for which the Interahamwe had been trained. Kambanda said many soldiers were themselves frightened of the Interahamwe.

Kambanda, during later questioning by investigators, in a slip of the tongue called Ngirumpatse President of the Republic.

On the question of roadblocks, the interim government decided that local authorities ought to decide where the roadblocks should be located and to make sure that those who were manning the roadblocks were accountable for the decisions they were making. This government policy was the subject of a directive finally published on 27 April. It took so long to prepare, Kambanda explained, because of a lack of computers and photocopiers. Kambanda said the "loan" of machines, readily available in a printing works in Kabgayi, the seat of the first Catholic bishop of Rwanda, allowed for the reproduction of the directive. This directive was intended to control an anarchic situation because barriers had been established without control or responsibility. It was important to let the prefets know how to proceed. But in the end, said Kambanda, the interim government never did manage to control the roadblocks.

The interim government established its office in the prefecture of Gitarama, at a Ministry of Youth training school at Murambi. The decision was taken for them by the army high command. In its wake the interim government brought to Gitarama not only Presidential Guard but an estimated thousand Interahamwe. Up until then the prefecture had been largely quiet, for the predominant political party in Gitarama was the MDR, which as elsewhere was split between pro- and anti-Hutu Power factions. The turning point for Gitarama had been a meeting held on 18 April at which the prefect, Fidele Uwizeye, and all the bourgmestres were summoned to see the Interim Government. Uwieye, who had wanted help to maintain security, was told that his local administrators had to get in line with the government programme.[3]

The interim youth minister, MRND stalwart Callixte Nzabonimana, was from Gitarama. He addressed a large public meeting at which he asked the local population why they had not done their "work" and suggested that the cattle of the Tutsi were just waiting to be eaten.[4] Nzabonimana openly spoke out at cabinet meetings saying that the Tutsi should be eliminated "without exception". He made no distinction between the RPF and the Tutsi, said Kambanda. He carried a weapon into cabinet meetings, and he boasted that he had visited every commune in Gitarama. Kambanda claimed to have asked Nzabonimana not to take part in massacres. Kambanda said other ministers tried not to associate with him and people treated him with disdain.

Two days after the interim government arrived in Gitarama, a massacre took place in which an estimated three thousand people who were fleeing the commune of Musambira were killed. A survivor recalled: "By the time we reached Kayumbo Bridge we found several vehicles of soldiers … waiting for us. There was also a big group of Interahamwe … they started shooting … afterwards the Interahamwe looted the bodies, taking money, bags, everything."[5]

Kambanda said that in places where the MRND was not so powerful the massacres were slow to begin. "It was started timidly by groups of Hutu", he said of the killing. In these areas, retired soldiers encouraged it. Once people realised that local authorities were involved they believed the killing of Tutsi was sanctioned at the highest level.[6] According to Kambanda, "The massacres were presented as though they had been decreed by the interim government or … they were the actions of the masses, and there was confusion between the Interahamwe and civil defence, but it was the MRND … the party did not want to look as though it was responsible."[7]

One of the first letters that Dr Theodore Sindikubwabo wrote as the new interim president of Rwanda, was to the UN Secretary-General. The letter, neatly typed, blamed the Belgian peacekeepers for failing to protect President Habyarimana and claimed that RPF troops were responsible for "horrible massacres".[8]

The threat of a UNAMIR withdrawal

On 12 April, the Belgian government told the UN Secretary-General Boutros Boutros-Ghali that it was pulling its soldiers out of UNAMIR;

the foreign minister, Willy Claes, gave the news to Boutros-Ghali at a meeting in Bonn. Claes argued that the whole of UNAMIR should also leave. Claes claims that Boutros-Ghali agreed.[9]

Boutros-Ghali claims that he challenged the idea of total evacuation and that he disagreed with Claes.[10] In any event, he concluded that the position of the remaining peacekeepers was untenable unless the Belgians were replaced with equally well-trained troops.[11] However the UN archives reveal that a senior adviser, Under-Secretary-General Chinmaya Gharekhan, travelling in Europe with Boutros-Ghali, told New York that the Secretary-General had decided that UNAMIR should be withdrawn.[12]

The Belgian foreign minister also spoke with his US counterpart, Secretary of State Warren Christopher. In Washington, with news of the president's assassination, there had been an immediate decision not to get involved, post-Somalia, in costly UN operations. And so, during a telephone conversation between Claes and Christopher, a deal was struck, whereby it was agreed that the US would not challenge or criticise the Belgian decision to pull out its troops. And afterwards, the US never did criticise Belgium for this action.[13]

At once the Belgians began a diplomatic offensive to persuade everyone at the UN, and particularly the countries represented on the Security Council, that the only solution was for a complete withdrawal of UNAMIR: otherwise all the peacekeepers would be killed in a bloodbath. No one challenged this assumption.

Colonel Luc Marchal was incredulous. He knew that the withdrawal of troops would mean that thousands upon thousands of Rwandans would die. The Belgian government was in possession of intelligence to know the foreseeable consequence of the decision. Military intelligence reports had by now described "massive massacres".[14]

By Tuesday, 12 April, UN military observers stationed in Gisenyi had reported "tens of thousands" killed. UNAMIR was also getting reports from Cyangugu where killings had started "in large scale".[15] "This ethnic massacre is said to be mainly caused by CDR supporters", UNAMIR's daily situation report for that day told New York.[16] On the following day, large-scale massacres were reported taking place in Kibuye and Gikongoro.

There was reluctance in the Security Council to leave UNAMIR in place; the US wanted UNAMIR's withdrawal. The UK warned about the dangers of a repetition of Somalia; peacekeeping was inadequate in the face of civil war and perhaps the majority of peacekeepers should depart, leaving behind a token force in Kigali.

This lack of enthusiasm was relayed to the UNAMIR force commander Major-General Dallaire in Kigali and he made his own stand on the night of 12 April. He told New York that even if the Belgians did pull out he was staying put.[17] He warned that a sudden disappearance of UNAMIR would result in violence of "incalculable proportions", and he recommended that UNAMIR "continue to assist, albeit with a revised and stronger mandate".[18] But there was no stronger mandate, though the arrival of the French and Belgian troops to evacuate foreigners had enabled UNAMIR to increase its monitoring of the sites in Kigali where Rwandans were sheltering.

There was one whisper of hope that Tuesday, when a number of senior officers of the Rwandan army and the temporary chief of the army, Colonel Marcel Gatsinzi, who had kept their distance from the interim government, offered the RPF a ceasefire. At first this group of moderate army officers had thought that the massacres were happening because the Presidential Guard had run amok. Now they tried to short-circuit the interim government by proposing a meeting with the RPF command to see how to bring peace and contribute to the creation of transitional institutions. But soon all those who had signed the document proposing the meeting were marginalised.

In New York, the Under-Secretary-General for Peacekeeping, Kofi Annan, questioned the Belgian view that a total withdrawal was advisable. In a cable to the Secretary-General on 12 April Annan told of a meeting that had been held at UN headquarters to discuss Rwanda between Annan and Marrack Goulding. Goulding was UN Under-Secretary-General and the head of the Department of Political Affairs (DPA), responsible for helping the Secretary-General with the maintenance of peace and security, preventive diplomacy and peace building. Goulding, the most senior British official in the Secretariat, was well acquainted with what was happening in Rwanda. Also at this meeting were Iqbal Riza and Major-General Maurice Baril, the Secretary-General's military adviser. This group was unanimous that a precipitous decision to withdraw UNAMIR was not the answer. Annan wrote to Boutros-Ghali that the Council was looking for guidance and needed a definitive recommendation from the Secretary-General.[19]

The refusal of Boutros-Ghali to cancel his tour of Europe and return to headquarters at this crucial time was considered a serious error and officials could not understand it. In New York and in Kigali contingency plans for possible withdrawal of the whole force were drawn up.

Then on 13 April, a week after it had begun, came the first official notification that genocide was under way. It arrived in a letter to the President of the Security Council from the RPF: "A crime of genocide has been committed against the Rwandese people in the presence of a UN international force, and the international community has stood by and only watched. Efforts have been mobilised to rescue foreign nationals from the horrifying events in Rwanda, but there has been no concrete action on the part of the international community to protect innocent Rwandese children, women and men who have been crying for help."[20]

The letter pointed to a moral responsibility to protect Rwandans from barbaric and savage criminals. The RPF would neutralise the elements in the Rwandan army that were responsible for massacres but the international community should mobilise to support this task. Calling for ceasefires would allow the criminals to continue committing atrocities. The RPF wanted a UN war crimes tribunal to apprehend those who had committed crimes against humanity and bring them to justice. "The perpetrators ... are known and with UN assistance they can be brought to justice."

That day a draft resolution was submitted to the Security Council by Nigeria suggesting that the peacekeepers be allowed to enforce public order. The resolution pointed to the thousands of innocent civilians being killed, but although it was circulated among ambassadors, it was never tabled.[21]

An ambassador from the US mission, Karl Inderfurth, told them that in Washington it was considered that peacekeeping was not appropriate for Rwanda. China was the only country not to have closed its embassy in Kigali and the Chinese delegate pointed out that there was no immediate danger to the peacekeepers; only the untrained contingent from Bangladesh was in a panic. The others – the Tunisians and the Ghanaians – were doing useful work.

Rwanda's ambassador on the Security Council circulated a letter written by the interim government's minister of foreign affairs, Jérôme Bicamumpaka, claiming that the country, with the help of the UN peacekeepers, was stabilising. The death of President Habyarimana had led the military and the people to act "spontaneously", attacking those "under suspicion", but a new government had been created and it was giving great hope to the people.

Dallaire was by now arguing forcefully for the peacekeepers to remain and in a cable to Annan on 14 April he called for resolve.[22] He sent headquarters a detailed plan of action, believing that even without the Belgians the peacekeepers could still make a difference, and among the useful functions they could perform he listed digging mass graves, defending the airport, providing aid, and ensuring the security of the civilian population.

The reluctance of the US about the mission was growing. On 14 April a US delegate told the Security Council that if a vote was taken, the US would vote for withdrawal. The UK again advised pulling out the bulk of the peacekeepers and leaving a small force of a few hundred. But a decision was delayed again.[23]

On 15 April the US again told the Council that there was no useful role for peacekeeping in the present circumstances. The Nigerian ambassador, Ibrahim Gambari, made a plea for reinforcements, arguing that the peacekeepers still had a vital role to play. The UK disagreed. The UN could hardly leave two battalions in Rwanda to be slaughtered. The US claimed to have an "independent assessment" of what was happening in Rwanda and based on this assessment there was no choice but to pull out all the peacekeepers.

Strangely the US ambassador to the UN, Madeleine Albright, did not mention this "assessment" in her memoir. "It would be weeks before most of us understood the nature and scale of the violence", she would claim, blaming the UN for her lack of knowledge.[24] Official reporting by the Secretariat was curtailed, she wrote.

This means the information collected from US satellite and other intelligence-gathering capabilities, prioritising Rwanda as part of the evacuation order of US citizens, had not been made widely available. There were intercepted telephone calls and satellite photographs that confirmed the existence of massacre sites. In Washington, apparently, there was a disagreement over "extreme estimates" made by Defense Intelligence Agency staff.[25]

The desperate campaign waged by Belgium to pull out the peacekeepers continued apace. The foreign minister Willy Claes wrote to the Secretary-General on 15 April to tell him the peacekeepers were powerless.

A ceasefire was impossible.[26] The Belgian ambassador to the UN, Paul Noterdaeme, went to see Annan to tell him that the situation in Rwanda was going to deteriorate. Annan told him that Dallaire and Booh-Booh took a less alarmist view.[27]

Boutros-Ghali continued his European tour and was now in Spain. Riza had assured ambassadors in the Security Council that the officials in the Secretariat were doing their best, while pointing out the problems of communicating both with UN representatives in the field and with the Secretary-General in Madrid.[28] In a cable to the Secretary-General, Annan wrote that the Council was expecting him to offer alternatives for action.[29]

By 16 April, without any assurances from New York, Dallaire had reorganised his headquarters staff, filling the officer positions that would be vacated by the Belgians. The lack of logistics was worrying and the lack of water for personal hygiene was a major factor of concern. He learned that only 10 per cent of stores would be left for them by the Belgians. Undeterred, Dallaire created Humanitarian Action Cell, a special unit to bring assistance where possible, putting four officers in charge of six UN military observer teams who would be mobile and would gather information on displaced people and try to build up humanitarian relief for the stricken population.[30] There was an estimated total of 14,500 people sheltering with UNAMIR and an incalculable number sheltering in churches and other sites in the city and elsewhere in Rwanda.

"UNAMIR must maintain a visible, armed and determined presence in Kigali. We cannot remain in the safety of our garrisons and leave the population to die at the hands of these dangerous and erratic military and local armed bands", Dallaire wrote in a letter to a peacekeeping officer who had abandoned a mission for fear of the danger to his men.[31]

The attempts to secure a ceasefire continued. This was the subject of most discussion in the Security Council. On 16 April low-level talks took place between the RPF and the Rwandan government troops. Col. Gatsinzi was offering an immediate cessation of hostilities but the RPF had a list of preconditions including the immediate end to the RTLM broadcasts, arrests of militia, the dissolution of the Presidential Guard, and the compiling of a list of all the Rwandan politicians who had been murdered. An estimate of the number of people killed in the massacres must be made, the RPF also insisted, and they wanted the interim government denounced as a fraud. As a first step, the killing must stop.[32]

Dallaire said he realised that Gatsinzi was fighting a losing battle with the extremists; rebuffed one more time by the RPF he became more vulnerable.[33]

Dallaire believed that Gatsinzi was determined to end the war. Gatsinzi had even suggested to him that the government forces should simply walk away from the battlefields and put resources into trying to put an end to the massacres.

Dallaire sensed that the extremist movement had become emboldened. On 16 April a broadcast on RTLM by the interim government called for citizens to take up arms nationwide and mount roadblocks. Dallaire says that at this point he realised that a fanatically dedicated group existed that was determined to exterminate an entire group. He asked himself whether or not the extremists, with their privileged seat in the Security Council, had correctly concluded that it was now most unlikely there would be international intervention, so they would be safe in stepping up the killing.

Several times Dallaire objected to the presence in the Security Council since January of the Rwandan UN ambassador, Jean-Damascène Bizimana. All information from within the Council was obviously being fed back to the "shrouded entity running the show in Rwanda". The extremists had direct access to this information, which allowed them to shadow Dallaire's every move.[34] Dallaire sometimes thought the extremists were better informed than he was about what was being decided in New York.[35]

The US ambassador to the UN, Madeleine Albright, wrote later that she thought it "disgraceful that Rwanda's lawless regime was still permitted to sit in the Council".[36] But as far as can be ascertained she made no attempt to get rid of him. For the three-month duration of the genocide Bizimana sat in the Council as a representative of the interim government that was perpetrating it. Bizimana listened to the secret discussions and asked for support for the interim government. He maintained that the large number of deaths in Rwanda were the consequence of a civil war.

Ten days into the crisis and many streets in Kigali were empty save for the dump trucks picking up the bodies. "The memory of those trucks is indelible", Dallaire wrote. "Blood, dark, half coagulated, oozed like thick paint from the back of them."[37]

In a cable to New York on 17 April, Dallaire's focus was the continuing and hopeless attempts for a ceasefire and the progress of the RPF troops. Dallaire thought the possibility of a ceasefire was remote. In paragraph 14 of the cable Dallaire described how every Tutsi going through a roadblock and showing an identity card was executed on the spot. The radio, RTLM, was broadcasting inflammatory speeches and songs exhorting the population to destroy all Tutsi. "The ethnic cleansing continues", Dallaire wrote. Massacres had been witnessed at a distance by UN troops. "The militia have displayed drunkenness, drug abuse and sadistic brutality. They do not respect the UN flag, the Red Cross or any other human symbol .... The moral dilemma over what to do about the thousands of refugees who have taken shelter in RGF/militia-controlled areas and are threatened with massacre poses the dilemma over how to extract them .... Most of the large concentrations of these refugees are in militia-controlled areas." Dallaire wanted guidance. Should UNAMIR engage in armed confrontation for which they were not equipped and at risk to their own troops, or should the peacekeepers leave people for possible extermination? If the mission was to change into one of peace enforcement to stop the massacres and rescue civilians, a change in mandate would be required. The force could not continue to sit on the fence.[38]

But the news from New York on 18 April was not good. Unless there was a ceasefire in the next few days, a total withdrawal of UNAMIR should be envisaged. Dallaire was asked to provide an assessment of the consequences of withdrawal for the Rwandans who had taken refuge with UNAMIR. "Appropriate handover arrangements should be negotiated with both sides", Dallaire was told.[39]

Within hours, a change of heart in the Rwandan army was noted by Dallaire, with renewed enthusiasm from battalion commanders to continue the war. Dallaire warned New York that a total evacuation of the UNAMIR force would cause enormous dangers for his troops.

"For humanitarian reasons it would be unethical to leave this terrible scene without at least giving a last hard and determined chance for a ceasefire and an embryo of a relief organisation." He pleaded that if UNAMIR was to be evacuated, a small team of perhaps 250 could be left behind. He said he could not stress that point emphatically enough.[40]

The genocide spreads

The genocide spread and in some places it settled into a routine. Every day the Interahamwe came to Camp Kanombe to refuel their vehicles.

Para-commandos were spotted in the first week continuing to train militia.[41] The roadblocks were well organised and there was communication between them. At every roadblock vehicles were inspected extensively. The overall man in charge set the tone for each individual barrier. Some were very, very aggressive and demanding. Some seemed specifically orientated to killing. The majority of the people killed at roadblocks were slain with machetes by youths, a few of whom were armed with rifles. There were many grenades. At some roadblocks bodies were piled in nearby ditches or ravines, and elsewhere the bodies were laid side by side. Many massacre sites were on side roads where people had been herded before being killed.

Army officers called on the civilian population to eliminate the enemy and its accomplices. They distributed weapons and gave orders to commit, aid, abet and participate in the massacres.[42] All over the country the Tutsi population was fleeing to locations they thought would be safe, often on the recommendation of the local civil and military authorities, but this concentration of the Tutsis made things more convenient for the killers. In some places Tutsi were attacked, abducted and massacred on the orders of the same authorities who offered them advice. The frequency and intensity of the massacres were increasing.

In Kigali in the first week the prefect of Kigali, Colonel Tharcisse Renzaho, told Philippe Gaillard, chief delegate of the ICRC, that they had picked up 67,000 bodies in the streets. In Kigali the death toll was an estimated ten thousand people a day. Renzaho visited roadblocks to sustain the militia's enthusiasm for murder and encouraged civilians to participate in the killings with his civilian defence force. He also ensured that the genocide had leaders who were committed by replacing officials who lacked the necessary zeal. Ensuring a steady flow of arms to militiamen and local officials was a critical element in Renzaho's coordination of the genocide in the city.[43]

Although Renzaho was conscious of the need to conceal his own role in the killings and also to limit international awareness of the genocide as it was taking place, there is ample and compelling evidence of his part in it. Renzaho was in control of the city. Anyone who wanted to leave had to have his authorisation. He sent the local officials, *conseillers de secteur*, and political leaders to collect weapons and ammunition from army headquarters to distribute at roadblocks.

"It was no coincidence that soldiers of his age and rank were chosen for civil defence", said Kambanda. They had a sort of respectability for they had taken part in "the war" in the 1960s. They were experienced, they knew their own regions, and they were popular. Many officers of this generation were recruited into the emerging "civil defence" network.

A fundamental role in the routine of genocide was given to the radio station RTLM. There was daily contact between the army high command and the director-general of the radio, Phocas Habimana, who regularly spoke with General Augustin Bizimungu, the army chief of staff. Habimana, who had previously been a senior official at the Ministry of Finance, was described as "authoritarian". He stayed at RTLM most of the time and became the "editorial director". It was Habimana who on the night of 6 April had decided that RTLM should play only classical music and that it would broadcast only "official" pronouncements.

When the genocide started, the journalists of RTLM were given rooms in the Hôtel des Diplomates, and vehicles with drivers and military protection. The security of the RTLM studio was protected by members of the Presidential Guard.

A daily morning briefing for journalists from RTLM and Radio Rwanda was held at the Ministry of Defence. The briefing would begin with an account of the progress in the civil war, and instructions were given to the journalists only to speak of the victories. Army officers telephoned the offices of RTLM to ask journalists to broadcast the names and addresses of people who had somehow escaped the cordon of roadblocks.

The most frequent source of information for the journalists was the Interahamwe. Militia would either telephone or turn up at the RTLM offices to hand over the "search notices". Each "search notice" contained information describing a vehicle of specific colour with a specific number plate which was going from one area of the country to another and which had to be stopped for it contained "inyenzi". The "search notices" also contained the names, addresses and descriptions of people still being sought. Requests from civil servants or military were broadcast calling for the re-supply of weapons, ammunition, or grenades to certain areas. The radio was the voice of genocide.

"We had the Interahamwe and the army telephoning us", said Georges Ruggiu. The Belgian journalist worked at RTLM throughout the genocide and would later testify at the International Criminal Tribunal for Rwanda. "We were asked not to say anything about the massacre of the civilians." Ruggiu explained: "We were engaged in a war of words. We did not have weapons, it was a media war which – it is a form of war, just like any other war. Our words were our weapons."

In mid-April the military took journalists from RTLM to tour Kigali's roadblocks. When they got to Nyamirambo, Ruggiu saw "a pile of people". "They were in the process of dying, and they were cut up into pieces and piled up, and they were not even killed. They were just expiring, as it were. We really saw people dying. They were just piled one on top of the other, but they were still breathing."[44]

He claims that he challenged the Interahamwe who were there. "Do you really see what you have done?", he asked them. "I told them, you see in Europe, even animals which are in pain, they are spared such agony. I said even in Europe when horses are suffering, they are killed so that they do not suffer, but here people are still breathing for the last gasps."

The Interahamwe looked proud of having carried out a commendable job. He asked them why they were doing it. "You could use your weapons, shoot them or kill them in a proper way, if killing could be considered as something proper or clean, and so they told me, these people do not merit that [a] bullet to be used. That is what they told me. And they said, bullets need not be used in killing these people … that is what they said."

Several tours of the roadblocks were organised by the army for the journalists of RTLM. On another occasion near Kigali market Ruggiu saw a total of 129 women in a grass field. They were being killed, one at a time, and one next to the other. The women were Tutsis, he was told, "the slops of the RPF". Ruggiu also visited the Interahamwe headquarters at a place called Gitega where there was a roadblock. The Interahamwe said to Ruggiu that if he wanted to see "the work" that they had been doing then he should go and look at the pile.

"So there was a heap of bodies, and they said that when they clear the pile of bodies, then they will create another pile of dead bodies. This is what happened", Ruggiu told the court. There was an FM radio at every roadblock and hundreds of roadblocks throughout the country.

Ruggiu was asked in court what the term "inyenzi" meant to him. He said that by the time of the genocide the word had come to mean not just RPF. "From what I gathered, *inyenzi* means cockroach. So it means a domestic insect that is harmful to the population, but, in fact, in the ordinary sense of the word in Rwanda, it meant Tutsi."

"How often was the term 'inyenzi' used in RTLM broadcasts after the 6th of April?"

"The word 'inyenzi' was used permanently in all programmes which mentioned the Tutsi and in all programmes at all times that were aired on RTLM", Ruggiu said. "In my own programmes, when you wanted to refer to enemies of the government or MRND or allies of the RPF or members of the RPF, the word 'inyenzi' was used."

RTLM radio called itself the voice of the "rubanda nyamwinshi", the majority people. One broadcast was repeated several times over: "The inyenzi have always been Tutsi. We will exterminate them. One can identify them because they are of one race. You can identify them by their height and their small nose. When you see that small nose, break it."[45]

Ruggiu described how the editorial policy of RTLM was aligned to that of the MRND. It was against the Arusha Accords and against all persons allied to the RPF. "And, finally, it was anti-Tutsi, therefore, anti the inyenzi", he said. Ruggiu claimed that the editorial policy was followed more scrupulously in late March. He could not explain why this should be other than to say this was because of "events".[46]

Witnesses would later testify that Ruggiu himself was "active" when he was at roadblocks, dressed in a military uniform, with a pistol at his side, and with his army escort. The escort was also "active", providing Interahamwe with the names of people who were still on wanted lists and giving out hand grenades.

Ruggiu would later provide information about Ferdinand Nahimana, the intellectual inspiration for the genocide, and how he became an adviser to the interim government during the genocide. Nahimana had turned up at RTLM on either 8 or 9 April. He had come from the French embassy by foot and explained that he had been in the embassy since the evening of the plane crash. Ruggiu saw him again in Gitarama and then later on during the genocide in May or June 1994 when he visited Kigali.

Félicien Kabuga was the chairman and director-general of RTLM. He presided over the radio station, represented it, and signed on its behalf, the agreements and conventions that were concluded with the Rwandan authorities in order for it to continue to broadcast.

As the RPF advance progressed, broadcasters used increasingly graphic images to portray its soldiers. Valérie Bemeriki, a fluent broadcaster, accused the RPF of being involved in cannibalism. "They mutilate the body and remove certain organs such as the heart, liver and stomach ... they eat human flesh, the inyenzi-inkotanyi ... eat people."[47] Bemeriki was known for her passionate pronouncements about the Tutsi. Years later and in a Kigali prison she was at pains to point out that she always checked her facts and reported the truth and that the massacres of unarmed Tutsi had been caused because of "battles" between government troops and the RPF.[48]

The broadcaster Kantano Habimana managed to captivate audiences. The raucous style of Noël Hitimana was popular and well known in Rwanda; he spent ten years working for Radio Rwanda. Hitimana was often drunk. Ruggiu was much less adept for he had no broadcasting experience, but he was a white, a Belgian and people were curious and interested in what he had to say. His presence gave the impression that there was Western backing for the radio station.

In one of his broadcasts he had this to say: "They are very bad people. They are a species of bad people. I do not know how God will help us exterminate them. This is why we should stand up and – [raise] up ourselves and exterminate those bad people. This species of bad people, the species called the inkotanyi. There is – I do not want people to misunderstand this and say that I mean Tutsis. No, I am talking about a species called inkotanyi. They are bad people. These people should perish because there is no alternative."[49]

The broadcasts encouraged the population to kill. "Keep it up, mobilise, work, you the youth from everywhere in the country, come and work with your army, come and work with your government, to defend your country. If you do not do so, where will you go? That is why we have to stand up. The government has to find weapons for us. We also have to make a contribution in support of the war effort to produce weapons and strategies to kill the inkotanyi wherever they are and exterminate all their accomplices."

The studios of RTLM were shelled on 18 April but it moved to a neighbouring office in the Ministry of Tourism. A generator was provided so that transmissions could continue. From the end of April until July, three months, the salaries of RTLM staff were paid by the interim government. The wages were in the form of new Rwandan notes. The Rwandan civil service was also paid in this way, the various administrative wings of the government working quite efficiently in Gitarama.

In order to improve coordination of the various parts of the administration, the interim government created a Council for Security comprising the prime minister Jean Kambanda, the minister of defence Major-General Augustin Bizimana, the minister of the interior Faustin Munyazesa, later replaced by Edouard Karemera, the minister of justice Agnès Ntamabyaliro, and the minister of foreign affairs Jérôme Bicamumpaka. Most days this inner group met at 9 a.m. Both the civil war and the massacres would be discussed and suggestions made. For instance, the minister of the interior thought that it might be a good idea to have a platoon in each commune to track "the enemy" telling the group this was quite feasible.

For the three months of the genocide, reports were submitted from the prefectures at least once a month for government scrutiny. "We discussed the evolution of the massacres in each prefecture", said Kambanda. Anyone who showed any obvious objections to these plans was considered to be pro-RPF and would have been eliminated.

The most important thing, said Kambanda, was for the interim government always to reach a consensus on decision-making. He kept a note of the cabinet meetings, and prided himself on his ability to keep accurate records and know that meetings were run properly. He wanted there to be adequate government records.[50] Each morning he met his own intelligence chief who would give him a verbal report, but who always included one in writing.

The story of Butare

Rwanda's second city is Butare, the country's intellectual heartland and known for its liberal traditions and tolerance. With a high percentage of Tutsi residents, Butare had the only Tutsi prefect in the country, Jean-Baptiste Habyalimana. As the killing spread, thousands of people fled to Butare seeking protection from the terror in Kigali, Gikongoro and Gitarama.

Prefect Habyalimana tried to calm people, and ordered that meetings be held to try to stop violence erupting. For two weeks he tried to prevent the spread of the genocide. Then on 17 April in a broadcast on RTLM Valérie Bemeriki accused Habyalimana of working with the RPF. The following day he was dismissed by the interim government. Kambanda signed a decree appointing six new prefects for the prefectures of Kigali, Butare, Gisenyi, Ruhengeri, Byumba and Kibungo.[51]

Prime minister Kambanda arrived in Butare on 19 April for the inauguration of the new prefect, Sylvian Nsabimana, an agronomist who claimed only to have heard of his appointment on the radio. Kambanda was accompanied by the interim president, Theodore Sindikubwabo. They both gave rousing speeches, which were broadcast by RTLM.

That day two military planes landed at Butare airport carrying several hundred Presidential Guard and Interahamwe. More militia from Kigali arrived in buses. Habyalimana was arrested and put in a cell in the prefecture. He was taken to Gitarama where, during a cabinet meeting, the justice minister Agnès Ntamabyaliro asked what should be done with him. Kambanda claims that he called for Habyalimana's release but that, being a Tutsi, he was killed after he was released. He should not have been allowed to leave without some sort of security for he was, Kambanda explained, "a known Tutsi".[52]

Butare was first and foremost a university town, the home of the National University of Rwanda and the Group Scolaire, Rwanda's first high school. Immediately on the news of the President's death, the Tutsi students at the university had organised four teams of guards to keep watch at night. Their plans did not help. On the evening of Thursday, 21 April, soldiers came to the university and started to round up all the Tutsi students as they entered the cafeteria, checking their names on a list. Then Hutu Power students went to search for any Tutsi who might be hiding. The Tutsi were taken to the arboretum and shot.

In Butare there were places that became killing grounds: behind the national museum, at the university arboretum, near the Groupe Scolaire. The initial killings in Butare were systematic and they targeted political and intellectual leaders and the business community. There were both Hutu and Tutsi targets; they included those who had opposed Habyarimana, or who had opposed Hutu Power, and anyone who had believed in the Arusha Accords. Professors from the university, lawyers, doctors and journalists were slain. Soon soldiers were supervising the militia that were now sweeping through residential areas and then the poorer parts of town.

By 22 April, roadblocks had been erected, including one on a main road, run by Presidential Guard. There were soon mass killings throughout the prefecture of Butare. Today, out of twenty communes eighteen have genocide sites containing between 5,000 and 40,000 victims.[53] These sites are at churches, health centres, seminaries, communal offices, playing fields, markets and schools.

In one commune, that of Nyakizu, a densely populated and poverty-stricken place in the southwestern part of the prefecture, an estimated 20,000 people were killed at a Catholic church compound called Cyahinda in three days.[54]

The Catholic church at Cyahinda was a large brick building adjacent to a complex of school buildings and a clinic. Thousands of Tutsi had fled there for sanctuary; some of them had been directed to the church by their local authorities. At the church they were attacked by armed groups of local people and gendarmes. A major attack began on 19 April when soldiers arrived in army jeeps. They brought with them heavy weapons with which to fire at the church from across the valley. The killing at Cyahinda was completed that night. "It was a strictly military operation", someone recalled.[55]

Those who tried to escape from the Cyahinda church compound once the killing began found that Interahamwe blocked their path. One witness saw three buses full of gendarmes arrive. The job of the Interahamwe was to loot and to finish off the injured.

In the prefecture of Butare, in the commune of Runyinya, in the Karama sector, an estimated 40,000 people were killed.[56] The killing started just after the removal of the moderate prefect of Butare when the church compound was sealed by gendarmes and military reservists, trapping an estimated 70,000 people inside. "It was mainly the women and children put in the protected room. The men tried to fight back. But the only weapons … were stones", said one survivor.

"They shot from 10.30 a.m. until 5 p.m., until they ran out of bullets. For hours and hours there was an endless hail of bullets." This witness managed to escape and described hundreds of abandoned children crying over the bodies of their parents. Thousands of people who were injured were crying out in pain and could not move.[57] According to one witness, soldiers ordered some people to dig their own graves. "In every pit there were at least twenty people, including mothers with their children still strapped at their backs", a witness told an ICTR courtroom.[58]

Escape was virtually impossible. On the way to the border with Burundi from Butare there were twenty-five roadblocks. Dr Rony Zachariah from MSF drove along that road on 19 April and described how it was "spotted with corpses". In some of the piles of bodies there were between sixty and eighty people. At the border he saw a group of militia chasing about sixty people who were running along the road "like cattle in a stampede", he said.[59]

The genocide bureaucracy

The interim prime minister, Jean Kambanda, later described five levels of command for the massacres. From the beginning of the killing, Kambanda said he felt the influence of the Crisis Committee of the army, with its ghostly structure, even though it was officially disbanded when the interim government was sworn into office.[60]

The second level of command was the military hierarchy. Then there were the political leaders who put the government in place and who were of course under the orders of the military. The fourth level was the government. Lastly there was the "civil defence" network.

For the control of civil defence, Kambanda said there was also a ghostly structure. The civil defence network had three heads. In this way no one was able to tell who was effectively in charge. "There was the Interahamwe, others who killed, and the military and among the latter there were deserters or those who were on special missions, and the young gangs who enrolled for combat at the front but who were formed into killing gangs instead", he said.

Kambanda said that the Crisis Committee was the supreme power over the army and the government and that it indirectly controlled the civil defence. The army indirectly controlled the Interahamwe because many Interahamwe wanted to join the army. Kambanda was in no doubt that Bagosora was responsible for the Crisis Committee. Kambanda was given a twenty-four-hour bodyguard by the minister of defence and it turned out that the captain of this guard was Bagosora's assistant. Kambanda thought that he was there to spy on him rather than protect him.

It was Mathieu Ngirumpatse who nominated the interim government as though he controlled all the political parties. Bagosora initially had control of the army, at least until Colonel Marcel Gatsinzi was ousted. The minister of defence, Major-General Augustin Bizimana, had returned to

Rwanda from the Cameroon where he had been attending the Standing Advisory Committee on Security Questions in Central Africa, and when he did, Kambanda said, things fell into place. Kambanda described him as a good organiser and orator, and from then on, Kambanda said he had less contact with Bagosora. Kambanda was on good terms with Bizimana and had "privileged relations" with him.

There was no real direction for the massacres: it was a "decentralised structure", Kambanda explained. What the interim government had done was to appoint army officers, on the recommendation of the minister of defence, one to each prefecture. These soldiers were to be in charge of the "civil defence". The minister of defence was in overall control and he received his orders from his party, the MRND. The party was represented by three influential people who followed the interim government to Gitarama. They were Mathieu Ngirumpatse, Edouard Karemera and Joseph Nzirorera. Some years later these three would stand together in an international courtroom where it was alleged they had built a wave of anti-Tutsi sentiment throughout the Hutu population in Rwanda by using the structures of the party.[61] And now the MRND single party was back in power. Karemera, first vice-president of the MRND, had helped to create the interim government and had proposed that a president be nominated under the terms of the 1991 constitution. In May Karemera would become minister of the interior of the interim government.

The military officer chosen for the prefecture of Gikongoro was Major Aloys Simba, who had been one of the officers who seized power with Habyarimana in 1973. Simba was now retired from the army but he had made a successful career in the MRND in Gikongoro, his home prefecture. In Butare Colonel Alphonse Nteziryayo was in charge of civilian self-defence. He took up residence in the Hôtel Ibis, which became the informal local headquarters of the genocide. He received support from the Butare politician Pauline Nyiramasuhuko, who was the minister of family and women's affairs. She ran a network of killers in Butare and her son was an Interahamwe leader.[62] In Cyangugu the civil defence was coordinated by a young lieutenant called Samuel Imanishimwe who was helped by the prefect, Emmanuel Bagambiki, a former director of the intelligence services and a previous prefect in Kigali. In Gitarama there was Major Jean-Damascène Ukurikiyeyezu. In Kigali there was Colonel Tharcisse Renzaho. In Gisenyi there was Laurent Serubuga, former deputy chief of staff of the army, another of those who had seized power with Habyarimana in 1973, and Colonel Anatole Nsengiyumva. In the prefecture of Kibuye the civil defence was handled by Edoward Karemera, who became minister of the interior and who was the first vice-president of the MRND; there was also Eliézer Niyitegeka, who was the minister of information, a former journalist with Radio Rwanda. Kibuye was their home prefecture. In Kibungo the coordinator of the civil defence was Colonel Pierre-Célestin Rwagafilita.

Karemera was a lawyer and it had been Karemera who proposed the nomination of Sindikubwabo as president under the terms of the constitution of 1991, instead of the Arusha Accords.

Only once during the genocide does there appear to have been confrontation between the interim government and the military, and that had involved the nomination of the army high command, traditionally a political decision. Towards the end of April the cabinet was discussing a list of nominees given to them by the minister of defence, Major-General Augustin Bizimana when they heard the noise of a helicopter outside. Its three passengers, Colonel Bagosora, Colonel Léonidas Rusatira and Marc Twagiramukiza, wanted to meet Kambanda. He refused. The other ministers had been terrified from the moment they had heard the helicopter. Later they told Kambanda they thought his refusal to meet Bagosora's delegation had been suicidal.

It was Bizimana who went to meet Bagosora and the others who had turned up in the helicopter. When he returned he said they had wanted changes to the nomination list: they wanted a temporary triumvirate to be put in charge of the army until proper discussions could take place. This idea was rejected by the ministers. Kambanda was convinced that Bagosora was behind these proposed changes. Kambanda thought Bagosora was hoping that he would be nominated head of the army, and that they would bring him out of retirement and nominate him for the rank of general. Bagosora would then support Rusatira's hopes of becoming a general as well. Kambanda said that to have appointed Bagosora as head of the army at this moment would have looked terrible in the eyes of the international community. Kambanda did not meet Bagosora again until they were in exile.

"I evaluated the risks that day", said Kambanda. "I told myself that in any event we were a puppet government that they had put in place, a government that one could manipulate and so I needed to show that I was reasonable, with my own opinions and that I thought for myself."

Major-General Dallaire visited the interim government in Gitarama. He described it as located in a peaceful, modern schoolyard in a flower garden where middle-aged, well-dressed men and women went about their business in no apparent hurry. Dallaire had gone to Gitarama to talk to Kambanda about the roadblocks. Kambanda told Dallaire that the "self-defence personnel" had an important security job to perform in weeding out rebel infiltrators.[63] Dallaire was surprised to note that there seemed to be no direct communications between the Rwandan military high command and the interim government.[64]

The peacekeeping mission is reduced

In mid-April Major-General Dallaire began to send in UNAMIR's radio logs – daily military situation reports – to New York. "One would have had to have been blind or illiterate not to know what was going on in Rwanda", he wrote.[65] He described the militia as a virus that was now malignant and out of control.[66]

On 20 April, peacekeepers debriefed three missionaries who had been rescued by a team of UN military observers from Gitarama. The missionaries told them that at Ngenda, near the border with Burundi, two hundred men women and children had been killed by the Interahamwe. More than fifty people had been killed in Kilinda, including medical doctors. A church building at Nyange had been bulldozed: the people inside crushed to death. On 21 April in UNAMIR's daily situation report there is mention of "mass killing" in Butare, Gitarama and Gikongoro.

In New York that day, the Security Council took its first decision in the crisis, voting to reduce the peacekeepers of UNAMIR to a residual group of 250 that could help to negotiate and in the best case to monitor a ceasefire.

That night Dallaire was told in a telephone call with New York that the reinforcement option he wanted would never see the light of day. In a report to the Security Council Boutros-Ghali had suggested only "massive reinforcements" in order to "coerce the opposing factions". This report described "unruly Presidential Guards" and said that authority in Rwanda had collapsed. The death of the prime minister had been a "tragic consequence of the violence".

Dallaire had not even asked for massive reinforcements to coerce the warring factions. What Dallaire had wanted was a modest number of 5,500 troops to protect the sites where Rwandans were trapped. Over the phone Dallaire was told that too many countries had turned to Belgium for advice and that the Belgian campaign had worked. Willy Claes had personally telephoned a series of foreign ministries telling them that all the peacekeepers would be massacred.

For the abandonment of Rwanda Dallaire blames three permanent members of the UN Security Council: the US, France and the UK. They had led the UN to aid and abet a genocide. "No amount of its cash and aid will ever wash its hands clean of Rwandan blood", he angrily wrote later.[67]

Dallaire said that for the first weeks of the crisis, the use of the word "genocide" had eluded him. Maybe it was simple denial that anything like the Holocaust could ever happen again.[68] He thought that the word was first used by Oxfam on 24 April.[69] "Calling it ethnic cleansing just did not seem to be hitting the mark", he wrote later. He spoke with Oxfam personnel in London and he queried with New York whether or not this was genocide.

And now, with the withdrawal of the bulk of his force he had to tell his men – many broken by what they were living through, some who had risked their lives on missions of rescue – that the world would not be supporting them in their humanitarian efforts. He told them there was no shame in their withdrawal.

As the peacekeepers started to evacuate, the RPF and the Rwandan government forces (RGF) were lining up for a major battle in the city. The RGF was reporting heavy losses but moving reinforcements from Ruhengeri and Gitarama to Kigali. Negotiations were taking place in Arusha between the RPF and RGF which Dallaire considered no more than an attempt by the opposing armies to outwit regional diplomats and Security Council members. In this way they could carry on with their war so that the RPF could control an increasing amount of territory.[70]

In order to maximise the potential of his remaining tiny force comprising mostly soldiers from Ghana, Dallaire met with the interim government, hoping to obtain permission to evacuate refugees in Kigali from either side to safe areas. "The government did not seem to have fully appreciated the tactical situation of the war. They do not seem to be concerned or dismayed by the horrendous ethnic killing." Asked about an exchange of people, the prime minister told Dallaire the government was unable to control the militias. The roadblocks were because "local people want protection against the RPF".

The interim government was worried instead about a state funeral for the late President Habyarimana. "All of this in a nation which has lost as many as 100,000 killed … in the last two weeks", wrote Dallaire.[71]

The daily report to New York for 23 April described Rwandan soldiers carrying out "atrocities" in the south. That day Dallaire travelled to see the RPF military leader Kagame. In his memoir he described his journey north to Mulindi: "… we passed over bridges in swamps that had been lifted by the force of the bodies piling up on the struts. We had inched our way through villages of dead humans. We had walked our vehicles through desperate mobs screaming for food and protection. We created paths amongst the dead and half-dead with our hands … my courageous men had been wading through scenes such as this for weeks in order to save expatriates and members of religious orders."

At the military headquarters of the RPF he found Major-General Kagame relaxed and confident. The RPF was disappointed that the "international community" had not stated clearly its disgust with the decapitation of the opposition political parties and the total survival of the MRND and its leaders. Dallaire was told that the militia was linked to the army and that the RPF would sort out the militia in its own way.[72]

Dallaire thought that Bagosora avoided him. Finally they met at around noon on 28 April. Bagosora had just received a call from the US under-secretary of state for Africa, Prudence Bushnell, telling him to stop the massacres and sign a ceasefire agreement. Bagosora told Dallaire that he had informed her that he was not authorised to sign anything. He was outraged that she had attempted to impose her will. Bagosora told Dallaire that the RPF was intending to conquer the whole country. His side had never refused to share power with the RPF. It was all the fault of the RPF for refusing to negotiate with the interim government.

There were conditions for a ceasefire, said Bagosora: an end to massacres, the return of the displaced, the installation of the transitional government under the Arusha Accords, and a return to pre-6 April positions for both armies.

Bagosora wrote a message that day to the army high command telling them of the phone call from the US. Bagosora wrote that he told Bushnell that the RPF was the cause of "everything". The whole world was condemning Rwanda and protecting the attacker. "We need strong diplomatic action to counteract RPF lies", he wrote.[73]

By 29 April, the swift military success of the RPF in the country had created an atmosphere of doom and gloom among some troops and officers within the Rwandan army. There were fears that the RPF would take the whole country, and young officers were fearing retaliation against prisoners of war. The hardliners in the army were even suggesting a ceasefire. Some officers were planning to massacre all the people in Kigali who were sheltering in hotels and churches, the vast majority of them Tutsi.

There were reports to UNAMIR that massacres were on the increase in Butare.[74] The army was lacking direction and leadership, and military training of young men was taking place in the main barracks in Kigali. The attitude towards UNAMIR hardened. A group of UN military observers were trying to give out rations to a group of children when Rwanda army officers furiously drove them back. The ICRC was delivering food to the concentrations of people sheltering in Kigali, but only after discussions with the prefect of Kigali, Colonel Tharcisse Renzaho.

On 26 April, Agence France Presse reported that, according to the ICRC, 100,000 people had been killed. That day in New York the RPF representative, Claude Dusaidi, who had been waiting outside the Security Council chamber every day since the genocide began, wrote a carefully drafted letter to the President of the Security Council, ambassador Colin Keating, with a copy to the Secretary-General. The letter was headed *Genocide in Rwanda,* and it began: "When the institution of the UN was created after the Second World War, one of its fundamental objectives was to see to it that what happened to the Jews in Nazi Germany would never happen again. Today, in Rwanda, we are witnessing the implementation of a carefully planned campaign to exterminate the Tutsi ethnic group. Mr President, the mass killings of Rwandan Tutsi for no reason other than their ethnicity, is genocide. The International Community, under the Genocide Convention, is obliged to suppress and punish genocide. The perpetrators of this horrendous crime are the Rwandan army, particularly the Presidential Guard and the MRND-CDR militia". The letter went on to say that the names of those who had planned and implemented the crime were known; they included senior officers of the Rwandan army as well as extremist Hutu politicians of the so-called interim government who should be denounced, arrested and brought to justice.

The letter pointed out that the Security Council had put more emphasis on obtaining a ceasefire between the RPF and the Rwandan army and yet the casualties of the combat were insignificant compared with the slaughter of thousands of innocent Tutsi children, women and men by the Rwandan army. "We appeal to the Security Council to focus more on efforts to stop the genocide and to support the efforts of those who seek to stop this insanity."

A plea to focus on the genocide was made in the Security Council on 28 April when the ambassador of the Czech Republic, Karel Kovanda, complained that the Council had avoided the question of mass killing. Kovanda pointed out that so far the Council had spent 80 per cent of its efforts pulling out the peacekeepers and 20 per cent of its efforts in trying to get a ceasefire in the civil war. Kovanda had collated the information that was coming out of human rights groups, and he had been told that a genocide by the interim government was underway. After this meeting Kovanda was told by British and American diplomats that on no account was he to use such inflammatory language outside the Council. It was not helpful.[75]

By now ambassador Colin Keating, the President of the Security Council, had received a briefing from a representative from MSF-Belgium who had come to New York to see him. Keating was given details of a massacre at the University Hospital, Butare, on the night of 22 April witnessed by medical co-ordinator Dr Rony Zachariah, who afterwards had decided to pull out MSF from Butare. Zachariah had watched powerless while 170 of his wounded patients, all Tutsi and including children, were brutally removed from the wards and either beaten or hacked to death. Tutsi nurses were also taken. One of the nurses taken was a Hutu married to a Tutsi and expecting a baby. She had to be killed because her baby would have been Tutsi at birth. Zachariah heard a soldier say, "This hospital stinks with Tutsi. We must clean up."[76]

The word "genocide" was increasingly being used. On 28 April Oxfam issued a press release with the headline, "Oxfam fears genocide is happening in Rwanda". It began by pointing out that the death toll was likely to be far higher than expected and that the pattern of systematic killing of the Tutsi minority group amounted to genocide. There was a flicker of interest in the western press. But another story now grabbed the headlines: with thousands of people from eastern Rwanda fleeing the RPF advance, this was the fastest exodus of people the world had seen.[77] The refugees fled in order, in groups organised by local authorities according to cells of residence, and with Hutu Power firmly in control. Anyone who wanted to go back home was either maimed or executed.

A late night in the Security Council

On Friday, 29 April, the Security Council finally addressed the question of genocide. In two days Keating was to lose the presidency of the Council because of the monthly alphabetic rotation. He believed that if the Council could be persuaded that genocide was happening in Rwanda, they were bound, under the terms of the 1948 Convention on the Prevention and Punishment of Genocide, to do something about it. All but three members of the Council – Djibouti, Nigeria and Oman – had signed the Genocide Convention. And so Keating, supported by Argentina, Spain and the Czech Republic, proposed that a presidential statement should be issued from the Security Council that recognised that genocide was taking place. There were strenuous objections. The British ambassador, David Hannay, said that were Keating's statement to be issued, the Council would be a laughing stock. The US also objected to the use of the word and the French wanted the blame for the killing to be apportioned to the RPF.[78] The Rwandan ambassador said that the deaths were the result of civil war. Djibouti, a French ally, said that the statement Keating proposed was "sensationalist".

In a small back room behind the chamber of the Security Council they sat and argued for hours about the use of the word "genocide". Only when Keating proposed public exposure was compromise reached. In a last resort, Keating now proposed a Security Council resolution. A resolution requires twenty-four hours' notice. This meant that the council would have to reconvene the following night, a Saturday. There would be press coverage and a public debate. Some Council members would not be willing to say in public what they said in private. There was a compromise. Thanks to the drafting ability of the British, a statement was issued that while using wording from the 1948 Convention on the Prevention and Punishment of the Crime of Genocide managed to avoid using the word itself.

The statement read: "... the Security Council recalls that the killing of members of an ethnic group with the intention of destroying such a group in whole or in part constitutes a crime punishable under international law".[79]

The statement paved the way for a resolution which Keating submitted on 1 May. This called for an immediate expansion of the UN presence in Kigali and gave it a powerful mandate. The only support he was sure of was from Argentina, the Czech Republic and Spain.[80]

The evidence of genocide was now leaking. An estimated 40,000 bodies had been taken out of Lake Victoria. Thousands of bodies were floating down the Akagera River into Tanzania. In Kigali it was estimated 20,000 unburied bodies were lying in the streets.

Oxfam estimated that the whereabouts of half a million Tutsi was unknown.[81]

While everything just got worse, in defiance of the Security Council which had mandated a small force of 270, Dallaire and the deputy force commander, Brigadier-General Henry Kwami Anyidoho of Ghana, were now in command of 470 peacekeepers and military observers. The overwhelming number of these soldiers came from Ghana, and the battalion was the backbone of the residual force. The steadfastness of the government of Ghana in allowing some 334 of its soldiers to stay in Rwanda and the determination of Anyidoho ensured that UNAMIR did not capitulate, and the UN flag continued to fly over the Kigali headquarters.[82]

10

INTERNATIONAL SPIN

On 29 April, 1994 the International Committee of the Red Cross (ICRC), issued the most strongly worded statement in its history. It contained the following description: "Whole families are exterminated, babies, children, old people, women are massacred in the most atrocious conditions, often cut with a machete or a knife, or blown apart by grenades, or burned or buried alive. The cruelty knows no limits".

There was no accurate figure of how many people were dead but hundreds of thousands had been killed. A million more people had fled their homes and were destitute. The ICRC was in its own words providing a drop of humanity in an ocean of appalling suffering.[1] It went on: "The ICRC considers that this situation is unacceptable and that no effort should be spared to save lives before it is too late".

In a clear message to the Security Council the ICRC demanded that every measure be taken to put an end immediately to the "terrifying mechanism" of the massacres. If the Security Council did not act then the entire region would go up in flames.

In the Security Council the focus of attention suddenly turned to an unexpected intercession from the Secretary-General. On the same day that the ICRC issued its statement, Boutros Boutros-Ghali wrote a letter to the Council President demanding "forceful action" in order to "restore law and order and put an end to the massacres". This was the first time that officially the civil war and the massacres had been considered two separate issues. The letter was greeted by the ambassadors in the Council with a stunned silence. Even his senior staff were surprised for while Boutros-Ghali had suggested "forceful action", he had provided no options. It was customary for recommendations to come from the Secretariat, where there were already options under discussion.

The Security Council held a meeting about Rwanda on Tuesday, 3 May. France's opinion was that outside intervention would have to be primarily humanitarian. It was not realistic to bring peace between two factions. The US thought that the Council should send a delegation to Rwanda; this would provide some "symbolism" and avoid newspaper headlines such as "Shame on the UN". Nigeria supported this idea.[2] The UK thought neighbouring countries could help. Even if the Organization of African Unity could not meet for another week, it was unlikely the Council would come up with anything very significant before then. The UK warned that the UN must be careful about using words like "forceful action" – words used by the Secretary-General in his letter – for they would hardly encourage troop contributors. Brazil and China agreed wholeheartedly. Russia thought that the Council had no choice but to consult with the Organization of African Unity. China too stressed the support of African countries. The idea of an arms embargo was raised. China and the US thought it important, but France thought it of little use as most of the killing was done by hand. Colin Keating told the Council that forceful action could not be ruled out. He wanted UN action and a more detailed plan of what could be done from the Secretary-General.

In a letter to New York the RPF rejected the idea of UN intervention, considering the idea a trick, a deliberate attempt to manipulate the UN process in order to protect and support the murderers in the interim government.[3] The time for intervention was long past. The genocide was almost complete. The RPF was now demanding the instant recall of the Secretary-General's special representative Jacques-Roger Booh-Booh for his "partisan behaviour". If the UN had any dealings with the interim government then the RPF would request that even UNAMIR be withdrawn. The UN had to deal with the humanitarian crisis, not deploy an "intervention force".

The RPF was particularly suspicious that the call for "forceful action" had been made by Boutros-Ghali. The RPF leadership believed that the idea had come up at recent meetings between the interim government and the governments of France and Egypt. A UN "intervention force" would be convenient as the Rwandan government forces were losing the war. A UN buffer would conveniently prevent the RPF from taking the whole country. The Rwandan government forces were calling for a ceasefire and a return to the pre-war positions of 6 April, 1994.

There were ceasefire negotiations in early May but the RPF refused adamantly to deal with the interim government and the army chief of staff, Major-General Augustin Bizimana, would not negotiate without the interim government. The diplomatic route looked hopeless, especially as Dallaire claimed that by 7 May he was aware that the Ugandan National Resistance Army was providing help to the RPF.

The Kibuye massacres

The interim prime minister, Jean Kambanda, visited the prefecture of Kibuye on 3 May, to show his solidarity with the prefect, Clement Kayishema, for "the work" that was being accomplished there.

As soon as the genocide started, Kayishema, a medical doctor, had stationed gendarmes in most of the communes giving explicit instructions that people fleeing were to seek protection in Kibuye town. Tens of thousands of people had followed these instructions. Kayishema waited two weeks, possibly to make sure that as many people as possible fell into the trap, and then he launched attacks.

In the commune of Gitesi, in the Gatwaro stadium, an estimated 20,000 people were sheltering. They thought that the gendarmes surrounding the stadium were there for their protection. But then the water was cut off. Children began to die of hunger. No one could escape. People who went out to find food never returned. The killing began on Monday, 18 April with grenades being thrown into the crowds, and then the firing began, the soldiers shooting from above the stadium on a hill. Interahamwe waited outside the stadium to kill those trying to escape.

It is estimated that 12,000 people were killed on this one day. The killing continued the following day. The stench was terrible and many of the bodies were eventually taken in Ministry of Public Transport lorries to be thrown into pits.

Although Tutsi fought for their lives in many places and struggled with their attackers, the best known resistance was in Bisesero, a wooded mountainous ridge in Kibuye where many Tutsi fled and tried to hide.

The local militia was not enough to overcome their number and so Interahamwe were brought in from Gisenyi, from Cyangugu and from Kigali.[4] Many of the Tutsi in the hills were by this time starving to death.

One survivor said: "When we saw the attack coming we fled ... they followed us, killing people, especially children, old men and old women who could not run".[5] It is estimated that 50,000 people lost their lives in the hills of Bisesero.[6]

When the prime minister visited Kibuye on 3 May a meeting was organised in the prefecture office.[7] During the meeting a doctor from the Kibuye hospital had got to his feet with a question. He wanted to know what should happen to the children who had survived massacres and who had been brought to Kibuye hospital. The doctor said that since the children had arrived the Interahamwe had been trying to get into the hospital. The doctor wanted to know what the government was going to do to protect these children. Kambanda sat in silence. It was Eliézer Niyitegeka, the interim government's minister of information, and Donat Murego, who was the executive secretary of the MDR, who responded to the doctor.[8] They insulted him, telling him that he was a traitor, that the children were "enemies" and that no one should help them.

Not one person at the meeting came to the defence of the children. When the doctor returned to the hospital the children were no longer there. A nurse told him that Interahamwe had come with machetes and clubs, "power members" from Rutsiro and Kibuye, who searched the wards, found the children, took them to an enclosure, and killed them.[9]

Those involved in the genocide in Kibuye would later earn the distinction of accomplishing the most comprehensive killing of Tutsi during the whole period. Entire Tutsi communities were wiped out with no witnesses left to tell what happened. From a population of 252,000 Tutsi in a 1991 census, by the end of June there were an estimated 8,000 left alive.[10]

Kambanda admitted in his plea bargain with the ICTR that he had personally been an eye-witness to massacres, that he had knowledge of mass killings through regular reports from the prefects to the minister of the interior, and through discussion held during the course of cabinet meetings. The interim government had decided that each prefecture would have a designated minister who would visit and call on the civilian population to be vigilant against the enemy and "its accomplices".

He described how one minister, Pauline Nyiramasuhuko, had been open and frank at cabinet meetings, saying that she personally was in favour of getting rid of all Tutsi. Without the Tutsi, she told ministers, all of Rwanda's problems would be over. Outside her house in Butare was a road block where people were frequently killed. A former social worker, at the time of the genocide she was studying to be a lawyer. Her husband was the rector of Butare University and they owned an hotel. It was for all these reasons that people listened to her.

Kambanda was asked by one of his interrogators: "You see we have clearly established that in the council of ministers everyone who was there knew what was happening, that there existed ethnic massacres in Rwanda, knew that there was a genocide underway … and you could keep quiet … said nothing?"

"I don't remember, it would surprise me, if anyone had said something", Kambanda replied.

"Were there people who said it?"

"I … I think that even if there had been objections, it would not have stopped her …. She was responsible for her own behaviour and I was responsible for mine."

Kambanda explained that the problem in Rwanda was because there was a war between Hutu and Tutsi. He was on the side of the Hutu. Everyone knew their ethnic origin. "I always knew mine", he said. "If there had not been a war there would have been no problem."

Kambanda said of Bisesero, "It had always been a difficult region". They determined to rid the area of the resisting Tutsi. Joseph Nzirorera said that no Tutsi should remain in the Bisesero hills. Lt.-Col. Anatole Nsengiyumva called on the Interahamwe and Impuzamugambi militia to go to Bisesero.

After one cabinet meeting a loudspeaker van toured Gisenyi and called on all the youth of the MRND, the youth of the CDR and the Impuzamugambi to join up. All the volunteers were gathered together in the Umuganda stadium, put on buses, given weapons, and taken to Bisesero. Nsengiyumva provided weapons and the fuel needed for transport.[11]

Sanctuary?

The intent to eliminate all the remaining Tutsi in Rwanda was stalled in the city of Kigali. There were UN peacekeepers there, as well as the medical teams of the ICRC and MSF, and too many prying western eyes for anyone to attempt the large-scale massacres that were happening elsewhere. Thousands of people were trapped in the city, in schools, churches and hotels at the whim and mercy of the Interahamwe militia.

The interim prime minister, Jean Kambanda, said that he knew that in Kigali the people sheltering in the churches were "in full view". The prefect, Colonel Tharcisse Renzaho, who collected the faxes that arrived in the ministries from abroad, showed him a fax from the US government that demanded protection for one of the sites where people were sheltering, the Hôtel des Mille Collines. Renzaho assured Kambanda that he would look after the people in the hotel. Kambanda said a directive had gone out over RTLM that these people should not be harmed. "Renzaho knew the pressures we were under", said Kambanda.

The peacekeepers did not have enough manpower to protect all the sites where people were gathered but patrols were sent around to check on security and drop off food and supplies. Major-General Dallaire even ordered unarmed military observers to sleep in the orphanages to deter the killers. A group of Tunisians held at bay the military and militia wanting to get at the people at the Hôtel des Mille Collines, where 550 people were sheltering.

The hotel was the focus of much western international press attention because several high-profile people were sheltering there, including prominent opposition politicians, both Hutu and Tutsi, and the public prosecutor for Kigali, François-Xavier Nsanzuwera, who had made an arrest in the murder of the politician Félicien Gatabazi. Unknown to the extremists, there was an outside telephone line still working from the hotel.

The army high command made frequent visits to the hotel and there were daily threats that everyone would be killed. Outside, a roadblock was manned by Interahamwe who, when told early on by Dallaire that the hotel was to be under UN protection, had laughed.[12]

The largest concentration of people trapped in Kigali was at the St Famille-St Paul complex where 6,000 people were sheltering. They were overwhelmingly Tutsi, along with Hutu opponents of the regime.[13] On 15 April, Interahamwe and Presidential Guard had selected 120 people from the group, using prepared lists, and everyone who was taken away was shot dead. Another 12 people died and 113 were injured when on 1 May the church site was shelled – the front line in the war between the RPF and the Rwandan government cut the city in two. The ICRC hospital was completely overwhelmed and despair set in among the peacekeepers and the medical staff of the ICRC.

On 9 May there were more victims of the civil war. Three to four artillery rounds fired by the RPF landed on the government sector where the Central Hospital in Kigali was located, killing forty people standing in a line waiting for medicines. A bomb landed in the middle of a tent where thirty injured were waiting for attention. And a peacekeeper, a Ghanaian private named Mensah-Baidoo, was killed when RPF shells fell on the Amahoro stadium.

Dallaire came up with the idea of exchanging some of the people trapped in this government zone for those who were prisoners in RPF conquered territory. Such an operation was fraught with danger and not all the peacekeepers agreed that the idea was a good one – while truces might be agreed by both sides to stop the fighting to allow UN convoys of people across the front line, the militia posed a great danger – but Dallaire was desperate.

In early May an attempt was made to evacuate people from the Hôtel des Mille Collines – some 70 people from among the hundreds there. Only those with the requisite entry visas to Belgium would be allowed to leave. A UNAMIR soldier from Poland, Major Stefan Stec, standing in the crowded hotel lobby, had read out loud the list of names of those people who were to be put on a convoy to the airport. Both the RPF and Rwandan government forces had agreed to allow safe passage. But at a roundabout on the outskirts of town the convoy was stopped at a roadblock by Interahamwe, alerted to the convoy by RTLM, and all the passengers were pulled out of the cars. Some of them were beaten, twelve were injured and the baggage was looted. Calm was restored only through the intervention of Tharcisse Renzaho, and even then it took four hours of negotiation with the militia to avoid bloodshed. The convoy returned to the hotel. The Interahamwe was quite clearly in control of some parts of the city.

In order to get agreement for further attempts to make exchanges of people, Dallaire met with Renzaho and Major-General Augustin Bizimungu, chief of staff of the army. Both of them were uneasy about the militia and to Dallaire it seemed that the two of them were having to defer to a body more powerful than either the Rwanda government forces or the interim government.[14] Dallaire thought that Bizimungu in particular was letting the militia and its leaders run the show, although he still had a grip on the army and the gendarmerie.

Dallaire asked for a meeting with the Interahamwe, and Bizimungu and Colonel Théoneste Bagosora introduced him to three young men in the Hôtel des Diplomates. Dallaire had already taken the bullets from his gun in case his temptation to shoot them was too great.[15] They were introduced and Dallaire noted that one of the young men had dried blood on his shirt. Dallaire was told they were Robert Kajuga, President of the national Interahamwe, Bernard Maniragaba and Ephren Nkezabera. They told Dallaire that they were at his disposal. They had "sensitised" their people to stop the massacres. Kajuga told him that the Interahamwe had no problem with UNAMIR.[16]

Dallaire then went to the Hôtel des Mille Collines where he met Froduald Karamira, the vice-president of the MDR, who gave him the interim government's tacit approval for the transfer of "prisoners". Dallaire concluded that the links between the army, the militia and the interim government were real.[17]

There were several more meetings between the Interahamwe and peacekeepers in UNAMIR's Humanitarian Action Cell, led by Colonel Clayton Yaache of Ghana, which concluded that the army lacked control of the militia groups.[18] Yaache had also met Bagosora who had insisted that the government was committed to allowing "freedom of movement to its citizens".[19]

Major Don MacNeil, a Canadian officer who was also a part of the Humanitarian Action Cell, described how agreement for the safe passage of civilians could not be negotiated with the former government leadership alone, but with "militia and self-defence groups" dressed in various uniforms. At one meeting a high ranking officer of the army had been shouted down by local Interahamwe.[20]

Dallaire's reinforcement plea

In the first week of May, Dallaire sent a detailed plan for reinforcements to DPKO in New York. Entitled "Proposed Future Mandate and Force Structure of UNAMIR", it called for a full and effective force that would include four mechanised battalions, or, alternatively, a minimum viable force of five infantry battalions of which three would be mechanised. Dallaire warned that even if a ceasefire were to come into immediate effect it would still be difficult to control the militia. What was needed was combat power to face the militias and undertake deterrent operations such as arms seizures. The plan required approximately 4,000 men. Military units had to be deployed to areas where the displaced were sheltering. And the prospect for success depended upon earliest deployment.[21] Dallaire did not require the enforcement powers of the UN Charter. What he needed was latitude in the interpretation of the more pacific provisions known as Chapter VI. The urgent task was for something to be done about those preventing aid reaching the threatened and the dying. Rwanda was in need of massive and immediate humanitarian assistance. It wanted a reasonably capable force, strong, self-protected, self-sufficient and highly mobile, to establish safe havens and provide security for people in danger.[22]

On 6 May a group of non-permanent members of the Security Council, Spain, New Zealand, Argentina, and the Czech Republic, presented a resolution that called for reinforcements. But British and US diplomats told everyone that action in Rwanda must be taken through the efforts of African countries, and that the Organization of African Unity should have a role to play. On 11 May, in another secret and informal meeting, Madeleine Albright, the US ambassador, came up with an alternative idea: instead of flying troops to Kigali, which would be too difficult because of the civil war, "protective zones" should be created along the border with Burundi where an international force could provide assistance to those in need. The UK called for a more formal report from the Secretariat and a budget outline.[23]

When told of the US idea of protective zones Dallaire argued that this would require a whole new set of negotiations with neighbouring states. In any event the people would not be able to get to the protective zones because they would be killed on the way. Big, isolated camps were not the solution. What was needed was an "ubiquitous locally overwhelming presence of UN forces with equipment, a mandate and manpower to deter subversive elements". He provided the figures: in the Rwandan government zone there were an estimated 416,000 people sheltering and at risk of continuing massacres. In the RPF zone there were 256,000 displaced from their homes. He provided a map to show where these people were located. Time was running out, he wrote. An absolute priority was to get APCs, vehicles, radios, and stores into Rwanda because if, as seemed likely, troops would come from neighbouring countries they would have inadequate resources. In the same cable, dated 12 May, Dallaire reported that massacres were continuing.[24]

The US put every obstacle in the way. On 13 May, a delegation of nine senior US officials from the US State Department and the Department of Defense turned up at UN headquarters. They had come to tell DPKO that they were "very nervous" about the proposed plan for Rwanda. It was unwise, they said. Establishing adequate security in Rwanda would depend on the availability of troops and commitment to the plan from the warring sides. Dallaire's troop estimates were inadequate. They still favoured setting up safe havens on the borders. The officials in DPKO argued that this approach did not meet the major concern of protecting the people. The US then proposed that a team of unarmed military observers be sent to Rwanda for two weeks so that the Council could make up its mind definitively.

Madeleine Albright explained later that the plan put to the Council by the Secretariat "did not make sense to US military planners". The Pentagon's view was that it was not possible to have a humanitarian operation in the midst of a civil war.[25] The "protected zones" idea – the brainchild of a task force under Richard Clarke at the US National Security Council, who was also responsible for the US policy to withdraw the whole of UNAMIR – was the best the situation offered. "Once we knew the Belgians were leaving, we were left with a rump mission incapable of doing anything to help people. They were doing nothing to stop the killing", he said.

"What we offered was a peacekeeping force that would have been effective. What [the UN] offered was exactly what we said it would be, a force that would take months to get there".[26] He thought the outside-in approach would have saved some lives. Of the "protected zones", he would do absolutely the same again, he said.

There was a widespread belief in the US government that Rwanda could turn into another Somalia, that what would start as a small engagement of foreign troops would escalate quickly out of control. The Pentagon even refused a request for help to jam the broadcasts of RTLM because officials there thought this an "ineffective and expensive mechanism".[27] Dallaire thought that the US were so determined to deny help that they might be in league with the RPF, hoping for a free hand in order for them to conquer the whole country.[28]

After the genocide Dallaire's basic reinforcement plan was assessed by a panel of military experts. It concluded that a force of 5,000, operating with air support, logistics, and effective command and control, could have averted the deaths of half a million people.[29]

The western media's response

Major-General Dallaire believed that perhaps with greater public awareness there may have been some attempt to help. But the mobilisation of public opinion was not helped by inadequate international press coverage. There were no headlines about genocide. There were graphic reports about corpses piling up on the streets and news stories about the scale of the killing, but there was little explanation in the commentary. The western news agenda was largely focused elsewhere, particularly on Bosnia-Herzegovina, as Serbian forces massively attacked the safe area of Gorazde.

What western press coverage there was on Rwanda, instead of identifying the killing as a result of a planned and well-organised campaign of systematic extermination against a minority, showed the journalists at first interpreting the violence as the latest bloody chapter in an age old conflict. The killing was described as tribal bloodletting that foreigners were powerless to prevent.[30] This bolstered arguments that only a massive and dramatic intervention would succeed and that this was out of the question. The crucial issue of providing Dallaire's beleaguered force with either supplies or reinforcements to continue to try to save as many people as possible was simply not taken up as an issue. No one knew what the choices were.

The *New York Times* described Rwanda on 15 April as being in an "uncontrollable spasm of lawlessness and terror". No member of the UN with an army strong enough to make a difference was willing to risk the lives of its troops for a country in such a state.[31] One week later, when genocide had been recognised, an editorial in the same newspaper stated: "What looks very much like genocide has been taking place in Rwanda ... the world has few ways of responding effectively when violence within a nation leads to massacres and the breakdown of civil order". It went on to describe how the Security Council had thrown in the towel and said that without a rapid reaction force, the world had little choice but to stand aside and "hope for the best".[32]

In London the *Guardian* reported on 29 April that the aid agency Oxfam and a UNAMIR source in Kigali had determined that genocide was underway in Rwanda. The story merited ten paragraphs on an inside page.[33] An editorial some days later declared: "Glum pragmatism dictates that there is precious little the international community can do to stem the fighting in Rwanda at this stage".[34]

Several reporters said that there was resistance to the story from their editors. A British journalist, Scott Petersen, was unable to get his story printed about Oxfam having determined that the genocide of the Tutsi minority group was underway in Rwanda.[35] Another journalist on a London daily was told by her editor that there was "compassion fatigue about Africa".[36]

The first international inquiry into the genocide concluded that the western media's failure to adequately report that genocide was taking place, and thereby generate the public pressure for something to be done about it, had contributed to international indifference and inaction, and possibly to the crime itself. The press had been fundamentally irresponsible, it concluded.[37]

In April the journalist Aidan Hartley was sent to Rwanda by the Reuters News Agency from Nairobi to cover the evacuation of foreigners, and he remembers being told by his editors that this was "your classic Bongo story". There would be no interest in what was happening in Rwanda "unless they start raping white nuns". Hartley was told that his job was "to cover the whites, get the nuns evacuated" and that would be the end of it. Everyone knew that small wars in small states in Africa were less likely than ever to get coverage after what had happened in Somalia.[38]

Hartley reported the evacuation. He met the Secretary-General's special representative Jacques-Roger Booh-Booh at the Hôtel Meridien whom he described in a state of paralysed terror. Then he had to leave. Most western journalists were evacuated from the Hôtel des Mille Collines and taken to the airport by UNAMIR on 14 April. The big news story was now South Africa where universal suffrage was bringing apartheid to an end: there were 2,500 accredited press for the inauguration of Nelson Mandela as President on 10 May.[39] Once the ceremonies in South Africa were over, attention turned to Rwanda, where the magnitude of the killing was becoming apparent. By early May an estimated 5,000 bodies a day were coming down the Akagera river.[40]

Hartley returned to Rwanda in May. He was taken south from Kigali by RPF soldiers to a red brick church at Nyamata, which was full of decomposing bodies. There was a human head on the altar instead of a crucifix. "I had no idea of the scale of what I was witnessing", he wrote later.

Hartley also visited the St Famille church complex in Kigali where he was told that during the night young Tutsi men would be taken from the church by the militia. Some nights the militia would hammer holes through the church walls and drag youths away. At the gates there was a checkpoint of children with bows and arrows, guns and clubs.[41]

"Suddenly the truth dawned on me that there was a mad logic about it", Hartley wrote later. "The point was not to win the war but to wipe out the Tutsi. Time and again Hutu forces held a position long enough only so that the slaughter of civilians could be completed. Then they fell back, driving the remaining population before them into exile, taking their nation with them on foot, robbing the RPF of a people to govern."[42]

Hartley would come to realise that Rwanda represented one of the twentieth century's great acts of inhumanity, and yet he found little interest in it among his editors. Senior staff in Reuters wanted the Rwandan coverage to be wound down.[43] The message was clear enough to the genocidaires.

The international response

On 11 May, the UN High Commissioner for Human Rights José Ayala-Lasso arrived in Rwanda to assess the situation for himself. He met Philippe Gaillard, the chief delegate of the ICRC, who told him that by now 250,000 people had died. He was told he was exaggerating.[44]

But the ICRC was now in five locations apart from its hospital in Kigali.[45] It was providing help in the prefectures of Byumba, Kibungo in the east, Gisenyi in the north, and at the Catholic centre in Kabgayi, where 38,000 people were trapped.

Gaillard travelled to Kabgayi and saw the thousands crammed into schools and the health centre. About a dozen people a day were dying from starvation and the corpses remained among the living, bloated and unburied. Every day soldiers came to take away Tutsi. At night soldiers went through classrooms looking for victims. Gaillard tried to persuade ministers from the interim government to see Kabgayi for themselves.

In Cyangugu prefecture ICRC delegates had found a stadium with an estimated 8,000 people including seriously malnourished children and hundreds of people needing medical help. There was one water tap. Soldiers were guarding the site, working closely with the Interahamwe militia who roamed the camp abducting people.

Gaillard said that the poor of Rwanda were the damned of the earth for having accepted the racist insanities that had poured over the airwaves.[46] This was a genocide in full view; everyone could see the pictures of the bodies clogging the rivers.

Ayala-Lasso wrote a report after his visit to Rwanda to appeal to both sides to avoid human rights abuses. There had been "wanton killing" of 200,000 civilians, he reported, a figure which could now well exceed 500, 000. He noted all the relevant international human rights instruments to which Rwanda was a party, including the 1948 Convention on the Prevention and Punishment of the Crime of Genocide.

A campaign for something to be done was by now underway in France. A French doctor, Jean-Hervé Bradol, who had worked at the ICRC hospital in Kigali, returned to Paris determined to expose what was going on in Rwanda. Bradol appeared on television news to say that military intervention was not needed to stop a civil war, but to stop genocide. He accused the French government of having armed and trained the perpetrators.[47] He explained that the killing was a political act, a planned extermination.

In London the aid agency Oxfam held a vigil and delivered a letter to the prime minister, John Major. The letter, dated 3 May, called the killing genocide.

The UN Secretary-General started to adopt a higher profile and appeared on US television to say that he had written letters to heads of state all over the world to get help for Rwanda but that there was general fatigue. There had to be intervention, he said. "It is a question of genocide."[48]

UN responses to Dallaire's reinforcement plea

On 13 May the Secretary-General presented a report to the Security Council containing Dallaire's detailed plan for action and recommending his call for 5,500 reinforcements for UNAMIR. It was hoped that, within a week of obtaining Security Council approval, several APCs could be deployed and 400 Ghanaian troops flown to Kigali to protect the airport and all the sites in the city where thousands of people were trapped.[49] The report was critical of the US idea of safe havens on the borders. The overwhelming majority of people in need of help were inside the country and if they tried to get to the borders they would be killed on the way.

But before the vote was taken, and as part of what could be regarded as a concerted international campaign of spin, a representative of the interim government flew to New York and appeared at the Council table. Jérôme Bicamumpaka, the interim foreign minister, told the ambassadors that the death toll was exaggerated. They must look closer into the events in Rwanda. They should understand that the tragedy derived from the "age-old history of the nation". The hatred that had erupted was "forged over four centuries of cruel and ruthless domination of the Hutu majority by the haughty and domineering Tutsi minority". The apocalypse had come in the form of an "inter-ethnic war of unbelievable cruelty" and unleashed "the animal instinct of a people afraid of being enslaved again". Bicamumpaka accused the RPF of shamelessly misleading the world. The only way of ensuring a ceasefire was to use an international buffer force from neutral countries.[50]

Bicamumpaka, a Brussels-trained economist, was accompanied to New York by Jean-Bosco Barayagwiza, who for years had been the director of foreign policy at the foreign ministry. He was also the founder of the extremist CDR, a shareholder in RTLM, a man who promoted the killing of Tutsi at public meetings and supervised roadblocks manned by the Impuzamugami militia.[51] He and Barayagwiza had already been received in Paris where on 27 April they had met President François Mitterrand, prime minister Edouard Balladur and foreign minister, Alain Juppé.[52]

In the early hours of 17 May, eight weeks after the genocide began, and twenty-seven days after UNAMIR had been reduced, the Security Council finally authorised the 5,500 reinforcements, expanding the peacekeeping mandate to provide security and protection for civilians at risk in Rwanda, including the establishment and maintenance, where feasible, of secure humanitarian areas.

The resolution had come after five hours of debate. And although it appeared to indicate action, in reality all it provided for was the authorisation of a deployment of troops. The actual provision of troops was conditional on a further report by the Secretary-General on the possible cooperation of the parties to the conflict, which would require a team of UN military observers to visit Rwanda. The US had wanted to know who would pay for the mission and was insisting on the necessity of the consent of the parties. The UK was cautious, insisting that it should be made quite clear why this was not an enforcement operation. Its representative counselled against the use of the words "decisive action".

The New Zealand ambassador, Colin Keating, wrote to his capital calling the resolution "a sham" which they would not be able to explain to the world.[53] The US and the UK had weakened it, he said.

Major-General Dallaire wondered years later why the world had been "so feeble, fearful and self-centred in the face of the atrocities".[54]

The civil-defence network strengthens its grip

The interim government issued a directive on 25 May to all the prefects to provide detailed plans for civil defence. With the world becoming better informed there was a desire for less conspicuous anarchy. The prime minister had made a similar attempt at the end of April with a directive asking for an end to"violence, pillage and other acts of cruelty".

Harking back to a speech at Butare university ten days earlier, at which he had said that every Rwandan was needed to fight the RPF, Kambanda's directive included the phrase "Wimaigihugu amaraso imbwa zikayangwera ubusa", interpreted as "if you refuse to spill your own blood for your country then the dogs will drink your blood for nothing." The enemy was supported by foreign governments, the people were warned. Rwanda's greatest weapon was its people. The people could only be utilised with organisation and training.

"This is why the communal authorities and prefectures should in the next 15 days have complete mobilisation, organisation and training. The following principles must be taken into account: the tactical organisation and strategy of this popular resistance must be carried out in the utmost secrecy." The directive called for physical, moral and ideological training, and training in the use of weapons.

Civil defence representatives had to be chosen in each sector after meetings had been held in each cell. There were to be five representatives chosen in each cell after cell meetings. A coordinator had to be elected who would be responsible for education, communication and information and who would report on all meetings. A reservist preferably should be the deputy. At the communal level the committee of coordination would comprise four people. The bourgmestre would supervise. These plans were remarkably similar to those outlined in a 1993 diary, belonging to Bagosora, which contained a sketch of a scheme about training and arming of civilians with the assistance of the Rwandan armed forces. The diary, found abandoned in Kigali, would later be produced as evidence against Bagosora at his trial.[55]

Essentially, there was now to be a less public and smaller scale method to eliminating Tutsi. And so it was: by the end of April most of the large-scale massacres were over.

Rescue missions

For three months the peacekeepers of UNAMIR were swamped with requests from all over the world, from nations and agencies, asking them to rescue certain people. Some of these referrals were related to foreign nationals belonging to religious orders, and students and teachers who had refused to leave during the evacuation of foreigners. Most requests involved Rwandans, mostly Tutsi, who had worked for or knew the ex-pats who had left so hurriedly.

There were inherent risks in such rescue attempts. The militia in Kigali would frequently execute on sight any Tutsi found travelling in UNAMIR vehicles or seen in public. And there were increased dangers when the RPF managed to acquire UN vehicles to infiltrate fighters behind RGF lines.

The rescue missions sometimes involved negotiating twenty or thirty roadblocks. On one occasion a drunken militia disarmed the bodyguard of an official from the Kigali prefecture. The militia fired his weapon into an orphanage. Captain Diagne Mbaye of Senegal saved dozens of lives braving fire, mines, and the militia but on 30 May he was killed by an RPF mortar fragment. It was for lack of petrol, not of courage, that more rescue missions were not attempted.

By June the peacekeepers had received 971 requests for rescue, all of them people who were well connected in some way. Dallaire began to resent this. In June, for instance, he received a message from Kofi Annan asking that he provide protection at the Rwanda Catholic church in Kabgayi where in the large seminary 30,000 people, including many clergy, were sheltering. By then the RPF during its advance had surrounded the site and the Pope himself had requested extra security. Dallaire responded that he would send UN military observers there as often as he could spare them but could do nothing additionally until he got more troops.

He wondered whether or not the apparent cynical manoeuvring by France, Belgium and the US, the RPF and the RGF, proved that the peacekeepers were sacrificial lambs, allowing everyone to say that something was being done. The UN was no more than a camouflage, a cover-up.[56] He felt he had been duped:

"It took every ounce of our effort, resources and courage to produce tiny results, yet all around us hundreds of thousands of human beings were being ripped apart and millions were running for their lives .... I had pushed my people to do real things that ultimately saved human lives, but which in the scheme of the killing seemed nearly insignificant, and all the time I had thought I was leading the effort to try to solve the crisis".[57]

Another cable to headquarters made the point: "UNAMIR personnel, since the start of the war, have on a daily basis risked their lives to save people ... we will do everything within our abilities to continue...".[58]

Plans were devised by UNAMIR's Humanitarian Action Cell to create secure zones and provide basic needs for people who were dying of hunger and disease; there were 91 places in Rwanda where terrified people were sheltering, hundreds of thousands under threat from militia and military. Dallaire was trying to provide security to four camps and mobile patrols for others in Kigali.[59]

On 25 May the ICRC sent a list of the estimated numbers of people trapped in large concentrations. "The lives of countless civilians, mainly Tutsi, are still at risk", an accompanying letter pointed out.

One of the peacekeepers in HAC recalled: "All that was needed was a shuttle convoy from Uganda of the most basic things – blankets, food and medicine. People were not only dying because of genocide but from disease, lack of clean water and food." It was estimated that in May 5,000 people a day were dying from the want of basic necessities.

On 1 June, sixty people in the St André Church in Kigali were shot, some of them trying to hide in the cellar. More than 100 people were taken away.

The Director of MSF, Philippe Biberson, wrote to Kofi Annan to tell him what had happened and to plead for action. "Tomorrow, perhaps, in Kigali the only Tutsi left will be those injured in the ICRC hospital", he wrote. "Do all in your power to accelerate the arrival of reinforcements ... if they do not arrive next week there will be no more Tutsi to treat in Kigali".[60]

The first successful transfer of people across the front line was achieved by UNAMIR on 27 May, taking RPF sympathisers from the Hôtel des Mille Collines to a town southeast of Kigali and bringing Hutus from the Amahoro to a drop off point outside the city, still in RGF hands. This involved three hundred people. In total the peacekeepers rescued 10,000 people in these exchanges.[61]

The UN discusses genocide

On 24 May the UN Human Rights Commission, which a year earlier had refused to discuss Rwanda in public session, held an emergency meeting in Geneva, convened by Canada. It heard direct testimony about the genocide.

The French minister for human rights, Lucette Michaux-Chevry, agreed that the word genocide was appropriate and claimed that France had provided "exceptional assistance to the victims of the conflict". Dallaire wryly observed that the minister must have been talking about Hutu extremists who were sitting it out in France. Geraldine Ferraro led the US delegation and to everyone's surprise, not least Dallaire's, announced that she supported UNAMIR's efforts. A Special Rapporteur, René Degni-Ségui, was appointed to investigate whether a genocide had in fact occurred.

At the end of the month of May Dallaire's anger at the total failure of the US to provide anything at all was expressed to Brian Atwood, the US under-secretary for foreign aid, whom Dallaire flew to see in Nairobi. Dallaire told Atwood that it would be so easy for the US to provide the necessary equipment and airlift for UNAMIR. Without strategic lift no one would get there. If the millions of Rwandans now on the move were pushed westward into Zaire then the world would face a terrible regional problem. Atwood and his delegation listened politely.[62] Charles Petrie, deputy director of the UN Rwanda Emergency Office that had opened in Nairobi, told Atwood that to protect the safe havens in Rwanda all that was needed was about thirty APCs to allow Ghanaians back in.

Every effort was made in DPKO to find transport for a rescue mission. Kofi Annan faxed forty-four member states, those with known spare military capacity, to ask for vehicles for the troops available for Rwanda. By 10 June Ghana, Senegal, Ethiopia, Zambia and Nigeria had all offered troops.[63] There were two replies to the request for equipment. The US offered 50 APCs in storage in Turkey, from their vast unused Cold War stocks. For these they would charge a lease-hold rate of US $4 million and an additional US $6 million to cover the cost of transport. The vehicles arrived after the genocide was over and they were stripped of machine guns, radio, tools, spare parts and training manuals. Major-General Dallaire described them as tons of rusting metal.[64] The UK offered fifty trucks in return for a sizeable amount of money. They were fit only to be museum relics, Dallaire said. The British quietly withdrew the request for money, he said, and some vehicles did arrive but one at a time they broke down.[65]

Every day of delay in providing equipment meant that more people were massacred or simply died from not being re-supplied in their hiding places. Dallaire's last cable in May read: "This situation is a disgrace that the force commander will express to all to hear … the killings will most certainly continue, with several hundreds of thousands of people in advanced stages of malnutrition."[66]

The first official acknowledgement of genocide finally came in a report to the Security Council on 31 May. It was based on the information provided by Iqbal Riza and Maurice Baril, the Secretary-General's military adviser who had completed a visit to Rwanda between 22–27 May. There was little doubt about their findings. There had been large-scale killing of one ethnic group.

The report determined that an immediate priority was to relieve the suffering and to secure assemblies of civilians still in peril. There were plans that had been drawn up by UNAMIR. There should be urgent and decisive action. The report noted how the "the international community appears paralysed". And then, in the penultimate paragraph, were the following words: "We all must recognise that … we have failed in our response to the agony of Rwanda, and thus have acquiesced in the continued loss of human lives."

There would be a review of the whole system, Boutros Boutros-Ghali promised.[67]

Moves towards exile

The RPF advance continued and for the interim government and the Rwandan military the situation became desperate. There was an emergency meeting of the Rwandan army high command on 5 June in Kigali. The interim prime minister attended, with the minister of defence, Augustin Bizimana, and the minister of the interior, Edouard Karemera.

One suggestion was to do away with civil authority altogether and replace all the prefects and the bourgmestres with military officers, but there were not enough officers left. The RPF had targeted the officer corps and some units had no officers at all. They would have to use the 450 candidate officers in the École Supérieure Militaire.

The country was now under a Security Council embargo on weapons, imposed in resolution 918. "We saw defeat coming even at the beginning", said Kambanda. There was so much desertion in the army that a need was identified for military prisons for the "re-education" of undisciplined soldiers. Six hundred new recruits were being trained but this would hardly compensate the losses. An increasing number of families of soldiers were escaping to Gisenyi.

Kambanda said he first considered exile at the end of June just after he had visited his home commune to arrange to have his family evacuated to the Ivory Coast, via Kinshasa. His brother, who was married to a Tutsi, told him that at first her family had sheltered with him but he had eventually asked them to leave. Kambanda said his brother had no choice. "He did not want them to die in his house … he did not want to have to see them die." Kambanda's mother and the Tutsi wife had fled together, with the help of Kambanda, who ensured them a military escort.

Kambanda said that it was only when he got home to Butare that he thought about everything that had happened. At first the hunt for Tutsi had been through the roadblocks, then there was an attempt to eliminate them in their homes and now there was a hunt for those who had escaped, some of whom were sheltering with Hutu. There was a campaign to ensure that the whole hill "was clean". His brother had been told to take part in it. He told Kambanda that 20,000 people were sheltering in a local seminary armed only with stones and their attackers had machetes. When soldiers arrived all the refugees were killed.

At the end of June, and for the first time in his life, Kambanda travelled north, to the Gishwati Forest, where President Habyarimana owned a farm. He found the president's brother-in-law, Protais Zigiranyirazo, there and he invited Kambanda to his home. Zigiranyirazo's mother was seriously ill and when she died some days later Kambanda felt an obligation to help with the funeral arrangements. Zigiranyirazo was shocked at the low turn-out at the funeral. Government ministers and some local dignitaries did not attend the service. Zigiranyirazo complained. Some of the ministers owed their jobs to him, he told Kambanda. Kambanda thought that Zigiranyirazo had asked him to his home to show how family members, President Habyarimana's in-laws, were a power in the land.

A fundraiser was held at the end of June at the Hôtel Méridien in Gisenyi. Several interim government ministers were there, and the military was represented by Colonel Anatole Nsengiyumva. The MRND Secretary-General Joseph Nzirorera was also present. They said they would use the money raised to purchase weapons and ammunition for their campaign in the Bisesero hills where Kambanda said the Tutsi continued to resist. Weapons were eventually acquired, said Kambanda, coming into Rwanda through Goma, and were received by Joseph Nzirorera. Colonel Nsengiyumva requisitioned brewery lorries to transport the weapons at night.

"Opération Turquoise"

On 10 June, Dallaire flew to Nairobi to meet major humanitarian groups and diplomats. He gave a detailed briefing about the military situation and the genocide, and outlined his plan to provide support for the protection of Rwandans in danger. In a press conference he told international journalists that they had dropped the ball. They were allowing "fence-sitting politicians off the hook for the Rwandan genocide".[68] He needed troops right now.

Then to Dallaire's astonishment (a few days later), he was told that the French government had decided to launch its own military operation for Rwanda. The French had announced they were to secure humanitarian areas and protect the displaced people. The idea had received the enthusiastic endorsement of Secretary-General Boutros Boutros-Ghali, who made no reference to Dallaire or to what his mission was doing.[69] Dallaire's anger spilled over in a cable sent to headquarters on 20 June: "One wonders how the UN and the international community has permitted itself to get into such a situation in the first place, as an early and determined effort to get troops and resources here on the ground under UNAMIR's mandate could have avoided all this and already saved so many lives ...".[70]

Dallaire believed that the interim government, the RGF, Boutros-Ghali and France had all connived behind his back to secure this French intervention.[71] Even the RPF was better informed than he was, their two representatives in Europe having been briefed on the plan before Dallaire heard about it.[72]

Dallaire thought that the French, who had declared their operation humanitarian, were simply using a humanitarian cloak to secure an intervention which would enable the RGF to hold onto a sliver of the country. They really wanted to split Rwanda in two, one part Tutsi and the other Hutu, he believed. If they were genuinely concerned about the humanitarian aspects they could have reinforced UNAMIR.

When news of the French intervention was announced over RTLM the troops at Camp Kigali went mad with joy for they believed that the French were coming to save them.[73] Jean Kambanda thought that the intervention would create a common front along the western frontier of the country to protect three prefectures – Cyangugu, Gikongoro and Kibuye – from the ongoing RPF onslaught. He was right.

The announcement of the French intervention seriously undermined UNAMIR's rescue units. Dallaire would now have to send home his French-speaking African officers who would be at risk from possible RPF hostility. These soldiers had been remarkable, responsible for saving so many lives, the team leaders on dozens of escorts, rescue and reconnaissance. They were described by Dallaire as "dynamic, courageous, determined". Duly, they were evacuated, and Dallaire was close to capitulating.

The French operation included everything UNAMIR needed. There were more than 2,500 elite soldiers from the French Foreign Legion, paratroopers, marines and special forces, all equipped with state-of-the-art weaponry, communications, one hundred armoured vehicles, heavy mortars, helicopters, and even jet aircraft. There was an armada of cargo aircraft.

What was achieved by "Opération Turquoise", as the French intervention was called, was in fact nothing less than a resurgence in the genocide. The peacekeepers were told by militia leaders that there was no point in resuming transfers of orphans and the displaced.[74]

A huge tide of refugees was now fleeing the RPF advance and France went back to the Security Council on 1 July to announce that they would have to create a safe zone in south-western Rwanda to "protect the people from fighting". This they did, and it provided a sanctuary for the killers.

By 3 July Camp Kigali, the heart of the extremist military machine, had started to empty. Rwandan soldiers were leaving the city, followed by militia in their retreat. That day the RTLM transmitter was dismantled from the roof of the studios and was taken to Mount Muhe in Gisenyi. The broadcasting equipment was loaded into buses that were commandeered by the army, the same buses used to transport military equipment. The RTLM equipment was quickly reinstalled in Mount Muhe to ensure that the radio was not off the air for too long. The journalists Georges Ruggiu and Valérie Bemeriki were given army protection for their move north.

Kambanda was in Kigali just before it fell, staying in the Hôtel des Diplomates, one of the last Hutu Power bastions in the city. The hotel was bombed that night and the guests sheltered in the cellar.

The following day, 4 July, the RPF took Kigali. The city was quiet at last. And so the interim government, along with the national treasury, its killers, its militia and its army, was able to move safely into Zaire. In all two million people fled Rwanda, incited to do so by RTLM which was continuing to broadcast to the "Hutu Nation", warning the population to take refuge in Zaire because the Tutsi RPF was going to kill all the Hutu. To those watching on the border it seemed as though the whole country was emptying. Kambanda announced: "We have lost the military battle but the war is by no means over because we have the people behind us".[75]

Like the genocide the exodus was unparalleled in its scale and speed. It was a politically ordered evacuation, during which the former leaders kept almost total control of the population.[76]

On 17 July, the bulk of the Rwandan army fled to Goma, an estimated 20,000 soldiers in intact combat units, bringing with them their heavy weapons. Other less organised troops, between 5,000 and 7,000, fled to Bukavu. In eastern Rwanda about 1,000 troops along the Tanzania frontier launched sporadic attacks against the RPF. An additional 3,000 soldiers were in the Benaco region of Tanzania. In Gikongoro the French created a humanitarian protection zone: there were an estimated 5,000 militia, primarily in the Nyungwe Forest.

The total number of troops who fled Rwanda was thought to be in the region of 37,000. Only about 10,000 of these were well-disciplined and trained. The whereabouts of the military officers implicated in the genocide were unknown.[77]

On 20 July, 1994 a unilateral ceasefire was declared by the RPF. No crowds were cheering and the refugee movements continued, as Rwandans fled the country in their thousands towards neighbouring Zaire and Burundi. The refugee population in Zaire was soon estimated to be 1.8 million, bringing the total population of Rwandans now outside their country to 2.5 million.

This massive exodus finally pushed Rwanda to the top of the international news agenda. By the end of July there were some five hundred journalists and technicians in Goma, Zaire, with scores of satellite transmission dishes at the airport filming the catastrophe which was described as "biblical" in its scale. The conditions in the camps were horrific; hundreds of thousands of people settled on a barren plain surrounded by volcanoes, where filth and overcrowding were endemic. Every day an estimated three thousand people were dying of cholera and dead bodies lined the roads.

The apocalyptic scenes on the nightly news led to calls for something to be done and so, on the day following the ceasefire, the US began a huge airlift of humanitarian aid to the camps. It took three days to get the planes on the ground in Goma and food unloaded, but at least the US had immediately spent some US$400 million and sent 4,000 military to help the relief workers. The UNHCR also operated in Goma, along with dozens of independent relief agencies.

There was no comparable TV coverage or help for the people in Rwanda itself, where an estimated 2 million people were displaced from their homes. Their condition was disastrous. There was no clean water. Livestock had been killed and the crops laid to waste. Everywhere there were skeletons or corpses, the rotting bodies being eaten by wild dogs and vultures.[78]

On 21 July, a day after the RPF ceasefire, a new government was sworn into office. The ceremony took place amid massive security, with dignitaries sheltered from the sun under a canopy erected outside the CND building where the RPF battalion had been billeted. One of the guests was Major-General Roméo Dallaire. The speeches were entirely in Kinyarwanda and Dallaire remembers only how solemn the occasion was.[79] The new government was called the Broad-Based Government of National Unity. A prominent businessman, Pasteur Bizimungu, was sworn in as president. Once a part of the elite, Bizimungu had fled to Uganda in August 1990, exposing Habyarimana's corruption and telling the RPF that the rotten regime in Kigali was ready to collapse. The minister of defence was Major-General Paul Kagame who was also in the newly created post of vice-president. Faustin Twagiramungu, who had escaped the elimination of the opposition on 7 April, was appointed prime minister, as intended under the Arusha Accords.

All political parties, apart from the MRND, were represented in the seventeen-member government. It had no offices, no telephones and no electricity, because the country had been ransacked. There were also revenge killings and executions. The ranks of the RPF, some of whose entire families had been wiped out, had been swollen by new recruits who were less disciplined, and thousands of civilian Hutu people became victims of reprisal killings, in some cases amounting to massacres, which occurred during, and continued after, the RPF advance.[80]

The immediate security concern of the new government was the continuing threat from Hutu Power, whose ideology was still flourishing in the refugee camps in neighbouring Zaire. Extremists among the exiled local officials and militia quickly established their authority and controlled the camps' populations. Handsome profits were made by monopolising the distribution of international aid and creating a trade in purloined humanitarian provisions, profits which were routinely diverted into arms purchases. Extortion, rapes and killings were rife: in the first month that the camps were established, four thousand people were murdered, some of them simply for wanting to return home.[81]

The exiled army with its heavy weaponry began to regroup, most notably in the Mugunga camp south of Goma. In October 1994 it was reported to the UN that the most dangerous and influential group in the camps was the Interahamwe, operating in civilian clothes and melting away in the crowds. "Pre-war each of the 145 communes had organised between 100–150 political activists", the report noted. There was increasing organisation, with cooperation between the political leaders, the military and the Interahamwe.[82]

It was the French government which facilitated the cohesive migration of the interim government, in effect the political, military and administrative leadership of the genocide. With the Hutu Power movement transforming itself in the camps and with the active support of the government in Zaire, plans were now being laid to re-conquer Rwanda and a series of attacks began along the western borders. The political leadership had created its own camp in Lac Vert, south of Goma. The militia were now integrated into the army and young recruits came to train every day from the refugee camps.

11

THE SILENCE

An accurate death toll for the Rwandan genocide may never be possible. The figure of 800,000 is now generally accepted, though it remains unclear why this number is so commonly used. It is a statistic provided by Human Rights Watch but it seems to be based on a census of Tutsi in 1991 and does not estimate the number of other victims who died in the genocide.[1] A higher figure is given by several experts present in Rwanda while the genocide took place. Philippe Gaillard, the Chief Delegate of the International Committee of the Red Cross (ICRC), who had an intimate knowledge of the country, its politics and population, and was probably the first person to recognise that genocide was likely,[2] estimates that up to one million people were killed. This figure is confirmed by Charles Petrie, the deputy co-ordinator of the UN Rwanda Emergency Office.

In a preliminary report published by the Rwanda Ministry of Local Government in December 2001, endorsed by the national Rwanda government, the figure of just over one million is cited. This figure is based on a census carried out six years after the genocide in July 2000, during which the names of 951,018 victims were established. The report recommended further investigation, saying that the census encountered "constraints that mean it is not perfect". It cites, for example, "the lack of reliable information in some regions where entire families were wiped out; omissions due to memory lapse; refusal to talk for fear of being arrested; or, in certain urban areas, the indifference of the population". This was why the eventual figure was thought to be more than a million.

The genocide had started in October 1990 in the prefectures of Gisenyi, Byumba and Ruhengeri with the outbreak of civil war. The vast majority of victims, some 99.2%, were killed between April and December 1994. According to the report, 93.7% of the victims were killed because they were identified as Tutsis; 1% because they were related to, married to or friends with Tutsis; 0.8% because they looked like Tutsis; and 0.8% because they were opponents of the Hutu regime at the time or were hiding people from the killers. These figures remain strongly contested by exiled opponents of the current government.

The report further claimed that young people were particularly targeted. The survey found that 53.7% of the victims were between 0 and 24 years old, while 41.3% were aged between 25 and 65 years. More men (56.4%) were killed than women (43.3%). The majority (48.2%) of genocide victims were poor rural dwellers, followed by students in secondary and higher education (21.2%). Pre-school children and elderly people over 65 represent 16.8% of victims, according to the report. Most victims were killed by machete (37.9%), followed by clubs (16.8%) and firearms (14.8%). Some 0.5% of the victims were women who had been raped or cut open. Other victims were forced to commit suicide, beaten to death, thrown alive into rivers or lakes, or burned alive. Infants and babies were thrown against walls or crushed to death.

One of the first Rwandans to investigate in any detail what had happened was a senior RPF official, Tito Rutaremara. He documented fifty-six common ways in which the militia killed people using machetes, screwdrivers, clubs with nails and other implements including hammers. Rutaremara thought that the more he studied the genocide, the more he might understand it. In the end he decided that it was beyond his understanding. "There was one woman who pulled out another's uterus," he said. The aggressor was a thirty-five year old from Murambi and when Rutaremara went to the prison to see what she looked like she appeared quite normal to him. "Rwanda destroyed its humanity," he said. "Our generation is lost. The people are going to have to slowly come to realize they must not kill."[3]

The sexual crimes in the genocide were unparalleled. The rape of women was so extensive that the International Criminal Tribunal for Rwanda (ICTR), thanks largely to representations by human rights groups, would later make an historic determination that systematic rape was a crime against humanity and that sexual violence constituted genocide in the same way as other acts. The tribunal indicated that the crime had been to mutilate women before they were killed with the intent to destroy the Tutsi group, while inflicting acute suffering on its members in the process.[4]

That genocide had occurred in Rwanda was officially recognised by an impartial Commission of Experts, created by the Security Council in July 1994, and in a report to the Council in October 1994 it determined that "a concerted, planned, systematic and methodical" campaign against the Tutsi and Hutu opponents of the extremists had taken place. There were ample grounds to prove that the 1948 Convention on the Prevention and Punishment of the Crime of Genocide had been violated between 6 April and 5 July, 1994. A provisional list of massacre sites was produced.[5] Corpses were still piled high in classrooms and churches, and strewn across the country in an apocalyptic landscape. Impartial justice for Rwanda was essential.[6]

And there was an overwhelming need for justice which, under the circumstances, seemed impossible. The number of people who had directly taken part in crimes against humanity was enormous. In post-genocide Rwanda there were no functioning institutions. No justice system or police force existed that could apply Rwandan law in order to arrest those who participated. Very few judges and prosecutors, police inspectors and court clerks remained in the country or were alive. No bar association existed, and there were hardly any lawyers.

Francois-Xavier Nsanzuwera, the Kigali prosecutor, had survived the genocide and was back in his office despite even the door frames and windows having been looted. A journalist had to give him a copy of the penal code.[7] Thousands of people were thrown into prison by RPF soldiers on the basis of denunciations. If this had not been the case, it was argued, there would have been more revenge killing. There was soon an unprecedented number of people in prison accused of the gravest of crimes against humanity. Before 1994 there had been capacity for an estimated 13,000 to 15,000 in Rwanda's twenty prisons and "centres of re-education and production", but more than 100,000 were incarcerated after the genocide. Their conditions were appalling and thousands of people died, many as a result of contracting gangrene from being permanently on wet and dirty floors and others who probably suffocated through lack of space. The efforts of the ICRC and medical NGOs checked the death rate among detainees.[8] It was estimated that two hundred years would be needed to process all the cases.

It was not until March 2001, in order to expedite the trials, that a law was adopted to bring justice to survivors by providing for what were called "Gacaca" courts, a system of local justice based on traditional methods, in which each community elects people of integrity from the community to decide the punishment of transgressors. The system was also intended to provide a record of events for the survivors, so they would know how their loved ones had died.

The Gacaca system had been preceded by a genocide law promulgated in 1996. One of its provisions was that suspects who confessed would have an automatic reduction in sentence, a rule that was not extended to category one prisoners, those convicted of helping to organise the genocide, who were subject to the death penalty. The regular courts in Rwanda were to be responsible for the fate of the three thousand category one prisoners, those deemed to have wielded power and influence during the genocide. The first trials held in Rwanda's national courts included that of former vice-president of the Mouvement Démocratique Républicain (MDR), Froduald Karamira, who was convicted on charges of genocide and incitement to commit genocide. It was Karamira who was said to have devised the phrase "All Hutu are one power". At a rally in Kigali in 1993 he had warned that "the enemy is among the people". Karamira showed no remorse. He was sentenced to death and was executed in public by firing squad on 24 April, 1998, along with twenty-one others in stadiums throughout the country.

Accounting for genocide

With hindsight, the decision in 1993 by the UN Security Council to send a small mission of peacekeepers to Rwanda and keep them there in an increasingly hostile environment was a terrible error. The mission, established to monitor Rwanda's transition from dictatorship to democracy, was suitable for only the most benign environment. This feeble UN effort actually encouraged the conspirators, signalling that they had nothing much to fear from the outside world. Many more Rwandans who died in the genocide might well have believed that with the UN in their country they would be safe.

The catastrophic failure over Rwanda has been examined by the UN, in an independent inquiry seeking to establish the role of the organisation in what happened. The Report of the Independent Inquiry into the actions of the UN during the 1994 genocide in Rwanda was authorised by Kofi Annan, who became Secretary-General in December 1996 after the US vetoed a second term for Dr. Boutros Boutros-Ghali.

This report, published in December 1999, called the genocide one of the most abhorrent events of the twentieth century. The report left no doubt that each part of the UN system, and in particular the Secretary-General, the Secretariat, the Security Council and the member states, had to assume and acknowledge their responsibility in the failure to prevent genocide.[9] The circumstances of the genocide have also been considered by an international panel created by the Organization of African Unity and a report, "Rwanda: The Preventable Genocide", was published in Addis Ababa in July 2000.[10] It showed how the potential to prevent the genocide was very real; it would have been possible to at least minimize significantly the carnage once it began. Those who most egregiously failed to use their power and influence included the governments of France, Belgium, the US, the UK, the Catholic Church and the UN Secretariat.

Two key member states also conducted enquiries – France and Belgium. The investigation by a Senate Commission in Belgium made public important diplomatic traffic between New York, Brussels and Kigali. It examined the decision by the Belgian government of prime minister Jean-Luc Dehaene to withdraw the Belgian troops from UNAMIR and the subsequent diplomatic offensive to persuade other troop contributors to do the same. In April 1994 hardly a voice had been raised in Belgium against the decision to abandon the mission, including in the media.[11]

Six years later, in April 2000, the Belgium government formally apologised to Rwanda. At a ceremony in Kigali the prime minister, Guy Verhofstadt, said: "I accept … the responsibility of my country, of the political and the military authorities. Belgium was at the heart of the UN mission … Belgium and the international community must recognise the errors made … we should have done more". He asked the people of Rwanda for forgiveness. Verhofstadt had previously worked on Belgium's

Senate Commission to investigate the genocide. He said the knowledge of what had happened changed him forever.[12]

As for France, in an unprecedented decision in 1997 parliament agreed to investigate the French policy towards Rwanda in a joint enquiry between the foreign affairs commission and that of the armed forces. A Mission of Information was to concentrate on the military operations of France, other countries and the UN in Rwanda between 1990 and 1994. The commission considered that the genocide was one of the greatest tragedies of the century and the delay in an enquiry, given the close relations between France and Rwanda, was "regrettable". There followed hours of public testimony with officials, diplomats and military personnel and many more interviews at the UN in New York and in Rwanda. Among the conclusions reached by the French Senate was the fact that policy towards Rwanda had been guided by President François Mitterrand.[13] The wide powers of the president over foreign affairs and the military meant that politicians had not been adequately informed of the complexity and the specifics of the Rwandan crisis. There was input from the French foreign ministry, and the ministries of defence, finance and co-operation, and from the French intelligence service, the DGSE, but overall co-ordination rested with Mitterrand. In future, the commission concluded, parliament should have better control over military operations.

The President of the Senate enquiry, a socialist deputy and former minister of defence, Paul Quilès, would eventually announce the result on French television: "France in no way incited, encouraged, helped or supported those who orchestrated the genocide", Quilès maintained. The report, published in December 1998, concluded that the French government was not implicated in the genocide. The only admission was the following: "the threat of a possible genocide had been underestimated while openly racist extremist branches multiplied in most of the political parties".[14]

The close involvement of France with the Rwandan regime heightens its responsibility in this tragedy, and the conclusion of the French Senate is surely, given the evidence, quite inadmissible. The overwhelmingly military nature of French support – with equipment and expertise labelled as "coopération" – had been a consideration during the Senate enquiry. It uncovered thirty-one direct transfers of weapons to Rwanda that had taken place in disregard of the correct export procedures.[15] Some answers seemed hard to come by. The report noted on weapons transfers: "The mission does not believe that it has uncovered the whole truth on this subject and particularly it does not claim, in respect of arms transfers, to have elucidated all the cases evoked in various articles ... about parallel markets and deliveries carried out at the time of the massacres in April 1994, or after the embargo announced by the UN on 17 May". There is most certainly a huge amount of information still hidden from view in French archives and the documentary evidence provided in the annexes to the Senate report is sparse, given the potential for disclosure. The Rwandan army, as far as the Senate discovered, was a "military protégé" of France and there had been French people involved who had been determined to prevent an RPF victory at all costs.

In 1994 senior French military officers had been embedded in the Rwandan armed forces. There are believed to have been at least forty senior French military personnel involved in advising Rwandan armed forces. Dallaire testified to more than twenty French advisors at lieutenant-colonel rank and very senior NCOs integrated into the units of the government forces. Dallaire notes that the Belgians too had people "in the entrails of the gendarmerie and right into the army headquarters of the RGF".[16]

The presence in Rwanda of a French mercenary, Captain Paul Barril, gives yet another dimension to the tragedy. He was spotted in Kigali at the end of 1993, telling people that he had been taken on as an "advisor" to President Juvénal Habyarimana.[17] Barril was a notorious figure. A former number two of the French Groupe d'Intervention de la Gendarmerie Nationale (GIGN), police special forces, Barril had been implicated in a corruption scandal in 1982 and was said to have been part of a plot to manufacture evidence against alleged Irish terrorists. Afterwards he helped to create an anti-terrorist cell in the Elysée Palace that answered only to President Mitterrand. Barril next went freelance creating his own private security companies. He had been working for the Rwandans since 1989 when he was taken on by President Habyarimana to reorganise the intelligence service operated from within the Presidential Guard. In 1994 Barril's services were required again when the interim government asked him to help them recuperate $US 1.65 million from an arms dealer who had apparently been paid by Rwanda for weapons, but who had failed to deliver the merchandise. Barril later claimed to have been in Kigali on

7 April, and again on 27 April when he said he had been at the French embassy "safeguarding the image of France".[18]

Barril did not give evidence to the Senate enquiry.

It would appear that French policy, largely run by a circle of Franco-African experts and businessmen, and unaccountable to either parliament or the public, centred on the Africa Unit, established in the president's Elysée Palace. There is evidence that this parallel structure used its own group of special forces in Rwanda: French soldiers, probably legionnaires, were living under assumed names near a major military camp, conducting special operations, and keeping watch on hangars full of weapons.[19]

Throughout three months of the genocide, the French government continued to confer legitimacy on the interim government of Rwanda, while seemingly ignoring the reality of what was happening. On 13 May, 1994 Bernard Kouchner, the founder of Médecins Sans Frontières (MSF), had arrived unannounced in Kigali and told Dallaire that the French government, concerned about nightly news bulletins on Rwandan massacres, was seriously looking at changing its attitude towards the Rwandan government. What would help was a demonstration of goodwill, and Kouchner suggested that perhaps the government of Rwanda could be associated with the release of some of the 400 orphans trapped at a Kigali orphanage. These children could then be flown to France. To help obtain their release Kouchner went to see Colonel Théoneste Bagosora at the Hôtel des Diplomates to discuss the complex problem of moving the children from behind the roadblocks to the airport. Kouchner and Bagosora agreed that the operation was a priority.[20] Dallaire said that Kouchner had advised him that it was in his own interests that these orphans were safely released: the "gesture" would help Dallaire in France, where, Kouchner told him, he was seen in a very bad light.[21]

France, a staunch and seemingly unquestioning ally of Rwanda, had not wavered despite previous frequent and serious human rights abuses. Before the genocide of 1994 there was a pattern to the killing, the methods described in human rights reports. There was detailed evidence that 2,000 Rwandan civilians had been killed in atrocious massacres. In France there had been considerable lobbying by human rights groups to try to trigger a change in the French policy to Rwanda.[22] Not one public government statement even commented: France cut no aid, withdrew no troops. As far as can be ascertained, the French policy seemed to based on the fact that Rwanda was at a crossroads between anglophone and francophone Africa. French military help to Rwanda was not exceptional given similar involvement with other African allies. A strong French interest on the continent was a key pillar of French foreign policy.

In the Security Council in New York, France did not take advantage of its position on the Council to provide crucial information about Rwanda that it surely possessed. Until France decided to push for its own military operation, Operation Turquoise, it kept a relatively low profile in the Council. The French ambassador to the UN, Jean-Bernard Mérimée, blamed the UK and the US ambassadors for the failure over Rwanda. "I remember very well", he said, "the attitude of Madeleine Albright and David Hannay ... they didn't want to set foot in there".[23]

The Crash

We may never know who was responsible for shooting down the president's plane in Kigali at 8. 30 pm on 6 April 1994. All that is certain is that several eye witnesses saw two missiles fired and then hit the Falcon jet as it was coming in to land. As the wrecked plane lay smouldering in the presidential garden, the rumours began and today there is a plethora of speculation about who was responsible. The unlikelihood of an international investigation would give it the appearance of a perfect crime.

One of the first people at the crash site was the head of the French military mission to Rwanda, Lt.-Colonel Grégoire de Saint Quentin. Formerly of the French National Gendarmerie, de Saint Quentin was attached to the Rwandan para commando battalion. He had gone to the site to retrieve the bodies of the French crew and had returned the next day to get the black box, without success.[24] One ICTR prosecution witness, who claims to have been at the presidential villa, said that on the night of the crash two French officers had arrived to obtain the aircraft's black box.[25]

In those early hours, before returning to headquarters from the École Supérieure Militaire, Dallaire had been ushered into a side room to find two officers from the French military assistance mission in Rwanda offering him help with an investigation, telling him that there was a French military and technical team in Bangui, the capital of the Central African

Republic, some six hours away. Dallaire declined. An enquiry should be international. But there was no UN enquiry into the crash. There were UN peacekeepers, sent by Dallaire that night to the crash site, but they were prevented by Presidential Guard from reaching the wreckage. Dallaire sent peacekeepers to the place from where the missiles were probably fired. Nothing was found. It was May before the UN got access to the plane. Later it emerged that news was broadcast by RTLM that those responsible were from the RPF, and that Belgian UNAMIR troops had been in on the plot. It was a story that spread like wildfire. Dallaire would later testify that nothing was done to counteract it and that it was broadcast repeatedly.

Belgian military intelligence had instigated an immediate enquiry, and agents the next day reported to Brussels that in all likelihood the plane had been downed by soldiers who had not wanted the peace agreement to work. Five days later, on 12 April, another report informed headquarters that everyone believed that Colonel Bagosora was responsible for the assassination. Yet another report on 15 April, classified "B", indicating high grade intelligence, gave details of an informer, who had been in contact with a former Rwandan minister and a high-ranking officer of the Rwandan armed forces. These two revealed that Bagosora was behind the attack, and that whoever was in the control tower was also involved.[26] On 22 April Belgian agents produced revised information, also classified "B". "We therefore, need to review our position regarding those responsible for the attack against the presidential plane. Now, everything points to the fact that the perpetrators are part of the faction of the Bahutus inside the Rwandan army, and this is strange … [it] leads us to believe that there was no improvisation in the events." These intelligence agents told Brussels that half an hour after the crash and well before the official announcement over the radio, ethnic cleansing started inside the country, and was carried out brutally on the basis of preestablished lists. The group responsible was gravitating around the president's wife, whose brothers and cousins had become senior authorities or dignitaries in the regime. "These high dignitaries were involved in terror and money and it was difficult for them to give up their privileges and advantages", the 22 April report noted.

The intelligence gathered elsewhere led to no firm conclusions and US experts were apparently baffled. A declassified US State Department document, dated 18 May, 1994, and addressed to Assistant Secretary of

State George Moose, states: "Who killed the president? The assassins of Presidents Habyarimana and Ntaryamira may never be known. The black box from the aeroplane has probably been recovered by Rwandan government officials who controlled the airport when the plane was shot down, or, according to unconfirmed reports, by French military officials who later secured the airport and removed the body of the French pilot from Habyarimana's plane after the crash."

The French ambassador to Rwanda, Jean-Philippe Marlaud, while conceding there was no material evidence available, seems to have believed that the RPF was the most likely culprit. At the end of April, in a note to the foreign ministry in Paris, Marlaud wrote that the case against the Habyarimana inner circle was thin. Marlaud thought that "given the events immediately after the crash, with the authorities in disarray", a coup d'état was unlikely. The army commander was on the plane and his death had seriously weakened the Rwandan armed forces. If Rwandan army officers had been responsible, a less costly way could have been found to scupper the accords. Marlaud thought that what was happening was a repetition of events in February 1993. At that time the RPF had suddenly advanced on Kigali but only after goading the government side. The RPF had "pushed the other side to extremes", looking for a suitable excuse to invade. This time the Rwandan government had been fearful of a trap. Marlaud told Paris that after the assassination of the president there had been murderous reprisals by a section of the Presidential Guard against the opposition and the Tutsi. These reprisals had given the RPF the pretext it had wanted all along. Marlaud advised: "the Hutu, as long as they think the RPF are trying to take power, will react with ethnic massacres". The only hope for Rwanda was an end to the fighting.[27]

At a press conference in Nairobi, three weeks after the genocide began, Mathieu Ngirumpatse, the president of the MRND, and Justin Mugenzi, the minister of commerce in the interim government, gave their own version. Rwanda had suffered an attempted coup organised by the prime minister, Agathe Uwilingiyimana. Ngirumpatse further claimed that the ten Belgian peacekeepers killed in the early hours of 7 April "had died in battle" after one of them fired on a Rwandan soldier. The massacres taking place at present were the result of "popular anger", which was difficult to control, but the interim government was determined to hunt down those responsible. The RPF had assassinated the president with the connivance of Uganda. The Rwandan government, claimed Ngirumpatse, had the black box, but had no time to mount an inquiry.[28]

The idea of an attempted coup organized by the prime minister was the version preferred by the president's widow, living in a recently purchased flat in Paris. Agathe Kanziga, evacuated by a French plane four days after the crash, had announced that the Belgians were implicated because their troops had been in charge of security at the airport, a statement she would later retract under pressure from the French government. The coup, Kanziga explained, had involved soldiers from the south who had turned out to be loyal to the president. Kanziga had hired the French mercenary, Paul Barril, to find out who had killed her husband. Later, on 28 June, Barril gave a press conference in Paris. Holding up a black box, he said it had come from the Falcon. Barril alleged that the RPF had shot down the presidential jet.

A different version of events was given to ICTR investigators when they had interviewed Jean Kambanda, the prime minister in the interim government. Kambanda had said that while he was in exile he had learned that President Sese Seko Mobutu of neighbouring Zaire had warned President Habyarimana not to go to Dar-Es-Salaam on 6 April, but that Habyarimana had said he had no choice. Mobuto said the warning had come from a very senior official in the Elysée Palace in Paris. There was a link between this warning, said Mobutu, and the subsequent suicide in the Elysée of a senior high-ranking official working for President François Mitterrand, a man who had killed himself on 7 April after learning about the downing of the Falcon.

This man was François de Grossouvre, a presidential advisor on African affairs.[29] Too many threads link this man to Rwanda not to raise serious questions about the policies that were formulated in these presidential offices.[30]

There is also another explanation, and this one which was first reported in Brussels by the Africa Editor of *Le Soir*, the journalist Colette Braeckman. Some weeks after the crash, in mid-June 1984, Braeckman reported in her newspaper that she had received a letter from someone calling himself "Thadée", who claimed to be a militia leader in Kigali. He told her that two members of the French Détachement d'Assistance Militaire et l'Instruction (DAMI), had launched the missiles on behalf the CDR party. Only four members of the CDR were involved. Those who fired the missiles had worn Belgian army uniforms stolen from the hotel Le

Méridien. They were spotted leaving Masaka hill by members of the Presidential Guard. The missiles had been portable, probably SAM, originally from the Soviet Union. Braeckman reported that during the three days after the missile attack some 3,000 people living in the Masaka area were murdered.[31]

The academic Gérard Prunier, an expert on the Great Lakes region of Africa, would tell the French Senate that there were witnesses who saw white men on Masaka hill on the evening of 6 April. It would have been possible to hire mercenaries to do this, said Prunier, and if mercenaries had been involved then Paul Barril would know them. Prunier believed that Habyarimana had become a handicap for Hutu Power. In 1998 the French Senate commission drew no conclusions about the assassination of Habyarimana. The final report revealed that the view of the commissioners was only a hope that one day others would pursue the truth.

The International Civil Aviation Authority (ICAO) did not conduct an enquiry. The aircraft was a state aircraft in its own territory and so it was not covered by the ICAO international convention. No investigation was required and none was undertaken.[32] There was a flicker of interest at the ICAO, but only at the request of Belgium and the crash was discussed by the ICAO council on 25 April, 1994. The minutes record that the council President suspended further consideration until Belgium provided more information. To date, no further information from Belgium has been received.

It would be ten years before the attack on the Falcon jet was headline news again. In March 2004, to coincide with this anniversary, *Le Monde* ran a story that there was evidence to prove that the RPF was responsible for the assassination on 6 April 1994.[33] A six-year investigation by a French judge, Jean-Louis Bruguière, an anti-terrorism expert, had been conducted on behalf of one of the families of the French crew. The full Bruguière report had yet to be made public and *Le Monde* journalist Stephen Smith had been allowed to read sections of it. A part of the *Le Monde* story concerned abandoned launchers of the ground-to air missiles, those that apparently had struck the jet. The missiles were part of a batch bought in Moscow in 1987 and then supplied by the Ugandan government to the RPF. The launchers, complete with their serial numbers, had been discovered on 25 April, 1994 – less than three weeks after the crash – by a peasant looking for wood. The missile parts were taken to an army camp where a Rwanda soldier, Lieutenant Augustin Munyaneza, had examined them and written a report.

The information was not new; these missile parts were the subject of a series of documents published in an annexe to the French Senate enquiry in 1998. The original source of the serial numbers of these missile launchers was Colonel Théoneste Bagosora who had given the information to a Belgian political scientist, Professor Filip Reyntjens.

One of Bruguière's informants was Paul Barril. Barril told journalists that he was a good friend to the judge for they had been chasing terrorists for years. According to *Le Monde*, hundreds of witnesses were interviewed in the enquiry, including some key RPF "dissidents". There was a former commando in the RPF, Abdul Ruzibiza, who claimed that a "network commando" unit had been created within the RPF to carry out the assassination and that a team had gone to Masaka Hill, just a few kilometres from the airport, to fire the missiles. Another RPF "dissident", Jean-Pierre Mugabe, a political refugee in the US, accused the RPF leadership of having been so determined to seize power that they had been prepared to sacrifice the Tutsi in Rwanda. Mugabe also gave details to Bruguière for inclusion in his report.

There were voices of dissent. A French lawyer representing Jacqueline Héraud, the widow of the Falcon's pilot, said that the enquiry had not come to a conclusion. In an interview, Laurent Curt said there were still a number of leads to follow. At issue was not how the plane was destroyed but who did it. The delay in finalising the report had more to do with the information obtained by Bruguière that implicated people in France who had known what was to happen and yet had failed to do anything to prevent it. Curt believed that neither the flight data recorder nor the cockpit voice recorder was of any use in identifying the killers. Curt confirmed that Bruguière was in possession of transcripts of the conversation in the Kigali control tower on the night of 6 April, but said that this information added nothing new.[34]

One further revelation in *Le Monde* was that the jet's black box had been in the possession of the UN all along and was to be found in a filing cabinet in the Department of Peacekeeping Operations in the Secretariat building in New York. There were claims of a UN cover-up. But as it turned out a statement issued later from the UN's Office of Internal Oversight Services (OIOS), revealed that the particular black box that was found did not come from the Falcon jet and that there would have to be a review in the department of "the information flow".[35]

The current president of Rwanda, Paul Kagame, has vehemently denied RPF involvement in the attack. He has said that given the means the Rwandan government would mount an enquiry, seeking UN help in this endeavour. "In the interests of truth and to put the matter finally to rest, the government of Rwanda supports a full investigation conducted by the ICTR involving all political and military groups that were present in Rwanda in 1994 … the Rwandan government will co-operate, as it has done in the past."[36] Regarding the assassination, Kagame believed that there had been a split at the heart of the regime: Habyarimana had begun to push for a change of direction but a group of extremists had been intent on destroying the Arusha Accords. Habyarimana finally reached the point where he was arguing that if the Arusha Accords were accepted, then solutions to the political impasse over the extremist CND could be found later. That was why Habyarimana had taken his army chief to Dar-es-Salaam on 6 April. Habyarimana may have realised that Colonel Deogratias Nsabimana was conspiring against him. He feared for his life.

The former ICTR prosecutor, Swiss advocate Carla Del Ponte, appointed by the Security Council in 1999, argued when she was in office against the tribunal mounting an investigation. Although the attack set everything in motion, she said, an enquiry did not fall within the tribunal mandate.

Accountability

The 1994 genocide in Rwanda should have been condemned internationally in the strongest possible terms. From the moment the extent of the killing was evident, certainly two weeks into the slaughter all countries, at the very least, should have severed diplomatic ties with the interim government and expelled Rwandan ambassadors. Anyone who was trying to represent a government presiding over – in fact perpetrating – genocide should have had no place in the civilized world. Instead there was silence. From start to finish, all governments continued to recognize the interim government as legitimate.

The interim government of Rwanda was represented in the Security Council, in the General Assembly, in Geneva in the UN Commission for

Human Rights and other parts of the UN system: its representatives had sat with the Organization of African Unity and it had been represented in the various capitals of Europe and the US.

A change in attitude did not come until the RPF was on the verge of taking the capital. The first indication came from the US State Department when it unexpectedly cancelled invitations to Rwandan diplomats abroad to attend the US Independence Day celebrations on 4 July.[37]

So many questions remain. Although no one – including the RPF – could have predicted the scale of the killings in Rwanda, there were significant warnings that a disaster of some sort was imminent. The evidence about the continuing threats to Rwandan civilians was provided in human rights reports. There was detailed information available about militia training, arms dumps, political murders, hate propaganda and death lists.

This must call into question the policies devised towards Rwanda by the UK government, under the then prime minister John Major, and the US administration of President Bill Clinton. Both played a major role shaping UN policy before and during the genocide, and yet little is known about how decisions were arrived at, the information upon which they were based and why the respective ambassadors in the Council – David Hannay and Madeleine Albright – acted in the way that they did.

They had been reluctant about the UN mission for Rwanda from the beginning, arguing in 1993 that with 70,000 peacekeepers deployed the UN was over-stretched. These states had also argued that in Rwanda, with a peace agreement in place, and the obvious goodwill of all the parties, there should be a more limited role for UNAMIR than that envisaged in the Arusha Accords.

Then there is the difficult issue of early warning. In the UN Secretariat there was the information about Rwanda provided to US and UK diplomats by the Belgian UN ambassador, Paul Noterdaeme, who in February 1994 was instructed by his foreign ministry to warn that UNAMIR was in deep trouble. The rising level of extremism was increasingly dangerous. A stronger mandate and reinforcements were urgently necessary. The US and the UK ambassadors rejected these ideas on economic grounds.

After the genocide began, the policy of the UK and the US of insisting on a ceasefire in the renewed civil war was critical. This paid little heed to the fact that massacres of civilians were taking place nowhere near the fighting. Every effort was made by some of the non-permanent members of the council – New Zealand, Spain, Nigeria – to get the US and the UK to focus not on the civil war, but on the daily murder of thousands upon thousands of civilians. Their objective by mid-April was to call what was happening a genocide so as to build international support for reinforcement of UNAMIR.[38] There was resistance from the US and the UK about the use of the word. This indicated that officials may have believed that there was either a legal or a moral obligation to act once a genocide determination had been made.

Neither the US or the UK paid any attention at all to either stabilising or reinforcing the residual force of UN peacekeepers that had stayed behind. This was why Dallaire and his tiny garrison were abandoned. In the secret and informal meetings of the council their respective ambassadors were keen to downplay the fact of genocide and both were reluctant to take even the slightest action – such as jamming the hate radio.

Then there is the vexed question of when the US and the UK knew that what was happening was genocide. Sources close to the Clinton administration have shown how quickly senior officials understood the magnitude of the killing.[39] In the UK sources have also confirmed that within two weeks genocide was apparent, the information coming from reputable sources: the ICRC and Oxfam.[40] To continue then to depict the genocide as the latest round in a chaotic and bloody civil war served only to obscure the reality of the situation and fuel the impression that anything other than massive external intervention would be unable to prevent the slaughter.

In the House of Commons on 9 May, 1994 the parliamentary under-secretary of state for foreign and commonwealth affairs, Mark Lennox-Boyd, had observed in a written answer: "There are estimates that more than 200,000 may have perished in recent fighting in Rwanda … It is a horrific and tragic civil war." At the time several British ministers and officials were making confident assertions that intervention would make no difference.

The British public had depended on the media to know what was going on. But in the press there was a failure from the beginning to adequately report the scale and the nature of the genocide. The mass killings were described as incomprehensible to outsiders: the killing was not or negotiable nor amenable to reason. The newspapers described "hopeless, helpless horror", taking place in a relatively unknown country, far away.

In May, when there were African troops available for Rwanda with offers from ten countries, neither the US nor the UK, both with the capacity to do so, was willing to provide either airlift or equipment. The US did offer to lease to the UN armoured personnel carriers that were in storage in Germany, and the UK was willing to provide fifty trucks, but none of this equipment arrived in time to save any lives.

Also in May, the US actively blocked action for Rwanda by insisting in the council that any UN operation should involve "protected sites" on the borders, thereby preventing any help at all for Dallaire and the remaining peacekeepers. For this the presidency of Bill Clinton and his senior officials must bear full responsibility. Madeleine Albright would later claim that it would be weeks before she understood the nature and scale of the violence, blaming the UN for a lack of information.[41] President Bill Clinton also seems to be convinced that the fault was a lack of information. "All over the world there were people like me", he would say on a visit to Rwanda in 1998, "sitting in offices, day after day after day, who did not fully appreciate the depth and speed with which you were being engulfed by this unimaginable terror".

And so Dallaire was, in his own words, "left to hang out and dry" by those countries who were in positions of power in the Council, with the means to help, and yet who refused to do so. The UK and the US possessed the military and logistical capabilities that could have made a significant difference. Instead policies were adopted that did not impede the genocide and then helped to prolong it. It would appear that a serious assessment of the situation was missing, while the press variously blamed either the "UN peacekeepers" or "the UN" for the tragic failure.

Nearly a month after the Security Council's decision on 17 May to deploy 5,500 troops to Rwanda, the news on BBC television, in a first in–depth and critical report concerning the delay by the UN in finding troops to go, was the following: "the worse the suffering gets for millions of Rwandans, the more innocent people who are massacred, the more paralysed the United Nations seems to be."[42] One print journalist said the lack of action was because Rwanda "was not important enough". It was a former Belgian colony. It was in the francophone sphere, and was therefore of little interest to the Foreign Office.[43]

While at the UN there has been a willingness to uncover what happened, in Washington and London there is a lack of interest in who was responsible for the policies towards Rwanda and how they were decided.[44] Requests in the US for a congressional investigation into the Clinton administration's decision-making are ignored. Only a fraction of the government documents regarding the issue have been released in the US.

In Washington from 7 April there were intercepted communications from Rwandan officials in Kigali ordering massacres in outlying districts, and within a day or two the Defence Intelligence Agency had photographs of massacre sites with thousands of bodies. This intelligence targeting was part of the operation to evacuate the US citizens.[45] The deputy chief of the US embassy in Kigali, Joyce Leader, when she was back in Washington, reported that genocide was taking place.

If neither the White House nor the State Department was made aware in the first weeks that a genocide was underway then this indicates a critical lack of coordination, although it has been speculated that there was so much intelligence to analyse that this part of it became buried.[46] One former US official has claimed that the government knew of the extent and nature of the killing within ten to fourteen days after 6 April.[47] There has been no official explanation why an American operative had arrived in Kigali before the crash of the president's plane with a "Noncombatant Evacuation Order" (NEO), to rescue all 257 US nationals present in the country.

In the UK the Labour prime minister, Tony Blair, has said that in retrospect, if nearly a million people were being murdered in Rwanda today, as they had been in 1994, then the British government would have both a political and a moral duty to prevent or suppress the killing.[48] In January 2000, Blair declared the establishment of an annual Holocaust Memorial Day for, as he pointed out, the lessons that the Holocaust taught us for our own time must never be forgotten.[49] And yet there exists no apparent awareness to understand his predecessor's failure over Rwanda, or how it might help to formulate government policy for the future in trying to predict genocide, or even to support an initiative to build up a genocide prevention capability into the UN.[50]

There is one indication of an awareness in the UK government that grievous mistakes were made. In a telling paragraph in the 2005 Report of the Commission for Africa, commissioned by Blair, are the words: "Just 5,000 troops with robust peace enforcement capabilities could have saved half a million lives in Rwanda. Evidence shows that prevention can work".[51]

Otherwise the genocide is airbrushed from history. Although the government of Prime Minister John Major had prided itself on the promotion of human rights, Rwanda is somehow missing from the writings and memoirs of key figures. In John Major's 1999 autobiography, the chapter called "The Wider World" has no reference to the genocide. In Malcolm Rifkind's case, the UK defence secretary in 1994 did not consider events in Rwanda significant enough to warrant a mention in a keynote speech on British foreign policy made less than a year after the genocide ended. As the genocide had progressed the foreign secretary, Douglas Hurd, wrote a newspaper article in which he made it quite clear that the responsibility belonged to "the UN". It was "the UN" that should pay more attention to preventive diplomacy. And "the UN" could only act, he pointed out, if member states were prepared to support it with money, resources and troops, and with their political muscle.[52] In his memoirs, Hurd would devote a few lines to Rwanda, although the word was not mentioned in the index. "I could not honestly list Rwanda among the major preoccupations at the Foreign Office", he wrote. And then in an astonishing admission from a former foreign secretary of a permanent member of the Security Council, Hurd wrote that Rwanda was a country with which the UK was "little concerned". News about Rwanda had come through imperfectly and late. "It never occurred to us, the Americans or anyone else to send combatant troops to Rwanda to stop the killing. I record this as a bleak fact". Furthermore, Hurd insisted that it was nonsense to say that the lesson had been learned and that, as President Clinton had asserted, the next time the West would not stand idly by. Hurd writes: "The doctrine of humanitarian intervention will never be universal; it will always depend on time, place and circumstance ... we deceive ourselves with our own speeches."[53]

Of pivotal importance for Britain's African policy was Lynda Chalker, head of the Overseas Development Agency, who has not yet shared her knowledge of these events. In July, 1994, Chalker had told an audience on BBC Newsnight that "the UN should get its procurement right".

There are people who were in office at the time who have spoken anonymously. A retired senior civil servant said that there was a warning given to the Cabinet Office before the genocide started. "We weren't indifferent", said one source, "it's just that we didn't know what to do". There was an assumption that there would be massive loss of life, similar to that in Burundi in October 1993. "But", said another, "when it got to 100,000 dead, we thought it was a bit persistent".

The focus had been to get the Arusha Accords implemented. This was confirmed by David Hannay, Britain's UN ambassador. The UK had been "extremely unsighted" over Rwanda, for there was no British embassy there. Telegrams about Rwanda were not treated as "high grade". There had been inadequate briefings given to the Council, Hannay said. Even if the genocide had been acknowledged, then there was nothing the UN could have done, given a Hutu government intent on it.[54]

Britain's stringent laws on government secrecy will ensure that we will never know how the UK's policy towards the genocide in Rwanda was made. Even when the official records are available the full story may not emerge for it has been claimed that the relevant documents in Whitehall already show evidence of weeding.

As permanent members of the UN Security Council, the UK and the US could have taken action in accordance with the 1948 Convention on the Prevention and the Punishment of the Crime of Genocide, a legally binding treaty. The post-Holocaust promise of "never again" is enshrined in the convention, establishing a collective commitment to prevent ongoing and systematic murder of any group of people. In 1994 the US and the UK undermined international law over Rwanda. While these states resisted even using the word genocide, this would appear to indicate that they were aware that it carried some form of obligation to act.

In both London and Washington, and at the UN in New York, there were politicians and civil servants who took decisions that cost the lives of an incalculable number of people. They should bear full responsibility for those decisions.

12

JUDGEMENT

Seven months after the genocide was over, on 19 February, 1995, Colonel Théoneste Bagosora was spotted boarding a plane in Kinshasa, Zaire, on his way to Cameroon. It was one of a number of trips he had made to meet up with former colleagues: Ferdinand Nahimana the propagandist; Joseph Nzirorera, the secretary-general of the MRND; Lieutenant-Colonel Anatole Nsengiyumva; Majors Léonard Nkundiye and Protais Mpiranya; Jean-Bosco Barayagwiza, founding member of the CDR. And Bagosora's brother, Pasteur Musabe, was also there.

They were gaining weight now, and living an almost idle existence. They held fundraisers and they managed to collect thousands of dollars for Hutu Power, the cause which they knew lived on with the estimated 2.5 million Rwandans and their exiled army in refugee camps. In reality they were not defeated, just chased out of the country.

The president of Cameroon, Paul Biya, was reluctant to take action against the group of exiled Rwandans, even though the Belgian government was pushing hard to get Bagosora to stand trial for the murder of the peacekeepers. Bagosora was also under surveillance by agents from the government in Kigali. Finally arrested in Yaoundé on 10 March, 1996, he had been trying to cash American Express travellers cheques that had been taken from the Rwandan state treasury in Kigali.

In Cameroon eleven more Rwandans were taken into custody two weeks later in a surprise operation involving 100 gendarmes organised by the Cameroon Justice Minister, Douala Moutone. The arrests came at dawn and included Ferdinand Nahimana and Jean-Bosco Barayagwiza. Several others, Nziorera, Mpiranya and Nkundiye among them, managed to escape.

There were conflicting claims over this group of prisoners languishing in Cameroon's central gaol in Yaoundé. The government in Kigali immediately despatched a high level delegation to Cameroon to secure their arrest and return them to Rwanda for trial. But the government of Cameroon, and President Biya, were under a barrage of media criticism for having taken part in an "anti-Hutu" campaign. There were claims that the "Tutsi regime" in Kigali was trying to neutralise resistance and hostility. In the journal *Africa International* it was pointed out that the Hutu were after all the majority people in Rwanda. From prison, Barayagwiza told the *Cameroon Tribune*: "The Hutu community is ready to negotiate with those Tutsi who have taken power in Kigali, to talk about power sharing …".[1]

International pressure on Biya increased. The Chief Prosecutor of the International Criminal Tribunal for Rwanda (ICTR), a South African judge, Richard Goldstone, was also asking for extradition. Goldstone first sent a written request, followed by a visit to Yaoundé. There were continued delays. Next, an ICTR judge, a Swede, Lennart Aspegren, so worried at how long this was taking, went to Cameroon. There he managed to persuade the ministry of justice to allow him access to the prison where he held a special session of the ICTR, and acting under international law, ordered the provisional detention of Bagosora and his transfer to international custody. Aspegren requested the Cameroon government to effect as soon as possible the tribunal's order of 17 May, 1996 for the transfer of Bagosora to Arusha. Only in January 1997 was a decree issued to transfer him to ICTR custody. He was moved immediately to Arusha and locked in a cell in a special compound called the UN Detention Facility, built inside a top security prison just outside the town.

The tribunal had been created by the Security Council on 8 November, 1994 under Resolution 955, to put on trial those responsible for genocide and other serious crimes against international humanitarian law. By now the fact of genocide in Rwanda had been fully and officially recognised.

The ICTR was the second international criminal tribunal since the establishment of the UN, the first having been established to deal with crimes against humanity in the former Yugoslavia. The scope of the ICTR was however limited. Article 1 of its statute read: "The International Criminal Tribunal for Rwanda shall have the power to prosecute persons responsible for serious violations of international humanitarian law committed in the territory of Rwanda, and Rwandan citizens responsible for such violations ... between 1 January and 31 December, 1994".

The post-genocide government in Rwanda argued unsuccessfully that the court's jurisdiction should cover the period 1 October, 1990 to 17 July, 1994. The ICTR's restricted mandate meant that the human rights abuses detailed in reports prior to the 1994 genocide would remain unpunished. Yet the creation of the ICTR was at least a signal that in some instances the rule of international law would be upheld.

The statute for the tribunal was based in large part on the UN Commission of Experts October 1994 report which had maintained that there were "substantial grounds" to conclude that the RPF had also committed serious breaches of international law. While the killings were not systematic or even approved by government or army commanders, the commission recommended that an investigation into the violations of international humanitarian law, and of human rights law attributed to the RPF, be continued by the Prosecutor. This was largely due to French pressure in the Security Council pushing for the tribunal to investigate the alleged violations of humanitarian law by the RPF during the genocide and afterwards.

The investigation into the circumstances of the genocide by the ICTR got off to a slow start. Judge Richard Goldstone says that at the beginning he was visited "by serious historians and professors from universities, particularly from Belgium and France" who told him that stories of genocide were untrue. But gradually evidence was assembled, witnesses were found, and some documents were obtained. Goldstone believes today that the tribunal did manage to establish "historical truth".[2]

It was not an easy task. In January 1995 an ICTR prosecutor's office was established in Kigali, but it lacked funding. In April, a year after the genocide began, Goldstone was obliged to travel to New York to complain that investigations were impossible due to a lack of money.

The Kigali offices of the ICTR had five staff where 100 were needed. There were apparently 400 suspects at large and identified in Africa, Europe and North America. Three years after the genocide, on 9 April, 1997, the Rwandan survivors group Ibuka demonstrated outside the prosecutor's office in Kigali to object that many key leaders of the genocide had still not been investigated and prosecuted. The ICTR was remote to them. It had been established in Arusha, Tanzania, some 800 kilometers away, in the place where the peace agreement had been negotiated and signed.

At the beginning Goldstone had issued a press release to announce that the immediate and primary focus of his investigation and prosecution would be directed at those who had planned and executed the genocide. He acknowledged that a significant number of these people now resided outside Rwanda. But although the investigation had begun with the intention of prioritising the conspiracy to commit genocide, a decision was eventually taken that a more important consideration was to secure a conviction as soon as possible.

The first case to be completed by the court was that of a bourgmestre from the Taba commune in Gitarama, Jean-Paul Akayesu, convicted on 2 September, 1998 for the crime of genocide and sentenced to life imprisonment, confirmed on appeal. Akayesu, a teacher and school inspector was not a part of the national leadership. He had pleaded not guilty.

The Akayesu case was the first time that the crime of genocide had been tried in an international court. The crime had been defined by the 1948 Genocide Convention, but since that time no international court had adjudicated on the basis of the convention's provisions. Akayesu was found guilty of "genocide, direct and public incitement to commit genocide, and crimes against humanity (extermination, murder, torture, rape and other inhumane acts)".[3] A major contribution of the Akayesu case was its analysis and application of the terms of the 1948 convention.

Another milestone concerned the conviction in December 2003 of Ferdinand Nahimana, Jean-Bosco Barayagwiza and Hassan Ngeze.[4] These three were held to account for the racist campaign waged in newspapers and the vitriolic radio station, Radio-Télévision Libre des Mille Collines (RTLM). The judgement, after a three year trial, determined that there had been collaboration between them as a group, either as a trio or in pairs. Ngeze, the owner of an overtly racist magazine, *Kangura,* Barayagwiza, a lawyer, diplomat, and an RTLM director and Nahimana, a propagandist and history professor were found to have promoted the targeting of the Tutsi population for destruction. This was the first time since Julius Streicher, notorious for his anti-Semitic journal *Der Stürmer*, and hanged as a war criminal in 1946, that journalists had stood accused in an international criminal court for using words to kill. The court heard that the broadcasts of the hate radio were an integral part of the genocide conspiracy and once the genocide began the radio had a fundamental role in naming victims. The first target of RTLM had been democracy itself, with an immediate campaign against the Arusha Accords.

The media trial was part of a prosecution strategy to speed up the process by arranging the accused into small groups based on different issues. In this way it was hoped that a nationwide conspiracy would be revealed. The trials of the interim government ministers and other political leaders take place in two courtrooms with a total of seven defendants. In one court the MRND president, Mathieu Ngirumpatse, arrested in Mali in 1998 and Joseph Nzirorera, the party's secretary-general, joined Edouard Karemera, who was the MRND's vice-president.

In another courtroom Jerome Bicamumpaka, the former foreign minister, Casimir Bizimungu, minister of health, the minister of commerce, Justin Mugenzi, and the former minister of public service, Prosper Mugiraneza, were on trial each charged with six counts including genocide and crimes against humanity.

Another trial, known as Military Two, saw the chief of staff of the Rwanda army, Augustin Bizimungu, arrested in Angola in 2002, joined by the former head of the gendarmerie, General Augustin Ndindiliyimana, arrested in Belgium two years earlier. The former commander of the reconnaissance battalion, Major François-Xavier Nzuwonemeye, and his deputy Innocent Sagahutu were included in this case. The defendants in these trials plead not guilty.

The prosecution case is the result of some eleven years' investigation. The case relies in large part on the expert report of the historian Alison des Forges, advisor to Human Rights Watch, and on a series of Rwandan witnesses to the events themselves. Some of these witnesses who have been called to testify are former senior Interahamwe. Some witnesses travel from Rwanda where they are held on death row, killers found guilty of the crime of genocide in the national courts.[5] An overwhelming number of witnesses appear in court anonymously, hidden from view in a curtained witness box. A bullet-proof screen separates the public gallery from the courtroom. The witnesses testify in more than one trial and some testify by video conferencing from Europe. Two informers have testified: Omar

Serushago, a former militia leader from Gisenyi, and Georges Ruggiu, who worked on RTLM. Both were witnesses for the prosecution.

One witness was held back. He was Michel Bagaragaza, a close relative of the Habyarimana family and now cooperating with the ICTR. In what has been described as his confidential confession he has given a version of what he says happened in the presidential palace on the night of the crash. It was the president's brother in law, Protais Zigiranyirazo, who after the plane crash had ordered the head of the Presidential Guard, Protais Mpiranya, to send soldiers to kill opposition politicians. The list was drawn up in the presence of the widow of President Habyarimana, Agathe Kanziga and his daughter Jeanne.[6] Zigiranyirazo was arrested in Brussels in 2001 and is to stand trial in 2006. Bagaragaza, the most senior member of the inner circle ever to cooperate, is held in secret in a prison in The Hague waiting to testify in this trial. The prosecutor of the ICTR announced that there were concerns for his security in the light of his voluntary surrender to the tribunal.[7]

Among those now in custody at the UN Detention Facility are: Colonel Tharcisse Renzaho, préfet of Kigali, arrested in 2002 in the Democratic Republic of Congo; Joseph Serugendo, former technical director of RTLM, arrested in Gabon in 2005. Those who evade international justice include the billionaire businessman Felicien Kabuga and his son in law, Augustin Ngirabatware, the former minister of planning. The former minister of defence, August Bizimana, and the former commander of the presidential guards, Major Protais Mpiranya, are still at large.

The ICTR has achieved a total of seventy-two arrests in twenty countries. It has completed a total of twenty-six cases.

Planning Genocide

The prosecution case relies on the fact that the massacres perpetrated in Rwanda in 1994 were the result of a strategy and that strategy was adopted and elaborated by political, civil, and military authorities. In the trial of government defendants, the prosecution lawyer Don Webster would argue forcefully in an opening statement to the court in November 2003: "It was a plan. It was a plan that had been organised at the highest level and its object was the extermination of Tutsi. The effects of it had been seen all over Rwanda." There had been a central role for the Interahamwe.

Webster told the court that one defendant Mathieu Ngirumpatse, the president of the MRND, had been the head of the Interahamwe. Another, Joseph Nzirorera, had been the national secretary of the MRND, and had been the head of the Interahamwe, certainly in his home town of Ruhengeri. With Édouard Karemera, he said, these were the leaders of the Interahamwe. These MRND leaders had come together in the interim government, and brought with them fellow travellers from the Hutu Power wings of the opposition parties.[8]

"Through intimidation and entreaty", Webster had continued, "through lies and subterfuge, through fear and coercion, [they] moulded the impoverished unlettered farmers and landless, unemployed peasants of Rwanda into an army of brutes and killers." Webster described how "civil defence" had been the means by which the interim government had eventually turned everyone into an Interahamwe: "All of the youth throughout the country who could be recruited by their bourgmestres, by their conseillers, by their préfets, became Interahamwe, and the interim government itself became an expanded government of Interahamwe." It was the MRND that had "nursed and cultivated and trained and armed and paid for" the Interahamwe. They had stoked the fires of ethnic hatred in order to use these militias to attack the Tutsi. The conspirators knew what they were doing.

"They wanted to destroy the Tutsi," Webster said. "Part of the destruction, part of that project, was not only killing the Tutsi; it was obliterating them. The whole project involved chasing Tutsis from their homes, setting fire to their homes, stealing their property, corralling them into public spaces where they could be grouped and killed more effectively."

The defendants deny the accusations against them. They deny the planning of genocide. They complain about too much hearsay evidence in the courts and they say witnesses are unreliable and too often convicted murderers sent from Rwanda and told what to say. The genocide plot was a propaganda thesis. Or as one defence lawyer, Christopher Black, representing General Augustin Ndindiliyimana, would one day say of the prosecution case: "They have not established a conspiracy. It never existed. We know that after ten years of the cases there is not one scintilla of evidence published anywhere in the world indicating that."

The foundation upon which the defence case is seen to rest is the denial of culpability for the downing of Habyarimana's plane on 6 April, 1994. The denial of responsibility for the crash is a claim that is variously, repeatedly and vigorously made in court by the defendants and their lawyers. As Black claimed to the court during the Military Two court case, the assassination of two sitting presidents and other leaders – the event that sparked the massacres – had been the subject of a cover-up. He argued that the responsibility for the missile attack had to be an integral part of the trials, to be the subject of full and fair testimony.

While blaming the RPF leadership for the crash the defendants can claim that they were responsible for starting the killing. It was the fury of the people, the revenge for the death of their beloved leader that caused so many massacres. The people feared that the "the Tutsi RPF" were coming back to enslave them. In this way the defence lawyers hope to show that the genocide was more complex than it might appear. Both sides are responsible for killing. They point repeatedly to the failure by the ICTR to prosecute a case against RPF commanders who committed crimes against humanity. They believe that international opinion has been tricked into thinking that a genocide took place by an effective and educated "pro-Tutsi lobby". With a denial of culpability in the crash the defendants are able to challenge the legitimacy of the court, for neither the court nor anyone else has carried out an investigation into the death of the president. It must therefore be a conspiracy to stifle the truth.

Just before he gave evidence in his own defence, Bagosora said in an interview with a Canadian journalist: "Here, at this tribunal, we have victor's justice ... This is not justice. But I hope to give my truth, the whole story ... There is the truth of the victor, the truth of the vanquished and the truth of international history, and I'm working for the historic truth".[9] Bagosora said he was now "in the hands of the United States".

Denial

The trial of Colonel Théoneste Bagosora began at the ICTR on 2 April, 2002. It is known by the name "Military One" to indicate the importance of the defendants in the dock. It is expected to last five years. Bagosora was charged with twelve counts, including genocide, conspiracy to commit genocide, public incitement to commit genocide, crimes against humanity for murder, extermination, rape, persecution and other inhumane acts, and violations of the Geneva Conventions. According to his indictment he had assumed de facto control of political and military affairs once the genocide began.

Bagosora is joined by three other senior commanders in the former Rwandan army, Lieutenant-Colonel Anatole Nsengiyumva, Major Aloys Ntabakuze, and Brigadier-General Gratien Kabiligi. They have yet to be judged.

Bagosora decided to testify in his own defence and he began to do so on 24 October, 2005, at the start of the defence case. Bagosora's examination in chief was conducted by his lawyer, Raphael Constant, of French Martinique. The cross-examination for the prosecution team was conducted by a Canadian, Drew White. Bagosora was in the box for seventeen days.

In the examination in chief, Constant had taken Bagosora through the events of 1994 during which Bagosora had questioned the very basis of the prosecution case, arguing that the prosecutors had failed to prove that the killings met the legal definition of genocide.

Bagosora began his evidence by telling the court that the reason he had decided to testify was to counteract the false accusations levelled against him by ill-intentioned people. Then he immediately challenged the court saying it was "common knowledge" that the president of Rwanda, Paul Kagame was responsible for the attack on the plane, the event that had triggered the killings. And yet the ICTR has so far "done nothing concrete to arrest that criminal". He blamed the court for spending time trying "the Hutu who are the vanquished, at the same time as courting the Tutsi criminals who won the war, which they themselves planned, carried out and won at the price of scores of losses, with human lives and material damage". It was the first of several statements in the course of his testimony.

He said that as the "directeur du cabinet" at the ministry of defence, he had acted within the confines of the law and military regulations. What occurred in Rwanda was something other than planned genocide; it was a reaction to the circumstances in which the Rwandan people found themselves, and it was spontaneous.

"Me, I don't believe that genocide took place", Bagosora said. "Most reasonable people think there were excessive massacres."

On the events of 6 April Bagosora explained that there had been total disarray. The only person who would have been able to contain the wave of violence was Habyarimana. Bagosora tried to explain to the court: "The elimination of Habyarimana was tantamount to actually getting rid of the only person who, at that time, because up to that time he was the only person who could contain the violence in Rwanda."

Bagosora denied that civil defence had been organised at a national level, explaining that the roadblocks were set up on the initiative of the local authorities at the lowest, grassroots level because the people had to make sure that there were no "infiltrations". The communication with the population had broken down.

After the government had left Kigali on 12 April, the capital had fallen into the hands of people who could not be controlled. Bagosora said that if he had been consulted he would not have accepted that the government leave the capital. He painted a picture of the interim government functioning as any other government and that his own role was to fulfil the normal tasks of government. He denied ever having been present at the roadblocks.

"My duties prior to the 6th of April, 1994 and also post 6th April, 1994 did not change", he told the court. "I did not have the power to go and give orders to combating units", he had said.

For the deaths of the Belgian peacekeepers on 7 April, Bagosora blamed Dallaire. He said that Dallaire should have tried to rescue them. For the death of the prime minister, Bagosora blamed the UN peacekeepers for abandoning their mission.

These peacekeepers, the escort for the prime minister, he explained, had been killed by chance. In Bagosora's own words: "Nobody thought that they were coming. Nobody, nobody could know that they would go to Agathe's house and come to the Kigali camp. So what I am saying here is that those who say that the ten Belgian troops were killed for the UNAMIR mission to fail I think they are mistaken or they are trying to mislead public opinion … we are not the ones who wanted the UN troops to leave because we ourselves already said we were not ready to wage war. We needed sufficient … a sufficient force which in the event of need would stand between us and the RPF."

Bagosora blamed the soldiers of UNAMIR for failing in the first hours to protect the opposition politicians from their assassins. Bagosora explained the killings as follows: "Personally, I think there was some settlement of scores arising from neighbourhood conflicts disputes or arising from politics or perhaps even for other reasons that I cannot define, but I believe there was a settlement of the scores, political scores or for other matters."

Bagosora blamed the population of Rwanda at local level for the massacres. Bagosora blamed the US for the "international failure". When Prudence Bushnell, the deputy assistant secretary of the Africa bureau in the State Department had called him on 28 April, she had told him that the Rwandan government army was going to lose the war. It was then he realised, said Bagosora, that the US was siding with the RPF.

Once more he turned to the subject of the missile attack on the presidential aircraft. "Personally", said Bagosora, "I suspected the RPF". He listed in court the names of the "RPF dissidents" who he claimed had provided direct witness testimony to Judge Jean-Louis Bruguière.

Drew White's cross examination for the prosecution was methodical and thorough. He pointed out to the court that from June 1988 to a period in June 1992 Bagosora had been the commander of the anti-aircraft battalion at Camp Kanombe: "As the commander of the anti-aircraft battalion you were familiar [with] the flight paths and the approaches of the aircraft to the Kanombe international airport, weren't you? There was an airport with just one strip. And one does not need to be a specialist to know that there is just one runway. And that runway goes directly over the Kanombe military camp, right?"

Bagosora told the court that Bruguière had the proof of who was responsible for the attack on the plane. The real culprits, he said, were "circulating misleading information so that people should go after the wrong information and so cover up the true information".

It was the first time that Bagosora had been questioned publicly, and a milestone in the history of the trials. White levelled at Bagosora some fierce and determined accusation:

"Colonel, I'm going to suggest to you that there was a coup on the night of April 6th, 1994. It was a coup by the Rwandan armed forces over the political authorities of the Rwandan government. And that you were the head of that coup. That you took over the power of the country of Rwanda on the night of April 6th, 1994." Bagosora denied it.

"Colonel, I'm going to suggest to you that it was no coincidence that the prime minister was killed after you took effective power and control of Rwanda on the night of April 6th, 1994", said White. Bagosora denied it.

White took Bagosora through his military career and talked to him of the time in 1973 when he had joined Juvenal Habyarimana and other military officers in a coup d'état against the then president Gregoire Kayibanda. White had asked Bagosora what was necessary to mount a coup. "As a matter of principle, a coup d'état is not legal", Bagosora conceded, then he added: "It is double or quits. If you succeed, fine. If you fail, you are done in." White said: "... in your direct testimony you told us, precisely, that you knew what was necessary to have a successful coup. And so now I'm trying to find out, in your mind, what is necessary to have a successful coup d'état?"

Bagosora replied: "You need to have enough military strength, as well as sufficient political credibility. You need a combination of both ... You ... must be convinced that if you have to address the population, they will believe you."

White was scathing about Bagosora's denial of culpability in the genocide. "Even more particularly, I suggest to you that in your testimony you have evaded truthful responses, you have fabricated new versions of events, you have reconstructed events to suit your own whims, you have changed dates, times, places, and vehicles, and there is absolutely nothing of any substance that you have said that we can rely on."

All the prisoners deny conspiracy to murder and none has shown any remorse for what happened in 1994. Their denials echo throughout the courtrooms, are translated and transcribed and filed for posterity.

NOTES

1 GENOCIDES

1 ICTR case no. 97-23-S. Judgement and Sentence. Kambanda pleaded guilty to six counts including genocide, conspiracy to commit genocide, direct and public incitement to commit genocide, complicity in genocide, crimes against humanity (murder), crimes against humanity (extermination).

2 ICTR case no. ICTR-97-23-1. Prosecutor v. Kambanda. Plea Agreement between Jean Kambanda and the Office of the Prosecutor. 29 April, 1998. Under seal. Author's archive.

3 ICTR Transcript. Interrogation of Jean Kambanda. Author's archive.

4 Mary Kimani. Internews news agency. 5 December, 2000.

5 Colonel Théoneste Bagosora, "The Assassination of President Habyarimana or the ultimate Tutsi operation to take power by force in Rwanda." Unpublished pamphlet, p. 12. Author's archive.

6 J.-B. Piollet, *Les Missions Catholique Françaises au XIXe siècle*, Les Missions d'Afrique, 1902.

7 Jan Vansina, *Le Rwanda ancien: Le Royaume Ngiyinya*, Paris: Karthala, 2001.

8 Antoine Lema, *Africa Divided: The Creation of Ethnic Groups*, Lund University Press, Sweden: 1993, p. 53.

9 There are no typical Hutu or Tutsi surnames. There are no surnames in Rwanda. Women do not take the name of their husbands, and children do not bear the name of their parents.

10 Peter Uvin, *Aiding Violence. The Development Enterprise in Rwanda*, New York: Kumarian Press, 1998, p. 31.
11 Colin Waugh, *Paul Kagame and Rwanda. Power, Genocide and the Rwandan Patriotic Front,* Jefferson NC: McFarland, 2004.
12 UN Doc. Trusteeship Council. T/Pet. 3/107. Petition from B. K. Kavuste from Kigeri High School, Kigezi, Uganda.
13 UN Doc. General Assembly, *Question of the Future of Ruanda-Urundi. Report of the UN Commission for Ruanda-Urundi established under General Assembly Resolution 1743.* (XV1) (A/5126) 30 May, 1962.
14 Josias Semujanga, *Origins of Rwandan Genocide*, New York: Humanity Books, 2003, p. 172. He claims the genocides were: 1959–60; 1963–64; 1973; 1990–93 and 1994.
15 Ibid, p. 184.
16 Lema, *Africa Divided.* p. 43.
17 Semujanga, *Rwandan Genocide*, p. 185.
18 Bagosora, "The Assassination of President Habyarimana", p. 7.
19 Ibid, p. 16.
20 Uvin, *Aiding Violence*, p. 37.
21 "L'Extermination des Tutsi", *Le Monde*, 4 February, 1964.
22 Michael Bower, Gary Freeman and Kay Miller, *Passing By: The United States and Genocide in Burundi.* Special Report, Humanitarian Policy Studies. Carnegie Endowment for International Peace, 1972.
23 Leo Kuper, *The Prevention of Genocide*, New Haven CT and London: Yale University Press, 1985, p. 154.
24 ICTR transcript. Interrogation of Jean Kambanda.
25 Gérard Prunier, *The Rwandan Crisis 1959–1994. History of a Genocide*, London: Hurst and Company, 1995.
26 ICTR transcript. Interrogation of Jean Kambanda.
27 In Rwanda there were ten prefectures, each governed by a prefect. The prefectures were further subdivided into communes which were placed under the authority of bourgmestres. The bourgmestre of each commune was appointed by the president of the republic. A bourgmestre was responsible for public order. Each commune was further subdivided into sectors and cells.
28 Herman J. Cohen. *Intervening in Africa. Superpower peacemaking in a Troubled Continent*, London: Macmillan Press, 2000, p. 167.
29 "Juvénal Habyarimana", obituary, *Le Monde*, April 8, 1994.

30 Prunier, *The Rwanda Crisis*, p. 82. Prunier interviewed a former civil servant in Kigali who told him that Habyarimana feared that the blood of his predecessor could cause him harm and fearing the shedding of Kayibanda's blood he starved Kayibanda to death.
31 André Gakwaya, Rwandan journalist. Unpublished manuscript. Author's archive.
32 Prunier, *The Rwanda Crisis*, p. 75.
33 US Department of State. Human Rights Report. 1978.
34 Robert E. Gribbin. "In the Aftermath of Genocide. The US Role in Rwanda". iUniverse. 2005.
35 François Misser, *Vers un Nouveau Rwanda? Entretiens avec Paul Kagame*, Editions Luc Pire, Karthala, p. 82.
36 ICTR defence testimony Théoneste Bagosora. Cross-examination Drew White. Military One.
37 Vénuste Nshimiyimana, *Prélude de Génocide Rwandais. Enquête sur les Circonstances Politiques et Militaires du Meurtre du Président Habyarimana.* Paris: Quorum, 1995, p. 77.
38 Prunier, *The Rwanda Crisis.*
39 Prunier, *The Rwanda Crisis.*
40 Interviews. Kigali, December 2001.
41 While the percentage of Tutsi in Rwanda was officially at 9 per cent, research by the UNDP showed this figure to be nearer 20 per cent. In some places the number of Tutsi was as high as 30 per cent, principally in the west, in Kibuye. In the north-west there was an estimated 5 per cent.
42 Amnesty International, *Rwanda: Persecution of Tutsi Minority and Repression of Government Critics, 1990–1992*, May 1992.
43 ICTR prosecution witness statement. GS.
44 ICTR prosecution witness statement. DAT.
45 ICTR prosecution witness statement. DBN.
46 International Federation of Human Rights (FIDH), *Report of the International Commission of Investigation on Human Rights Violations in Rwanda between 1 October, 1990 to January 1993, Final Reports.* New York: Human Rights Watch/Africa, March 1993, p. 20. Author's archive.
47 Assemblée Nationale, Mission d'Information Commune, *Enquête sur la Tragédie Rwandaise (1990–1994)*, Paris, p. 133.
48 Ibid, p. 276.
49 Misser, *Vers un Nouveau Rwanda?*, p. 62.

50 Interview with Col. Charles Uwihoreye, Minister for Prisons, Ministry of Internal Affairs. Kigali, December 2001.
51 Prunier, *The Rwanda Crisis*, p. 93.
52 *Rwanda Rushya*, no. 10, 1991. The editor André Kameya was killed during the genocide in 1994.
53 Gakwaya, unpublished MS, p. 55.

2 CIVIL DEFENCE

1 ICTR prosecution testimony. Military One. Witness ZF.
2 ICTR transcript. Interrogation of Jean Kambanda.
3 Ibid.
4 Rwandan Republic. Note to His Excellency the President. Subject: study of the means necessary for defence and to allow the population to counter any attack from inside or outside the country. Undated. Col. Augustin Ndindiliyimana. Author's archive.
5 Rwandan Republic. To the Presidential Minister in charge of Defence and Security. Subject: Minutes of Meeting. Rapporteur: Lt. Gregoire Rutakamize. 9 July, 1991. Author's archive.
6 Rwandan Republic. Account of a Seminar of Prefects. 11–12 September, 1991. Author's archive.
7 Rwandan Republic. Note to H. E. President of the Republic. Confidential. Subject: A law for civil defence. Kigali, 22 October, 1991. Author's archive.
8 Prefecture of Kibuye. Letter to the Minister of the Interior, Kigali. From: Prefect of Kibuye. Subject: Recommendations of council for security. Signed Gaspar Ruhumliza. 26 November, 1991. Author's archive.
9 Law proposal, 1991, Organisation of National Defence. Author's archive.
10 Daniela Kroslak, *The Responsibility of External Bystanders in Cases of Genocide: The French in Rwanda, 1990–94*, unpublished Ph.D thesis, University of Wales, Aberystwyth, 2003.
11 French Republic. Embassy of France in Rwanda. Cover Sheet and attachments. 5 July, 1991. Signed Col. Galinie, Head of the Military Assistance Mission. Author's archive.
12 Prunier, *The Rwanda Crisis*, footnote p. 149.
13 Interview. Kigali, December 2001.

14 Human Rights Watch/Fédération Internationale des Ligues des Droits de l'Homme, *Leave None to Tell the Story. Genocide in Rwanda*, 1999, p. 62.
15 Interview with Major-General Marcel Gatsinzi. Kigali, December 2001.
16 Vénuste Nshimiyimana, *Prélude du Génocide Rwandais.*
17 ICTR prosecution testimony. Military One. Witness ZF.
18 ICTR prosecution witness statement. AK.
19 Assemblée Nationale, *Enquête sur la Tragédie Rwandaise*, p. 209.
20 Prunier, *The Rwanda Crisis*, p. 124.
21 MDR, Bureau de Poste, Kigali. Letter to the Minister of the Interior. 7 July, 1991. Signed: Thaddée Bagaragaza et al. Author's archive.
22 Prunier, *The Rwanda Crisis*, p. 125.
23 Rwandan Republic. Army High Command. Letter to Minister of Defence. Subject: Activities of the private press. Major-General Juvénal Habyarimana, pp. Colonel Laurent Serubuga. Kigali, 29 November, 1991.
24 The threat was typed on Ministry of Defence notepaper and signed, "The companions in arms of Colonel Rwendeye." Author's archive.
25 Press Release, Kigali, 2 December, 1991. Executive Committee, Rwandan Association of Journalists. Signed: Abbe André Sibomana, Gaspard Karemera, Sixbert Musangamfura, André Kameya, Perè Guy Theunis. Author's archive.
26 Human Rights Watch, *Leave None to Tell the Story*, p. 58.
27 ICTR prosecution testimony. Media Trial. Witness X.
28 ICTR transcript. Interrogation of Jean Kambanda.
29 ICTR prosecution witness statement. KL.
30 Both men are dead.
31 Janvier Africa, in *Courier International*, 30 June–6 July, 1994.
32 ICTR prosecution testimony. Military One. Omar Serushago.
33 André Guichaoua, ed., *Les Crises Politiques au Burundi et au Rwanda, (1993–1994)*, Université des Sciences et Technologies de Lille. Paris: Karthala, 1995. 2nd Edition, p. 265.
34 FIDH, *Report of the International Commission*, pp. 44–5.
35 Rwambuka was assassinated on 25 August, 1992.
36 Veronique Tadjo, *The Shadow of Imana. Travels in the heart of Rwanda*, translated by Veronique Wakerley, London: Heinemann, 2002. According to Professor Filip Reyntjens, Locatelli's presumed killers were apprehended and then released without their identity being established. (ICTR testimony of Professor Filip Reyntjens.)

37 Martre served until March 1993 when he retired. He was replaced by Jean-Michel Marlaud.
38 Linda Melvern, *A People Betrayed:The Role of the West in Rwanda's Genocide*, London and New York: Zed Books, 2000, p. 45.
39 Gakwaya, unpublished MS, p. 72.
40 Linda Melvern. A People Betrayed. The Role of the West in Rwanda's Genocide. P 43 Zed Books. 2000)
41 Rwandan Patriotic Front. Press release. Death commando unit and massacres of civilians in Rwanda. Paris, 4 November, 1991. Signed: Dr Jacques Bihozagara. Author's archive.
42 Marie-France Cros, "Rwanda: M. Kuypers dénonce l'entourage du Président", *La Libre Belgique*, 3–4 December, 1992.
43 ICTR defence testimony. Théoneste Bagosora. Military One.
44 Gakwaya, unpublished MS.
45 Nick Gordon, *Murders in the Mist*, London: Hodder and Stoughton, 1993.
46 Nshimiyimana, *Prélude du Génocide Rwandais*, p. 82.
47 Ibid.
48 Ibid, p. 83.
49 French translation of an article, "Ibikorwa bya escadron de la mort byashyizwe ahagaragara", published in *Kinyarwanda in Umurava-magazine*, no. 14, 25 December, 1992. Author's archive.
50 Africa listed the following officers killed for this reason; Colonels Mayuya, Rwanyagasore, Kamanzi, Haguma, Gacinya, Turatsinze and Major Muhirwa.
51 Janvier Africa, "Ibikorwa bya escradon de la mort byashyizwe ahagaragara", published in *Kinyarwanda in Umurava-magazine*, no. 14, 25 December, 1992.
52 ICTR prosecution testimony. Military One. Witness ZF.
53 Ibid.
54 Gakwaya, unpublished MS, p. 69.
55 Interviews, Kigali, December 2001.
56 ICTR defence testimony Théoneste Bagosora. Cross-examination Drew White.
57 In August 1993, just before the Arusha Accords were concluded Gasana fled to Switzerland claiming to be in fear of his life.
58 Rwandan Republic. Ministry of Defence. G2. Note to Army Chief. Network of Subversion, 6 June, 1992. Secret. Signed AN. Author's archive.
59 Rwandan Republic. Ministry of Defence. G2. Note to the Minister of

Defence. Subject: Situation at the Front. Copy to the President. Kigali, 23 June, 1992. Signed AN. Author's archive.

60 Rwandan Republic. Ministry of Defence. G2. Note to Army Chief. Subject: The organisation of services. Copy to the President. Kigali, 2 July, 1992. Signed AN. Author's archive.

61 Rwandan Republic. Ministry of Defence. G2. Note to the Minister of Defence. Subject: Situation of the enemy. 14 July, 1992. Signed AN. Author's archive.

62 Rwandan Republic. Ministry of Defence. G2. Note to Army Chief. Subject: State of mind of soldiers and civil population. July 27, 1992. Signed AN. Copy for the President of the Republic. Author's archive.

63 Rwandan Republic. Ministry of Defence. G2. Subject: Situation for May. 31 May, 1992. Unsigned. Author's archive.

64 Rwandan Republic. Ministry of Defence. G2 Meeting of 26 October, 1991. Secret. Rapporteur Anatole Nsengiyumva. Author's archive.

65 Rwandan Republic. Ministry of Defence. G2. Subject: Tension at the UNR. Campus of Nyakinama. Signed Laurent Serubuga. 31 May, 1992. Author's archive.

66 Cohen, *Intervening in Africa*, p. 171.

67 Colette Braeckman, "Des Escradons de la mort au Rwanda", *Le Soir*, Brussels, 12 October, 1992.

68 ICTR Defence Attorney, Don Webster, Government One.

69 FIDH, *Report of the International Commission*, pp. 24–5.

70 Rwanda Republic. Ministry of Defence. Letter to the Minister of Defence. From Colonel Déogratias Nsabimana. Subject: Training of PL CRAP, 2 October, 1992. Author's archive.

71 ICTR prosecution witness statement. Witness ZF.

72 Bruce D. Jones, *Peacemaking in Rwanda. The Dynamics of Failure*, Colorado: Lynne Rienner, 2001, p. 83.

73 ICTR transcript. Interrogation of Jean Kambanda.

74 Walter A. Dorn, Jonathan Matloff, Jennifer Matthews, "Preventing the Bloodbath: Could the UN have predicted and prevented the Rwandan Genocide", Cornell University, Peace Studies Program, Occasional Paper, no. 24, November 1999, note p. 35.

75 Jones, *Peacemaking in Rwanda*, p. 34.

76 Melvern, *A People Betrayed*, p. 101.

77 Cohen, *Intervening in Africa*, p. 176.

78 Jones, *Peacemaking in Rwanda*, p. 72.
79 Interview. Kigali, December 2001.
80 Melvern, *A People Betrayed*, p. 54.
81 Bagosora, "The Assassination of President Habyarimana".
82 Jones, *Peacemaking in Rwanda*, p. 72.
83 ICTR defence testimony. Théoneste Bagosora. Military One.
84 Bagosora, "The Assassination of President Habyarimana".
85 Prunier, *The Rwanda Crisis*, note p. 19.
86 Rwandan Republic. Ministry of Defence. To the Minister of Defence. Subject: Psychological Preparation. 21 September, 1992. Signed Déogratias Nsabimana. Author's archive.
87 Rwandan Republic. Ministry of Defence. G2. To The Minister of Defence. 9 December, 1992. Signed Déogratias Nsabimana. Author's archive.
88 Stephen Smith, "Massacres au Rwanda", *Libération*, 9 February, 1993.
89 Prunier, *The Rwanda Crisis*, p. 178.
90 Ibid, p. 180.
91 Rwanda Republic. Ministry of Defence. National Gendarmerie. Account of meeting of National Gendarmerie, Kigali, 27 March, 1993. Author's archive.
92 Human Rights Watch, *Leave None to Tell the Story*, pp. 107–8.
93 ICTR defence testimony. Théoneste Bagosora. Examination in Chief. Raphael Constant.
94 Prefecture of Kigali. To the Minister of the Interior. Subject: Probable attack by the RPF from 11 May, 1993. signed Lt.-Col. Tharcisse Renzaho. Author's archive.
95 Note to Army Command. Network of RPF in Kigali. Secret. 24 June, 1993. Signed Tharcisse Renzaho. Author's archive.
96 Rwandan Republic. Periodic report on the internal situation. April–December 1972. To the Director of National Security, Kigali. Signed: S/Lt. Tharcisse Renzaho. Author's archive.
97 Ubutabera. Edition 46. "Chronicles and reports on International Criminal Justice" in Diplomatie Judiciare/Judicial Diplomacy.
98 ICTR defence testimony. Théoneste Bagosora. Cross-examination Drew White.
99 Rwandan Republic. Ministry of Defence. G2. Note to High Command. Subject: Internal State Security. Confidential. Signed Anatole Nsengiyumva. Author's archive.
100 He was replaced as head of G2 by Col. Aloys Ntiwiragabo.

101 Rwandan Republic. Ministry of Defence. Operational command, Gisenyi. Subject: Appreciation of the situation. Secret. 27 June, 1993. Signed Lt.-Col. Anatole Nsengiyumva. Author's archive.
102 Rwandan Republic. Ministry of Defence. To the Prime Minister. Subject: Report on state security. Kigali, 25 February, 1993. Signed Dr James Gasana. Author's archive.
103 FIDH, *Report of the International Commission*, p. 60.
104 Human Rights Watch, *Leave None to Tell the Story*, p. 113.
105 Ibid, p. 115.
106 Ibid, p. 113.
107 Letter from Félician Semusambi, Owner of the newspaper, *Umuranga*, Bureau de Poste 1128. Subject: Request for an Inquiry into the violence in Gikondo, Kicukiro and Kimihurura. Kigali, 13 July, 1992. Author's archive.
108 Gakwaya, unpublished MS, p. 74.
109 Rwandan Fr 175=US$1.
110 ICTR prosecution testimony. Military One. Omar Serushago.
111 Rwandan Republic. Ministry of Defence. Operations command. Gisenyi. To the Minister of Defence. Subject: Civil Defence. Very Secret. 14 December, 1993. Signed Anatole Nsengiyumva. Author's archive.
112 ICTR transcript. Interrogation of Jean Kambanda.

3 A PROGRAMME OF HATRED

1 ICTR case no. 99-52-T. The Prosecutor v. Ferdinand Nahimana, Jean-Bosco Barayagwiza, Hassan Ngeze. Judgement and Sentence. December 2003, p. 41.
2 African Rights, *Rwanda. Death, Despair and Defiance*. London: African Rights, 1995, p. 70.
3 Ibid, p. 76.
4 ICTR judgement, 95-52-T, p. 77.
5 African Rights, full text of commandments, in Rwanda, p. 42.
6 *Kangura*, no. six, December 1990. Prunier, *The Rwanda Crisis*, p. 166.
7 Jean-Pierre Chrétien, Jean-Francois Dupaquier, Marcel Kabanda and Joseph Ngarambe, *Rwanda: Les Médias du Génocide*, Paris: Karthala/Reporters Sans Frontieres, 1995, p. 220.
8 Ibid, p. 156.

9 ICTR. Prosecution Opening Statement. Media Trial.
10 Ibid.
11 Prunier, *The Rwanda Crisis*, p 166.
12 ICTR prosecution testimony, Media Trial. Witness X.
13 Ibid.
14 ICTR defence testimony. Théoneste Bagosora. Military One.
15 ICTR testimony, Media Trial. Witness X.
16 ICTR. Prosecution Opening Statement. Media Trial. Bernard Muna.
17 ICTR prosecution testimony. Military One. Georges Ruggiu.
18 ICTR prosecution testimony. Media Trial. Witness SA.
19 ICTR prosecution testimony. Media Trial. Witness X. February 2002.
20 Ibid.
21 ICTR. Prosecution Opening Statement. Media Trial. Muna.
22 ICTR prosecution testimony. Media Trial. Witness X.
23 Jones, *Peacemaking in Rwanda*, p. 117.
24 Belgian Senate, *Commission d'enquête parlementaire concernant les événements du Rwanda*. Report, 6 December, 1997, p. 607.
25 Jacques Castonguay, *Les Casques Bleus au Rwanda*, Paris: Editions l'Harmattan, 1998, p. 68.
26 Rwandan Republic. Ministry of Defence. Cabinet of Minister. To the President. Subject: Arms for the autodefense of the population. Kigali, 18 November, 1991. Signed Colonel L. Rusatira. Author's archive.
27 Pierre Galand and Michel Chossudovsky, *L'Usage de la Dette Extérieure du Rwanda (1990/1994). La Responsabilité des Bailleurs de Fonds. Analyse et Recommandations.* Brussels and Ottawa. Rapport Préliminaire, November 1996. Author's archive.
28 Melvern, *A People Betrayed*, p. 67.
29 ICTR transcript. Interrogation of Jean Kambanda.
30 For a more detailed story on these arms deals, see Melvern, *A People Betrayed*, p. 32.
31 Interviews. New York, December 2001.
32 Testimony of Eric Gillet. Belgian Senate, *Commission d'enquête parlementaire*, p. 193.
33 Dr Greg Stanton. Email message to author. June 2003.
34 Assemblée Nationale, *Enquête sur la Tragedie*, Vol. 1, p. 82.
35 The official groups included: The Association for the Defence of Human Rights (ARDO), the Rwandese Association for the Defence of Human

Rights and Civil Liberties (ADL), the Association of Peace Volunteers (AVP) and the Collective of the Leagues and Association for the Defence of Human Rights in Rwanda (CLADO).

36 *Rapport sur les Droits de l'homme au Rwanda, Septembre 1991–Septembre 1992*, Kigali: Association Rwandaise pour la defénse des droits de la personne et des libertés publiques (ADL), December 1992.

37 African Rights, *Rwanda*, p. 49.

38 FIDH, *Report of the International Commission.*

39 African Rights, *Rwanda*, p. 34.

40 Africa Watch, "Beyond the Rhetoric: Continuing Human Rights Abuses in Rwanda", Report no. 7, June 1993.

41 For Genocide Convention see: William A. Schabas, *Genocide in International Law*, Cambridge: Cambridge University Press, 2000.

42 The reports were as follows: Amnesty International, *A Spate of Detentions and Trials in 1990 to Suppress Fundamental Rights* (AFR 47/07/1990, October 1990); Africa Watch, *Rwanda; Talking Peace and Waging War, Human Rights since the October 1990 Invasion* (February 1992); Amnesty International, *Rwanda, Persecution of the Tutsi Minority and repression of government critics. 1990–1992* (AFR 47/02/92, May 1992); UN Commission on Human Rights, *Report by Mr. B. W. Ndiaye, Special Rapporteur on his Mission to Rwanda, April 8–17, 1993* (E/CN.4/1994/7/Addi), 11 August 1993; Human Rights Watch Arms Project, *Arming Rwanda: The Arms Trade and Human Rights Abuses in the Rwandan War*, January 1994; International Federation of Human Rights (FIDH), *Report of the International Commission.*

43 UN Doc. Economic and Social Councils Commission on Human Rights. Report by Mr. B. W. Ndiaye, Special Rapporteur, on his mission to Rwanda from 8–17 April, 1993. (E/CN.4/1994/7/ Add.1) 11 August, 1993.

44 Interview with Bacre Waly Ndiaye, New York, October 2002.

45 Assemblée Nationale, *Enquête sur la Tragédie*, Vol. 1, pp. 322, 330.

46 Human Rights Watch, *World Report, 1994*, p. 39.

4 MISSION IMPOSSIBLE

1 "Remember Rwanda, Major-General Dallaire Pleads", *Globe and Mail*, Toronto, 2 February, 1998.

2 Organization of African Unity, *Rwanda, The Preventable Genocide*, chapter 13, p. 4.
3 UN DOC. DPKO. UNOMR Reconnaissance Mission to Rwanda. Fax to Jonah/Annan. 20 August–3 September, 1993.
4 Jones, *Peacemaking in Rwanda*, p. 105.
5 Michael Barnett, *Eyewitness to a Genocide*, Africa and London: Cornell University Press, 2002, p. 70.
6 Linda Melvern, *The Ultimate Crime. Who Betrayed the UN and Why*, London: Allison and Busby, 1995.
7 UN DOC. Security Council. Report of the Secretary-General on Rwanda, requesting establishment of a United Nations Assistance Mission for Rwanda (UNAMIR) and the integration of UNOMUR into UNAMIR. S/26488, 24 September, 1993.
8 Melvern, *The Ultimate Crime*, pp. 84–5.
9 Ibid, p. 330.
10 Ibid, p. 323.
11 Ibid, p. 325.
12 Barnett, *Eyewitness to a Genocide.*
13 Melvern, *The Ultimate Crime*, pp. 315–31.
14 Report of the Commission of Inquiry Established in Pursuant to Security Council Resolution 885 (1993) to investigate armed attacks on UNOSOM II Personnel which led to casualties among them. New York, 24 February, 1994. Unpublished. Author's archive.
15 Melvern, *A People Betrayed*, p. 79.
16 In October 1993 the non-permanent members were: Cape Verde, Djibouti, Japan, Morocco, Pakistan, Hungary, Brazil, Venezuela, New Zealand and Spain.
17 Security Council Resolution 872. 5 October, 1993.
18 Ahmedou Ould-Abdallah, *Burundi on the Brink 1993–95*, Washington DC: United States Institute of Peace, 2000, p. 35.
19 Hutu Power is the name given to an ideology whose adherents were rabidly anti-Tutsi. Racist and nationalistic, they were opposed to democracy and believed that the way to avoid it was through the elimination of all Tutsi and pro-democracy Hutu.
20 African Rights, *Rwanda*, p. 87.
21 Human Rights Watch, *Leave None to Tell the Story*, p. 138.
22 Ould-Abdallah, *Burundi on the Brink.*

23 Geraldine Brooks, "Peacekeeping Mission of UN is Pursued on a Wing and A Prayer", *Wall Street Journal*, 28 December, 1993.
24 Ibid.
25 Nshimiyimana, *Prélude du Génocide Rwandais*, p. 66.
26 Lt.-Gen. Roméo Dallaire, *Shake Hands with the Devil: The Failure of Humanity in Rwanda*, Canada: Random House, 2003, p. 111.
27 UN Doc. UNAMIR outgoing code cable. To Annan/DPKO/New York, from Dallaire/UAMIR/Kigali. 6 January, 1994.
28 Nshimiyimana, *Prélude du Génocide Rwandais*, note p. 66.
29 Dallaire, *Shake Hands with the Devil*, p. 111.
30 UN Archives. UNAMIR Force Commander's Papers. Box 1, G60132. To Maurice Baril. From Dallaire. Subject: Military Situation Overview. 30 November, 1993. MIR 144.
31 UN Archives. UNAMIR Force Commander's papers. Box 1, G60132. File 8007.1 To Distribution list. From Force Commander. Subject: Militia. 25 November, 1993.
32 UN Doc. DPKO. UNAMIR Outgoing code cable. From Booh-Booh, SRSG. To Jonah, USG, DPA. Report of the Secretary-General on Rwanda, 16 December, 1993.
33 Anonymous letter. To the Commander of UNAMIR. Subject: Machiavellian plan of President Habyarimana. Kigali, 3 December, 1993. Author's archive.
34 Rwanda Republic. Ministry of Defence. G2. Destination List A and the Minister of Defence. Kigali 29 December, 1993. Signed Déogratias Nsabimana. Author's archive.
35 African Rights, *Rwanda*, p. 49.
36 Ibid, pp. 59–60.
37 Cohen, *Intervening in Africa. Superpower Peacemaking in a Troubled Continent*, p. 175.
38 Les Familles des Paras, *Rwanda. Lettre Ouverte aux parlementaires. Le texte du rapport du group "Rwanda" du Sénat*, Brussels: Editions Luc Pire, 1997, p. 69.
39 ICTR transcript. Interrogation of Jean Kambanda.
40 Rwanda Republic. Ministry of Defence. Para-commando battalion. Subject: Account of Meeting, Camp Kanombe. November 30, 1993. Signed Major Aloys Ntabakuze.
41 Rwandan Republic. Account of a meeting of Intelligence Services.Cabinet.

Ministry of Defence. Kigali, 13 September, 1993. Signed Lt.-Col. Laurent Rutayisire.

42 Dallaire, *Shake Hands with the Devil*, p. 120.
43 Les Familles des Paras, *Rwanda*, p. 39.
44 Colonel Luc Marchal, *Rwanda: la descente aux enfers*, Brussels: Editions Labor 2001, p 45.
45 Ibid.
46 The decision by the Belgian government to send troops to Rwanda was taken on 19 November, 1993.
47 Belgian Senate, *Commission d'enquête parlementaire*, p. 361.
48 Les Familles des Paras, *Rwanda*.
49 Interview with Roméo Dallaire. London, September 1994.
50 Dallaire, *Shake Hands with the Devil*, p. 122.

5 MORNING PRAYERS

1 Melvern, *A People Betrayed*, p. 32.
2 Boutros Boutros-Ghali, *Unvanquished. A US-UN Saga,* London: I. B. Tauris, 1999, p. 9.
3 "New chief of UN Pyramid", *Observer*, profile, Boutros Boutros-Ghali. 24 November, 1991.
4 Interview. London, June 2003.
5 Nshimiyimana, *Prélude du Génocide Rwandais*, p. 35.
6 ICTR witness statement. J.-R. Booh-Booh.
7 Dallaire, *Shake Hands with the Devil*, p. 114.
8 Ibid, pp. 171–2.
9 Ibid, p. 209.
10 Interview with Roméo Dallaire. New York, January 2003.
11 *Report of the Independent Inquiry into the Actions of the United Nations during the 1994 Genocide in Rwanda.* UN Doc. 15 December 1999.
12 Interviews. UN Secretariat, DPKO. New York. April–July 1994.
13 US Senate. Committee on Foreign Relations. Reform of UN Peace-keeping Operations: A Mandate for Change. A Staff Report to the Committee. 103rd Cong. Ist Session, August 1993.
14 UN Doc. DPKO. Situation Report. No. 6. 23 To Annan from Dallaire. November 1993.

15 Colin Keating. "Lessons from the Security Council's Role in the Rwanda Crisis", in David M. Malone, ed., The UN Security Council. *From the Cold War to the Twentyfirst Century*. Boulder, CO: Lynne Riener, 2004.
16 UN. DPKO. Outgoing code cable. From Annan. J.-R. Booh-Booh, 17 December, 1993.
17 Dallaire, *Shake Hands with the Devil*, p. 50.
18 Interviews. Geneva, July 1999. New York, December 2001.
19 Report of the Secretary-General on UNAMIR. S/26927. UN Doc. 30 December, 1993.
20 *The United Nations and Rwanda 1993–1994*, p. 237.
21 UN Independent Inquiry, 1999, p. 29.
22 Marchal, *Rwanda*, p. 101.
23 Ibid, p. 105.
24 Ibid, p. 107.
25 Rwanda Republic. Ministry of Defence. G1. Subject: Situation of Rwandan Army Officers. 5 March, 1994. Author's archive.
26 Mel McNulty, "France's Rwanda debacle", p. 12. *War Studies*, Vol. 2, no. 2, Spring 1997.
27 Prunier, *The Rwanda Crisis 1959–1994*, p. 216.
28 Ministry of Defence. Letter to Minister of Defence. Subject: New RPF plan. Kigali, 16 August, 1993. Signed Déogratias Nsabimana. Author's archive.
29 ICTR transcript. Interrogation of Jean Kambanda.
30 Les Familles des Paras, *Rwanda*, p. 68.
31 Dallaire, *Shake Hands with the Devil*, p. 139.
32 ICTR case no. ICTR-96-7-1. The Prosecutor Against Théoneste Bagosora, 1999, p. 26.
33 Dallaire, *Shake Hands with the Devil*, p. 143.
34 ICTR prosecution witness statement. (Each cell contains an average ten households.)
35 Dallaire, *Shake Hands with the Devil*, p. 144.
36 Ibid, p. 147.
37 Michael Barnett, *Eyewitness to a Genocide*, p. 83.
38 UN Doc. DPKO. UNAMIR outgoing code cable. To Annan. From Booh-Booh. Subject: Initiatives undertaken relating to latest security information. 13 January, 1994.

39 Interview, Karel Kovanda, Ambassador Czech Republic. June, 2003 in Colin Keating, "Lessons from the Security Council's Role in the Rwanda Crisis".
40 UN Doc. DPKO. UNAMIR outgoing code cable. To Annan from Booh-Booh. Subject: Contacts with informant. 15 January, 1994.
41 The four children survived.
42 Marchal, *Rwanda*, p. 179.
43 Philip Gourevitch, *We wish to inform you that tomorrow we will be killed with our families. Stories from Rwanda*, London: Picador, 1999, pp. 104–5. See also Gourevitch, "The Optimist", *The New Yorker*, Vol. 79, 3 November, 2003, pp. 50–73.
44 Interviews. DPKO, New York, December 1996.
45 Barnett, *Eyewitness to a Genocide*, p. 83.

6 ON THE EDGE

1 Lindsey Hilsum, "Rwanda tribal rampage fear after two politicians are killed", *Guardian*, 23 February, 1994.
2 Dallaire, *Shake Hands with the Devil*, p. 184.
3 Ibid.
4 Ibid, p. 185.
5 Belgian Senate, *Commission d'enquête parlementaire*, p. 87.
6 Les Familles des Paras, *Rwanda*, p. 93.
7 UN Doc. DPKO. UNAMIR Interoffice Memorandum to SRSG from FC. Subject: Recovery of illegal weapons. 31 January, 1994.
8 UN Doc. DPKO. Outgoing code cable. To BB/Dallaire. From Annan. 16 February, 1994.
9 Interview with Roméo Dallaire. New York, January 2003.
10 UN Archives. Force Commander's Papers. Box 1. G60132. To Annan from BB. 15 February, 1994.
11 UN Archives. Force Commander's Papers. Box 1. G60132. Memorandum to CAO from Force Commander. 13 January, 1994.
12 Interview with Roméo Dallaire. London, September 1994.
13 UN Archives. Force Commander's Papers. Box 1. G60132. To SRSG from FC. 27 January, 1994.
14 Les Familles des Paras, *Rwanda*, p. 83.

15 ICTR prosecution testimony. Media Trial. Witness: François-Xavier Nsanzuwera.
16 Rwandan Republic. Constitutional Court. Letter to the President from the President of the Constitutional Court, Joseph Kavaruganda. Subject Death threats. Kigali 25 March, 1994. Author's archive.
17 *The United Nations and Rwanda 1993–1994*, p. 25.
18 UN Archives. UNAMIR, Force Commander's papers. Box 1. G60132. Force Commander. Notes on the meeting with Paul Kagame. 22 January, 1994.
19 Marchal, *Rwanda,* p. 109.
20 Ibid.
21 UN Archives. Force Commander's papers. Box 1. R75755. MIR 297. To Annan from BB. 8 February, 1994.
22 Dallaire, *Shake Hands with the Devil*, p. 201.
23 UN Doc. DPKO. UNAMIR outgoing code cable. To Annan from Booh-Booh. 21 January, 1994. Attachment: Interoffice Memo. To SRSG. From FC. 21 January, 1994.
24 UN Doc. DPKO. UNAMIR Interoffice memorandum. To SRSG from FC. 31 January, 1994.
25 UN Archives. UNAMIR Force Commander's papers. Box 1. G60132. Internal Memorandum. From Force Commander to Distribution List. Four hour supper with Minister of Transport André Ntagerura at Péché Mignon. 15 January, 1994.
26 Interview with Roméo Dallaire. Nottingham, January 2002.
27 ICTR testimony. Maxwell Hkole, Commander of Investigations, Military One.
28 Tony Marley Interview, PBS Frontline at www.pbs.org.
29 UN Doc. DPKO. Outgoing code cable. To Barril from Dallaire. Subject: Deterrent Operations. 3 February, 1994.
30 UN Archives. UNAMIR Force Commander's papers. Box 1. G60132. Interoffice memorandum. To CAO from FC. February 4, 1994.
31 UN Archives. UNAMIR Force Commander's papers. Box 1 G60132. Interoffice memorandum. From Force Commander to Distribution List. Notes from meeting with Minister of Defence. 4 February, 1994.
32 ICTR prosecution testimony. Witness XXQ.
33 ICTR prosecution testimony. Witness XXQ.
34 Les Familles des Paras, *Rwanda*, p. 78.

35 ICTR prosecution testimony. Media Trial. Omar Serushago.
36 Interview, Gikondo, Kigali, December, 2001.
37 UN Doc. DPKO. Outgoing Facsimile. To Annan from Dallaire. Incident Report. 24 February, 1994.
38 Interview with Paul Kagame. Kigali, October 1997.
39 Melvern, *A People Betrayed*, p. 101.
40 ICTR prosecution testimony. Witness XXQ.
41 ICTR prosecution testimony. Witness LAI.
42 ICTR prosecution testimony. Lt.-Gen. Roméo Dallaire. Cross-examination.
43 Belgian Senate, *Commission d'enquête parlementaire*, p. 242. The UN Independent Inquiry gives the date as 14 February.
44 Ibid, p. 394.
45 Les Familles des Paras, *Rwanda*, p. 95.
46 Report of the Internal Commission of Enquiry, Belgian military authorities. Secret. President. General Vytterhoeven, p. 44.
47 Ibid.
48 Belgian Senate, *Commission d'enquête parlementaire*, pp. 392–3. The telex was sent by the Chef de Cabinet, M. Willems.
49 Les Familles des Paras, *Rwanda*, p. 78.
50 ICTR prosecution testimony. Faustin Twagiramungu.
51 UN Doc. DPKO. UNAMIR Daily Situation Report. MIR 715.
52 Ibid.
53 UN Doc. DPKO. UNAMIR outgoing code cable. From Booh-Booh. To Annan/Goulding. Weekly Situation Report. 22 March–28 March, 1994.
54 ICTR prosecution testimony. François–Xavier Nsanzuwera.
55 Ibid.
56 UN Archives. UNAMIR Force Commander's papers. UN Confidential. Interoffice memo. File no. 1000. The Military Situation and Assessment of RGF and RPF Intentions. 23 February, 1994.
57 UN Doc. DPKO. UNAMIR outgoing code cable. From Dallaire to Annan. Subject: Reinforcement of the KWSA. 27 February, 1994.
58 UN Doc. DPKO. UNAMIR outgoing code cable. To Annan/Goulding. From Booh-Booh. Subject: Meeting with Ambassadors of Belgium, France, Germany.
59 UN Archives. UNAMIR Force Commander's papers. Box 1. R75755.

Code cable from J.-R. Booh-Booh to Kofi Annan. MIR 409. 24 February, 1994.

60 UN Doc. DPKO. UNAMIR Weekly Situation Report. 22–28 February. To Annan from JRBB.

61 UN Archives. UNAMIR. To J. C. Aime, Office of the Secretary- General. From J.-R. Booh-Booh. 28 February, 1994.

62 Dallaire, *Shake Hands with the Devil*, p. 198.

63 ICTR. Case file of exhibits. Office of the Prosecutor. Military One. Document code: BELSGR-1.

64 Mouvement Démocratique Républicain (MDR), B.P. 2278 Kigali. Dossier "Interahamwe Za Muvoma". Kigali, May 1992. Author's archive.

65 Zero Network was the name given to the secret communications link between the extremists. Marchal was not to know this at the time.

66 Interview. Kigali, December 2001.

67 Les Familles des Paras, *Rwanda*, p. 82.

68 Ibid, p. 74.

69 Ibid, p. 57.

70 Dallaire, *Shake Hands with the Devil*, p. 90.

71 Rwanda Republic. Rwandan Ministry of Defence. Army Command, Officer Situation List. 1 March, 1994, pp. 1–15. Dated 5 March, 1994. Author's archive.

72 Les Familles des Paras, *Rwanda*, p. 134.

73 BBC Summary of World Broadcasts, AL/1948 A/3. 17 March, 1994.

74 Jones, *Peacemaking in Rwanda,* p. 82.

75 Bruce D. Jones, "The Arusha Peace Process", in Howard Adelman and Astri Suhrke, eds, *The Path of Genocide, The Rwanda crisis from Uganda to Zaire*, New Brunswick, NJ: Transaction, 1999, p. 141.

76 UN Archives, UNAMIR. Cable to Annan/Goulding. From J.-R. Booh-Booh. March 29, 1994. Box 1 R75755.

77 UN Archives. UNAMIR. Force Commander's papers. Box 1 R75755. Outgoing code cable. To Annan from J.-R. Booh-Booh. 15 February, 1994.

78 Dallaire, *Shake Hands with the Devil*, p. 212.

79 Les Familles des Paras, *Rwanda*, p. 84.

80 African Rights, *Rwanda*, p. 92.

81 Marchal statement to Belgium judicial authorities. 11 February, 1997.

82 Republic of Rwanda. Prefecture of the town of Kigali. Subject: List of

People. Kigali, 31 March, 1994. Signed Col. Tharcisse Renzaho. Author's archive.

83 Army Command, Officer Situation List, p. 2.

84 Rakiya Omar, Director, African Rights. Letter to Ambassador Pierre-Richard Prosper, Ambassador-at-Large for War Crimes Issues, US Department of State. July 2003.

85 ICTR defence testimony. Cross-examination of Théoneste Bagosora. Drew White.

86 Marchal, *Rwanda*, p. 71.

87 UN Doc. DPKO. Interoffice Memorandum. To Kofi Annan From Benon Sevan, UN Security Co-ordinator. 1 March, 1994.

88 Uwilingiyimana became Prime Minister on 18 July, 1993.

89 ICTR prosecution witness statement. PA.

90 Nshimiyimana, *Prélude du Génocide Rwandais*, p. 86.

91 Ibid, p. 88.

92 ICTR prosecution testimony. Media Trial. Witness Marcel Kabanda.

93 ICTR prosecution witness statement. AI.

94 Nshimiyimana, *Prélude du Génocide Rwandais*, p. 38.

95 ICTR witness statement. Jacques-Roger Booh-Booh.

96 Ibid.

97 ICTR testimony. Media Trial. Stephen Rapp, prosecution closing arguments.

98 UN Doc. UNAMIR daily situation report, 3 April, 1994.

99 Nshimiyimana, *Prélude du Génocide Rwandais*, note p. 51.

100 Marchal, *Rwanda*, p. 213. and Marchal Statement to Belgian judicial authorities. 11 February, 1997.

101 Les Familles des Paras, *Rwanda*, p. 84.

102 ICTR prosecution witness statement. Author's archive.

103 The Arusha Accords provided for: The MDR four portfolios with the prime minister and foreign minister; the RPF five portfolios, including the vice prime minister; the MRND five portfolios including defence and public works, and the presidency; PSD three, including finance; the PL three portfolios, including justice.

104 UN Doc. DPKO Files. RPF. Letter to the Secretary-General of the UN. Subject: Complaint against Dr Booh-Booh. Mulindi, 5 April, 1994. Received Office of Kofi Annan. Copy sent to Marrack Goulding. 5 April, 1994. Signed: Colonel Alexis Kanyarengwe, President RPF.

105 The non-permanent members of the Security Council in April 1994 were: Czech Republic, Djibouti, New Zealand, Nigeria, Oman, Pakistan, Spain, Argentina, Brazil and Rwanda.
106 Michael Barnett, *Eyewitness to a Genocide*, p. 76.
107 UN Doc. DPKO. Account of meeting between the Secretary-General with His Excellency André Ntagerura, Minister of Transport and communications of Rwanda. Note taken by Fabienne Segui Horton. 1 March, 1994.
108 Melvern, *A People Betrayed*.
109 UN Doc. DPKO. UNAMIR outgoing code cable. To Annan/Goulding. From Booh-Booh. Subject: Meeting with US Assistant Secretary for Africa. 21 March, 1994. Signed: Sammy Kum Buo.
110 Linda Melvern, Paul Williams, "Britannia Waived the Rules: The Major government and the 1994 Rwandan Genocide", in *African Affairs*, Spring 2004.
111 Rt. Hon. Peter Hain MP, Minister of State for Foreign Affairs, Presentation Speech. Inaugural Aegis Award to Major-General Roméo Dallaire. Westminster, January 2002.
112 Interview, FCO official. London, December 2003.
113 Interview with Boutros-Ghali. Paris, December 1999.
114 Boutros-Ghali, *Unvanquished,* p. 140.
115 Marchal, *Rwanda*, p. 214.
116 Interview with Anastase Gasana. New York.
117 Interviews. Kigali, November 2002.
118 Ibid.
119 Communiqué published after the regional summit held on 6 April in Dar-es-Salaam on the situation in Burundi and Rwanda. Author's archive (French version).

7 CRASH

1 Dallaire, *Shake Hands with the Devil*, p. 221.
2 Belgian military, crash enquiry, secret. Witness statements.
3 ICTR witness testimony. Also Nshimiyimana (*Prélude du Génocide Rwandais*, p. 77*)* claims to have spoken to a witness who said that the lights of the runway went out as the plane approached the airport.

4 ICTR prosecution witness statement. GX.
5 Dallaire, *Shake Hands with the Devil*, p. 221.
6 Interview, Westminster, March 2003.
7 Marchal, *Rwanda*.
8 ICTR prosecution witness statement. IB.
9 UN Doc. DPKO outgoing code cable. To Baril from Dallaire. 7 April, 1994. Significant Incident Report – Reported Death of President of Rwanda.
10 He is also listed in: Rwandan Republic, Ministry of Defence, Army Command, Officer's Army List. Author's archive.
11 Dallaire, *Shake Hands with the Devil*, p. 228.
12 ICTR prosecution witness statement. KQ.
13 ICTR prosecution testimony. Witness DBQ.
14 ICTR prosecution testimony. Military One. Witness DP.
15 ICTR prosecution testimony. Witness DA.
16 Interview, Kigali, September 2002.
17 Filip Reyntjens, *Rwanda. Trois Jours qui ont fait basucler l'histoire*. Paris: Editions L'Harmattan, 1995.
18 Bagosora, "The Assassination of President Habyarimana".
19 Interview. Kigali, December 2001.
20 Ibid.
21 Ibid.
22 Dallaire, *Shake Hands with the Devil*, p. 223.
23 Among those present at this meeting were General Ndindiliyimana, the head of the gendarmerie and colonels Bagosora, Muberuka, Murasampongo, Ndengeyinka, Rwabalinda, Rwarakabije, and Major Kayumba.
24 ICTR defence testimony. Théoneste Bagosora.
25 ICTR prosecution witness statement. IZ.
26 ICTR case no. ICTR-96-7-1. The Prosecutor Against Théoneste Bagosora, ICTR Criminal Registry. August 1999, p. 40.
27 ICTR witness statement. Jacques-Roger Booh-Booh.
28 ICTR prosecution witness statement. LS.
29 ICTR prosecution witness statement. PY.
30 ICTR prosecution witness testimony. XXQ.
31 Ibid.
32 Statement. Assassinat de Joseph Kavaruganda le 7 April, 1994. Arrestation et Assassinat. Signed Mrs Annonciata Kavaruganda, and Jean Marcel Kavaruganda, 19 September, 1996. Unpublished. Author's archive.

33 Belgian Military Auditorat General pres la Cour Militaire. Dissier No Iere Bureau – 86426. Unpublished.
34 Statement, Assassinat de Joseph Kavaruganda.
35 ICTR prosecution testimony. Military One. Witness DBQ.
36 Ibid.
37 ICTR prosecution witness statement. DBQ.
38 ICTR prosecution testimony. Military One. Witness DBQ.
39 ICTR prosecution testimony. Witness XAQ.
40 ICTR prosecution witness statement. GS.
41 ICTR prosecution testimony. Military One. Witness DBQ.
42 ICTR prosecution testimony. Witness DBQ.
43 Ibid.
44 ICTR prosecution testimony. Witness XXY.
45 Human Rights Watch, *Leave None to Tell the Story*, p. 195.
46 ICTR prosecution witness statement. DBQ.
47 ICTR case no. ICTR-96-7-1. The Prosecutor Against Théoneste Bagosora, ICTR Criminal Registry. August 1999, p. 32.
48 UN Doc. DPKO outgoing code cable. To Baril from Dallaire. 7 April, 1994. Significant Incident Report – Reported Death of President of Rwanda.
49 ICTR prosecution witness statement. CW.
50 Interview in Gikondo. Kigali, December 2001.
51 Astri Suhrke, "Dilemmas of Protection: The Log of the Kigali Battalion", in *The Path of a Genocide. The Rwanda Crisis from Uganda to Zaire*, ed. Howard Adelman, New Jersey: Transaction Publishers, 1999, p. 259.
52 Army Command Officer's Army List: Captain Sedecias. Company Commander.
53 Statement. Assassinat de Joseph Kavaruganda.
54 Kavaruganda was killed later that morning. His wife and children reached the Canadian embassy and were eventually evacuated from Rwanda with the help of UNAMIR.
55 UN Doc. DPKO outgoing code cable. To Baril from Dallaire. Significant Incident Report: Reported Death of President of Rwanda. 7 April, 1994.
56 Reyntjens, *Rwanda*, p. 129.
57 African Rights, *Rwanda*, p. 936.
58 Human Rights Watch, *Leave None to Tell the Story*. This is sourced to Tribunal de Première Instance de Bruxelles, déposition de témoin. 18 September, 1995. Dossier 57/95.

59 ICTR prosecution witness statement. WL.
60 ICTR prosecution witness statement. ET.
61 Interviews Kigali, December 2001.
62 ICTR prosecution witness statement. DT.
63 ICTR testimony. Cross-examination of Théoneste Bagosora. Drew White.
64 Interview transcript. BBC, Summary of World Broadcasts. AL/1996. 8 April, 1994.
65 African Rights, *Rwanda*, p. 179.
66 Samantha Power, *A Problem from Hell: America and the Age of Genocide*, New York: Basic Books, 2002, p. 332.
67 Melvern, *A People Betrayed*.
68 For a fuller account see *A People Betrayed*, pp. 118–26.
69 Les Familles des Paras, *Rwanda*, p. 103.
70 Melvern, *A People Betrayed*.
71 ICTR transcript. Interrogation of Jean Kambanda.
72 ICTR case no. 96-7-I. Bagosora Indictment.
73 Bagosora would later give conflicting accounts about why he had been unable to contact Bizimana in these crucial forty-eight hours. He said that Bizimana had not sent "contact details". In another part of his testimony Bagosora explained that the telephones were not working. ICTR testimony. Théoneste Bagosora.
74 Ibid.
75 The members of the Crisis Committee were: Major-General Augustin Ndindiliyimana, Colonels, Théoneste Bagosora, Marcel Gatsinzi, Léonidas Rusatira, Balthazar Ndengeyinka, Félicien Muberuka, Tharcisse Renzaho, Joseph Murasampongo, Lieutenant. Colonels, (army) Ephrem Rwabalinda, Cyprien Kayumba, (Gendarmerie) Lt.-Col. Paul Rwarakabije, Major Theophile Gakara.
76 ICTR testimony. Théoneste Bagosora. Supplementary-examination. Counsel for co-accused.
77 Interview with Dallaire.
78 Dallaire, *Shake Hands with the Devil*, p. 237.
79 Ibid, p. 237.
80 ICTR prosecution testimony. Professor Filip Reyntjens.
81 ICTR prosecution witness statement. HA.
82 ICTR prosecution witness statement. AX.
83 ICTR prosecution testimony. Lt.-Gen. Roméo Dallaire.

84 UN Doc. DPKO outgoing code cable. To SG from Annan. 7 April, 1994.
85 Marchal, *Rwanda*, p. 227.
86 ICTR prosecution witness statement. DU.
87 Dallaire, *Shake Hands with the Devil*, p. 231.
88 On 6 April, 1994 UNAMIR strength stood at: Austria 15, Bangladesh 942, Belgium 440, Botswana 9, Brazil 13, Canada 2, the Congo 26, Egypt 10, Fiji 1, Ghana 843, Hungary 4, Malawi 5, Mali 10, the Netherlands 9, Nigeria 15, Poland 5, Romania 5, the Russian Federation 15, Senegal 35, Slovakia 5, Togo 15, Tunisia 61, Uruguay, 25, and Zimbabwe 29.
89 Reyntjens, *Rwanda*, p. 82.
90 UN Doc. UNAMIR. From Booh-Booh to Annan. Subject: Draft Report of the SG on UNAMIR. 13 April, 1994.
91 Reyntjens, *Rwanda*, p. 133.
92 Rwandan Republic. General Marcel Gatsinzi. Report. Unpublished. Author's archive. P. 2.
93 Reyntjens, *Rwanda*, p. 85.
94 ICTR case no. 96-7-I. Bagosora Indictment.
95 Ibid.
96 ICTR prosecution witness statement. DAK.
97 Ibid.
98 ICTR prosecution witness statement. GS.
99 ICTR prosecution witness statement. HT.
100 ICTR prosecution witness statement. HP.
101 ICTR prosecution witness statement. WD.
102 ICTR prosecution testimony. Lt-Gen. Roméo Dallaire.

8 ZERO NETWORK

1 ICTR prosecution witness statement. OR.
2 ICTR prosecution testimony. Military One. Witness ZF.
3 Ibid.
4 ICTR prosecution witness statement. BW.
5 ICTR prosecution testimony. Military One. Witness ZF
6 ICTR prosecution witness statement. OW.
7 ICTR prosecution testimony. Military One. Witness ZF.
8 African Rights, *Rwanda*, p. 547.

9 Ibid, p. 557.
10 ICTR prosecution testimony. Military One. Witness DO.
11 Ibid.
12 ICTR prosecution testimony. Military One. Witness AOB.
13 Ibid.
14 ICTR prosecution testimony. Witness Omar Serhsago.
15 African Rights, *Rwanda*, pp. 544–7.
16 ICTR prosecution testimony. Military One. Witness ZF.
17 Ibid.
18 Author communication with Austrian UNMO. December 2002.
19 Dallaire, *Shake Hands with the Devil*, p. 314.
20 African Rights, *Rwanda*, p. 577.
21 Ibid, p. 299.
22 Ibid, p. 417.
23 Ibid, p. 186.
24 Ibid, p. 457.
25 Ibid, p. 480.
26 Interviews. Kigali, September 2002.
27 ICTR prosecution testimony. Witness WVG.
28 André Guichaoua, *Les Crises Politiques au Burundi et au Rwanda*, p. 775.
29 André Kameya was killed on 17 June, 1994.
30 ICTR prosecution testimony. Witness XXQ.
31 ICTR case no. 97-23-DP. Jean Kambanda. Defence Document. Author's archive.
32 ICTR transcript. Interrogation of Jean Kambanda.
33 Human Rights Watch, *Leave None to Tell the Story*.
34 ICTR transcript. Interrogation of Jean Kambanda.
35 Human Rights Watch, *Leave None to Tell the Story*, p. 199.
36 Reyntjens, *Rwanda*, p. 39.
37 Article 19, *Broadcasting Genocide: Censorship, Propaganda and State-Sponsored Violence in Rwanda, 1990–1994*, London, 1996, pp. 110–11.
38 ICTR prosecution witness statement. DAR.
39 Renzaho, *Guerre Civile et les Massacres Interethniques d'Avril 1994*, unpublished. Author's archive.
40 ICTR prosecution testimony. Witness GLJ.
41 ICTR prosecution testimony. Witness BJ.
42 ICTR case no. 96-7-I. Bagosora Indictment.

43 Interview. Kigali, December 2001.
44 Melvern, *A People Betrayed.*
45 Ibid.
46 US National Security Archive. Memo from Deputy Assistant Secretary of State Prudence Bushnell. To Under-Secretary of State Warren Christopher. Death of Rwanda and Burundi President in Plane Crash outside Kigali. 6 April, 1994.
47 Belgian Senate, *Commission d'enquête parlementaire*, p. 536.
48 Ibid, p. 535.
49 Assemblée Nationale, *Enquête sur la Tragédie Rwandaise, (1990–1994).*
50 Belgian Senate, *Commission d'enquête parlementaire*, p. 536.
51 Ibid, p. 565.
52 Ibid, p. 537.
53 UN Doc. DPKO outgoing code cable. To Secretary-General, Geneva. From Annan. Subject: Rwanda. 7 April, 1994.
54 UN Doc. DPKO outgoing code cable. To Annan/Goulding. From Booh-Booh. Subject: An update on the current situation in Rwanda and military aspects of the mission. 8 April, 1994.
55 Colin Waugh, *Paul Kagame and Rwanda.*
56 Ibid.
57 UN Doc. DPKO. UNAMIR outgoing code cable. To Annan/Goulding/Hanson. From Booh-Booh. Subject: Supplementary report on UNAMIR Humanitarian Activities. 8 April, 1994.
58 Dallaire, *Shake Hands with the Devil*, p. 271.
59 Letter to His Excellency Mr Colin Keating, President of the Security Council. From the Secretary-General, 8 April, 1994. UN Doc. Author's archive.
60 UN Doc. DPKO outgoing code cable. To the SG, Geneva, from Annan. Subject: Rwanda. 8 April, 1994.
61 UN Doc. DPKO outgoing code cable. To the SG, Geneva, from Annan. Subject: Rwanda. Continuation of our earlier cable of today. 8 April, 1994.
62 UN Security Council, *Report of the Independent Inquiry into the actions of the United Nations during the 1994 genocide in Rwanda*, 15 December, 1999, p. 16.
63 A list of these people is to be found in Guichaoua, *Les Crises Politiques au Burundi et au Rwanda*, pp. 697–701.
64 Compte-Rendu du Colonel Cussac et Lt-Col Maurin. Paris, le 19 Avril, 1994. Mission d'Assistance Militaire à Kigali. Assemblée Nationale,

Mission d'Information Commune, Enquête sur la Tragédie Rwandaise (1990–1994), 1998.

65 Under local authority divisions in Rwanda Gikondo is a sector, a part of the Commune of Kicukiro.

66 ICTR prosecution witness statement. UU.

67 Genocide in Rwanda. Documentation of Two Massacres during April 1994. Issue Brief. US Committee For Refugees.

68 Ibid.

69 *Genocide in Rwanda. Documentation of Two Massacres during April 1994.* Issue Brief. US Committee For Refugees.

70 Jean Hélène, "Le Rwanda a feu et a sang", *Le Monde*, 12 April, 1994.

71 Philippe Gaillard. Communication with author, November 2003.

72 Interview with Jean-Philippe Ceppi. July, 2001.

73 Linda Melvern. "Major Stefan Stec. Peacekeeper on a "Mission Impossible" in Rwanda. Obituaries. *The Independent*, 7 Ocotber, 2005.

74 Hélène, "Le Rwanda a feu et a sang".

75 Rwandan Republic. Presidency of the Republic. Bureau de Poste, 15 Kigali. Déclaration à la Nation. Author's archive.

76 ICTR opening statement. Don Webster. Government One. And ICTR prosecution testimony. Witness AAA.

77 UN Doc. DPKO. UNAMIR outgoing code cable. From Booh-Booh. To Annan/Goulding. Subject: Current situation in Rwanda. 9 April, 1994.

78 Melvern, *A People Betrayed*, chapter 1.

79 Interview. Kigali, December 2001.

80 ICTR case no. 96-7-I. Bagosora Indictment.

81 ICTR defence testimony. Cross-examination of Théoneste Bagosora. Drew White.

82 Unsigned document: "Enseignements à Tirer. Mission d'Assistance Militaire à Kigali. Assemblée Nationale, Mission d'Information Commune, Enquête sur la Tragédie Rwandaise (1990–1994).

83 Interview with Eric Bertin. December 1999.

84 Alan J. Kuperman, *The Limit of Humanitarian Intervention, Genocide in Rwanda*, Washington DC: Brookings Institution Press, 2001.

85 National Security Archive. Washington DC Executive Summary, Memorandum for Under Secretary of Defense for International Security Affairs. From Deputy Assistant Secretary of Defence for Middle East Africa. Prepared by Lt.-Col. Harvin. 11 April, 1994.

86 Agnès Callamard, *French Policy on Rwanda. In The Path of a Genocide. The Rwanda Crisis from Uganda to Zaire*, New Jersey: Transaction Publishers, 1999, p. 175.
87 Dallaire, *Shake Hands with the Devil*, p. 290.
88 Father Wolfgang Schonecke. Jesuit Refugee Service. "African Churches draw lessons from Rwanda war". December, 1994. Author's archive. The detailed role of the Catholic Church in Rwanda is beyond the scope of this book.
89 ICTR interrogation of Jean Kambanda.
90 ICTR prosecution witness statement. ZA.
91 Rakiya Omar, *Tribute to Courage*, Africa Rights, 2003.
92 Ibid.

9 APOCALYPSE TWO

1 ICTR transcript. Interrogation of Jean Kambanda.
2 Defence of Jean Kambanda. Appeal document. Author's archive.
3 ICTR opening statement. Don Webster. Government One.
4 African Rights, *Rwanda*, p. 361.
5 Ibid, p. 363.
6 ICTR transcript. Interrogation of Jean Kambanda.
7 Defence of Jean Kambanda. Appeal document. Author's archive.
8 Rwandan Republic. Presidency of the Rwandan Republic. Bureau de Poste. 15. Kigali. To H. E. Boutros Boutros-Ghali. From Dr Theodore Sindikubwabo. 13 April, 1994. Author's archive.
9 Belgian Senate, *Commission d'enquête parlementaire*, p. 543. Also Les Familles des Paras, *Rwanda*, p. 126.
10 *The United Nations and Rwanda 1993–1994*, p. 113.
11 Boutros-Ghali, *Unvanquished*, p. 132.
12 UN Doc. DPKO. Cable. To Annan/Goulding. From the Secretary-General. 13 April, 1994.
13 Robert E. Gribbin. "In the Aftermath of Genocide. The US Role in Rwanda", pp. 77–78.
14 Les Familles des Paras, *Rwanda*, p. 129. (Report dated 9 April, 1994.)
15 UN Doc. DPKO. UNAMIR Daily Situation Report. 11 April, 1994.
16 UN Doc. DPKO. UNAMIR Daily Situation Report. 12 April, 1994.

17 Melvern, *A People Betrayed.*

18 UN Doc. DPKO. UNAMIR Daily Situation Report. 13 April. To Annan/Goulding. Attached: Draft. Special Report of the Secretary-General to the Security Council. Overview. Para 15.

19 UN Doc. DPKO. To SG. From Annan. Rwanda. April 12, 1994.

20 Rwandese Patriotic Front. Letter to the President of the Security Council, Ambassador Colin Keating (New Zealand). From Claude Dusaidi, Director for External Relations and RPF Representative to the UN. Author's archive.

21 An account of the secret and informal meetings of the Security Council was leaked to the author. See *A People Betrayed.*

22 UN Doc. DPKO. UNAMIR outgoing code-cable. To Annan. From Dallaire. April 14, 1994.

23 UN Doc. DPKO outgoing code cable. To Dallaire/Booh-Booh. From Annan. Security Council consultations. 14 April, 1994.

24 Madeleine Albright, "Madam Secretary. A Memoir", New York: Talk Miramax, 2003, p. 148.

25 Kuperman, *The Limits of Humanitarian Intervention.*

26 Letter, Belgian Foreign Minister Willy Claes. To the SG. 15 April. French. Author's translation.

27 Melvern, *A People Betrayed*, p. 162.

28 UN Doc. DPKO. Proceedings of the SC. To Dallaire from Annan. 13 April, 1994.

29 UN Doc. DPKO. Outgoing code cable. To the Secretary-General. From Annan. 13 April, 1994.

30 UN Doc. DPKO. UNAMIR Daily Situation Report. 16 April, 1994.

31 Force Commander's Letter. Author's archive.

32 Preconditions for an Eventual Meeting and Discussion on a Ceasefire. Kigali, 15 April, Dr Jacques Bihozagara. 15 April, 1994.

33 Dallaire, *Shake Hands with the Devil*, p. 301.

34 Ibid, p. 195.

35 Ibid, p. 357.

36 Albright, *Madam Secretary.*

37 Dallaire, *Shake Hands with the Devil*, p. 305.

38 UN Doc. DPKO. UNAMIR outgoing code cable. The Military Assessment of the Situation as of 17 April, 1994. To Baril. (Only) From Dallaire. 17 April, 1994.

39 UN Doc. DPKO. outgoing code cable. To BB/Dallaire. From Annan. Subject: Status of UNAMIR. 18 April, 1994.
40 UN Doc. DPKO outgoing code cable. To Annan. From Dallaire. Military Assessment of Situation. 19 April, 1994.
41 ICTR witness statement. AJ.
42 Ibid.
43 Rakiya Omar, Director, Africa Rights. Letter to Ambassador Pierre-Richard Prosper, Ambassador-at-Large for War Crimes Issues, U.S Department of State. July, 2003.
44 ICTR testimony. Military One. Georges Ruggiu.
45 ICTR testimony. Media Trial. Matthias Ruzinda.
46 ICTR testimony. Georges Ruggiu.
47 ICTR testimony. Media trial. Jean-Pierre Chrètien.
48 Darryl Li, "Echoes of Violence", *Dissent*, Winter 2002.
49 ICTR testimony. Media trial. Georges Ruggiu.
50 In his interrogation Kambanda claims that most of his documents were taken from him in exile by an officer of the Zairian army.
51 Rwandan Republic. Decree. Nomination of Prefets. Signed Jean Kambanda 18 April, 1994. Author's archive.
52 ICTR interrogation of Jean Kambanda.
53 Commission of the Memorial of the Genocide: Rousseau Report, Minister of Higher Education, established 1995, author's archive.
54 Ibid.
55 African Rights, *Rwanda*, p. 339.
56 Rousseau Report, author's archive.
57 African Rights, *Rwanda*, p. 346.
58 ICTR prosecution testimony. Military One. Witness DW.
59 Human Rights Watch, *Leave None to Tell the Story*, p. 463.
60 ICTR transcript. Interrogation of Jean Kambanda.
61 ICTR opening statement. Don Webster. Government One.
62 Human Rights Watch, *Leave None to Tell the Story*, p. 517.
63 Dallaire, *Shake Hands with the Devil*, p. 330.
64 UN Doc. DPKO. UNAMIR Daily Situation Report. 24 April, 1994.
65 Dallaire, *Shake Hands with the Devil*, p. 306.
66 UN Doc. DPKO. Outgoing code cable To Annan. From Dallaire. 25 April, 1994.
67 Dallaire, *Shake Hands with the Devil*, p. 323.

68 Ibid, p. 306.
69 Ibid, p. 333.
70 Ibid, p. 324.
71 UN Doc. DPKO. To Annan. From Dallaire. Current assessment of situation in Rwanda, 24 April, 1994.
72 Ibid.
73 Rwanda Republic. Ministry of Defence. Military Intelligence Report. Secret. Author's archive.
74 UN Doc. DPKO. UNAMIR Special Situation Report covering 28 April. Dated 29 April.
75 Interview with ambassador Karel Kovanda. New York, July 1994.
76 Dr Rony Zachariah, medical co-ordinator. MSF-France. Wauter Van Emplem, Emergency Desk, MSF-Holland. "Eye witness accounts of massacres/Human Rights Violations." Chronological recollection of events, Butare Rwanda. Unpublished.
77 Linda Melvern, "Missing the Story: The Media and the Rwandan Genocide", in *Dimensions of Western Military Intervention*, eds, Colin McInnes and Nicholas J. Wheeler, Frank Cass, 2002.
78 Linda Melvern, "Death by Diplomacy", *Scotsman*, 4 January, 1995. For a fuller account see also *A People Betrayed*.
79 *The United Nations and Rwanda, 1993–1996*, p. 271.
80 Melvern, "Death by Diplomacy".
81 Oxfam Press Release, "Oxfam Fears Genocide is Happening in Rwanda", 28 April, 1994.
82 The following countries provided troops for UNAMIR during the duration of the genocide (figures calculated on 25 May 1994): Ghana 334, Tunisia, 40, Canada 11, Togo 18, Senegal 12, Bangladesh 11, Zimbabwe 8, Mali 9, Austria 7, Congo 7, Nigeria 7, Russia 4, Poland 3, Egypt 2, Malawi 2, Fifi 1.

10 INTERNATIONAL SPIN

1 International Committee of the Red Cross. "Cri d'alarme du CICR au nom des victimes de la tragédie rwandaise", Geneva, 28 April, 1994. French version. Author's archive.
2 UN Doc. DPKO. Security Council. Informal Consultations. 3 May, 1994.
3 Rwandan Patriotic Front. Letter to H. E. Boutros-Ghali. Signed: Gerald

Gahima, Political Bureau. 3 May, 1994.

4 ICTR testimony. Don Webster. Opening statement. Government One.

5 African Rights, *Rwanda*, 1995, p. 661.

6 Ibid, p. 662.

7 ICTR case no. ICTR 97-23-1. Prosecutor v. Jean Kambanda. Plea Agreement between Jean Kambanda and the Office of the Prosecutor. Under Seal. Author's archive, p. 9.

8 Also present were: Edouard Karemera, Vice-President of the MRND and Emmanuel Ndindabahizi, Minister of Finance.

9 ICTR case no. 97-23-DP. Defence of Jean Kambanda. Affair. Quoted in Kambanda appeal document.

10 African Rights, *Rwanda*, p. 394.

11 ICTR transcript. Interrogation of Jean Kambanda.

12 Dallaire, *Shake Hands with the Devil*, p. 268.

13 African Rights, *Rwanda*, p. 687.

14 Dallaire, *Shake Hands with the Devil*, p. 334.

15 Ibid, p. 345.

16 Ibid, p. 346.

17 Ibid, p. 347.

18 UN Doc. DPKO UNAMIR Interoffice Memorandum. To Force Commander. From CHO. 16 May, 1994.

19 UN Doc. DPKO. UNAMIR. Interoffice Memorandum. To Force Commander. From CHO. 17 May, 1994.

20 Major Don MacNeil, Liaison Officer, UNAMIR. "The Role of UNAMIR", in *Genocide in Rwanda. A Collective Memory*, eds, John A. Berry and Carol Pott Berry, Washington DC: Howard University Press, 1999.

21 UN Doc. DPKO. Code cable. To the SG, Johannesburg. From Annan. Subject; Rwanda. 7 May, 1994.

22 UN Doc. DPKO. Draft. UNAMIR Future Force Structure. 4 May, 1994.

23 UN Doc. DPKO. Security Council Consultations. Thursday, 12 May, 1994.

24 UNAMIR outgoing code cable. Most Immediate. From Dallaire. To Annan. Informal Consultation on the Non-paper. Author's archive.

25 Albright, *Madam Secretary*, p. 151.

26 Samantha Power, "Bystanders to Genocide", *The Atlantic Monthly*, September 2001.

27 Ibid.

28 Dallaire, *Shake Hands with the Devil*, p. 346.
29 Scott R. Feil, *Preventing Genocide: How the Use of Force Might Have Succeeded in Rwanda*, Pre-publication Draft, December 1997. New York: Carnegie Commission on Preventing Deadly Conflict.
30 Linda Melvern, "Missing the Story: The Media and the Rwanda Genocide", in *Dimensions of Western Military Intervention*, eds, Colin McInnes and Nicholas J. Wheeler, London: Frank Cass, 2002.
31 Elaine Sciolino, "For the West, Rwanda is not worth the Political Candle", *New York Times*, 15 April, 1994.
32 "Cold Choices in Rwanda", *New York Times*, 23 April, 1994.
33 Peter Smerdon, "It's Genocide, says UN as Rwandan butchery continues", *Guardian*, 29 April, 1994.
34 "The Orphan of Africa", *Guardian*, 4 May, 1994.
35 Scott Petersen, "Me Against my Brother", London and New York: Routledge, 2001, p. 253.
36 Interview. Reporting The World Conference, Marlow, Buckinghamshire. June, 2001.
37 DANIDA, *The International Response to Conflict and Genocide: Lessons from the Rwandan Experience*. Copenhagen. Chapter 2, p. 36.
38 Aidan Hartley, *The Zanzibar Chest. A Memoir of Love and War*, London: Harper Collins, 2003, p. 371.
39 Steven Livingstone and Todd Eachus, "Rwanda: US Policy and Television Coverage", in Howard Adelman and Astri Suhrke, eds, *The Path of a Genocide. The Rwanda Crisis from Uganda to Zaire*, p. 209.
40 ICTR. Media Trial. Judgement and Sentence, p. 38.
41 Aidan Hartley, *The Zanzibar Chest*, p. 381.
42 Ibid, p. 371.
43 Ibid, pp. 396–7.
44 Communication with Philippe Gaillard. November 2003.
45 ICRC Geneva. Compilation of Press Communications relative to Rwanda, 1993–August 1996. (In French.) Author's archive.
46 Interview with Philippe Gaillard. Switzerland, July 1998.
47 "20 Heures". Presented by Patrick Poivre d'Arvor, 16 May, 1994.
48 "Nightline" (ABC). 4 May, 1994. Transcript 3378. Author's archive.
49 *The United Nations and Rwanda, 1993–96.*
50 UN Doc. UN Security Council. S/PV. 3377. Monday, 16 May, 1994.
51 ICTR Media Trial. The Prosecutor v. Ferdinand Nahimana, Jean-Bosco

Barayagwiza and Hassan Ngeze. Summary of Judgement, 2003.

52 Prunier, *The Rwanda Crisis, 1959–1994*, p. 277.

53 New Zealand Mission to the UN. Notes made by Ambassador Colin Keating. Cable to Wellington, 17 May, 1994. Author's archive.

54 Dallaire, *Shake Hands with the Devil*, p. 355.

55 ICTR testimony. Cross-examination of Théoneste Bagosora. Drew White.

56 Melvern, *The Ultimate Crime*, p. 355.

57 Dallaire, *Shake Hands with the Devil*, p. 414.

58 UN Doc. UNAMIR outgoing code cable. Most Immediate. To Annan. From Dallaire. Situation Report on Rescue Missions. 20 May, 1994. Author's archive.

59 UN Doc. DPKO. Outgoing code cable. To Annan. From Dallaire. 18 May, 1994.

60 UN Doc. DPKO. Letter to Kofi Annan. From MSF Director, Philippe Biberson. 11 June, 1994.

61 Dallaire, *Shake Hands with the Devil*, p. 405.

62 Ibid, p. 400.

63 UN Doc. DPKO. To the Secretary-General. From Annan. UNAMIR Troop Contribution Status. 10 June, 1994.

64 Dallaire, *Shake Hands with the Devil*, p. 376.

65 Ibid.

66 UN Doc. DPKO. UNAMIR outgoing code cable. To Annan/Baril. From Dallaire. Subject: Re-assessment of New Phase Two. No distribution. 31 May, 1994.

67 Report of the Secretary-General on the situation in Rwanda, covering the political mission he sent to Rwanda to move the warring parties towards a ceasefire and recommending that the expanded mandate for UNAMIR be authorised for an initial period of six months. S/10994 640, 31 May, 1994. Blue Book Series, p. 290.

68 Dallaire, *Shake Hands with the Devil*, p. 417.

69 UN Doc. DPKO. UNAMIR outgoing code cable. To Annan. From Dallaire. 20 June, 1994.

70 UN Doc. DPKO. UNAMIR outgoing code cable. To Annan. From Dallaire. An assessment of the proposed French-led initiative in Rwanda Crisis. 20 June, 1994.

71 Dallaire, *Shake Hands with the Devil*, p. 418.

72 Ibid, p. 438.
73 Ibid, p. 426.
74 Ibid, p. 445.
75 In Tanzania there were an estimated 500,000 people. In Burundi, 200,000, and in Bukavu, 200,000. Melvern, *A People Betrayed*, p. 218.
76 Ian Martin, "Hard Choices After Genocide. Human Rights and Humanitarian Dilemmas", in *Hard Choices: Moral Dilemmas in Humanitarian Intervention*, ed. Jonathan Moore, Oxford: Rowan and Littlefield, 1998.
77 US Doc. Background Paper for US Mission, USUN. Subject: Former Rwandan Army (ex-FAR) Capabilities and Intentions. 1 September, 1994. Author's archive.
78 Shaharyar Khan, "The Shallow Graves of Rwanda", London: I. B. Tauris, 2000.
79 Dallaire, *Shake Hands with the Devil*, p. 475.
80 Ian Martin, *After Genocide. The United Nations Field Operation in Rwanda*, Human Rights Centre, University of Essex.
81 UN Doc. DPKO. Report of the UN technical Team on the Security Situation in the Rwanda refugee camps in Zaire. 19 October, 1994. Author's archive.
82 Ibid.

11 THE SILENCE

1 Human Rights Watch. "Leave none to tell the story. Genocide in Rwanda". New York. 1999 p 15.
2 Philippe Gaillard told Richard Dowden, Africa Editor of The Independent newspaper in January 1994 that genocide was likely. Dowden did not believe him. See Dowden: Comment: The Rwandan Genocide: How the Press missed the story: A Memoir. African Affairs (2004) 103, 283–290. Royal African Society.
3 Interview with author. Kigali. October, 1997.
4 UN Doc. Press briefing of Under-Secretary-General for Legal Affairs. Hans Corell. September 3, 1998.
5 UN Doc. Letter dated 1 October from the Secretary-General to the president of the Security Council transmitting the interim report of the Commission of Experts on the evidence of grave violations of international

humanitarian law in Rwanda including possible acts of genocide. S/1194/1125. 4 October, 1994.

6 Bouchet-Saulnier F. and F. Laffont. "*Maudits soient les yeux fermés*" Paris: Editions JC Lattès. 1995.

7 Ibid.

8 Ian Martin. "After Genocide. The United Nations Human Rights Field Operation in Rwanda". Human Rights Centre. University of Essex. Number 20. 1997 Author's archive.

9 UN Doc. Security Council. Report of the Independent Inquiry into the actions of the United Nations during the 1994 genocide in Rwanda. S/19991257. December 16, 1999.

10 Organization of African Unity. *"Rwanda. The Preventable Genocide"*. The Report of the International Panel of Eminent Personalities to Investigate the 1994 Genocide in Rwanda and the surrounding events. July 2000.

11 David Rieff. "Hope is not enough", Prospect. October 2003.

12 Joseph Ndahimana, "Les effects indésirable d'une demande de pardon". *Le Libre Belgique.* 8–9 April 2000.

13 Gérald Papy, "*Kigali: le Belgique demande pardon au people rwandais*". La libre Belgique. 8–9 April 2000. Full text: p. 10.

14 Assemblée Nationale. Mission d'Information Commune. Enquête sur la Tragedie Rwandaise, (1990–1994). Paris. Part 1, p. 363.

15 Assemblée Nationale, p. 187.

16 ICTR Prosecution Testimony. Lt.–General Roméo Dallaire.

17 Mel McNulty, "France's Rwanda Débacle", War Studies, Vol. 2, No. 2, Spring 1998, p. 12.

18 Christian Chatillon. Playboy. Interview with Paul Barril. Reproduced in Réseau Voltaire. 20 September, 2004.

19 Interviews Kigali, December 2004.

20 ICTR prosecution testimony. Lt.-General Roméo Dallaire.

21 Ibid.

22 Daniela Kroslak, "The Responsibility of External Bystanders in Cases of Genocide: The French in Rwanda, 1990–1994. (Unpublished Ph.D. Thesis, University of Wales, Aberystwyth, 2002.)

23 Kroslak.

24 Assemblée Nationale. Annexe 6. 1998.

25 ICTR prosecution witness statement. IB.

26 ICTR Defence Testimony. Théoneste Bagosora. Military One.

27 République Française. Note au Ministère des Affaires étrangères. 25 April, 1994. Signed Marlaud. Assemblée Nationale, Mission d'Information Commune, Enquête sur la Tragédie Rwandaise (1990–1994), Paris. Annexe 6. 1998.
28 AFP-RTR 27 April, 1994. "Agathe Uwilingiyimana voulait "organiser un coup d'état, selon le partidu president Habyarimana".
29 François-Xavier Verschave. *"La Francafrique. Le plus long scandale de la Republique"*, Paris: Stock, 1998, p. 190.
30 Daniela Kroslak, "*The Responsibility of External Bystanders in Cases of Genocide: The French in Rwanda, 1990–1994*" (Unpublished Ph. D. Thesis, University of Wales, Aberystwyth, 2002), p. 329.
31 Colette Braeckman. "L'avion rwandais abattu par des Français?" *Le Soir* 17 June, 1994.
32 Richard Menzel. Technical Officer. ICAO. Email message to author: 29 November, 2005.
33 Stephen Smith: "L'enquêsur l'attentat qui fit basculer le Rwanda dans le génocide". *Le Monde*, 10 March, 2004.
34 Mehdi Ba. "L'évocation du rapport Bruguière est un mensonge éhonté". Golias No. 101. March–April 2005.
35 UN Document. Press Release.
36 François Misser. "Vers un nouveau Rwanda? Entretiens avec Paul Kagame". Brussels: Editions Luc Pire, p. 79.
37 Rwandan Embassy in Washington. "Attitude of Washington vis-à-vis the Interim Government". Letter from Ambassador Aloys Uwamani to The Minister of Foreign Affairs. 11 July, 1994.
38 Colin Keating. "Lessons from the Security Council's Role in the Rwanda Crisis". In David M Malone, ed., "The UN Security Council. From the Cold War to the twenty-first century". Boulder, Co: Lynne Rienner Publishers, 2004.
39 Samantha Power. "Bystanders to Genocide", *Atlantic Monthly*. September 2001.
40 Interviews with author. Anonymous sources. London. September 2003.
41 Madeleine Albright. "Madam Secretary. A Memoir". New York. Talk Miramax. 2003.
42 Jon Leyne on BBC1 News, 12.6.1994. Nicola McPake. "Failing to uncover the truth: The British media and the Rwandan genocide". Dissertation. University of Stirling.

43 Richard Dowden. "Comment: The Rwandan Genocide: How the Press Missed the Story: A Memoir. African Affairs, (2004), 103, 283–290. Royal Africa Society 2004.

44 Linda Melvern. "Death by Diplomacy", The Scotsman, January 1995. See also Melvern: 'The UN and Rwanda", The London Review of Books, December 1996; "A People Betrayed. The Role of the West in Rwanda's Genocide". Zed Books. 2000. Mark Curtis "Britain's Bit Part in Rwanda's Tragedy", Africa Analysis, Vol. 27 January, 1995. Linda Melvern and Paul Williams. "Britannia Waived the Rules: The Major Government and the 1994 Rwandan Genocide", African Affairs, Spring 2004. For US reaction see: Michael Barnett. "Eyewitness to a Genocide. The United Nations and Rwanda", New York. Cornell. 2001. PBS-Frontline. "The Triumph of Evil". January 26, 1999. Samantha Power, "A Problem from Hell, America and the Age of Genocide", Flamingo 2002.

45 Alan J. Kuperman. "The Limits of Humanitarian Intervention. Genocide in Rwanda". Brookings Institution Press. Washington DC. 2001.

46 Kuperman.

47 Interview with James Woods. Deputy Assistant Secretary for African Affairs, Department of Defense. Interview. PBS Frontline. At www.pbs.org.

48 Prime Minister Tony Blair. Speech to the Labour Party Annual Conference, Brighton, 2 October, 2001.

49 Stephen Castle. Clare Garner. "Britain declares annual Holocaust Memorial Day". The Independent. 27 January, 2000.

50 In 2004, for the tenth anniversary of the genocide the government designated Holocaust Memorial Day: "From the Holocaust to Rwanda: Lessons learned, lessons still to learn".

51 Our Common Interest. Report of the Commission for Africa. March 11, 2005, p. 37.

52 Douglas Hurd. "Why the UN is more important to the world than ever", Evening Standard, 20 June 1994.

53 Douglas Hurd, "Memoirs", Little,Brown. London. 2003.

54 Linda Melvern. "A People Betrayed. The Role of the West in Rwanda's Genocide", London. Zed Books 2000.

12 JUDGEMENT

1 Jean-Marie Aboganena. "*Quelle diplomatie pour le Cameroun*", Africa International. Numero 294. May 1996.
2 Richard Goldstone. "Justice now, and for posterity". International Herald Tribune. 15–16 October 2005.
3 ICTR-96-4-1. Judgment in the case against Akayesu.
4 Ngeze and Nahimana were sentenced to life imprisonment, Barayagwiza to a 27 year sentence. All three cases are on appeal.
5 The statute of the ICTR does not permit capital punishment. The government of Rwanda held that conviction with execution ought to be among the possible verdicts. This possibility was rejected by the Security Council given European opposition.
6 Thierry Cruvellier. The Secret of the Akazu. *International Justice Tribune.* 21 November, 2005.
7 "Tribunal confirms transfer of suspect to The Hague". Hirondelle Press Agency in Arusha. 19 August, 2005.
8 ICTR Prosecution Opening Statement. Don Webster. Karemera et al. ICTR 98-44-T. November 2003.
9 Allan Thompson: "Rwandan "kingpin" plays it cool". Ex-Colonel accused of plotting the 1994 genocide smiles for reporter's camera and mocks Dallaire". *The Toronto Star*, 10 July, 2005.

SOURCES

UNITED NATIONS BOOKS, AVAILABLE REPORTS AND DOCUMENTS:

Security Council

An Agenda for Peace: Preventive Diplomacy, Peacemaking and Peacekeeping. Report of the Secretary-General pursuant to the statement adopted by the Summit Meeting of the Security Council on 31 January, 1992 (A/47/277 – S/24111), 17 June, 1992.

Effective Planning, Budgeting and Administration of Peacekeeping Operations. Report of the Secretary-General (A/48/1994), 25 May, 1994.

Rwanda

Interim report of the Commission of Experts established in accordance with Security Council resolution 935 (S/1994/1125) 4 October, 1994.

Final report of the Commission of Experts established pursuant to Security Council resolution 935 (S/1994/1405), 9 December, 1994.

Report of the Independent Inquiry into the Actions of the United Nations during the 1994 Genocide in Rwanda. 15 December, 1999.

Somalia

Report of the Commission of Inquiry Established Pursuant to Security Council Resolution 885 (1993) To Investigate Armed Attacks on UNOSOM II Personnel Which Led To Casualties Among Them. 24 February, 1994.

Economic and Social Council. Commission on Human Rights

Report by Mr. B.W. Ndiaye, Special Rapporteur, on his mission to Rwanda from 8–17 April, 1993 (E/CN4/1994/7/Add 1), 11 August, 1993.

Report of the United Nations High Commissioner for Human Rights, Mr José Ayala Lasso, on his mission to Rwanda, 11–12 May, 1994 (E/CN.4/S-3/3), 19 May, 1994.

Revised and updated report on the question of the prevention and punishment of the crime of genocide. B. Whitaker (E/CN.4/1985/6), 2 July, 1985.

Report on the situation of human rights in Rwanda submitted by M. René Dégni-Ségui, Special Rapporteur, under paragraph 20 of resolution S–3/1 of 25 May, 1994 (E/CN.4/1995/7), 28 June, 1994. Further reports: 12 August, 1994 (E/CN.4/1995/12) and 11 November, 1994 (E/CN.4/1995/70).

United Nations books

The United Nations and Rwanda, 1993–1996. The United Nations Blue Book series, Vol. 10. New York: UN Department of Public Information, 1996 (Contains all the Secretary-General's reports and letters to the Security Council in relation to UNAMIR together with all relevant resolutions.)

The Blue Helmets: A Review of United Nations Peacekeeping (3rd edn). New York: UN Publications, 1996.

Comprehensive report on lessons learned from United Nations Assistance Mission for Rwanda (UNAMIR), October 1993–April 1996. New York: United Nations, 1996.

REPORTS

ADL, *Rapport sur les droits de l'homme au Rwanda. September 1991–September 1992.* Kigali: Association Rwandaise pour la défense des droits de la personne et des libertés publiques (AD1), December 1992.

Amnesty International, Rwanda: Amnesty International's Concerns Since the Beginning of an Insurgency in October, 1990. March 1991 (AI Index: AFR *47/05/91).*

— *Rwanda: Persecution of Tutsi Minority and Repression of Government Critics, 1990–1992.* May 1992.

— *Rwanda: Mass Murder by Government Supporters and Troops in April and May, 1994.* 23 May, 1994.

— *A Call for UN human rights action on Rwanda and Burundi.* May 1994.

Article 19, *Broadcasting Genocide: Censorship, Propaganda and State-Sponsored Violence in Rwanda 1990–1994. Article 19,* October 1996.

Assemblée Nationale, Mission d'Information Commune, *Enquête sur la Tragédie Rwandaise (1990–1994)*, Paris.

Belgian Senate, *Commission d'enquête parlementaire concernant les événements du Rwanda.* Report, 6 December, 1997.

Chossudovsky, Michel and Pierre Galand, *L'Usage de la Dette Extérieure du Rwanda (1990/1994) La Responsabilité des Bailleurs de Fonds. Analyse et Recommandations.* Brussels and Ottawa. Rapport Préliminaire, November 1996.

Fédération Internationale des Droits de l'Homme (FIDH). Rapport sur la Commission d'enquête sur les violations des droits de l'homme au Rwanda depuis le 1er Octobre, 1990: Paris and New York.

Feil, Colonel Scott R., *Preventing Genocide. How the Use of Force Might Have Succeeded in Rwanda.* Pre-publication Draft, December 1997. New York: Carnegie Commission on Preventing Deadly Conflict.

Genocide in Rwanda. Documentation of Two Massacres during April 1994. Issue Brief, US Committee for Refugees, November 1994.

Human Rights Watch, *Genocide in Rwanda April–May 1994.* May 1994. Human Rights Watch, *Rwanda: Talking Peace and Waging War.* 27 February, 1992.

Human Rights Watch, *World Report, 1994.* December 1993.

Human Rights Watch Arms Project, *Arming Rwanda. The Arms Trade and Human Rights Abuses in the Rwandan War*, Vol. 6, no. 1, January 1994.

International Federation of Human Rights (FIDH), Africa Watch, InterAfrican Union of Human Rights, and International Centre of Rights of the Person and of Democratic Development, *Report of the International Commission of Investigation of Human Rights Violations in Rwanda since 1 October, 1990,* 7–21 January, 1993. See also: *Report of the International Commission of Investigation on Human Rights Violations in Rwanda since 1 October, 1990. 7–21 January, 1993. Final Reports,* New York: Human Rights Watch/Africa, March 1993.

International Monetary Fund, *Rwanda. Briefing Paper 1992 Article IV Consultation and Discussions on a Second Annual Arrangement under the Structural Adjustment Facility.* 14 May, 1992.

The International Response to Conflict and Genocide: Lessons from the Rwanda Experience. Joint Emergency Assistance to Rwanda. Copenhagen, March 1996. Study I: "Historical Perspective: Some Explanatory Factors", Tor

Sellström and Lennart Wohlgemuth. Study II: "Early Warning and Conflict Management", Howard Adelman. Study III: "Humanitarian Aid and Effects", John Bourton, Emery Brusset, Alistair Hallam. Study IV: "Rebuilding Post-War Rwanda", Krishna Kumar, David Tardif-Douglin, Kim Maynard, Peter Manikas, Annette Sheckler and Carolyn Knapp. Synthesis Report, John Eriksson (ISBN 87 7265 335). (This study was initiated in 1995 by the Nordic countries, eventually sponsored by nineteen countries and eighteen international agencies. France withdrew its support for the report after examining the draft.)

Minear, Larry, and Philippe Guillot, *Soldiers to the Rescue. Humanitarian Lessons from Rwanda.* Paris: Development Centre of the Organization for Economic Cooperation and Development, 1996.

Reporters sans Frontières, "Rwanda: Médias de la haine ou presse démocratique?" Report of mission 16–24, September, 1994.

Segal, Aaron, *Massacre in Rwanda*, Fabian Society, April, 1964.

UN Report on the Fifth Annual Peacekeeping Mission 3–11 November, 1995. United Nations Association of the USA, January 1996.

US Department of State, *Annual Report on Human Rights, 1993.*

Watson, Catherine, *Exile from Rwanda. Background to an Invasion.* US Committee for Refugees, Issue Paper. Washington, DC, February 1991.

PAPERS

Gaillard, Philippe, *Rwanda 1994: La vraie vie est absente (Arthur Rimbaud) Cycle de Conférence les Mardi de Musée. M. Philippe Gaillard, délégué du CIRC, chef de délégation au Rwanda de juillet 1993 à juillet 1994.* Unpublished.

Kroslak, Daniela, *The Media in Wartime. International History and International Politics*, University of Wales, Aberystwyth, 1997. Unpublished.

— "Evaluating the Moral Responsibility of France in the 1994 Rwandan Genocide." Paper presented to the 23rd annual conference of the British International Studies Association (BISA), 14–16 December, 1998. Unpublished.

— *The Responsibility of External Bystanders in Cases of Genocide: The French in Rwanda, 1990–1994*, unpublished Ph. D. Thesis, University of Wales, Aberystwyth, 2002.

Mamdani, Mahmood, "From Conquest to Consent as the Basis of State Formation:

Reflections on Rwanda." Paper presented to the conference Crisis in the Great Lakes Region, organised by the Council for the Development of Social Research in Africa, Arusha, Tanzania, 4–7 September, 1995.

McPake, "Failing to uncover the truth: The British media and the Rwandan genocide". Unpublished dissertation. University of Stirling.

Mfizi, Christophe, *Le Réseau Zéro, Lettre Ouverte à M. le Président du Mouvement Républicain National pour la Démocratie et le Développement (MRNDD),* Editions Uruhimbi, BP 1067 Kigali, Rwanda, 1992.

Tarling, Serena I. M, *Blinkered vision: how British journalists saw and reported the Rwandan genocide*, Napier University. MA Thesis. Print, Media and Communications department, Napier University, Edinburgh.

JOURNALS

Africa Confidential, "Rwanda: Civilian Slaughter", Vol. 35, no. 9, 6 May, 1994.

Barnett, Michael N., "The UN Security Council, Indifference, and the Genocide in Rwanda". *Cultural Anthropology,* Vol. 12, no. 4, 1997.

Blankfort, Lowell, "Almost a Million dead, Rwanda Seeks Justice", *World Outlook,* 2 December 1995 (UNA-US).

Bradol, Jean-Hervé, "Rwanda, Avril–Mai 1994. Limites et Ambiguités de l'Action Humanitaire. Crises Politiques, Massacres et Exodes Massifs", *Le Temps Modernes*, no. 583, 1995.

Burkhalter, Holly J., "The Question of Genocide. The Clinton Administration and Rwanda", *World Policy Journal*, Vol. 11, no. 4, Winter 1994–95.

Clapham, Christopher, "Rwanda: The Perils of Peacemaking", *Journal of Peace Research,* Vol. 35, no. 2, 1998.

Destexhe, Alain, "The Third Genocide", *Foreign Policy*, no. 97, Winter 1994–95.

Heusch, Luc de, "Rwanda. Responsibilities for a Genocide", *Anthropology Today,* Vol. II, no. 4, August 1994.

Jones, Bruce, "'Intervention Without Borders'. Humanitarian Intervention in Rwanda, 1990–94'", *Millennium,* Vol. 24, No. 2, Summer 1995.

Leitenberg, Milton, "Rwanda, 1994: International Incompetence Produces Genocide", *Peacekeeping and International Relations*, November–December 1994.

Lemarchand, René, "The Apocalypse in Rwanda", *Cultural Survival Quarterly,* Summer/Fall, 1994.

Mel, McNulty, "France's Rwanda Debacle", *War Studies*, Vol. 2, no. 2, Spring 1997.

Mamdani, Mahmood, "From Conquest to Consent as the Basis of State Formation: Reflections on Rwanda", *New Left Review*, no. 216, 1996.

Melvern, Linda, "The UN and Rwanda", *London Review of Books*, 12 December, 1996.

— "Genocide Behind the Thin Blue Line", *Security Dialogue,* Vol. 28, no. 3, September 1997.

— " Is anyone interested in Rwanda?", *British Journalism Review,* July 2001.

— "The Security Council: behind the scenes", *International Affairs*, 77, 2001.

— with Paul Williams, "Britannia Waived the Rules: The Major Government and the 1994 Genocide in Rwanda", *African Affairs*, Vol. 103, no. 410, January 2004.

Smith, David Norman, "The Genesis of Genocide in Rwanda: The Fatal Dialectic of Class and Ethnicity", *Humanity and Society*, Vol. 19, no. 4, November 1995.

Suhrke, Astri, "Dilemmas of Protection: The Log of the Kigali Battalion", *Security Dialogue,* Vol. 29, no. 1, March 1998.

van Hoyweghen, Saskia, "The Disintegration of the Catholic Church of Rwanda. A Study of the Fragmentation of Political and Religious Authority", *African Affairs,* no. 95, 1996, pp. 379–401.

BOOKS

Adelman, Howard and Suhrke, Astri, ed.s, *The Path of a Genocide. The Rwanda Crisis from Uganda to Zaire,* New Brunswick, NJ: Transaction, 1999.

Abdulai, Napoleon, ed., *Genocide in Rwanda*, Africa Research and Information Centre, 1994.

African Rights, *Rwanda. Death, Despair and Defiance*, London: African Rights, 1995.

Albright, Madeleine, *Madam Secretary: A Memoir*, New York: Talk Miramax, 2003.

Anyidoho, Henry Kwami, *Guns Over Kigali*, Accra: Woeli Publishing Services, 1997.

Barnett, Michael, "The Politics of Indifference at the United Nations and Genocide in Rwanda and Bosnia", in Thomas Cushman and Stjepan

Mestrovic, eds, *This Time We Knew: Western Responses to Genocide in Bosnia*, New York: New York University Press, 1996.

— *Eyewitness to a Genocide. The UN and Rwanda,* Ithaca, New York: Cornell University Press 2002.

Berry, John A and Carol Pott Berry, eds, *Genocide in Rwanda. A Collective Memory*, Washington DC: Howard University Press, 1999.

Blumenthal, Sidney, *The Clinton Wars. An Insider's Account of the White House Years*, London: Viking, 2003.

Bowen, Michael, Gary Freeman and Kay Miller, *Passing By. The United States and Genocide in Burundi, 1972.* Special Report. Humanitarian Policy Studies. Carnegie Endowment for International Peace.

Boutros-Ghali, Boutros, *Unvanquished. A US-UN Saga*, London: I.B. Tauris, 1999.

Braeckman, Colette, *Rwanda, Histoire d'un Génocide.* Paris: Fayard, 1994.

— *Terreur Africaine. Burundi, Rwanda, Zaire: les racines de la violence*, Paris: Fayard, 1996.

Castonguay, Jacques, *Les Casques Bleus au Rwanda*, Paris: Editions l'Harmattan, 1998.

Chrétien, Jean-Pierre, *Le Défi de l'Ethnisme. Rwanda et Burundi, 1990–1996,* Paris: Karthala, 1997.

Chrétien, Jean-Pierre, Jean-Francois Dupaquier, Marcel Kabanda and Joseph Ngarambe (Reporters sans Frontières), *Rwanda: Les Médias du Génocide*, Paris: Karthala, 1995.

Clapham, Christopher, ed., *African Guerrillas*, Oxford: James Currey; 1998.

Cohen, Herman J, *Intervening in Africa. Superpower Peacemaking in a Troubled Continent*, Basingstoke: Macmillan, 2000.

Dallaire, Lt.-Gen Roméo, *Shake Hands wirh the Devil. The Failure of Humanity in Rwanda*, Canada: Random House, 2003.

Destexhe Alain, *Rwanda: essai sur le génocide*, Editions Complexe, 1994.

— *Qui a Tué Nos Paras?* Brussels: Editions Luc Pire, 1996.

Durch, William J., ed., *UN Peacekeeping: American Politics and the Uncivil Wars of the 1990s.* Henry L. Stimson Center, New York: St Martin's Press, 1996.

Eltringham, N. P., *Accounting for Horror: Post-Genocide Debates in Rwanda*, London: Pluto, 2004.

Fein, Helen, *Accounting for Genocide after 1945. Theories and Some Findings*, International Journal on Group Rights, Vol. 1. Amsterdam: Martinus Nijhoff, 1993.

Gordon, Nick, *Murders in the Mist*, London: Hodder and Stoughton, 1993.

Gourevitch, Philip, *We wish to inform you that tomorrow we will be killed with our families. Stories from Rwanda*, London: Picador 1999.

Gouteux, Jean-Paul, *Un Génocide secret d'Etat*, Editions Sociales, 1998.

Gribbin, Robert E., "In the Aftermath of Genocide. The US Role in Rwanda", Universe, 2005.

Guichaoua, André, ed., *Les Crises Politiques au Burundi et au Rwanda (1993–1994),* Université des Sciences et Technologies de Lille, Paris: Karthala, 1995.

Hartley, Aidan, *The Zanzibar Chest. A Memoir of Love and War*, London: HarperCollins, 2003.

Horowitz, Irving, *Taking Lives: Genocide and State Power*, New Brunswick, NJ: Transaction, 1981.

Human Rights Watch/Fédération Internationale des Ligues des Droits de l'Homme, *Leave None to Tell the Story. Genocide in Rwanda*, 1999.

Jones, Bruce D., *Peacemaking in Rwanda. The Dynamics of Failure*, Boulder, Colorado: Lynne Rienner, 2001.

Klinghoffer, Arthur Jay, *The International Dimension of Genocide in Rwanda*, London: Macmillan, 1998.

Kuper, Leo, *The Prevention of Genocide*, New Haven, CT, and London: Yale University Press, 1985.

Kuperman, Alan J., *The Limits of Humanitarian Intervention. Genocide in Rwanda*, Washington DC: Brookings Institute, 2001.

Lema, Antoine, *Africa Divided*, Sweden: Lund University Press, 1993.

Lemarchand, René, *Rwanda and Burundi*, London: Pall Mall, London, 1970.

Les Familles des Paras, *Rwanda. Lettre Ouverte aux parlementaires. Le texte du rapport du groupe "Rwanda" du Sénat*, Brussels: Editions Luc Pire, 1997.

Marchal, Colonel Luc, *Rwanda: la descente aux enfers. Témoinage d'un peacekeeper Decembre 1993–Avril 1994*, Brussels: Labor, 2001.

Malone, David M., ed, *The UN Security Council from the Cold War to the Twenty-First Century*, Boulder Colorado: Lynne Rienner, 2004.

Marrus, Michael, The *Holocaust in History*, Harmondsworth: Penguin, 1996.

Melvern, Linda, *The Ultimate Crime. Who Betrayed the UN and Why*, London: Allison and Busby, 1995.

— *A People Betrayed. The Role of the West in Rwanda's Genocide*, London: Zed Books, 2000.

Misser, François, *Vers un Nouveau Rwanda? Entretiens avec Paul Kagame*, Brussels: Editions Luc Pire, 2000.

Moore, Jonathan, ed., *Hard Choices, Moral Dilemmas in Humanitarian Intervention*, Oxford: Rowman and Littlefield, 1998.

McInnes, Colin and Nicholas J. Wheeler, eds., *Dimensions of Western Military Intervention*, London: Frank Cass, 2002.

Newbury, Catharine, The *Cohesion of Oppression; Clientship and Ethnicity in Rwanda, 1860–1960,* Columbia University Press, 1988.

Nshimiyimana, Vénuste, *Prélude du Génocide Rwandais. Enquête sur les Circonstances Politiques et Militaires du Meutre du Président Habyarimana*, Paris: Quorum, 1995.

Ould-Abdallah, Ahmedou, *Burundi on the Brink 1993–95*, Washington DC: US Institute of Peace, 2000.

Petersen, Scott, *Me Against my Brother,* London: Routledge, 2001.

Piollet, J.-B., *Les Missions catholiques françaises au XIXe siècle,* Les Missions d'Afrique, 1902.

Porter, Jack Nusan, *Genocide and Human Rights. A Global Anthology,* University Press of America, 1982.

Power, Samantha: *A Problem from Hell: America and the Age of Genocide*, New York: Basic Books, 2002.

Prunier, Gérard, *The Rwanda Crisis 1959–1994. History of a Genocide*. London: Hurst and Company, 1995.

Reyntjens, Filip, *L'Afrique des Grands Lacs en crise. Rwanda, Burundi: 1988–1994,* Paris: Karthala, 1994.

— *Rwanda. Trois Jours qui on fait basculer l'histoire,* Paris: Editions l'Harmattan, 1995.

Schabas, William A. *Genocide in International Law*, Cambridge: Cambridge University Press, 2000.

Semujanga, Josias, *Origins of Rwandan Genocide*, New York: Humanity Books, 2003.

Speke, J. H., *Journal of the discovery of the source of the Nile*, London: J. M. Dent, 1969 (1st edn, 1863).

Tadjo, Veronique, *The Shadow of Imana. Travels in the heart of Rwanda*, translated by Veronique Wakerley, London: Heinemann, 2002.

Uvin, Peter, *Aiding Violence: The Development Enterprise in Rwanda*, New York: Kumarian Press, 1998.

Vansina, Jan, *Le Rwanda ancient: Le Royaume Ngiyinya*, Paris: Karthala, 2001.

Vassall-Adams, Guy, *Rwanda: An Agenda for International Action,* Oxford: Oxfam Publications, 1994.

Waugh, Colin, *Paul Kagame and Rwanda. Power, Genocide and the Rwandan Patriotic Front,* Jefferson NC: McFarland, 2004.

Wheeler, Nicholas J., *Saving Strangers: Humanitarian Intervention in International Society*, Oxford: Oxford University Press, 2000.

CHRONOLOGY

1500 lt is believed that from 1506 there was increasing unification of the kingdom of Rwanda. A society was created which would be compared with those in European feudal states.

1885 The Berlin Conference agrees that Ruanda-Urundi should become a German protectorate.

1894 The first European, a German, Count Gustav Adolf von Götzen, arrives at the Rwandan court.

1900 The Missionaries of Africa (White Fathers) found their first mission in Rwanda.

1907 The Germans establish a post in Kigali and a prominent explorer, Richard Kandt, is appointed the first Resident.

1910 The frontiers of the Belgian Congo, British Uganda and German East Africa – including Ruanda-Urundi – are fixed at a conference in Brussels.

1911 A popular uprising in northern Rwanda is crushed by the German Schütztruppe and Tutsi chiefs, leaving bitterness among northern Hutu.

1913 Coffee introduced as a cash crop.

1914 German control strengthens with the introduction of a head tax.

1916 Belgian troops drive out the Germans and occupy both Ruanda and Urundi.

1923 Ruandi-Urundi becomes a mandated territory of the League Of Nations under the supervision of Belgium.

1931 November: King Musinga is deposed by the Belgian administration and replaced with one of his sons.

1933 The Belgian administrators organize a census and everyone is issued with an identity card classifying people as Hutu, Tutsi or Twa.

1945 Transfer of the Belgian mandate to a UN Trust Territory.

1946 Dedication of Rwanda to Christ the King.

1948 The Convention on the Punishment and Prevention of the Crime of Genocide, voted by the General Assembly on 9 December. First UN Trusteeship Council visiting mission goes to Ruanda-Urundi and Tanganyika.

1957 Publication of the Hutu Manifesto.

1959 King Mutara Rudahigwa dies in suspicious circumstances.
Aug–Sept Political parties are created.
November There is a Hutu rebellion and thousands of Tutsi flee for their lives to Burundi.
Belgium places Rwanda under military rule.
Hutu now favoured by Belgian administrators.

1960 Rwanda's first municipal elections give Hutu a large majority.

1961

January The monarchy is formally abolished by a referendum and a republic is proclaimed.
There is a new wave of violence against the Tutsi.
More people flee from the country.

1962 Armed attacks by Tutsi exiles from Burundi.
There are internal reprisals and 2,000 Tutsi are killed.
Proclamation of the independence of Rwanda.
Grégoire Kayibanda is declared president.

1963 Further armed attacks from Tutsi into Rwanda.
Violence against Tutsi escalates and there are further massacres of Tutsi. A new wave of refugees.

1964 British philosopher Lord Bertrand Russell calls the killing of Tutsi in Rwanda the most horrible extermination of a people since the killing of the European Jews.

1967 Renewed massacres of Tutsi.

1972 Massacres of Hutu in Burundi.
Tutsi are purged from the administration in Rwanda.

1973 A purge of Tutsi from schools and the National University of Rwanda, Butare.
Coup d'état by Major Juvénal Habyarimana.

1975 Creation of the one-party MRND. France and Rwanda sign a military assistance agreement.

1978 Habyarimana promulgates a new constitution and becomes president of Rwanda after an election in which he is the sole candidate. Hutu are favoured in government.

1979 The Rwandan Alliance for National Unity (RANU) is created in Kenya.

1980 An attempted coup by Colonel Théoneste Lizinde, ex-security chief, and thirty conspirators.

1982 The Rwandan refugee communities in Uganda are attacked. Those who flee to the border are trapped.

1983 Re-election of President Juvénal Habyarimana with 99.98 per cent of the vote.

1986 The government in Kigali announces that Rwandan refugees will not be allowed home because the country is not big enough.

1987

1 July Celebrations for twenty-five years of independence.

1988 International conference held by Rwandan refugees in Washington, DC.
The RPF is created in Uganda. Re-electron of Habyarimana with more than 99 per cent of the vote.

1989 First meeting of a Rwanda-Uganda ministerial committee to discuss the refugee problem.

1990

July Habyarimana concedes the principle of multi-party democracy.

September Thirty-three intellectuals publish a letter to denounce the one-party system.
Pope John Paul II visits Rwanda.

October The RPF invades Rwanda, starting a civil war. France, Belgium and Zaire send troops.
Rwanda's ambassador to Egypt requests Boutros Boutros-Ghali, minister of state, to help Rwanda obtain arms.
First Egyptian weapons sold to Rwanda.
South Africa starts to sell arms to Rwanda.

Thousands of people, most of them Tutsi, are arrested in Rwanda.
More than 300 Tutsi are killed in Gisenyi.
Structural adjustment programme (SAP) for Rwanda is agreed.
The planning of a genocide of the Tutsi begins.

1991

January The RPF attack Ruhengeri prison.
Massacres of Tutsi take place in the prefectures of Gisenyi, Ruhengeri, Kibuye and Byumba.
A further arms deal is concluded with Egypt.

February Guerrilla attack by the RPF in response to massacres.
Summit in Dar-es-Salaam to discuss Rwanda crisis.

March A ceasefire agreement is signed in N'sele, Zaire, under OAU supervision, between the Rwandan government and the RPF but it soon breaks down. A further arms deal is concluded between Egypt and the Rwandan government.

April A further arms deal is concluded between Egypt and the Rwandan government.

June A new constitution is adopted bringing in multi-partyism.
A French intelligence report warns that an extremist group surrounding Agathe Habyarimana is encouraging ethnic hatred and is determined to resist democracy.

August Creation of political parties, the MDR, PSD, PL.

September The OAU creates a Neutral Military Observer Group (NMOG) to monitor the border between Rwanda and Uganda.

November A demonstration organized by opposition to the government brings thousands onto the streets of Kigali.

1992 On and off talks continue between the Rwanda government and the RPF at various locations for over a year and another ceasefire is signed; this one is largely observed. US assistant secretary of state for Africa, Herman Cohen, convenes an inter-agency forum in Washington to discuss Rwanda.

February Massacres of Tutsi take place in the Bugesera. Radio

Rwanda is blamed for incitement by human rights groups.
CDR and MRND militias are built up by Hutu Power supporters.

March Rwandan human rights groups link deaths in the Bugesera to local officials.
A further arms deal is concluded between Egypt and the Rwandan government.

April A new government is created with increased representation.
The president of the World Bank, Lewis Preston, writes to Habyarimana to ask him to stop military spending.

May Violent demonstrations by militia.
Agathe Uwilingiyimana, minister of education, attacked in her home.
Pitched battles between supporters of political parties.
The RPF meets with the OAU in Kampala.

June A further arms deal is concluded between Egypt and the Rwandan government.

August A defector, Christophe Mfizi, reveals that Rwanda is run by a ruthless and greedy oligarchy from the north.
Formal opening of the peace conference in Arusha, Tanzania.

October Professor Filip Reyntjens gives a press conference in Brussels to warn of death squads in Rwanda.

November The planning for a new radio station begins.
Political violence occurs. Hutu extremist militia grows.
Government opponents continue to demonstrate.
Prominent Hutu Dr Léon Mugesera appeals to Hutu to send the Tutsi back to Ethiopia via the rivers.
A further arms deal is concluded between Egypt and the Rwandan government.

1993

January The composition of a broad-based transitional government is agreed at the negotiations in Arusha.
More than 300 Tutsi killed in the north-west.
International human rights experts visit Rwanda.
Weapons are distributed to communal police in certain areas.

The importation of huge numbers of agricultural tools commences.

February The RPF launches a fresh offensive and their soldiers reach the outskirts of Kigali. French forces called in to help. More than one million people displaced because of the fighting.

March A new ceasefire is agreed.
At the UN Security Council in New York, France suggests the creation of a UN peacekeeping mission for Rwanda.
A human rights report is published revealing that 2,000 Tutsi have been killed since 1990.
A further arms deal is concluded between Egypt and the Rwandan government.

April The ICRC warns that because of the displaced people in Rwanda there is the risk of a major humanitarian catastrophe. Famine is imminent. UN Human Rights Commission Special Rapporteur on Extrajudicial, Summary or Arbitrary Executions, Bacre Waly Ndiaye, visits Rwanda.

May The Habyarimana regime enters into an arms deal for US$12 million with a French arms dealer.
The Secretary-General, in a report to the Security Council, recommends the creation of a UN observer mission for the Rwanda-Uganda border.

June The Security Council adopts resolution 846 creating the United Nations Observer Mission Uganda-Rwanda (UNOMUR).
Brigadier-General Roméo A. Dallaire appointed commander of UNOMUR.

July A new government is formed with Agathe Uwilingiyimana as prime minister. This results in divisions within the MDR.

August The Arusha Accords are signed between the Rwandan government and the RPF. Multi-party elections, which are to include the RPF, are scheduled to be held within twenty-two months.
Dallaire arrives in Kigali with a reconnaissance mission to evaluate the possible role of international peacekeepers.
Bacre Waly Ndiaye publishes a report for the UN Human Rights Commission which reveals that in Rwanda the

Convention on the Prevention and Punishment of the Crime of Genocide, 1948, is applicable.

September The Secretary-General recommends to the Security Council that a peacekeeping force be provided for Rwanda without delay.

October Eighteen elite US troops are killed in Somalia.
The US Security Council passes resolution 872 creating the UN Assistance Mission for Rwanda (UNAMIR), which is to help implement the Arusha Accords. UNOMUR is integrated into UNAMIR.
Dallaire is appointed force commander of UNAMIR.
The Hutu President Melchior Ndadaye is killed in Burundi. Thousands of people flee from Burundi to Rwanda.
Political violence in Rwanda escalates.

November The Organization of African Unity (OAU) Neutral Military Observer Group (NMOG) is integrated into UNAMIR. The Belgian troops arrive in Kigali.
The Secretary-General's special representative, Jacques-Roger Booh-Booh, arrives.
A series of killings takes place in northern communes.

December UNAMIR peacekeepers are in place in Rwanda. As part of the Arusha Accords a contingent of RPF troops is deployed in Kigali. French troops withdraw. A few remain.
Diplomats in Kigali and Dallaire receive an anonymous letter from within the Rwandan army warning of a plan to kill Tutsi in order to prevent the implementation of the Arusha Accords.

1994

January Rwanda takes its seat as a non-permanent member of the Security Council. The Security Council adopts resolution 893 approving deployment of a second infantry battalion to the de-militarized zone.
Investiture of Habyarimana as president.
Transitional government fails to take off, with each side blaming the other for blocking its formation.
Human Rights Watch Arms Project publishes a report on

the continuing arming of Rwanda.

The Belgian ambassador in Kigali, Johan Swinnen, warns Brussels that the new hate-radio is destabilizing Rwanda.

Violent demonstration in Kigali by the Interahamwe.

The CIA reports that if hostilities resume in Rwanda up to half a million people could die.

Dallaire informs UN headquarters there is an informer from the heart of Hutu Power who warns that a genocide against the Tutsi is planned. Dallaire tries to persuade UN headquarters that he be allowed to conduct arms seizures.

February Félicien Gatabazi of the PSD assassinated. Martin Bucyana, the president of the CDR, lynched.

Dallaire warns New York of the deteriorating situation, weapons distribution, death squad target lists, and pleads for reinforcements. USA issues a travel advisory for Rwanda.

The ICRC and MSF stockpile medicines and prepare for large numbers of casualties.

Belgian Foreign Minister Willy Claes visits Rwanda. Warns Boutros-Ghali that Dallaire needs a stronger mandate. Claes warns the USA that Habyarimana could be playing a double game.

March A joint communiqué is issued by Kigali diplomatic community asking for acceptance of the CDR.

Boutros-Ghali writes a report to the Security Council that the security situation is deteriorating and requests an extension of the mandate of UNAMIR for six months.

2 April Booh-Booh threatens that the UN will pull out unless the peace agreement is implemented.

5 April The Security Council, with resolution 909, renews the mandate for UNAMIR with a threat to pull out in six weeks unless the Arusha Accords are applied.

6 April President Habyarimana and President Ntariyamira of Burundi and a number of government officials returning from a summit in Tanzania are killed when the plane in which they are travelling is shot out of the sky on its approach to Kigali airport.

7 April Systematic killing begins of opposition politicians, pro-democracy Hutu and Tutsi.
Ten peacekeepers, the prime minister's escort, are killed in a Rwandan army barracks in Kigali.
RPF troops in Kigali engage Presidential Guard.
Armed militias begin an organized round-up and slaughter of Tutsis and political moderates in Kigali. The violence escalates and spreads. RTLM broadcasts that the RPF and the Belgian peacekeepers are responsible for the death of the president.

8 April Telephone lines are progressively cut.
Increasing numbers of people are killed.
Former parliament speaker Théodore Sindikubwabo announces the formation of an interim government and declares himself president.

9 April The RPF leaves its northern bases and attacks Byumba and Ruhengeri.
Interahamwe and Presidential Guard conduct massacre at Gikondo. Evacuation starts of foreign nationals.
Sindikubwabo meets Dallaire and asks him to negotiate a ceasefire with the RPF.

10 April Prisoners are put to work with refuse carts picking up bodies. Ambassador David Rawson closes the US embassy in Kigali.

11 April Dallaire obtains a ceasefire to facilitate the evacuation of ex-pats.
The Belgian peacekeepers abandon Kicukiro leaving behind 2,000 people.

12 April French embassy closes its doors.
The interim government flees to Gitarama as the RPF moves on the capital. Claes meets Boutros-Ghali in Bonn to tell him that Belgium is withdrawing soldiers from UNAMIR.

13 April ICRC-MSF convoy arrives in Kigali from Bujumbura with doctors and medicines.

14 April Belgium announces it is withdrawing its troops from UNAMIR.
In Kigali wounded people are dragged from a Red Cross

ambulance and killed.

18 April An attempt by the RPF to silence RTLM fails.
The interim government dismisses the prefect of Butare.

19 April The last Belgian peacekeepers leave Kigali.

20 April The last Belgian peacekeeper leaves Rwanda.

21 April The UN Security Council votes resolution 912 to withdraw the bulk of UNAMIR peacekeepers from Rwanda, authorizing 270 to remain.
The RPF takes Byumba.

22 April A second ICRC road convoy reaches Kigali from Burundi.

24 April MSF withdraws its medical team from Butare.
Oxfam emergencies officer Maurice Herson telephones Oxfam headquarters to say that genocide of the Tutsi is taking place in Rwanda.

28 April Oxfam issues a press release that the killing in Rwanda amounts to genocide.

28–29 April An estimated 250,000 people flee across the Rwandan border into Tanzania.
This is reportedly the largest mass exodus of people ever witnessed by the UNHCR.

29 April A long Security Council debate to discuss the use of the word genocide in a Presidential Statement. The UK and USA resist the use of the word. The Secretary-General asks the Security Council to re-examine its decision to reduce UNAMIR.

30 April The RPF takes the Tanzanian border town of Rusumo.

1 May Rwanda is at top of news schedules due to massive exodus of Rwandans into Tanzania.

4 May Boutros-Ghali appears on ABC *Nightline* and says that it is a question of genocide in Rwanda.

5 May A presidential directive on peacekeeping policy is launched.
In Kampala, Museveni accuses the interim government of Rwanda of genocide in Rwanda.

6 May UN human rights commissioner, José Ayala Lasso, says he is going to Rwanda.

13 May Boutros-Ghali suggests to the Council Dallaire's original plan to airlift 5,500 troops to Kigali.

16 May The RPF cuts the road between Kigali and Gitarama.

17 May The Security Council votes resolution 918 approving the deployment of 5,500 troops to Rwanda but no troops are available.

19 May Lasso produces a report which calls Rwanda a human rights tragedy.

21 May An ICRC convoy with medical aid reaches Kigali.

22 May The RPF takes control of the airport and the Kanombe military camp and extends control over the north and eastern part of the country. The government forces continue to flee south in front of an RPF advance.

22–27 May Under-Secretary-General lqbal Riza and the Secretary-General's military adviser, Major-General J. Maurice Baril, visit Rwanda.

23 May The RPF overruns the presidential palace.

24 May The UN Commission on Human Rights holds meeting to discuss Rwanda.

25 May The UN Commission on Human Rights appoints René Dégni-Ségui as special human rights envoy to Rwanda. Ghana, Ethiopia and Senegal make a firm commitment to provide 800 troops each to the UN efforts. Zimbabwe and Nigeria make similar commitments soon after.

29 May The RPF takes Nyanza.

31 May The Secretary-General reports to the Council on the special mission by Riza and Baril, recommending that the Council authorize an expanded mandate for UNAMIR.

2 June The RPF takes Kabgayi.

5 June The Canadian relief flight is forced to stop flying relief supplies into Kigali due to heavy fighting around the airport.

6 June Opening of the thirtieth OAU summit in Carthage, Tunisia. The Rwandan government army launch their last major attack against RPF troops in the region of Kabgayi.

8 June The Security Council adopts resolution 925, which extends the UNAMIR mandate until December 1994.

10 June Some members of the interim government leave Gitarama for Gisenyi.

11 June Special Rapporteur Dégni-Ségui begins a week-long field mission to Rwanda to investigate violations of human rights.

13 June The RPF takes Gitarama.

17 June France announces its plan to the UN Security Council to deploy troops to Rwanda as an interim peacekeeping force. The Secretary-General and the USA support the idea.

21 June First French troops arrive on the Zaire-Rwanda border.

22 June The UN Security Council, in resolution 929, approves the French proposal to dispatch troops to Rwanda under a UN peacekeeping mission.

24 June French military forces are deployed into eastern Rwanda through Goma and Bukavu in eastern Zaire.

28 June The report of the UN Commission on Human Rights Special Rapporteur is published in Geneva stating that the massacres that occurred throughout Rwanda were pre-planned and a systematic campaign of genocide.

1 July Security Council sets up a commission of experts to investigate acts of genocide in Rwanda.
Booh-Booh is replaced by Mohamed Shaharyar Khan of Pakistan as special representative.

2 July Boutros-Ghali supports the French proposal for a designated "safe zone" in south-western Rwanda to protect vulnerable populations in the region.

3 July The RPF takes Butare.

4 July The RPF wins control of Kigali. The RPF leadership states that it intends to establish a new government based on the framework of the Arusha Accords.

5 July The French establish a humanitarian zone in the south-west corner of the country.

6 July Canadian relief flights into Kigali are resumed.

7 July Kigali airport reopens.

13 July Ruhengeri is captured by the RPF.

13–14 July An estimated 1 million people begin to flee towards Zaire.

14 July An estimated 6,000 people per hour file into the French safe zone, including members of the militia and interim government officials.

25 July The Clinton administration publicly declares that it no longer recognizes the interim government of Rwanda.

16 July Thirteen ministers of the interim government take refuge in the French safe zone.

17 July The RPF takes Gisenyi, the last Rwandan stronghold of Hutu Power.

18 July The war comes to an end with the RPF defeat of the remnants of Rwandan government troops still in Rwanda.

19 July A new government of national unity is created and announces the end of compulsory identity cards.

22 July Clinton announces that US troops will be deployed to help the refugees in camps in Zaire.

16 August Dallaire leaves Rwanda. Canadian General Guy Touignant takes command of UNAMIR, which has 1,624 soldiers.

October An interim report is produced by the Commission of Experts which concludes that a genocide had taken place against the Tutsi.

November UN Security Council adopts resolution 955 on the establishment of an international criminal court for the criminals of Rwanda.

LIST OF ABBREVIATIONS

APCs	armored personnel carriers
BBTG	Broad-Based Transitional Government
CDR	Coalition pour la Défense de la République
CIA	Central Intelligence Agency
CND	Conseil National pour le Développement
CRAP	Commando de Reconnaissance et d'Action en Profondeur
DAMI	Détachement d'Assistance Militaire et d'Instruction
DMZ	demilitarized zone
DPA	UN Department of Political Affairs
DPKO	UN Department of Peacekeeping Operations
ESM	École Supérieure Militaire
ETD	École Technique Officielle
FAR	Forces Armées Rwandaises
FC	Force Commander
HAC	Humanitarian Assistance Cell
HPZ	Humanitarian Protection Zone. Area of Rwanda secured by Operation Turquoise
ICRC	International Committee of the Red Cross
ICTR	International Criminal Tribunal for Rwanda
IMF	International Monetary Fund
KIBAT	Nickname for the Belgian troops located in Kigali
KWSA	Kigali Weapons Secure Area

MILOB	Military Observer. Unarmed military officers loaned to the UN. Also known as United Nations Military Observers (UNMOs)
MDR	Mouvement Démocratique Républicain
MOG	Military Observer Group
MRND	Mouvement Révolutionnaire National pour le Développement
MSF	Médecins Sans Frontières (Doctors Without Borders)
NGOs	nongovernmental organizations
NRA	National Resistance Army
OAU	Organization of African Unity
OCHA	UN Office for the Coordination of Humanitarian Affairs
PDC	Parti Démocrate Chrétien
PL	Parti Libéral
PSD	Parti Social Démocrate
PDI	Islamic Democratic Party
RGF	Rwandan Government Forces
RPF	Rwandan Patriotic Front
RTLM	Radio-Télévision Libre des Mille Collines
SITREP	Situation Report (military), provides details of current situation
SRSG	Special Representative of the Secretary-General
UN	United Nations
UNAMIR	UN Assistance Mission for Rwanda
UNCIVPOL	United Nations Civilian Police
UNDP	UN Development Programme
UNHCR	UN High Commissioner for Refugees
UNMO	UN Military Observer
UNOMUR	UN Observer Mission to Uganda-Rwanda
UNREO	UN Rwanda Emergency Office

APPENDIX

CONVENTION ON THE PREVENTION AND PUNISHMENT OF THE CRIME OF GENOCIDE, 1948

The Contracting Parties,

Having considered the declaration made by the General Assembly of the United Nations in its resolution 96 (I) dated 11 December 1946 that genocide is a crime under international law, contrary to the spirit and aims of the United Nations and condemned by the civilized world,

Recognizing that at all periods of history genocide has inflicted great losses on humanity, and

Being convinced that, in order to liberate mankind from such an odious scourge, international co-operation is required,

Hereby agree as hereinafter provided:

Article I: The Contracting Parties confirm that genocide, whether committed in time of peace or in time of war, is a crime under international law which they undertake to prevent and to punish.

Article II: In the present Convention, genocide means any of the following acts committed with intent to destroy, in whole or in part, a national, ethnical, racial or religious group, as such:

(a) Killing members of the group;
(b) Causing serious bodily or mental harm to members of the group;
(c) Deliberately inflicting on the group conditions of life calculated to bring about its physical destruction in whole or in part;
(d) Imposing measures intended to prevent births within the group;
(e) Forcibly transferring children of the group to another group.

Article III: The following acts shall be punishable:

(a) Genocide;
(b) Conspiracy to commit genocide;
(c) Direct and public incitement to commit genocide;
(d) Attempt to commit genocide;
(e) Complicity in genocide.

Article IV: Persons committing genocide or any of the other acts enumerated in article III shall be punished, whether they are constitutionally responsible rulers, public officials or private individuals.

Article V: The Contracting Parties undertake to enact, in accordance with their respective Constitutions, the necessary legislation to give effect to the provisions of the present Convention, and, in particular, to provide effective penalties for persons guilty of genocide or any of the other acts enumerated in article III.

Article VI: Persons charged with genocide or any of the other acts enumerated in article III shall be tried by a competent tribunal of the State in the territory of which the act was committed, or by such international penal tribunal as may have jurisdiction with respect to those Contracting Parties which shall have accepted its jurisdiction.

Article VII: Genocide and the other acts enumerated in article III shall not be considered as political crimes for the purpose of extradition.

The Contracting Parties pledge themselves in such cases to grant extradition in accordance with their laws and treaties in force.

Article VIII: Any Contracting Party may call upon the competent organs of the United Nations to take such action under the Charter of the United Nations as they consider appropriate for the prevention and suppression of acts of genocide or any of the other acts enumerated in article III.

Article IX: Disputes between the Contracting Parties relating to the interpretation, application or fulfilment of the present Convention, including those relating to the responsibility of a State for genocide or for any of the other acts enumerated in article III, shall be submitted to the International Court of Justice at the request of any of the parties to the dispute.

Article X: The present Convention, of which the Chinese, English, French, Russian and Spanish texts are equally authentic, shall bear the date of 9 December 1948.

Article XI: The present Convention shall be open until 31 December 1949 for signature on behalf of any Member of the United Nations and of any nonmember State to which an invitation to sign has been addressed by the General Assembly.

The present Convention shall be ratified, and the instruments of ratification shall be deposited with the Secretary-General of the United Nations. After 1 January, 1950, the present Convention may be acceded to on behalf of any Member of the United Nations and of any non-member State which has received an invitation as aforesaid. Instruments of accession shall be deposited with the Secretary-General of the United Nations.

Article XII: Any Contracting Party may at any time, by notification addressed to the Secretary-General of the United Nations, extend the application of the present Convention to all or any of the territories for the conduct of whose foreign relations that Contracting Party is responsible.

Article XIII: On the day when the first twenty instruments of ratification or accession have been deposited, the Secretary-General shall draw up a proces-verbal and transmit a copy thereof to each Member of the United Nations and to each of the non-member States contemplated in article XI.

The present Convention shall come into force on the ninetieth day following the date of deposit of the twentieth instrument of ratification or accession.

Any ratification or accession effected, subsequent to the latter date shall become effective on the ninetieth day following the deposit of the instrument of ratification or accession.

Article XIV: The present Convention shall remain in effect for a period of ten years as from the date of its coming into force.

It shall thereafter remain in force for successive periods of five years for such Contracting Parties as have not denounced it at least six months before the expiration of the current period.

Denunciation shall be effected by a written notification addressed to the Secretary-General of the United Nations.

Article XV: If, as a result of denunciations, the number of Parties to the present Convention should become less than sixteen, the Convention shall cease to be in force as from the date on which the last of these denunciations shall become effective.

Article XVI: A request for the revision of the present Convention may be made at any time by any Contracting Party by means of a notification in writing addressed to the Secretary-General.

The General Assembly shall decide upon the steps, if any, to be taken in respect of such request.

Article XVII: The Secretary-General of the United Nations shall notify all Members of the United Nations and the non-member States contemplated in article XI of the following:

(a) Signatures, ratifications and accessions received in accordance with article XI;

(b) Notifications received in accordance with article XII;
(c) The date upon which the present Convention comes into force in accordance with article XIII;
(d) Denunciations received in accordance with article XIV;
(e) The abrogation of the Convention in accordance with article XV;
(f) Notifications received in accordance with article XVI.

Article XVIII: The original of the present Convention shall be deposited in the archives of the United Nations.

A certified copy of the Convention shall be transmitted to each Member of the United Nations and to each of the non-member States contemplated in article XI.

Article XIX: The present Convention shall be registered by the Secretary-General of the United Nations on the date of its coming into force.

ACKNOWLEDGEMENTS

My sincere thanks are due to those who provided me with information. In Kigali I gained access to the files and records that were left behind when the "genocidaires" fled. These neatly typed letters, memoranda, reports and other documents include evidence of the planning of genocide. I am grateful to those at the ICTR who broke convention and took the risk of providing me with a copy of the sealed 1,800-page interrogation of Jean-Kambanda. Other court records and statements about the conspirators were provided by those who thought that the story of the conspiracy to commit genocide should be made widely available as soon as possible. My investigation involved many interviews with people who shared their recollections and perspectives. I am most grateful to them.

I was lucky to receive encouragement and advice from the following people: Professor Ken Booth, Department of International Politics, University of Wales, Aberystwyth; Simon Burall, Director, One World Trust; Dr Gerald Caplan, author of the Organization of African Unity report, "Rwanda: The Preventable Genocide"; Professor Margaret Cox, School of Conservation Sciences, Bournemouth University and Chief Executive of the Inforce Foundation, the International Forensic Centre for Excellence for the Investigation of Genocide; Dr Eric Markusen, Senior Research Fellow, Department for Holocaust and Genocide Studies of the Danish Institute for International Studies; Ian Martin, former Chief of the post-genocide UN Human Rights Field Operation in Rwanda;

Gregory H. Stanton, President of Genocide Watch and the Coordinator of the International Campaign to End Genocide; Dr Roger Williamson, Associate Director, Wilton Park, UK.

I extend my sincere thanks to Edward Mortimer, Special Adviser to the UN Secretary-General, for his great help. He understood my concern about reporting what had happened as accurately as possible and for this to be done before too many years elapsed. I thank William W. Paterson who so generously helped to sort out the copies of the documents brought back from Rwanda. Charity Kagwi, who was part of the prosecution team in the media trial at the ICTR in Arusha, ensured that I received a copy of the judgement and sentencing in December 2003. I am grateful to her. Nigel Eltringham, who just completed his own book on the aftermath of the genocide, advised with key areas of research. I thank Farouk Sohawon in London for his continuing belief in this endeavour. Also André Gakwaya in Kigali for generously allowing me the use of his own investigation into the pre-genocide regime. I thank Francis van de Putte for his help with my research in Belgium.

In New York, Alexandra McCleod, UN librarian, is a constant source of help. I thank Derek Miller, Beverley R. Placzek, Danny Pelzig and Gloria Pelzig. William Wesbrooks and Dallett Norris never failed to lift my spirits.

I am particularly grateful to the Network for Social Change and The Funding Network for enabling me to travel to New York and Kigali to consult and collect documents. I thank Bevis Gillett for his belief in this project. For friendship and advice I thank Deborah Burton, Sue Snell, Mungo Soggot, and Sally Taylor. I thank Alan McClue, Forensic Research Co-ordinator Africa and Asia, The Centre for Forensic Science, Technology and Law, Bournemouth University, and specialist supporter Inforce. I would also like to thank his colleague, David Payne, for his specialist IT help. Alan and David were of enormous help at the most critical moments.

Paul Williams and I have worked together on the story of UK policy towards Rwanda in 1993–1994. I am grateful to him for this collaboration and value it highly.

I am fortunate that my nephew Michael Melvern is an extremely skilled IT consultant, and without his legendary calm and patience I would never have finished the book. I thank Peter Greaves, who suggested this book, and who has been an inspiration for ten years.

I thank Jane Hindle for her thoughtful editing of the manuscript. She made crucial changes. I thank my proofreader Jon Haynes for his patience and skill. One person who made a decisive difference to how this book turned out was Doris Hollander. Her comments on the early drafts were invaluable. Doris, and her husband Martin Page, were extraordinarily helpful and so many times they simply lifted my burden. I thank them sincerely for their dedication to the book.

I thank my mother, Mavius Melvern, for her love and support. This book could not have been written without the presence in my life of Phill Green and our son Laurence. Their love is essential to everything I do, including this book. It was their forbearance and good nature that gave me the strength to see it to the end.

Linda Melvern, London,
January 2006

INDEX